Des de Moor

Published by the Campaign for Real Ale Ltd
230 Hatfield Road
St Albans
Hertfordshire AL1 4LW
www.camra.org.uk/books
© Campaign for Real Ale 2011
Text © Des de Moor

ISBN 978-1-85249-285-4

A CIP catalogue record for this book is available from the British Library
Printed and bound in China by Latitude Press Ltd

Head of Publishing: Simon Hall
Project Editor: Katie Hunt
Editorial Assistance: Emma Haines
Design/Typography: Ian Midson
Cartography: Mark Walker
Cover Design: Dale Tomlinson
Head of Marketing: Tony Jerome

Every effort has been made to ensure the contents of this book are correct
at the time of printing. Nevertheless, the Publisher cannot be held
responsible for any errors or omissions, or for changes in the details given
in this guide, or for the consequences of any reliance on information
provided by the same. This does not affect your statutory rights.

The views and opinions expressed in this book are those of the author
alone and not necessarily those of the Campaign for Real Ale.

**CAMPAIGN
FOR
REAL ALE**

CONTENTS

INTRODUCTION

INTRODUCTION
ABOUT THIS GUIDE

London is indisputably one of the world's great cities and, as the capital of a country that's famed for its pubs and the last custodian of a unique family of beer styles, it should be one of the world's great beer cities, too. After a few challenging years, London's beer scene is once again buzzing, with some outstanding new young brewers, old stalwarts up to new tricks and a new generation of pubs and bars enthusiastically serving up London beers alongside some of the best and most innovative brews from Britain and elsewhere.

This book aims to make a contribution to the London beer renaissance by helping readers find and enjoy the very best beer London has to offer. As well as being a guide to an exciting variety of exceptional beer-focussed pubs and bars across the city, uniquely, it also profiles London's breweries and includes information on many of the brewers and beers drinkers in London are likely to encounter.

150 years ago, London was the beer capital of the world. The city's brewers pioneered industrial brewing, invented the first two global beer styles and sent their products to every inhabited continent on the planet. That global pre-eminence eventually declined and in the 20th century the city's domestic brewing dominance started to crumble too. London then became an early battleground, and remains a bastion, of the Campaign for Real Ale (CAMRA), the organisation that saved the traditional brewing technique of cask conditioning as well as helping inspire an international revival in craft brewing.

Today, London's size, prosperity and cosmopolitan character provide an eager market for brewers from Britain and the rest of the world. It's still the biggest city of the only nation where cask beer, with its unique character, remains an everyday drink. It's also an important export destination, with Belgian and German beers readily available and, increasingly, US beers too. The capital's beer outlets between them offer the widest range of beer anywhere in Europe – if you know where to look.

Thanks to the ubiquity of cask, craft beer is easy to find in London. Walk into a few pubs at random and you'll likely encounter a handpump or two dispensing cask ale. But if you want to get the best out of beer drinking in the city, this scattergun approach has its drawbacks. Firstly, cask beer is a living product

that requires careful handling in the pub cellar in order to be enjoyed at its best, and sadly not all pubs are as conscientious or as capable as they ought to be.

Secondly, you'll quickly notice the same few brands appearing again and again – some of them excellent beers when in top condition but hardly representative of a country with over 750 breweries. The range of styles, too, may be limited, with a frustratingly high proportion of 'brown bitters' and golden ales at strengths of between 3.7% and 4.5% ABV (see p254), some of them, if truth be told, rather difficult to tell apart aside from the name on the pump clip. Most of these usual suspects are brewed a long way outside London.

The reason for this is that the majority of London drinking establishments are owned by a handful of big businesses who control the range of beer landlords can sell. Some of these are breweries who predictably give precedence to their own products. The rest are pub-owning companies, 'pubcos', who can make the most money by procuring bulk supplies at a discount and selling them on at a large premium. They tend to play safe by stocking beers they think will have the broadest appeal, and although in recent years they've become more open to the potential of offering a better range, this tends to be limited to selected pubs that are confident of attracting more discerning customers.

< **Doggetts Coat & Badge (p111)**

London is a vibrant city with a thriving real ale scene

The primary intention of this guide is to steer the beer lover to places offering something more than the average pub. The longest section is a directory of over 250 pubs throughout Greater London which between them provide a mouthwatering selection of craft beers. Many are pubs offering a wide choice of cask ales in a decent variety of styles, particularly from small and local breweries. Brewery pubs aren't forgotten and some of the very best of them are featured as showcases for their owners' beer.

Cask ale isn't the end of the story either – new generation beer bars and the best of the specialist shops are included, reflecting the increased range of imported beers and non-cask craft beers on offer. In 1971 Britain produced only five bottle conditioned beers. The latest *Good Bottled Beer Guide* lists more than 1,300, and some of the best can be found using this book, alongside a huge range from elsewhere, from traditional Belgian Trappist ales to the latest hyper-hopped, wood aged novelties from California and Colorado.

Though the book lists plenty of outstanding pubs that even teetotallers will appreciate, it's not primarily a pub guide. Pubs can excel in all kinds of ways – sociability, architecture, history and heritage, entertainment, food, fine wines – but unless the beer offer fits the bill, they're not included here. Conversely, a small but significant proportion of the entries wouldn't qualify for a

standard pub guide: designer bars, social clubs, department stores and even cinemas and bowling alleys have been considered if they happen to do good beer. The huge diversity of places united by beery excellence, from glitzy Soho cocktail bars to basic corner boozers under the gloomy shadow of tower blocks, is a remarkable illustration of craft beer's growing appeal.

This growth is surely cause for optimism in an industry that sometimes seems beset with gloom, squeezed by duty rises, competition from other drinks and a global recession. The overall beer market in Britain is steadily declining at around 4% per year. Cask beer, though, is holding steady in overall terms, and increasing its market share: in 2010 it reached its highest share of beer sold in pubs for a decade. Heavily promoted industrial beer brands are shedding customers, while more discerning drinkers are turning to the depth and variety of flavour fine beer can offer.

Pub closures, too, are regularly in the news: former pub buildings converted into flats are a common sight on the streets. 5% of London's pubs closed between 2005 and 2009, by which stage the closure rate was estimated at 11 pubs a week. Beer duty, supermarket drink discounting, high property prices and money-grubbing pubcos are often singled out for blame but there are wider social trends affecting pubs, such as increasing numbers of home comforts that tempt us to remain indoors.

But reports of the death of the pub are premature. While researching this guide I encountered scores of inspirational pubs that have prospered, often in unlikely locations, by working hard to provide their customers with something special. Good food, events and little touches like books and newspapers are often part of this; a warm welcome, comfortable surroundings and an eagerness to take on the role of community hub are essentials. Quality specialist beer is often the jewel in the crown, and an excellent way of turning a pub on a site with no passing trade into a destination venue attracting customers from far and wide.

The book not only offers guidance on places to drink but on what to drink in them. The second major section lists around 140 breweries – in Britain and elsewhere – that regularly supply beer to London outlets, with notes on their key beers and tips about where to find them. Special attention is given to the breweries operating within Greater London itself, and it's here that the guide has one of the most exciting stories to tell.

From the dizzy heights of the late Victorian era, London brewing has suffered a century of decline. In 2006 it reached a depressingly low point when Young's, one of two remaining old-established independent brewers, merged with Wells in Bedford. This left just seven commercial breweries, of which only two were craft producers of any significant size. But since then seven more have appeared, alongside a would-be brewery that's currently commissioning its beers from outside London. All these new arrivals are small but rapidly expanding, working in a diverse range of styles and producing some truly impressive products. Most of the older breweries have developed significantly too, and London beers are now appearing on London bars in a way that hasn't been seen for several decades.

Finally, as excellent as London's beer is, it would be perverse, given the opportunity of exploring the city, to spend all your time in the pub. I've therefore included background detail about the city, its history, geography and culture, and pointed out other features of interest in the areas surrounding the listed outlets. These notes are necessarily brief and selective and I strongly recommend that to explore properly, you use this book in conjunction with a general guidebook (More information, p325). Searching for named places online is another option. Beer, as I state elsewhere, is also a cultural phenomenon and putting it in context can only enrich your appreciation of London's zythological bounty.

This book is published at a time when London's beer drinkers have much to celebrate. The capital's brewers are on a rising curve with an emerging younger audience for their work, enjoying it in a new generation of stylish and innovative beer bars. At the same time, the city's well-deserved reputation for traditional pubs endures, with many venerable institutions now benefitting from the renewed vibrancy of the beer scene. With this book to guide you to these places and more besides, I'm confident you'll get the most out of joining in the celebration.

Fuller's is the only surviving historic commercial real ale brewery in London

THE CITY THAT INVENTED ITSELF

London wasn't meant to exist. Those ancient urbanists, the Romans, rarely built on greenfield sites, preferring to redevelop existing settlements. When the legions crossed the Thames in the year 43 they found nothing of note on the little rise of Cornhill, on the north bank just east of the Walbrook stream. Belgic and Celtic farmers populated the wider area, but the river then was much broader, shallower and marshier than today, so settlements clung to higher ground. There may have been a farm on or close to the place where London later grew, with a name later borrowed into Latin as LONDINIVM.

The Roman army originally used several crossing points, but sometime after the year 50 a decision was taken to build a permanent crossing between Southwark and Cornhill, a few metres upstream from the present London Bridge. No military emplacement was intended for the north end of the bridge, so the officer who signed off the plans couldn't have had any idea he was ushering one of the greatest cities in human history into existence.

Unsurprisingly given its strategic importance, the road junction over the bridge attracted service industries and a small settlement grew. In 60 the fledgling town was sacked by the Celtic Iceni tribe: their leader, Queen Boudica, is another inadvertent godparent as her actions prompted London's rebuilding as a proper planned city, with a defensive wall that can still be traced today. The centre of administration moved here from Colchester and by the end of the 1st century it was the biggest city in and the *de facto* capital of the province of Britannia.

It's remarkable how the earliest development of London set so much of the tone for what was to follow, driven as it was by entrepreneurs who realised there was a living to be made in hawking goods and services from the roadside. The importance of London as a port also goes back to Roman times, the sheltered estuary and good connections to a new road network making it a more favourable entry point than the old Celtic ports on the south coast. A complex of wharves soon projected into the river, the first of many such encroachments that eventually

Layers of history: the Tower of London, built on the Roman city walls of Londinivm

created the narrower, deeper Thames we know today

Three centuries later, their empire crumbling around them, the Romans abandoned Britain and much of their city was eventually abandoned too, although the Germanic invaders that filled the vacuum continued to recognise it as a seat of power – the Guildhall is on the site of an Anglo-Saxon royal hall, and the Christian missionary Augustine established St Paul's Cathedral nearby in 604. The Anglo-Saxons at first avoided the ruined Roman city, building a new trading suburb known as Lundenwic along the Strand, in those days the actual riverfront, until it occurred to Alfred the Great that the old walls provided a readymade set of defences.

Following the unification of England in 974, London's prosperity ensured its importance as a political centre and royal residence. The old city lost its political role in 1052 when Edward the Confessor moved his court upstream to Thorney Island, next to a tiny abbey which was rapidly bolstered with royal patronage. Though much altered, the palace and the abbey still stand at Westminster, and the split between economic and political centres remains a persistent feature of London's geography. This split is also behind the typographical subtlety that distinguishes the city of London – the totality of continuous development – from the City of London, occupying the original Roman site.

In 1066 William the Bastard, Duke of Normandy, conquered England, building what was to become the most powerful fortress in Britain, the Tower of London, in the southeast corner of the City. The Normans gradually abandoned the old practice of peripatetic royal courts, and by the time Magna Carta was signed in 1215 Westminster had emerged as the single administrative capital, its palace the meeting place of Parliament. The City remained the population centre and the economic powerhouse, home to the powerful guilds that controlled manufacturing and trade in the medieval world, exploiting this position to lever autonomy from cash-strapped monarchs. Today the City of London retains a structure unique in English local government and even has its own police force.

London has long been the biggest city in Britain, but as the Middle Ages ended it lagged behind Paris and even Bruges and Novgorod in the world league tables. Under the Tudors and Stuarts it began to catch up, with the population spilling over the City walls into what became the East End. Southwark, to the south of the bridge, also flourished by providing services too disreputable for the City. The theatres for which it's best known signal London's emergence as a cultural crucible, a vibrant urban environment in which talents like William Shakespeare and Christopher Marlowe could flourish.

The river was central as both barrier and lifeline, now not only a conduit of trade but of England's growing sea power, with naval dockyards established at Deptford and Woolwich. As well as big ships it was busy with watermen constantly ferrying commuters, and with royals who took to wafting in sumptuous flotillas between the string of riverside palaces from Greenwich to Windsor.

With the population rocketing, overtaking Paris by 1650, the aristocratic owners of adjoining rural estates realised the true extent of their good fortune. The earl of Bedford got things started with the piazza at

The Thames by night

Covent Garden in the 1630s (p73), but a pair of disasters interrupted developments. The Great Plague of 1665 killed at least 100,000 people, perhaps 20% of the population. Next year came the Great Fire, which destroyed 80% of the largely wooden buildings within the City walls over the course of four days. The wealth of London is evident from the grand rebuilding that followed, its centrepiece Christopher Wren's spectacular new home for St Paul's. But the funds didn't stretch to realising Wren's ambitious master plan to build a new system of grand boulevards – something to ponder as you wander streets and alleys that still thread between the City's office blocks on their Roman and medieval alignments.

Post-Fire, the noxious industries were exiled east, while the west saw the onward march of property development through the 18th century. The now familiar pattern of streets, squares and terraces spread into the spaces between royal hunting grounds, themselves now remade into Royal Parks. New docks (p123) boosted the city's trading capacity, and as the Industrial Revolution took hold,

industry became bigger, more capital intensive and technologically advanced, feeding international markets secured by the country's growing naval might. London's famed cosmopolitan character grew as people flocked here from all over.

Better transport facilitated further expansion in the 19th century, with improved roads rapidly followed by railways that spawned commuter suburbs further and further out. 'Ribbon development' and sprawl swallowed scores of formerly separate villages and towns. Victorian London was the capital of a massive empire, dotted with sumptuous monuments to its own success, but at a cost. Beneath it was a sink of poverty, with millions packed into unhealthy slums of the sort that sparked Charles Dickens to righteous anger.

Amazingly, London had got this far without a single directing authority. It wasn't until 1855 that a Metropolitan Board of Works was set up to coordinate infrastructure such as sewers – just in time for the Great Stink of 1858 when the stench of raw sewage in the Thames even disrupted parliamentary proceedings. A fully fledged London County Council followed in

1889, but the capital's boundaries had outgrown it before it even met.

As London entered the 20th century, political pressure built to contain this relentless growth, and to protect the remaining undeveloped areas. The outbreak of another war in 1939 marked a watershed. German bombs rained on the city for 76 consecutive nights in the Blitz of 1940-41, destroying vast areas of the urban fabric, particularly around the docks and industrial areas. After the war a new order took hold, with an increased role for government. New planning controls locked the boundaries of the built-up area where they remain today, within a protected Green Belt. The slums the Luftwaffe had missed were cleared and many of their inhabitants leapfrogged to supposedly self-contained New Towns much further out.

London was now the capital of a humbler Britain, no longer a great imperial power. Its industry declined and by the 1970s it had even lost its ancient role as a port. But the City clung to pre-eminence as a financial and business centre that is still only rivalled by

New York City, handling the majority of the world's business in foreign exchange.

As the dowdy 1950s gave way to the 'Swinging 60s', London's art and culture flourished. The evolution of British popular music from trad jazz, skiffle and rhythm and blues to the 'British invasion', psychedelia and prog can be traced through London's pubs, clubs and recording studios, and it was in London that provincial bands like the Beatles achieved their creative peak. A few years later the city was the epicentre of punk. London has nurtured leading fashion designers, photographers, architects, artists and film makers, and provided the backdrop to countless novels from Martin Amis' *London Fields* to Monica Ali's *Brick Lane*. Between them the rich heritage and the contemporary cultural buzz now attract more international tourists than any other world city, driving an industry worth £10.6billion.

London's creativity has been informed by its ever changing complexion. From 1948 it became a new home to settlers from Britain's former colonies in the Caribbean and the Indian subcontinent, followed by significant groups from Cyprus, Vietnam, west Africa and, latterly, eastern Europe. Currently almost a third of Londoners were born outside the UK, and over 300 languages are spoken here. While new Londoners haven't always received the warmest of welcomes, historically they're only the most recent arrivals in the flow of humanity that's converged on the city over millennia. London has also been the scene of bitter struggles – as a political and economic centre it's a focus for political protest and occasionally violent conflict, from the anti-war demonstrations of the 1960s to the anti-globalisation protests and student riots of more recent years.

In 1964 it finally gained a local authority almost commensurate with its size, though still not quite matching its true boundaries, with the creation of the Greater London Council. By 1986 this body, under its left-wing leader Ken Livingstone, became such a thorn in the side of Margaret Thatcher's Conservative government that they abolished it, leaving London balkanised between 33 boroughs. Livingstone ultimately became the first Mayor of London when a new system of governance was created in 2000, serving two terms before being ousted by eccentric Tory Boris Johnson. Both are due to go head-to-head again in 2012.

Recent decades have seen large areas of the capital transformed as former docks, warehouses and industrial areas are regenerated, postwar social housing refurbished and Victorian inner city suburbs gentrified with new City and media wealth, driving up property prices to world-busting levels. The most obvious symbol of all this is the high-rise business district built around disused docks at Canary Wharf which has shifted the balance of the skyline eastwards.

London is now almost two millennia old and looks set to continue reinventing itself. The recession of 2009 caused renewed anxiety, not least because of the savage cuts in local authority services now being implemented. But the population is still predicted to grow from 7million to 8.6million by 2030, with another 700,000 more jobs. It remains to be seen whether the Olympic and Paralympic Games, which London is due to host in 2012, will be as much of a milestone as, say, the 1851 Great Exhibition, which ushered in the self-confident Victorian era, or the 1951 Festival of Britain aimed at bootstrapping the country out of postwar gloom.

The Queen Elizabeth Olympic Park now nearing completion (p135) will add to the variegated patchwork created by the city's haphazard growth. This complex texture, although confusing to navigate, is one of London's principal delights, blissfully free of the sort of unofficial apartheid that afflicts so many US cities. When you set your sights on a great pub, don't forget to enjoy the process of reaching it – you're quite likely to pass a pompous Victorian pile, a gloomy 1960s estate, a hidden green space, a poshed-up terrace, some striking contemporary architecture and a world famous landmark all within a few minutes' walk, and you'll undoubtedly hear snatches of some of those 300 languages along the way. Perhaps there's something to be said for unplanned cities after all.

A similarly varied and cosmopolitan patchwork also characterises London's eclectic beer scene, as we shall shortly see...

CITY OF BREWING

On Chiswell Street on the very northern edge of the City is an events and conference venue known as the Brewery, which is used, according to its website, for everything "from upscale state functions and company conferences to televised music events and discreet boardroom powwows." The biggest available option to potential hirers is the Porter Tun room, one of the largest unobstructed indoor spaces in London. Built between 1776-84, it has a floor area of 778 square metres, with the exposed timbers of a king-post roof, the widest timber span in the city except for Westminster Hall, over 18m above. Its name might sound like a piece of quaint nonsense dreamed up by the marketing team, but is in fact an accurate reflection of the room's original purpose.

For well over a century this room housed huge wooden vats known as 'tuns' in which thousands of barrels worth of porter beer sleepily matured. Still more beer slept in stone-lined cisterns in the basement, the largest of which held 625,000l – about 1.1 million pints. This was the heart of the Whitbread brewery, opened by Samuel Whitbread in 1750 as the first purpose-built mass production brewery in the world, and at its peak the most successful brewery in Britain.

London has many more such relics. The Truman brewery, now an entertainment, retail and business complex, is a little to the east, in Brick Lane. The Courage brewery by Tower Bridge fell early to the redevelopment of London's Docklands, and is now offices and flats. The Anchor Retail Park in Mile End Road bears the name of Charrington's former Anchor brewery, of which a couple of key buildings survive. At Romford in London's far eastern suburbia, the Brewery shopping complex with its mattress superstores and multiplex cinema occupies the site of Ind & Smith, later Ind Coope. Between them these sites testify to London's former status as the world capital of beer.

Brewing almost certainly goes back to London's beginnings. The practice was well-established by the Middle Ages though as elsewhere in Europe much of it took place in places like pubs and the domestic

brewhouses of institutions and upper class homes. The canons of St Paul's brewed a hundred times in 1286, producing 67,800 gallons (3,082hl, 542,400 pints) – the output of a small commercial brewery today.

The growing population created increasing opportunities for 'common brewers' – standalone operations making a living from supplying beer. Southwark was particularly noted for such breweries. Geoffrey Chaucer, writing in the 1390s, has the Miller in the *Canterbury Tales* apologise in advance for the potential effects of alcohol on his storytelling abilities with the words: "And therfore if that I mysspeke or seye, / Wyte it ['blame it on'] the ale of southwerk, I you preye." Brewing in

Truman brewery – now a retail venue

Southwark persisted into the 20th century and in 1867 the Hop Exchange, centre of London's hop trade, was built there. The tradition has recently been restored in a modest way by the Brew Wharf and Kernel breweries.

The Worshipful Company of Brewers is one of the earliest of the City trade guilds, dating back to the end of the 12th century and granted a royal charter in 1437. It still maintains a Hall north of the Guildhall, just within the old City walls, though most of the breweries were elsewhere. John Stow, whose 1598 *Survey of London* mentions 26 common brewers, notes they "remaine neare to the friendly water of Thames". This was principally for transport reasons – it's a misconception that the already sewage-laden river provided the principal ingredient of London's beer. Brewers were banned in 1345 from using public water conduits, so sunk their own artesian wells, tapping the aquifers within the chalk underlying the Thames basin.

In terms of scale, these early common brewers were comparable to many of today's microbreweries, producing 20-30 barrels (33-50hl, 5,760-8,640 pints) a week with a staff of four or five people. As the city and its demand for refreshment grew, the total number of brewers declined, some of the smaller operations failing and the surviving breweries growing to fill the gaps. William Bucknall ran such a brewery, just to the east of the City walls on Brick Lane, when in the 1650s he added one John Truman to his payroll. How breweries like this grew big enough to leave the impressive legacy visible today is partly answered by the story of porter.

The exact origin of porter is unclear. The standard account – that it was invented by Ralph Harwood, landlord of the Blue Last in Curtain Road, Shoreditch, in 1730 as an all-in-one replacement for a blend of pale, aged and fresh beer mixed at the point of dispense – is now thought to be unreliable. It's more likely to have been refined over time by several brewers from an existing style of aged dark beer, probably in the 1710s. Most authorities do agree that the most likely explanation of the name is its popularity with porters, the labourers who unloaded goods from ships and transported them by hand around London's streets.

Porter was a relatively strong beer of around 7% ABV, made with brown malt that had been roasted so ferociously it was 'blown' – popped like corn. This gave the fresh beer a pronounced smoky tang, so it was aged to mellow the flavour. The long maturation in wooden vessels populated by numerous wild yeasts and other microflora produced a flat beer – 'stale' was the contemporary term – with distinctive sour, vinous flavours, as still found in a few surviving old ales and Flemish brown ales. Later recipes included pale malts and the 'stale' quality was eventually offset by blending aged beer with a fresher brew.

The process favoured better-resourced brewers who could afford to lock up cash and storage space with stock that might take two years to recoup its investment, sometimes accounting for over 10% of a brewery's assets. The increasing size of the porter breweries drove technological development and capital investment in mechanical equipment, steam power, coke firing and more accurate instruments like thermometers and hydrometers. Economies of scale increased profitability, and porter tuns swelled accordingly, with brewers competing for the biggest.

Rewards for the successful were immense. In 1781, Samuel Johnson, acting as executor to his late friend Henry Thrale, described the latter's Anchor brewery at Southwark as not "a parcel of boilers and vats, but the potentiality of growing rich beyond the dreams of avarice." Barclay Perkins took it over and turned it into the biggest brewery in the world. Samuel Whitbread bought himself a career as an MP and a country estate. Benjamin Truman, son of John, used his brewing profits to subsidise Britain's wars, earning a knighthood from George III.

By the 1780s porter had travelled the world – to Australia and India, the Caribbean and Africa, the Baltic and, notably, to Ireland, where a strong variety, 'stout' porter, outlived its parent's eventual decline. Another famous globetrotting porter was Thrale's, and later Barclay Perkins', very strong version exported to Russia from the 1790s. Known as Imperial Russian Stout, it remained in production until 1993.

The Thames provided a natural route to the rest of the world for London-brewed beers

In the 19th century the porter brewers faced competition from a very different style of beer that was ultimately to prove their downfall, and once again it emerged from London. Pale ale first appeared in the 1650s, when the invention of coke made it possible to produce paler malts. In the 1780s George Hodgson's then relatively small brewery at Bow began exporting supplies of strong pale ale alongside other beers to the British colonies in India. The sea voyage proved to accelerate the beer's maturation and 'India Pale Ale' rocketed in popularity, eventually also generating interest in pale ales at home.

In the 1830s the water of Burton upon Trent in Staffordshire was found to be particularly suited to pale ale brewing and some of the big London breweries set up branches there, though all except Ind Coope abandoned the Midlands when they discovered 'Burtonising' London water with gypsum produced comparable results.

By the mid-19th century, London tastes were turning from porter to the fresher 'running ale' long known as 'mild', now being distributed via the new railway network in sparkling form using cask conditioning. Similarly fresh but paler, hoppier beers, known

in the trade simply as pale ale but rapidly labelled 'bitter' by drinkers, had a growing more upmarket following. With porter production declining steeply by 1900, even Whitbread dismantled its famous tuns.

Besides Ind Coope, companies successfully challenging the porter brewers with lighter beers included Charrington, opened at Bethnal Green in the 1730s and relocated to Mile End in 1757; Courage, at Horsleydown from 1787; the Stag brewery at Pimlico, in the hands of the Watney family since 1837; Mann Crossman Paulin's 1808 Albion brewery at Whitechapel; and Taylor Walker, founded in Stepney in 1796 but based at Limehouse since 1823.

Brewers increasingly got involved in retailing, first by providing cheap finance to would-be licensees in exchange for exclusive supply rights, then buying up their own pub estates by the end of the 19th century, at a time when the value of pubs was growing due to a new policy to restrict licenses.

Brewing in London kept on expanding, reaching a peak around 1905 when the capital's biggest brewers between them produced 3,328,949 barrels (5,448,133hl – almost a billion pints). For two centuries,

London had boasted the biggest brewers in the world, but after 1910 that distinction was lost. Limits on raw materials in World War I drove down the strength of all British beer, which became known almost exclusively as a low gravity, high volume product.

Mild and bitter dominated the interwar years, with porter now seen as an old man's drink. Its strength was much reduced – Whitbread's was down to 2.3% by 1930. Curiously, porter's cousin, Irish stout in the form of Guinness, was growing in popularity, not only with Irish expatriates but among other drinkers, assisted by clever and witty marketing. In 1933 its Dublin brewer established a British plant at Park Royal in West London.

That same decade saw Watney's first experiments with filtered, pasteurised and artificially carbonated keg ales at the Stag brewery in Mortlake (p280), which it had owned since 1889. After World War II, the big brewers saw keg as a response to the challenge of rapidly changing markets and drinking habits, and through the 1950s and 1960s a wave of consolidation and rationalisation swept the industry as it invested in both the hardware and marketing muscle needed to launch first keg bitters, then keg lagers.

Whitbread swallowed 27 smaller breweries across the country between 1948 and 1971, rapidly closing almost all of them. In 1955 Courage merged with and soon closed Barclay Perkins; in 1960 it took over Simonds of Reading and was itself taken over by Imperial Tobacco in 1970. Watney merged with Mann in 1958, soon afterwards taking over several regional breweries outside London. In 1959 Ind Coope took over Taylor Walker, closing the brewery the following year, then in 1961 merging itself with big regionals in Birmingham and Leeds to form Allied Breweries. Charrington merged with United Breweries in 1962, then with Bass of Burton to form Bass Charrington five years later. Finally, after a bitter bidding war, the Grand Metropolitan hotel group acquired Truman's in 1971, merging it with Watney Mann the following year.

1971 is a significant year in the history of brewing and beer appreciation as it marks the foundation of the Campaign for the Revitalisation of Ale, shortly to be renamed the Campaign for Real Ale (CAMRA). When CAMRA began campaigning it faced a situation where seven big brewery groups brewed 75% of Britain's beer and owned half its pubs. Six of these – Allied, Bass Charrington, Courage, Guinness, Watney and Whitbread – had significant facilities in London. The seventh, Scottish & Newcastle, owned a significant number of London pubs.

These groups were now managed by people dedicated to beer made at the cheapest possible cost and sold at the greatest possible profit, with no particular loyalty to the craft and tradition of brewing. Cask conditioned ale was an unwelcome anachronism and the future as they saw it was in pasteurised, artificially carbonated keg beers of little character, including heavily promoted, cheap, low gravity approximations of European golden lagers.

Two smallish London breweries retained their independence. One, Fuller's of Chiswick (p270), was making its own plans to convert to keg beer until CAMRA persuaded it to retain cask production. The other, Young's at Wandsworth, remained committed to a tradition that included cask ale (see Ram, p276). Both breweries became revered names among the growing number of dedicated real ale drinkers.

The success of CAMRA persuaded some of the big brewers to dabble with cask again, but their trajectory remained towards ever larger concentrations of production and the rationalisation of facilities. Sentiment was set aside as business logic questioned the need for capacity in a place with such high property prices and traffic congestion as London.

Whitbread stopped brewing at Chiswell Street in 1976 although retained the site as a corporate headquarters and an events venue, finally selling it on in 2005. Grand Metropolitan shut the Mann plant in 1979 then pulled out of brewing entirely in 1988 when Truman's closed. Courage left Southwark in 1981, Charrington shut up shop in 1985 and Allied quit Romford in 1993. Guinness – now merged with Grand Met to create global drinks combine Diageo – shut

Young's of Wandsworth was a traditional brewer that retained a comitment to cask ale

down Park Royal in 2005. Watney's Mortlake brewery, leased since 1988 by Anheuser Busch to brew a British version of American 'Budweiser', is the only remaining fragment of old school big brewing left in London, and it too now faces closure, probably at the end of 2011 (see Stag, p280).

The same issues that drove the exodus of the big brewers have also inhibited smaller scale brewing in the capital, despite growing interest in craft brewed beers. One notable early exception was Pitfield (p305), opened in Hoxton in 1981. Rocketing rents forced it out to rural Essex in 2006. Another of London's outstanding micros was O'Hanlon's (p304), founded in 1996, but that too relocated, moving to Devon in 2000. A handful of others emerged and then foundered.

Meantime (p275), established in Charlton in 2000, found more enduring success by focusing initially on craft brewed lager. Its founder Alastair Hook had previously opened the Freedom (p293) brewery in Fulham in 1995, relocated outside London in 2005, and the Mash brewpub at Oxford Circus in 1998,

closed in 2006. A few other brewpubs have opened and closed in the capital over the years; the longest lasting is currently Zerodegrees (p284) at Blackheath, opened in 2000.

In 2006 came the grave news that Young's was abandoning six centuries of brewing history on its Wandsworth site and merging with Charles Wells in Bedford. As 2007 began, London had only six working commercial breweries besides the doomed Mortlake plant, of which only two, Fuller's and Meantime, were of any significant size. The others were Zerodegrees; the Brew Wharf brewpub (p266) opened in 2005 at Borough Market; a tiny brewery installed the previous year at the Horseshoe pub in Hampstead (Camden Town, p268); and a small cask micro, Twickenham (p283), founded in far western suburbia in 2004. A century of relentless decline from the absolute heights of world leader to the humiliation of total poverty seemed near complete. Events since, however, have given much new cause for hope.

THE NEW CITY OF BEER

At the Great British Beer Festival at Earls Court in August 2006, Londoner Duncan Sambrook and two old friends were planning their evening's drinking when they noticed that, of all the many hundreds of breweries represented from Britain and across the world, only one – Fuller's – was from the same city in which the event took place. Mulling on this over a few pints, they concluded the proper response was to start a brewery. It might just have been the beer talking, but the idea took root in Duncan's mind and, just over two years later, became reality with the opening of Sambrook's in Battersea (p279), not far from the recently vacated site of Young's.

Sambrook's was the most substantial dot so far on a line that had already begun to turn modestly upwards. In March 2007, the Capital Pub Company included a small brewhouse in its refit of the Cock and Hen pub in Fulham; a couple of months later the experiment was repeated on a slightly larger scale at the Florence in Herne Hill (p270). The Fulham pub was sold on a year later without its brewery, but the Florence is still producing its own beer.

As Sambrook's was commissioning its kit, across the other side of London siblings James and Lizzie Brodie were busy restoring the brewery at the family's pub, the William IV in Leyton. Installed under the name Sweet William in 2000, it had been left derelict since the original partner pulled out in 2005. Just after Sambrook's sold its first beer, the rejuvenated East London brewery relaunched as Brodie's (p267).

Meanwhile still other brains and hands were at work. Gavin Happé and Chris Penny were devoting their weekends to refurbishing an old farm building in East London's Green Belt, which opened as the Ha'penny brewery (p272) in October 2009. Evin O'Riordan, a former seller of fine cheeses, was busy under a railway arch in Bermondsey perfecting his artisanal micro Kernel (p273), which first brewed commercially towards the end of 2009.

Andy Moffat was another man moved to fire up a mash tun by the glaring paucity of London breweries – he'd been particularly struck when visiting cities in the North of England at how local communities took pride

in their local microbrewed beer, yet in London even the beer in the good pubs seemed to come from Yorkshire or Cornwall. His answer was Redemption in Tottenham (p278), launched early in 2010.

An even more ambitious project now fermented under railway arches in Kentish Town. Jasper Cuppaidge, who'd begun brewing on a tiny kit in the cellar of his Hampstead pub the Horseshoe in 2004, was relearning his skills on the fully automated brewing kit at the Camden Town brewery (p268) – probably the most significant investment in an entirely new brewery in London since Guinness built Park Royal in the 1930s.

Camden Town produces not just cask ale but a range of craft brewed keg ales and lagers, following in the footsteps of the capital's most enduringly successful contemporary brewery, Meantime. 2010 also saw this veteran enjoying a significant expansion, with the opening of a new small run microbrewery at the Old Brewery in the heart of the Maritime Greenwich World Heritage Site. This was followed by a long-planned move to a new main site just outside Greenwich town centre, where the kit, according to Meantime founder Alastair Hook, is among the most advanced in Europe.

Indeed 2010 was, in the words of Gavin Happé, "the year it all got very strange," with numerous new London beers and brewers seemingly coming out of nowhere at once. They included a new beer under the old Truman name, actually contract brewed in Suffolk, though its creators, James Morgan and Michael-George Hemus, who licensed the brand from Heineken, intend to start brewing in London when they can (p281).

Just as this book was going to press in spring 2011, we received news of yet another London brewery: Moncada in north Kensington (p276), which should have launched its first beers by the time you read this.

Social movements are often woven from several independent strands into a recognisable phenomenon when someone good at making connections comes along. In the London brewing revival that person is arguably Phil Lowry, manager of beer importer,

The Great British Beer Festival 2006 at Earls Court, which featured only one London brewery

distributor and online retailer BEERmerchants.com. In March 2010 Phil realised some of his own brewing ambitions by persuading the owners of the Brew Wharf bar-restaurant in the Vinopolis complex at Borough Market to let him loose on their microbrewery, along with two friends. The trio junked the previous traditional recipes and launched a series of daringly experimental beers.

Phil made contact with some of the other brewers and, realising something was going on, he and Evin O'Riordan decided to try to bring it all together. In May 2010 they invited all the London brewers, old and new, to dinner, and were overwhelmed at the response, particularly when John Keeling and Derek Prentice, the top brewing team at Fuller's, turned up too. Derek, who started his career at the old Truman brewery and worked at Young's before moving to Fuller's, is something of a living icon of London's brewing tradition and, as often in this industry staffed by enthusiasts, John and Derek were pleased to offer moral support and technical advice to their younger colleagues.

Out of this came the London Brewers Alliance, aiming to "unite those who make local beer with those who love it, and represent the vibrant heritage and contemporary scene of beer brewing in the great city of London". So far it's proved an excellent networking opportunity for the brewers, spawning various

collaboration brews and much sharing of advice and support, enabling brewers to work with new styles and formats. "I brewed a strong imperial Märzen lager with Simon Siemsglüss of Zerodegrees using their lager yeast," says Evin. "And I don't usually do cask beers, so when I was asked to provide some cask, Andy from Redemption helped me. Since then we've brewed a Victorian mild together."

"I've been involved with the London Brewers Alliance from the beginning," adds Simon, "and it's been a really good thing both for me personally and for the brewery. The regular contact and sharing of ideas is really important."

That sharing has extended to tips about possible outlets, and joint promotion projects including a short film. Ultimately a London beer week is planned. All agree there's plenty of room in the marketplace for yet more London brewers, and that promotion under a joint London banner is mutually beneficial. "Everyone can feed off everyone else," says Andy Moffat, "and the popularity of a particular beer raises interest in London beers in general." Alastair Hook concurs: "We can only grow the category of craft beer by growing together, so the more the merrier as far as I'm concerned."

"London's a neglected market," says Duncan Sambrook. "My business partner David Welsh, who was once a director at Ringwood, was amazed at the contrast with Hampshire and

Wiltshire where you're always bumping into reps from other breweries. When we started selling we found there were more outlets than we originally thought – more free houses, and more opportunities to get guests in. The London market's so big, I think it could support all of us and more, so long as London beers retain a really high quality and push the boundaries of what microbrewers can do."

Quality is a recurring theme, and Phil Lowry sees the LBA as a potential 'kitemark' assuring great beer. "There's no point in brewing beer in London unless you can match the standard of Fuller's," he says, "and I genuinely think we reach that. There's not a bad brewer amongst us. London beer is the bollocks!"

Interestingly the Alliance encompasses home brewers: London Amateur Brewers is an affiliated organisation and its members have collaborated on some beers. Historically, home brewing has been less obvious a source of commercial craft brewers in the UK than in some other countries where craft brewing had been historically obliterated. But there are an increasing number of would-be British brewers now experimenting at home, and Phil saw it as important to give them the chance to network too. The amateur sector also boasts a rich vein of research into historic recipes.

One of the striking things about the emerging scene is its variety and eclecticism. Brewers like Sambrook's and Twickenham and to some extent Redemption have followed the traditional cask ale model, but alongside them are Brodie's, producing a constantly changing variety of innovative and experimental beers, and Camden Town and Meantime with their craft brewed lagers. Fuller's has its solid tradition and its internationally recognised cask ale brands, but with an increasing range of fine beers based on long maturation, wood ageing and historic styles.

Kernel has chosen the unusual route for Britain of specialising in hand made, artisanal bottled beers, but its characteristic styles mark the two poles of the emerging brewing culture. On the one hand it makes old fashioned porters and stouts, some of them recreated from historic London recipes. On the other it makes fragrantly hoppy pale ales inspired by contemporary North American models.

The transatlantic influence is a recurring theme. It seems the craft beer culture of the USA, which in its early days was inspired and supported by the rise of beer appreciation in Britain, is now returning the compliment. Phil's model for the Alliance was the San Francisco Brewers Guild, which facilitates collaboration and camaraderie among Bay Area brewers. While the use of American hops has been fully embraced at Brew Wharf, Brodie's and Kernel, their characteristic fruit flavours are also evident in some beers from Meantime, Redemption and Twickenham.

"The modern London style is reflective of the modern London community," says Phil, himself one of only a very few born and bred Londoners on the current scene. London boasts brewers from all over England as well as Scotland, Ireland, Australia, Denmark, Germany and the USA, all of them well schooled in world beers as well as indigenous styles and techniques.

That sophistication is increasingly reflected in the market, which is getting noticeably younger, more diverse and more adventurous. With women as well as men now embracing London beer culture, the old stereotype of middle aged, bearded real ale quaffers is increasingly remote from reality. Craft beer is being approached afresh by savvy consumers who appreciate quality, provenance, craftsmanship, natural ingredients, flavour and character above the bland, processed conformity of international brands.

And interestingly, it's not necessarily cask beer either. Bottled ranges, including bottle conditioned beers, are growing and becoming more varied and sophisticated. Craft keg on the US model is also on the increase, presenting a challenge to the received wisdom of British beer appreciation and campaigning.

This is illustrated very well in the profusion of great beer venues clustering around Borough Market, an appropriate spiritual home for the London beer renaissance given Southwark's historic links with brewing. The ancient wholesale fruit and vegetable market evolved a dual role in the 1990s as a foodie haven, packed with independent stalls selling specialist produce, much of it organic or otherwise ethically sourced. The area had long boasted a handful of good real ale pubs, but mainly serving a very traditional real ale clientele.

In 2000 Utobeer (p62) started selling specialist beers there, sending out the message that these products deserved their place alongside real bread, artisanal cheese, organic meat and single estate Fairtrade coffee. Six years later the same owners opened the Rake (p60) nearby, then one of a few bars in London to sell quality cask alongside a genuinely international imported range. Its success prompted other pubs and bars in the area to up their game. Now there's a whole new following for all of them – from cask ale stalwarts like the Market Porter (p59) to stylish new arrivals like the Draft House (p55) and the Dean Swift (p54). Even the Roxy (p61), a fashionable bar with its own digital cinema, sees the virtue in offering a respectable selection of specialist bottles.

Many of the places with the most eclectic and interesting beer lists are recent makeovers and relauches, often of decaying and insalubrious old boozers that people once crossed the street to avoid, like Cask (p115), the Jolly Butchers (p158) and the Southampton Arms (p157). The designer cool of Mason & Taylor (p103), the eccentric diner-inspired concept of the Draft Houses (p196, p197) or the wood and pewter poshness of the Fox & Anchor (p70) would have been unthinkable in a beer pub a decade ago.

Even more telling is the appropriation of craft beer credibility by the commercial sector. One of the biggest pub owning companies, Mitchells & Butlers, now boasts two chains of pubs with craft beer at the heart of the concept, Nicholson's and the 'unbranded' Castle pubs, the latter often setting out to attract a younger, trendier crowd (p34).

All this may of course be just a blip, a final frenetic tango in the twilight of the apocalypse. Certainly there are still challenges. All the brewers I spoke to agreed that finding a suitable site at the right price remained the biggest obstacle to brewing within London itself, and although the recession reined back rents slightly, with the population still growing, the issue isn't going to go away. High rents also affect the retail sector, with prime sites priced out of the reach of anyone except global chains with no interest in fine beer.

This is in addition to challenges faced by brewers all over Britain, such as high and rising duties, and the power of the pub owning companies to extract discounts from brewers and premiums from licensees. "The pubcos have to realise," says Gavin Happé, "that if they keep squeezing their tenants, people will simply stop putting themselves forward for the trade."

Meanwhile one of the best things you and I can do to ensure the brewers of London stay on that upward curve is to celebrate their craft and creativity by enjoying its results. Raise your glasses, please, for a toast to London brewing. You've certainly got a wide choice of appropriate libations – Sambrook's Wandle, Redemption Urban Dusk, Twickenham Naked Ladies, Kernel London 1890 Export Stout, Meantime Hospital Porter and Camden Town Hells Lager are all possibilities that spring to mind. But perhaps the most appropriately named beer with which to wish the London brewers health, long life and prosperity is also one of the oldest-established: Fuller's London Pride.

WEIGHTS & MEASURES

I've used both imperial and metric measurements throughout this book, most of which should be familiar, with the possible exception of those used for bulk beer.

Traditionally British brewers talk in terms of barrels, which contain 36 (imperial) gallons, or 288 (imperial) pints (163.7l). US beer barrels are considerably smaller, containing 31 US gallons, or 248 US pints, which are 20% smaller than imperial pints (117.3l).

The metric measurement used for bulk beer is the hectolitre (hl), which is simply 100l, so a barrel is about 1.64hl and a US barrel about 1.17hl. 1hl is 0.61 barrels, about 176 pints, and 0.85 US barrels, about 211 US pints.

PLACES TO DRINK

INTRODUCTION
A GUIDE TO DRINKING BEER IN LONDON

CHOOSING LONDON'S BEST BEER VENUES

Despite the lengthy toll of pub closures, there are still 6,000 pubs and bars in London. Most of these sell beer and a good proportion can manage at least a half decent pint. Yet just over 250 venues are listed in the following pages. The obvious question is: how were they chosen? The simple answer is: by their beer.

Collectively, these pubs, bars and other outlets offer one of the world's best beer menus, from a starry cast of brewers working in a vast spectrum of styles. Many of the outlets are here because of the variety of craft beers they stock – both the serious specialist places with something to excite even the most well travelled beer geek, and those with more modest but carefully chosen lists that widen the horizons of less dedicated drinkers. Others, including some outstanding examples of brewery-tied pubs, are recognised for making an excellent job of presenting a more limited range.

London is, of course, real ale territory so it's no surprise that the majority lead their beer offer with a choice of top quality, impeccably served cask beers. But the fun doesn't stop at the handpumps: the guide also lists establishments with notable bottled and imported beers to enjoy. The pleasures of drinking at home are recognised in the inclusion of some first rate specialist beer shops.

Many of the places listed are also of considerable interest for other reasons, among them food and other speciality drinks, history, architecture, location, views or activities like music or theatre, and where appropriate these are discussed in the text. But while such factors might have swayed the balance in one or two borderline cases, they've been insufficient on their own to qualify a venue for inclusion. Some of London's most famous pubs are absent, as I didn't judge their beer offer of sufficient interest.

Two further criteria have been applied. The first is that all venues, in their own way, should offer a welcoming and pleasant environment where the civilised drinker will feel at ease. Some are very small and informal, so don't always expect lightning fast service and four star attention, but you should at least be able to rely on a friendly welcome and staff that care a bit about the stuff they serve. Thankfully it seems that if they care enough to get the beer right, they almost always get the other stuff right too. If you find otherwise, I would very much like to hear about it (see Updates and Feedback below).

The second consideration is that I'd like to encourage you as much as possible to explore London itself as well as its beers. The selection is biased a little towards places where you might, or should, go for other reasons. So the central area is covered in some depth, and I've also tried to ensure there are listings in the most interesting and attractive outlying areas like Greenwich, Hampstead and Richmond, and near big sports and entertainment venues, transport hubs and major parks and green spaces. If there's an outstanding beer outlet elsewhere, then I've listed it as worthy of a special trip, but I've usually imposed higher standards on places in the outlying suburbs. In a few cases, I hope to nudge you into exploring parts of London that aren't on most visitors' itineraries, but should reward you in other ways besides beer.

PUBS & BARS

Pubs account for the vast majority of the places listed here. 'Pub' is a licensing term, short for 'public house', somewhere that's licensed to sell alcoholic drinks to the general public with or without food, and not just club members, hotel guests or restaurant diners.

However in general use the term conjures up much more than this. It will likely make you think of somewhere unpretentious, convivial and relaxed, and probably rather old

< **The island bar at the Alma (p144)**

The Bear (p172) offers fine beers with a gastro menu

fashioned and rustic, with padded benches around a roaring open fire, and horse brasses and tankards dangling from ancient ceiling beams. Or perhaps a street corner public bar with a lino floor, a well-used dartboard and an amusing little sign that says credit will gladly be granted to customers over the age of 80, if accompanied by both parents.

Pubs like these do indeed still exist in London, and we should be thankful for the best of them. But these stereotyped images never reflected the breadth of pub culture, and are seriously out of step with it today. As reported elsewhere, pubs are under more pressure than ever before, and have survived either by living up to expectations in the best possible way, or by finding new ways of doing things to match the changing tastes of their customers.

This process has now been going on long enough to establish a new set of pub clichés which might include bare floorboards, mismatched furniture with bulky stripped wood tables and saggy sofas, big jars of olives and wasabi peanuts behind the bar and chalked up menus listing belly pork, wild mushroom risotto and fish finger sandwiches. If done well, these too can be great places, though customers with creaky knees are well advised to steer clear of those sofas.

There are many, many other varieties: pubs that look like living rooms or children's play rooms, youth clubs or wood panelled gentlemen's clubs, quirky pubs with collections of bizarre artefacts, stripped down designer pubs with sparse touches of contemporary art, not to mention a good number that dazzle us with their architecture and fittings, whether that's spectacular late Victorian engraved glass screens and mosaic floors or the sumptuous marble of former banking halls. What all these places share with the stereotype is that they're convivial and relaxed, and, designer minimalism aside, mainly unpretentious too.

The guide breaks places with pub licenses down into four categories, though all of them have very fuzzy edges.

A **traditional pub** is the closest thing to the pub stereotype. Most are in purpose-built premises at least a century old. They include London's few remaining basic public bars as well as more luxuriously fitted places.

A **contemporary pub** still feels very much like a pub and is often in the same kind of building as a traditional pub. But it has a more modern interior, refitted in the past couple of decades and indeed quite likely to boast bare floorboards, mismatched furniture etc etc. Most take pride in their food but remain at least equally welcoming to non-diners.

The term **gastropub** was coined in the 1980s, and its always imprecise meaning has been further confused by the proliferation of elements of the original formula – indeed most of the clichés mentioned above derive from gastro practice. I've reserved it for pubs that genuinely aspire to be a dining destination in their own right, not just a pub with good food. However gastropubs are still pubs, and non-dining drinkers should be welcome too.

Some places with pub licenses don't feel at all like pubs, and I've designated these **bars**. Most follow non-native traditions, homaging Low Countries cafés, Bavarian *gäststätte* or US dive bars, for example. A few are flasher establishments in the international style.

Brewpubs are pubs where beer is brewed on the premises, and their breweries also qualify for extended treatment in the Brewers & Beers section (p240).

I've also noted **specialists**, places where the wide range of unusual beers on offer is the main attraction.

Some pubs, mainly traditional ones, are identified as **heritage pubs**. These are listed on the National and Regional Inventories of Historic Pub Interiors maintained by CAMRA's Pub Heritage Group. The National Inventory lists interiors that have remained wholly or largely intact since World War II, or which retain exceptional rooms or features that are of national historic importance. The Regional Inventory is the next tier down and includes interiors which, though altered, still have significant historic or architectural value. Note that the inventories only include purpose-built pub interiors, not buildings of historic architectural interest that have more recently been converted to pubs.

OTHER LICENSED VENUES

Clubs are licensed to sell alcohol to a restricted group of people, such as members, or people who've paid an admission fee to dance or listen to bands. The few listed here are members' clubs, but happily they extend their welcome to those in possession of CAMRA membership cards or guide books.

The few **restaurants** listed here are either attached to pubs or have a separate bar area where they will serve drinks without food, but this may be restricted and they may prioritise people waiting for a table at busy times.

In England **shops** that specialise in alcoholic drinks are known as 'off licenses' as their wares are only for consumption off the premises: unlike in some countries, you're not allowed to drink what you buy before you've left, though they may offer free tastings. Much of what's on offer will be bottled but some sell freshly poured cask beer in takeaway containers. Pubs too are usually permitted to make 'off sales' and some actively promote this.

ADMISSION

None of the places listed in this guide habitually charge you simply to get in, though the more upmarket places with table service

Ordering a drink at the Green Man (p79)

may occasionally make a cover charge. Occasionally a venue holding a special one-off event might charge admission.

ORDERING A DRINK

Some of what follows may seem like stating the bleeding obvious to anyone familiar with British pub culture, but is provided for the benefit of visitors and new arrivals.

The general rule in Britain is to go to the bar, look expectant but not too pushy as you wait your turn for the staff's attention, order your drink, wait until it's poured and pay for it immediately, before you start drinking it.

Some pubs do free tasters of draught beer to help you make up your mind. This is occasionally mentioned in the listings: if not, look out for a notice, or ask questions about the beer on offer. If they have a tasting policy, they'll usually offer you a try at this point, otherwise if it's an unfamiliar beer you'll have to go on the bar staff's recommendation.

If there's something genuinely wrong with the beer – and things do go wrong, especially with cask beer, even in the most scrupulous pubs – tell the bar staff before drinking a substantial amount. Places in this guide should change it without question. Of course if the beer's simply not to your taste that's your hard luck. See also under Measures and prices below.

Cash is the preferred method of payment, though more and more pubs are accepting

credit and debit cards. Some of them make an additional charge for transactions below a certain amount, often £10 (€11.50, $16). Some pubs will run a tab for card users, usually keeping your card behind the bar as a deposit – don't forget to leave without it. Don't assume a pub takes cards – check before you order. Cash machines (ATMs) in pubs invariably make an additional charge to your account.

Some pubs have table service for diners, either throughout or in a specific area. In this case they'll likely fetch drinks for you too and present you with a bill before you leave. A few bars extend this service to people just drinking, in cosmopolitan fashion. Look for obvious signs such as a notice asking you to wait to be seated. When in doubt go to the bar and ask.

MEASURES & PRICES

The last legal bastions of imperial measurements in British retail are draught beer, cider and perry and, curiously, fresh milk.

Draught beer can only be sold in measures of a third of an (imperial) pint (197ml, 6.67 oz) or multiples of a half pint (284ml, 10 oz). Measures of two thirds of a pint (394ml, 13.33 oz) are shortly to be introduced too.

In practice, the majority of pubs sell beer in pints (568ml, 20 oz) or halves. A few specialist beer pubs offer thirds, which are also seen at many CAMRA beer festivals. It remains to be seen how pubs will take to the two thirds measure.

All glasses used for draught beer should carry an official stamp. Traditional glassware in London is designed to be filled to the brim, with very little head. You may occasionally encounter 'oversized' lined glasses, particulary at beer festivals. Branded glasses for imported beers are lined with the nearest appropriate British measure.

Pubs are legally allowed to fill brim glasses to only 95% of a full measure, a law which CAMRA has campaigned to change. If you're unhappy with the measure you've been served, you're within your rights to ask for a top-up, and all the pubs listed here should be happy to oblige.

Confusingly, bottled and canned beer, and all other drinks, are sold in metric measures. Packaged beers can be sold in any quantity, so long as it's shown in millilitres on the package. Most British brewed beers come in bottles of 500ml (16.9 oz), and occasionally 330ml (11.2 oz) or 750ml (25.4 oz). Imperial sized bottles are sometimes still seen, but labelled in ml. Bottled beers are almost always available singly, even in supermarkets.

At the time of writing, a typical pint of draught cask beer in a London pub costs around £3.50 (€4.10, $5.70), but could vary by up to 50p either way. A 500ml bottle of speciality British beer might cost £1.80 (€2.10, $2.90) in a supermarket. Something rarer could be £3 (€3.50, $4.90) in a specialist shop and brewers are getting more confident about asking premium prices for premium products.

The currency conversions, incidentally, are based on an exchange rate of €1.17 and $1.63 but this may well change.

SEATS & RESERVATIONS

In pubs, you're generally free to occupy any unoccupied space, including stools and standing room at the bar, so long as you're not in the way and there's no reserved sign or other indication you shouldn't be there (areas reserved for diners when you're only drinking, for example). Unlike in some countries, prices aren't cheaper at the bar. At busy times it's usually fine to ask if you can share a table. Hopefully the sort of pubs where you could

cause inadvertent offence by sitting in the seat normally occupied by the Oldest Regular are long gone and certainly shouldn't be listed here.

Reservations purely for drinking purposes are still relatively rare though some popular venues will reserve tables, or even whole areas or rooms, for groups of various sizes on request. The German practice of permanently reserving tables for particular groups of regulars is not common in Britain.

Gastropubs and other places big on food will likely operate a reservations system for diners and you're advised to take advantage of this, particularly at popular times such as Thursday, Friday and Saturday evenings and Sunday lunchtimes.

TIPPING

Though I certainly don't want to discourage spontaneous generosity towards London's hard working bar staff, tipping isn't customary when simply ordering drinks at a bar. Attempts to do so won't cause offence – some places even have a receptacle for the purpose, especially if they're used to overseas visitors – but no one will think less of you if you don't. The normal way to show occasional and by no means obligatory additional appreciation is to ask "And one for yourself?" Don't be surprised if the equivalent amount in cash is then placed in a communal tips jar rather than consumed in liquid form.

If you've enjoyed table service and are presented with a bill, this may well include the automatic addition of a 10-15% optional service charge, and the menu should forewarn you of this. If not, it will very likely state prominently that service is not included, in which case 10-15% is the appropriate amount to add, particularly if it's for a large group.

Note the service charge is optional, and you are well within your rights not to pay all or part of it, even if automatically added, if you genuinely feel the service provided doesn't merit it. This is a right to be exercised with confidence and discretion and best reserved for venues to which you have no intention of returning. I hope such a situation will never arise in the places listed here.

FOOD

The overwhelming majority of places listed here offer decent homemade cooked food in which they take great pride, and a handful offer cuisine of quality and distinction matching that of many high-end restaurants.

By food, incidentally, I mean something more substantial than the ubiquitous prepacked snacks which include, for those unfamiliar with the repertoire, crisps (potato chips), nuts and pork scratchings (roasted strips of pork fat)...and even olives and spicy wasabi peanuts.

Though the quality has improved immensely in recent decades, it's fair to say most pub food is still cut from the same cloth, in the traditional British style usually designated 'pub grub'. Pub menus usually start at sandwiches, increasingly of the 'gourmet' variety, progressing to salads, jacket potatoes, and 'ploughman's lunches' (cheese and/or ham, salad, pickles and crusty bread). More substantial retro snacks like pork pies, Scotch eggs (hard boiled eggs with a sausagemeat and breadcrumb coating) and pickled eggs (as peculiar as they sound) are undergoing a resurgence. Sharing 'platters' facilitate communal grazing, probably on something unhealthy. Pubs with early opening will offer continental or full English cooked breakfasts and some may do American-style brunches of the Eggs Benedict variety, particularly at weekends.

Pub grub main courses typically involve sausage or pie and mash, shepherd's pie (minced meat covered with a layer of potato), fish and chips, burgers, curries, steaks and pasta dishes. Everywhere now has vegetarian options but this may well be the ubiquitous mushroom risotto: if there are signs of a special effort for veggies I've noted this. Some places go much further with varied and imaginative menus. Gastropubs usually opt for posher versions of pub grub staples, enhanced by more sophisticated dishes that tend towards British, French and Mediterranean in style. A subset of pubs offer full Thai menus and a few more specialise in proper pizzas.

Disappointingly few pubs promote beer as an accompaniment to food, although some put it in their pies and sausages. Places with beer matching suggestions are highlighted in the text. Some places promoting Belgian beer match it with classic dishes like *moules frites* (mussels and chips). A few, realising the affinity between beer and cheese, offer appropriate tasting plates.

Pubs with food invariably offer something special on Sunday daytimes – usually roast meat and/or poultry and 'all the trimmings' (roast potatoes, Yorkshire batter pudding, vegetables), though probably with a veggie option too. This may well be to the exclusion of the regular *carte*.

The listings identify the cooking style and note a few typical dishes to give you an idea of the type of food you'll encounter. Specific dishes may well change as menus are refreshed. There hasn't been space to include food service times but food is almost never available throughout a pub's opening hours. It may only be served lunchtimes, or evenings, or not at all on quieter days. Kitchens are often closed for a period in the late afternoon and as early as 8 or 9 in the evenings. Sunday lunch usually continues until stocks run out. If you're relying on eating it's always best to ring ahead and check times.

We generally haven't indicated costs of meals, which can vary enormously both from pub to pub and according to how much, and what, you choose from the menu. Expect to pay at least £8-9 (€9.50-10.70, $13-15.50) for a cheaper main course. Some dishes, like steaks, could be a lot more expensive. If you find a decent homemade lunchtime main course for under £5 (€6, $8), congratulate yourself on your good fortune.

AGE LIMITS & CHILDREN

The legal drinking age in the UK is 18. The only exception is for 16-17 year olds dining in the company of adults, who are permitted to drink, but not buy, beer, wine and cider with their meal.

These limits are much more strictly enforced than they used to be, and licensees risk losing their license and their livelihood if they fail to uphold them. If you look younger, expect to be asked for proof of age. Increasingly licensees operate 'Challenge 21' and 'Challenge 25' policies to shrink the margin of error.

Licensees are also under no obligation to serve you even if you are over 18, so long as they don't break equal opportunity laws by discriminating against you on the grounds of race, religion, gender, sexuality or disability. Some pubs have 'over 21s only' rules to discourage unruly barely legal teenagers.

At the same time as attitudes to underage drinking have hardened, those to children in pubs have become happily more relaxed. Thirty years ago, the inside of practically every pub in Britain was an adults-only zone, with children only permitted outdoors. Today most pubs welcome children, so long as they're accompanied by adults. A few go out of their way to be family friendly, with children's menus, baby changing facilities, toys, special seating and even playrooms.

However restrictions may apply. Some pubs only allow children if dining, and/or in designated areas. Children are never allowed at the bar itself, and there's usually a curfew in the early to mid evening. Even if a pub doesn't turn children away, parents or carers may decide it's not an appropriate place to take them. Children will be expected to be well behaved, and not to run about or make excessive noise, except in places like play areas. A few pubs maintain the traditional ban, and that's fine too, as some customers prefer to drink in exclusively adult company.

SMOKING

Smoking in enclosed public places has been banned throughout the UK since 2007 and licensees face fines and possible loss of license if they don't enforce this. Where they have the space, landlords often show great ingenuity in creating smoking areas that are as sheltered, warm and comfortable as they can be while still meeting the legal definition of outdoors. If no such space is available, smokers have to do without or stand outside on the street. Ask before taking your drink outside with you as local licensing rules sometimes prohibit this.

DISABLED ACCESS

Visitors from North America may be surprised at the lack of provision for people with disabilities. Only a minority of pubs are fully wheelchair accessible with disabled toilets.

Those without disabled toilets but where access is possible will gladly make an effort to get wheelchair users in if they can, but it's best to notify them in advance. Newly built or refurbished places are now legally obliged to be accessible, but there's no requirement to retrofit older premises. In pubs' defence, most are in old buildings where it's complicated and expensive to install accessibility features, particularly if they're protected under heritage regulations.

GETTING AROUND

Although many Londoners appear to believe otherwise, London's public transport system is extensive, comprehensive, reasonably well-integrated and relatively reliable. It includes the world's biggest metro network, the London Underground, with 260 stations and 402km (249 miles) of track, and an extensive bus network, with almost 7,000 buses on over 700 different routes. Its drawbacks are that it's quite expensive, indeed extortionate if you buy tickets as you go rather than using one of the prepay or zonal pass schemes; that it's prone to partial planned closures due to protracted rebuilding after a long period of underinvestment; and that during peak hours it can get horrifically overcrowded.

Public transport is still a far better option than driving, which requires struggling with the capital's congested roads and tortuous one way systems, and paying a hefty charge to take a car into the central area on weekday daytimes. Readers of this book have a particular reason not to contemplate getting behind the wheel: drink driving laws are strictly enforced, as well they should be.

I recommend beer explorers equip themselves with an Oyster card, Transport for London (TfL)'s smart ticketing card, even if only in town for a short period. The £3 refundable deposit is a small price to pay for much cheaper fares and increased convenience. You can load it with cash and then pay as you go by touching in and touching out, and/or use it to store a zonal pass for a specific period of time.

Many Londoners and visitors appear to believe London's only usable method of travel is the London Underground, and start to glaze over when you suggest they visit places that

Central London is well-signed for walkers trying to navigate the city

aren't on 'the Tube'. Such an attitude is to be discouraged. There are whole swathes of the capital, particularly in the south and east, that the Tube doesn't reach. The ingenious and iconic diagrammatic map originally developed in the 1930s by Harry Beck distorts distances to show stations and connections clearly: in fact more than 100 station to station journeys in central London are quicker on foot. And you can easily spend far too much time staring at tunnel walls and wondering what the seemingly endless lengths of wire are for, rather than enjoying the street life and views.

As well as the Tube, Oyster cards are valid on practically all local services operated as part of the National Rail network within Greater London; the London Overground, a network of conventional rail lines around the inner suburbs overseen by TfL; the intriguing driverless trains of the Docklands Light Railway (DLR); TramLink, the modern tram (streetcar) network in south London centred on Croydon; and London Buses. The buses in particular are much easier to navigate than they used to be, with individually named bus stops and much improved information.

Alternatively you could save money and help work off some of the calories from all that beer by travelling actively. While London's still got some way to go to catch up with cities like Amsterdam or Copenhagen, its current fastest growing transport mode is cycling, reflecting significant investment. The most obvious signs are the ranks of distinctive 'Boris Bikes' for hire throughout the central area, so nicknamed after current Mayor Boris Johnson, although the scheme was first proposed under his predecessor. You can hire these with a credit card or become a member and get a key. With the latter it costs only £1 or less to ride around all day so long as you don't keep a single bike for longer than 30 minutes. The scheme is currently being extended towards the Olympic venues.

There are also networks of signed cycle routes although they're rarely segregated from motor traffic as in some other countries. Cycle maps published by TfL will help you find your way. Note that while there's no specific blood alcohol limit for cyclists, it's illegal and also highly irresponsible to cycle while drunk.

Finally, don't forget walking, my principal transport mode when researching this book. It's not only the cheapest and most easily available mode, it's also the best way to immerse yourself in the city environment and enjoy a close-up view that you simply can't get even on a bike. Although London still has far too many spaces dominated by traffic, there's been significant investment in walking too. There's a surprisingly attractive network of signed green routes using footpaths, parks and open spaces, and streets too are getting more pedestrian friendly, particularly in town centres.

Full and detailed information on all these options, including walking and cycling information and a reliable journey planner, is available at ⊕ www.tfl.gov.uk or by calling ☎ 0843 222 1234.

OF CHAINS, TIES & FREEDOM

Who owns London's pubs? The answer used to be straightforward as nearly all of them were owned by breweries under what's known as the 'tied house system'. Brewing in the UK was a classic example of a 'vertically integrated' industry where production, distribution and retail are in the same hands. In London this system took hold from the 1890s. But brewers had been tying up the retail sector long before then by providing favourable finance deals to licensees on condition that they committed to selling the partner brewery's products, an arrangement still common in mainland Europe.

There are two kinds of brewery-tied houses. 'Managed houses' are effectively branches of the brewery, with licensees and staff on the brewery payroll. 'Tenancies' are separate businesses, leasing pubs from breweries at a favourable rent but obliged to buy their beer from the owner, usually at a premium. A handful of pubs have always been 'free houses', owned by non-brewing interests and therefore free to source beer on the open market, at cheaper prices than brewery tenants.

The tied house system extended breweries' control to the pub cellar and the bar counter, advantageous given their main product, cask beer, requires careful handling right up to the point of dispense (p250). Where there were lots of breweries, consumers still had the opportunity to exercise choice simply by visiting a different pub. But it discouraged the creation of new and innovative brewery start-ups as without an estate of pubs, potential outlets were very limited.

Following post-war consolidation, the tied house system became a major obstacle to consumer choice. By the early 1970s, six large groups between them owned over half the country's pubs. These brewers were unafraid to exploit their powerful position, streamlining their ranges to a handful of cheaply made products they could now sell at a premium to a captive audience.

Following the founding of CAMRA the clamour for quality and diversity grew, but newly-founded breweries hoping to satisfy it faced major challenges in getting their products to market. CAMRA and others campaigned against this anti-competitive situation, advocating a limit on the size of estates across which the tie could be enforced. The authorities eventually agreed and in 1989 the government introduced new regulations known as the Beer Orders, forcing breweries with large tied estates to release some of their pubs from the tie and to allow the others to stock a guest beer.

No one could have predicted quite how much this apparently modest intervention would rock the industry. The horrific prospect of allowing other brewers' beer into their pubs prompted the breweries to question the very fundamentals of vertical integration. Some of them shed all of their pubs and focused on their brewing businesses. Others, including a poignant roll call of old established independents, cashed in the property value of prime town centre brewing sites and focused on their pubs, contracting their old brands out to others.

Anyone who thought the outcome would be a nation of free houses with newly liberated landlords beaming a hearty welcome from behind an array of exotic pump clips soon had those illusions shattered. A whole new wave of consolidation followed, and the Big Six have since been succeeded by four global giants, most of whom don't own a significant pub estate. A similar process swept the retailing side of the industry, with a handful of big pub owning companies, 'pubcos', eventually emerging. These pubcos were as keen to streamline operations as their predecessors had been, striking favourable supply deals with a handful of breweries. So drinkers often still ended up facing the same old boring beers in thousands of pubs, but now outside the reach of the Beer Orders which only applied to brewers.

Following all this, Britain has two more categories of pubs. In addition to free houses, brewery managed houses and brewery tenancies, there are now pubco managed houses and tenancies, the latter now tied to a pubco for their beer supplies. About half the UK's pubs remain tied in one way or another; a good few of the remainder are chains of managed houses prone to homogeneity in

The Founders Arms (p112) is a Young's pub with a fantastic riverfront setting

the interests of economies of scale.

In retrospect, though, the shakeup has resulted in an overall widening of choice, and made the pub owners more susceptible to consumer demand, bolstered by continued campaigning and awareness raising by organisations like CAMRA and the independent brewers' trade organisation SIBA. There are certainly enhanced opportunities for new craft brewers, especially when coupled with the adoption in 2002 of Progressive Beer Duty, which halved the duty on beer for breweries producing less than 60,000hl (37,000 barrels) a year.

700 new breweries have opened in the UK since CAMRA was founded, some of them now selling significant quantities through big national pub estates that once would have been completely off limits. In the past few years the pubcos have belatedly discovered the advantages of offering a wider range of craft beer, supporting a growing market. Variety has been boosted by new links with specialist wholesalers, and initiatives like SIBA's

Direct Delivery Scheme, enabling small breweries to supply beer direct to nearby pubco tenants, thus avoiding all the negative impacts of trucking supplies long distances via central warehouses.

Such variety has been achieved, quite literally, at a cost – to breweries and licensees and to you, the drinker. Pubcos use their buying power and control of the routes to market to negotiate aggressively for substantial discounts from the brewer. They then sell on to the licensee at an eye-watering markup, as much as double the price the brewery would charge a free house. Nearly every pubco tenant I spoke to while researching this guide had something often rather impolite to say about the double squeeze they face from increasing rents and increasing beer prices. CAMRA and tenants' organisations are currently campaigning for at least an easing of the pubco tie.

London is no exception in having the bulk of its pubs in the hands of breweries, pubcos and major chains, a situation reflected in this book. Things are complicated a little further by the fact that some tied pubs are now leased by small companies that also run other pubs, perhaps leased from different owners or free of tie. The capital's handful of genuine independent free houses is disproportionately represented here as many of these remain bastions of quality and variety, just as they were before the Beer Orders. An exceptional few tied houses have long enjoyed special privileges in stocking a wide variety of cask beers.

The capital's stock of brewery pubs is dominated by two companies: London brewer **Fuller's** (p270) and former London brewer **Young's** (see Ram p277 and Wells & Young's p316). These can usually be relied upon to stock their owners' cask ales, sometimes alongside a guest beer. Aside from the beer range the pubs vary enormously, including both tenancies and managed houses, though the examples of the latter listed here tend to be quite prestigious, with a substantial food offering too.

Some London pubs are leased from the **Scottish & Newcastle** subsidiary of **Heineken**, the only multinational brewer to retain a substantial pub estate, although most of it is ultimately owned by the Royal Bank of Scotland. Apart from Caledonian (p290), Heineken retains no UK craft beer brands of any interest so its pubs don't figure largely here.

The pubco sector in London is dominated by three groups descended from the former Big Six – Enterprise, Mitchells & Butlers and Punch. However you're unlikely to see these names prominently displayed on pub premises.

Enterprise pubs are all tenancies, most formerly belonging to Bass or Whitbread. They're a diverse bunch, their character determined by the individual tenants. They have access to a wide range of beer, including through the SIBA Direct Delivery Scheme, though invoiced to tenants at premium prices. Several real ale stalwarts listed here are Enterprise tenancies (⊕ www.enterpriseinns.com).

Mitchells & Butlers is one of the successors of Bass, reviving the name of a Birmingham brewery taken over by Bass in

1961 and closed in 2002 when the parent was carved up between the predecessors of AB InBev and Molson Coors. Its pubs are all managed houses, but segmented into a number of separate brands, each with its own house style. Two of these brands feature prominently in this book (⊕ www.mbplc.com).

Nicholson's is the brand used for the more upmarket traditional pubs in important centres. Real ale figures highly in the formula and most stock at least eight cask beers. They offer a comprehensive menu of tarted-up pub grub, often including breakfast and making a feature of either pies or sausages. The Nicholson's brand had a good reputation for real ale in the 1990s and its recent rejuvenation is a welcome development, significantly increasing the availability of fine beer in some previously badly served areas of Central London. Other branches besides those listed here are worth checking out (⊕ www.nicholsonspubs.co.uk).

Castle pubs also feature real ale, and a range of keg and bottled imported beers too. But the brand is only used internally, as each pub is supposed to have a distinct identity. Once you've been in a few, though, you'll soon learn to spot them. They tend to be youthful, upmarket and contemporary in feel, with arty tendencies, although there are some very traditional places too. Cask beers often include some in unusual styles, and it's pleasing to see craft beer deployed to attract this sector of the market.

Punch, another inheritor of the Bass and Whitbread estates, is the UK's biggest pub-owning company, with approaching 7,000 pubs including both managed houses and tenancies. Early in 2011, it announced its intention to split its managed and tenanted pubs bewteen two separate companies. The tenancies, like Enterprise's, vary in character, though hitherto they've had a more restricted selection of cask ales, with a limited core range and bimonthly list of guests under the name Punch Finest Cask. However the company has just rolled out the SIBA Direct Delivery Scheme to its tenants. Like Enterprise, it imposes hefty mark-ups (⊕ www.punchtaverns.com).

The managed houses, like M&B's, are segmented under various brands, of which the most significant for our purposes is

Taylor Walker – another recent revival of a defunct brewery name, originally belonging to an East End brewery bought and closed by Ind Coope (since absorbed by Carlsberg) in 1960. The house style owes an obvious debt to M&B's Nicholson's model, though in my experience with a less varied choice of beers (⊕ www.taylor-walker.co.uk).

The other major player is **J D Wetherspoon**, which has no roots in the old tied house system. Founded in 1979 with a single North London pub by entrepreneur Tim Martin, who named it after one of his former school teachers, Wetherspoon now owns over 700 managed pubs, mainly large ones in buildings converted from other uses. Wetherspoon pubs have an instantly recognisable style that is readily ridiculed, particularly given its founder's penchant for loud shirts and louder opinions, but also has much to be said for it. Cask ale is a major feature, sourced from a wide range of often very small breweries and sold at bargain prices. Two beer festivals a year across the chain include such praiseworthy initiatives as inviting top brewers from abroad to create cask specials in British breweries. Food, from an extensive menu, is on sale usually from breakfast until 10 in the evening and while it's far from gourmet standard, it's very fairly priced. The venues are blissfully free of piped music and aim to be welcoming and accessible to all but also sometimes lack atmosphere and can seem corporate and downmarket. Currently CAMRA members receive Wetherspoon discount vouchers as a membership benefit. Some Wetherspoons that make an extra effort with their beer range are listed here, including one particularly remarkable example in the City which has made it to our Top 25. The rest can usually be relied upon as a good standby if you're after a beer in an unfamiliar place. **Lloyds No 1** bars are also part of the group, but have background music and a more limited beer range (⊕ www.jdwetherspoon.co.uk).

There are other, smaller chains and pubcos which are mentioned in the entries when relevant.

The Crosse Keys (p66), a good example of a J D Wetherspoon's pub

HOW TO USE THE LISTINGS

NAVIGATION

The listings cover Greater London, as first defined in 1964 and now administrated by the Greater London Authority, the Mayor of London and the 33 London Boroughs. This is a bigger area than the one covered by the familiar London Postal Districts, and for decades the Royal Mail caused confusion by insisting that postal addresses in outlying areas included former county names, even Middlesex, which had been entirely abolished as an administrative entity. This book is proud to risk the annoyance of boundary traditionalists and metric martyrs by counting places like Barnet, Bromley, Croydon, Enfield, Harrow, Kingston, Richmond, Twickenham and Upminster as London.

Greater London covers 1,572 square kilometres (607 square miles) and has a population of 7,754,000. Unfortunately there's no universally agreed system for subdividing it – the two most familiar, postal districts and boroughs, both have their drawbacks. So I've taken a pragmatic approach, doing what most Londoners do and thinking in terms of clusters around transport interchanges.

Central London includes anywhere within a short walk of a station in Transport for London's Fare Zone 1. All the listings within this section are arranged under subdivisions with at least two venues in each.

Outside the central area, the listings are divided into East, North and West London, all to the north of the river Thames; and Southeast and Southwest London, south of the river. These are also subdivided, though there are several instances of isolated venues collected at the end of each section under their locality names. These venues are in no way less worthy of attention, it's just that they don't form convenient clusters with others.

To make things clearer, look at the overview map inside the front cover, the maps that introduce each section and the more detailed maps for individual areas which show the location of venues. These maps alone might not be sufficient for foolproof navigation so should be used in conjunction with a street atlas or online mapping (see More information p325).

NAMES

Within each section, venue names are listed alphabetically, ignoring initial 'The', and also initial 'Ye', the faux archaism beloved of heritage tourism. Names are kept short, dispensing with suffixed phrases like 'pub and restaurant', though there are a few 'inns' and 'taverns' if the name looked naked without them. Punctuation of pub names is often inconsistent so has been regularised by dropping apostrophes.

VENUE CATEGORY

These give a general indication of what to expect and are explained in more detail on p28. They are: *Traditional pub*; *Contemporary pub*; *Gastropub*; *Brewpub*; *Bar*; *Specialist*; *Restaurant*; *Club*; *Shop*.

☆ **25** shows a place included on the London's Top 25 Pubs & Bars list (p39).
★ indicates a pub on CAMRA's National Inventory of Historic Pub Interiors.
☆ indicates a pub on the London Regional Inventory.

CONTACT DETAILS

The street address includes a full postcode. In urban areas postcodes specify a short stretch of street or even a single building, and are extremely useful with online mapping and services like the TfL journey planner. I've left out the word 'London' for places in the London Postal Districts (postcodes beginning E, EC, N, NW, SE, SW, W and WC).

Phone numbers 🔳 are shown with area code in brackets, usually 020. You don't need to dial the 020 if calling from another 020 number, but you will if calling from a mobile (cellphone). To call from outside the UK, dial the international access code (00 in Europe, 011 in North America), then 44 for the UK, then the number shown leaving out the initial 0.

Web addresses ⊕ occasionally cover a group of venues, for example www. jdwetherspoon.co.uk. Their home pages should have an obvious way of searching for a particular place.

If the venue uses facebook or twitter we've indicated this with **fbk** and **tw** and included the twitter username.

OPENING TIMES

Indicated by ☼. Shown using the 12-hour clock, but with am and pm omitted as they are usually obvious from the context. Core pub hours are typically 11 or 12 to 11 at night, and 12 to 10.30 on Sundays, but there are many variations, and some places may not open till late afternoon on certain days. Most venues listed are open daily but pubs in the City and some other areas of central London may shut at weekends.

POLICY ON CHILDREN

If there's nothing about children, then assume they're not permitted inside the pub, although they are welcome in outdoor areas. Otherwise we've summarised the policy as best we can, but see under Age limits & children (p29) for more advice. 'Children very welcome' indicates the pub makes a special effort.

FOOD & DRINK

CASK BEER

This includes the number of cask beers you can expect to find and the brewers of any permanent beers. 'Guests' suggests these are sourced from better-known breweries; 'unusual guests' suggests an increased likelihood of finding rarer beers from smaller micros. More information is usually given in the text. Note that pubs may not always have all their beers on, particularly at quieter times. If you're puzzled by the significance of the term 'cask beer' and why it receives such special attention, see p251.

✅ indicates the pub had Cask Marque accreditation at the time of writing. This is awarded by an independent body supported by the industry, based on a twice-yearly unannounced assessment. Some licensees are critical of the value of Cask Marque but I've found it to be a relatively reliable indicator of beer quality. However pubs have to pay to be assessed and some choose not to, so those that don't have it are not necessarily any worse than those that do (⊕ www.cask-marque.co.uk).

OTHER BEERS

Numbers of other specialist and craft beers available in keg or in bottle are shown, ignoring mainstream industrial products which will be of little interest to readers. For more on these beer 'formats', see p251.

ALSO

This guide is first and foremost a beer guide, but most of us appreciate other quality drinks too. Where a venue offers a particularly noteworthy selection of something else that I happened to notice (and I may well have missed a few), it's mentioned here. Real cider and perry, naturally fermented and served without gas pressure, are of interest to many beer drinkers and have been noted if present. 'Malts' means single malt whiskies and if mentioned implies there's rather more than the odd bottle of Glenfiddich or Glenmorangie.

Thankfully most British pubs have got over the idea that fermented grape juice means bag-in-a-box French dregs and Liebfräumilch so syrupy you could pour it on pancakes, so the presence of a few drinkable wines can usually be relied upon. 'Wines' indicates a more than average effort, and a few of the gastropubs have some very serious cellars.

Soft drinks, particularly low calorie ones that don't contain caffeine, remain a weak link in pub culture. Take it as read that most venues offer tea and coffee, though a few might look at you askance if you ask for one late at night when they're busy.

FOOD

See the discussion on food above (p29). Space precludes us listing food service times in detail so ring ahead and check.

Many pubs take pride in their food menus

FEATURES

Outdoor facilities are particularly attractive in good weather as well as being of newly enhanced interest to smokers so I've mentioned them here. The relative rarity of front terraces is one area where traditional British pub culture scores badly compared to most of its European counterparts, even in countries where the weather is at least as wretched. Still there are some splendid back gardens to be found. If nothing is listed under this category, nothing is provided, and smokers will just have to stand out on the street.

♿ indicates a fully accessible disabled toilet. Some pubs have only conventional toilets but flat access to all or part of the building, and this is noted where staff have pointed it out.

A summary of activities other than eating, drinking and socialising is shown in italics. Most of these are self-explanatory. The term 'functions' indicates a separate space is bookable, quite possibly for a fee, for private social events and other purposes.

TRANSPORT

The nearest convenient rail interchanges are indicated as follows:

⤾   National Rail

϶ London Underground or London Overground (note capital 'O' – some Londoners also use the term to cover National Rail).

DLR Docklands Light Railway

🚉 Tramlink

Some places are not within easy walking distance of rail services so bus connections are shown with 🚌 , the name of the bus stop (all now individually named in London), the route numbers if there's only one or two, and the stations they connect to. We've favoured non-walkers when listing buses: if you're more energetic you might want to check on the map first to judge if it's worth waiting for a bus.

🚲 indicates if there are recognised cycle routes nearby. NCN indicates a National Cycle Network route (☸ www.sustrans.org.uk). LCN+ is a London cycle network route, with the route number if known or nearby destinations

it links to. CS indicates one of the new Cycling Superhighways. You can also cycle to places not on specific routes using the street network. For more details see the cycle maps at ☸ www.tfl.gov.uk.

➠ indicates if there are recognised walking routes nearby, though of course everywhere else can be reached by walking too. Details of London's principal walking routes can be found at ☸ www.walklondon.org.uk. Some others are shown on Ordnance Survey Explorer maps (☸ www.ordnancesurvey.co.uk) and/or information can be found online by googling the route names shown.

OTHER PLACES TO TRY

A summary of information sources about other potential places of interest to beer drinkers in London is under More information (p325).

UPDATES & FEEDBACK

A book like this is inevitably out of date from the second the final pages are sent to the printer. Leases come up for renewal, businesses fail and policies change. More positively, new initiatives are launched and existing venues decide to up their game. Change is particularly likely in today's volatile market. And as I admit elsewhere, there are undoubtedly venues that were missed during compilation.

If you're making a special trip, the only reliable way of guarding against disappointment is to contact the venue first – phoning is more likely, in my experience, to bring quick results than emailing.

If you encounter any closures or significant changes in policy, know about or discover any new or existing venues you believe worthy of inclusion, feel strongly that one of the entries really shouldn't have been included, or have any other comments or feedback, then please email me at des@desdemoor.com or by writing care of CAMRA Books (p326).

London's beer scene deserves a definitive guide and I'm hopeful this one will run to further editions so all such communications will be very gratefully received. In the meantime I'll be doing my best to keep things up to date via my Beer Culture website at ☸ www.desdemoor.co.uk.

LONDON'S TOP 25 PUBS & BARS

Visiting every venue in this book on consecutive nights will take you the best part of nine months and undoubtedly contravene the Chief Medical Officer's guidelines on alcohol consumption. Those who would prefer to prioritise are referred to the list of 25 outstanding beer retailers below, whom I regard as essential calls for anyone on a beer odyssey in London. Most are specialist pubs and bars offering a notably wide range of unusual beers; a few are excellent brewery pubs and a couple of shops are included too. Their entries in the main listings are highlighted with ☆ **25**.

BREE LOUISE
Bloomsbury, Euston & St Pancras (p47)
17 cask beers largely from local producers.

BRICKLAYERS ARMS
Putney (p217)
12 cask beers served in a lovely old building.

CARPENTERS ARMS
Shoreditch & Hoxton (p102)
Delightful regenerated pub with good mix of cask and imported beers.

CASK
Westminster, Victoria & Pimlico (p115)
Connoisseur's choice with 10 casks and 400 bottles.

CROSSE KEYS
City (p66)
Top Wetherspoon with up to 25 casks in a spectacular setting.

DEAN SWIFT
Borough (p54)
Homely new generation specialist with rare casks and cool bottles.

The cosy Dean Swift, Borough

The Harp, CAMRA's Pub of the Year 2010

DOG AND BELL
Greenwich & Deptford (p179)
Civilised community pub with good cask and top Belgian bottles.

DOVE
Hackney (p126)
London's quirkiest Belgian specialist with cask beers too.

DRAFT HOUSE NORTHCOTE
Battersea & Clapham (p196)
Arguably the best of an exciting new trio of beer bars, 'the home of the third'.

EUSTON TAP
Bloomsbury, Euston & St Pancras (p49)
A TARDIS of rare delights with 8 casks, 19 specialist kegs and up to 100 bottles.

HARP
Covent Garden (p75)
Eight top local casks in CAMRA's National Pub of the Year 2010.

The bustling Market Porter, Borough

HOOPERS
Camberwell, Dulwich & Peckham (p174)
Refurbished local with rare casks and a classic bottled list.

HORSESHOE
Hampstead (p150)
Camden Town brewery's stylish pub with a well-chosen bottled range too.

KING WILLIAM IV
Leyton, Leytonstone & Walthamstow (p129)
Brodie's rambling, quirky brewpub with up to 20 beers on tap.

KRIS WINES
Kentish Town & Tufnell Park (p155)
Shop stocking 750 specialist bottles, including many rarities.

MAD BISHOP & BEAR
Paddington & Marylebone (p98)
An exemplary range of Fuller's cask and bottled beers in a station bar.

MARKET PORTER
Borough (p59)
12 handpumps constantly rotating through new and unusual cask delights.

NIGHTINGALE
Battersea & Clapham (p201)
Gem of a community pub and a showcase for Young's cask and bottled beers.

OLD BREWERY
Greenwich & Deptford (p180)
Meantime's upmarket beer hall in the heart of a World Heritage Site.

OLDE MITRE
Holborn & 'Legal London' (p83)
Historic, eccentric and a constant source of varied and unusual casks.

RAKE
Borough (p60)
London's international beer geek drop-in centre with a wide world beer range.

ROYAL OAK
Borough (p61)
Close to perfect traditional pub with fine cask and bottled beer from Harveys.

SOUTHAMPTON ARMS
Kentish Town & Tufnell Park (p157)
Outstanding contemporary ale house with 10 mainly local casks.

UTOBEER
Borough (p62)
Shop with more than 700 international beers in Borough Market's gourmet haven.

WHITE HORSE
Fulham & Hammersmith (p225)
Longstanding smart specialist beer champion with eight casks and 200 bottles.

The sophisticated White Horse, Parsons Green

CENTRAL LONDON

CENTRAL LONDON

There is no official definition of Central London, so I've based mine on Transport for London's Fare Zone 1, which includes all the mainline rail terminals and the area within the Circle Line, with extensions northeast to Angel and Hoxton, east to Shoreditch High Street and Aldgate East, southwest to Earl's Court and south to Vauxhall and Elephant & Castle. All the venues listed below are within a few minutes' walk of a Zone 1 station.

This area includes London's three historic cores of the City, Westminster and the Borough and the majority of its famous landmarks and attractions. It encompasses the key centres of government, finance and the law; several important higher education institutions; many of Britain's top national museums, galleries and performance spaces alongside its leading commercial entertainment district; and some of the best known shopping streets and stores in the world. Within it are the sites of the coronation of most British monarchs, the premières of most of William Shakespeare's plays, the maiden voyage of the world's first metro train and the perfection of porter beer. The thread that keeps it all together is the glorious Thames, with walking routes on both banks.

Note the subdivisions below (and throughout the rest of the book) are rather approximate and pragmatic, based on clusters around transport interchanges that can easily be connected on foot rather than on postcodes or the traditional definitions of London districts.

Old Doctor Butler's Head (p67)

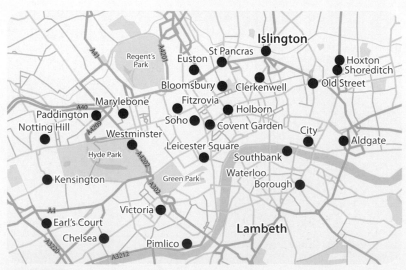

< **George (p56)**

ALDGATE

Originally the eastern gate through the old city walls, through which the Roman road into Essex passed, Aldgate most likely gets its name simply from 'Old gate'. An alternative suggestion that it was originally 'Ale gate' thanks to an adjoining pub might appeal more to readers of this guide. Today there's no gate but a series of traffic junctions on the inner London ring road and a tube station that's helped spread the name to the whole locality. Aldgate is right on the boundary between the City and the East End and was once thick with industries banned from the former. Today it still has an industrious feel and bustles with street markets, most famously Petticoat Lane, one of the oldest surviving markets in Britain. Just to the south is one of London's best known landmarks, the royal fortress of the Tower of London, which grew around William the Conqueror's 1070s White Tower into a fabled state treasury – it still houses the Crown Jewels – and a still more infamous prison and torture chamber.

DISPENSARY

Contemporary pub
19a Leman Street, E1 8EN
☎ (020) 7977 0486
⊕ www.thedispensarylondon.co.uk
✪ 11.30-11 Mon-Fri; Closed Sat & Sun.
Children welcome
Cask beers ✔ 4 (Nethergate, Adnams, unusual guests), **Other beers** 7-8 bottles, **Also** 1 real cider, 120 spirits, wines
🍴 Gastro/enhanced pub grub, 🪑 Benches on street
Seasonal special events including Oktoberfest German beer festival

Built in 1858 as the Eastern Dispensary, a charitable medical centre for East Enders, this imposing building was later a war hospital where Winston Churchill may have been treated, a Jewish community centre and an army surplus store. It became a pub in 1996 and was refurbished ten years later by current landlords David and Annie, who restored the tiled floors and Portland stone staircases, complimenting them with tasteful and slightly quirky modern furnishings and focusing on food and drink of quality and distinction.

Dispensary

❶ Dispensary
❷ Pride of Spitifields

Pride of Spitalfields

That includes quality beer, which has won them a local CAMRA award, including cask and bottle-conditioned house beer Florence Nighting Ale, commissioned from Nethergate. Changing guests, usually including a best bitter, a stronger beer and a dark choice, are often also from Nethergate or from Adnams – this was the first London pub to stock Explorer – and a variety of others including Ascot, Brodie's, Dark Star, Harveys, Itchen Valley, Redemption and Sambrook's. Imported bottles include Budvar and Brugse Zot. David was formerly a personal chef to the Rothschild family – coincidentally one of the original benefactors of the building – so unsurprisingly the food is impressive, and might include pumpkin ravioli, daube of beef, Thai spiced chicken or, in a pleasing nod to one of the historic local cultures, salt beef bagel.

Insider tip! There are free complimentary homemade tasters on Friday evenings, and also look for the Beer of the Week at a substantial discount.

⊖ Aldgate East 🚲 Links to LCN+11, 15, Wapping routes 🚶 Links to Jubilee Walkway, Thames Path

PRIDE OF SPITALFIELDS
Traditional pub
3 Heneage Street, E1 5LJ
📞 (020) 7247 8933
🕐 11-midnight Mon-Thu; 11am-2am Fri; 11-midnight Sun. *Children until early evening*

Cask beers ✔ 4 (Crouch Vale, Fuller's, Sharp's)
🍴 Sandwiches and hot specials, Sunday lunch (prebooking only)
Small functions

The story of Brick Lane is elegantly encapsulated in the history of the religious building on the corner of Fournier Street. Built in 1743 as a French Protestant chapel, it was later a centre for Jewish Christians, then a synagogue, and is now the London Jamme Masjid (mosque). The long street, linking Shoreditch and Whitechapel and at its most bustling on Sundays when it hosts a longstanding street market, is renowned for its Indian restaurants – most of them run by people with roots in Bangladesh's Sylhet region – but also mixes in 24-hour bagel bakeries, and art galleries, fashion and music shops focused on the regenerated site of the Truman brewery, closed in 1988. The mosaic is enriched by old Cockney fragments, such as this classic boozer tucked unexpectedly down a side street. Vintage photos of docks and railways and ancient invoices in frames hang above red upholstery and a wood burning stove, and there's a panelled snug with a display of old bottles. The pump clips rarely change – Brewers Gold, Doom Bar, Pride and ESB – but the beer is consistently reliable. The Carpenters Arms (p102) and Mason & Taylor (p103) aren't far away.

🚆 Liverpool Street ⊖ Aldgate East 🚲 Links to LCN+9, 39

BLOOMSBURY, EUSTON & ST PANCRAS

London got its first bypass in 1756: the New Road (modern Marylebone, Euston and Pentonville Roads), a toll-charging turnpike running east-west between Marylebone and Islington. The road effectively marks the northern boundary of Central London. Between it and Covent Garden is Bloomsbury, developed in the 18th century as terraces and squares, and perhaps now the capital's most extensive example of this style of Georgian development. It's certainly among the best known, thanks in part to the 'Bloomsbury Group' of writers, intellectuals and freethinkers such as E M Forster, John Maynard Keynes and Virginia Woolf that regularly soiréed here in the early 20th century. It's also home to the British Museum, University College London (UCL), the School of Oriental and African Studies (SOAS), University College Hospital and several similar institutions. There are rich pickings for beer lovers round here: the venues listed below include some just outside Bloomsbury but conveniently close to the big stations.

BETJEMAN ARMS
Contemporary pub
Unit 53 St Pancras International, Pancras Road, NW1 2QP
☎ (020) 7923 5440, ⊕ www.geronimo-inns.co.uk/thebetjemanarms/
✪ 11-11 Mon-Sat; 11-10.30 Sun. *Children welcome*
Cask beers ✔ 4 (Adnams, Sambrook's, Sharp's, guests), **Other beers** 3 keg (Meantime), 6 bottles, **Also** Wines

🍴 Gastro/enhanced pub grub menu, 🚆 Front terrace, rear patio on station concourse, ♿
Tue live piano, functions, annual beer event

The Midland Railway terminus at St Pancras, opened in 1868, is now rightly recognised as London's greatest monument to the Railway Age but was not always so appreciated – it was due for demolition in the 1960s and saved thanks to a campaign supported by

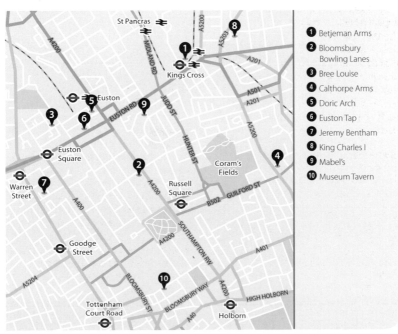

1 Betjeman Arms
2 Bloomsbury Bowling Lanes
3 Bree Louise
4 Calthorpe Arms
5 Doric Arch
6 Euston Tap
7 Jeremy Bentham
8 King Charles I
9 Mabel's
10 Museum Tavern

Betjeman Arms

poet and cultural commentator John Betjeman. Fronted on Euston Road by George Gilbert Scott's gobsmacking Gothic revival fantasy, the Midland Grand Hotel, it boasts a richly detailed brick concourse below William Henry Barlow's equally awe inspiring cast iron and glass arched roof, in its day the widest single span roof in the world. Below the platforms were acres of vaults used until the 1960s for storing beer delivered by rail from Burton upon Trent. In 2007 the previously underused station gained a new lease of life when it reopened, restored and with its vaults converted into a new concourse, as the first stop on the high speed line to the Channel Tunnel portal, a magnificent gateway to Europe.

The station famously boasts Europe's longest champagne bar but readers of this book may be more tempted by the Betjeman Arms just beyond the buffer stops of the international platforms, a better class of station bar that's firmly embedded in the station fabric and measures up well to its impressive setting.

Owners Geronimo Inns make a point of supporting cask ale and the offering includes Betjeman Ale (a rebadged Sharp's Cornish Coaster) alongside Adnams Bitter and guests usually from better known breweries – though the pub participates in its parent's intermittent beer festivals where all kinds of unusual beers are rapidly rotated. König

Ludwig Weissbier and Budvar Dark are good choices in bottle. Food from the open kitchen might include pumpkin and spinach gratin, lamb hotpot or grilled trout. Inside there are numerous light and comfortable spaces, including an eclectically furnished dining room and a boardroom bookable for private meetings. The pub is predictably popular as an informal rendezvous, including between your humble writer and publisher, who planned this very book at one of its tables.

Visitor's note: One of the most impressive covered drinking spaces in London is the pub's (no smoking) terrace on the concourse under Barlow's roof and in the shadow of Paul Day's towering 9m bronze statue *The Meeting Place*, intended to celebrate the romance of train travel. Another, smaller bronze honouring Betjeman is nearby, with floor plaques quoting his work.

Also worth noting is Sourced Market – ☎ (020) 7833 9353, ⊕ www.sourcedmarket.com – on the lower level opposite the domestic ticket office, not quite qualifying for a full entry but with about 50 interesting British and imported bottled beers. Even the bars on the Eurostar trains have something of note in classic Belgian ale Duvel, which is sadly more than you can say of the domestic services.

⇝ Kings Cross St Pancras ⊖ Kings Cross St Pancras ⊰ LCN+0, 6 ⤬ Jubilee Walkway, link to Jubilee Greenway

BLOOMSBURY BOWLING LANES

Bar
Tavistock Hotel, Bedford Way, WC1H 9EU
☎ (020) 7183 1979, ⊕ www.
bloomsburybowling.com, **fbk**, **tw** thelaneslive
✪ 2-midnight Mon-Thu; 2-2.30am Fri & Sat;
2-midnight Sun. *Children until 4pm*
Cask beer None, **Other beers** 4 keg,
5 international bottles, **Also** Bourbons,
cocktails, 'hard shakes'
🍴 Diner-style menu, ♿
*Bowling, private karaoke, Thu/Fri/Sat live music
and DJs, table football, pool*

This full scale 8-lane bowling alley, lounge,
karaoke suite and music venue in the
extensive basement of the Tavistock hotel,
decked out in finest retro kitsch 1950s
Americana and complete with "the only
vintage above lane ball return outside the US",
is remarkable enough in its own right. Hit the
twinkling bar, though, and you might be
surprised to encounter a well chosen range of
quality beers served by enthusiastic staff.
There's no cask, but there are keg craft beers
from Camden Town and Meantime beside
Czech brewer Bernard, and a small bottled
selection including curiosities like lovely Left
Hand Milk Stout from Colorado and top class
Bavarian wheat beer from Schneider. Food in
the diner style eatery is decent too, if less
unexpected: club sandwiches, burgers, pizzas,
burritos and the like. It's a fun, atmospheric
place that also offers five private lanes for hire.
The management is also connected with the
Euston Tap (below), which helps explain the
quality beer.

Visitor's note: You're not obliged to roll balls at
pins, but if you'd like to try your hand, there's
plenty of advice on offer to help you with your
pendulum motion, backswing and follow
through.

⭑ Euston ⊖ Russell Square 🚲 LCN+ 0, 6, 6A
🚶 Jubilee Walkway

BREE LOUISE ☆ 25

Contemporary pub, specialist
69 Cobourg Street, NW1 2HH
☎ (020) 7681 4930, ⊕ www.thebreelouise.com
✪ 11.30-11 Mon-Sat; 12-10.30 Sun. *Children
until early evening*
Cask beers ● 17 (Dark Star, Redemption,

Sambrook's, Windsor & Eton, unusual/local
guests), **Other beers** 4 keg, **Also** 11 real ciders/
perries, 20-30 whiskies
🍴 Pies and pub grub, 🪑 Benches on street
*Occasional brewery theme weekends and
tastings, board games*

This smallish and ordinary looking corner pub
in the streets just west of Euston station,
round the corner from the cluster of south
Indian vegetarian restaurants and sweet
shops in Drummond Street, dispenses what's
likely London's widest selection of locally and
independently brewed cask beer. Originally
the Jolly Gardeners, it's been under the
stewardship of current landlords Craig and
Karen since 2003, and in 2008 they decided to
go all out as cask ale specialists, buying out
the tie from building owners Enterprise for a
considerable annual fee so they could stock
what they liked. 17 beers are usually on, with
six on handpump and the others on gravity
from a stillage behind the bar. The pattern at
time of writing is three from Windsor & Eton,
two from Sambrook's, one from Redemption,
Dark Star Sixhop, and others that include at
least one mild and one porter or stout. Other
breweries supported include Art, Ascot,
BrewDog, Downton, Itchen Valley, Milestone,
Rebellion and Triple fff. The single, sparsely
decorated room is frequently crowded and
the tables favour group drinking, so you often
end up sharing, though groups can reserve in
advance. A relatively basic menu includes
pies, ploughman's and a long list of cheese
platters, but the beer, along with real cider, is
the main focus.

The pub's determination to support small
and local producers on such a scale easily
wins it an entry in the Top 25 but I'm obliged
to acknowledge it has come in for criticism,
including from some respected beer bloggers.
They've drawn attention to its unflattering
interior and the alleged variable serving
quality particularly of the beers on gravity,
with some suggestions that the range is
overambitious. Over several visits I've found it
basic but comfortable, with polite and
informed staff and a buzzing crowd to
provide the atmosphere. I've also had some
excellent pints there, but not every beer from
a small brewer is going to be a masterpiece.

Insider tip! Worthwhile discounts are granted to card-carrying CAMRA members.

⇌ Euston ⊖ Euston, Euston Square ᚛᚜ LCN+0, 6, 6A ✦ Jubilee Walkway

CALTHORPE ARMS
Traditional pub
252 Grays Inn Road, WC1X 8JR
☎ (020) 7278 4732
⊕ 11-11 Mon-Sat; 12-10.30 Sun. *Children until early evening*
Cask beers ✅ 4 (Wells & Young's, occasional guests), **Other beers** 7 bottles (mainly Wells & Young's)
⑩ Pub grub, ⊞ Tables on street
Quiz league, functions

As the stickers on the door attest, this unspoilt, friendly Young's local has spent at least 22 years in the *Good Beer Guide* and with good reason, as it's a fine showcase for the brewery's beers. Besides regulars Bitter and Special, there will likely be other Wells & Young's cask ales with occasional appearances by the likes of St Austell Tribute. Bottled beers are also popular here with Special London Ale and Double Chocolate Stout among the offerings. Pub grub runs to sausages, veggie chilli and scampi at bargain prices for the area, served in a pleasant brown wood and cream

single bar with a comfortably yellowed ceiling and traditional banquette seating. While landlord Adrian is pulling pints, some of his regulars may be pulling teeth as it's just down the road from the Eastman Dental Hospital. It's also near Calthorpe Gardens and opposite the London Welsh Centre.

⇌ Kings Cross, St Pancras ⊖ Russell Square ▯ Guilford Street (numerous Kings Cross) ᚛᚜ LCN+0

DORIC ARCH
Traditional pub
1 Eversholt Street, NW1 2DN
☎ (020) 7383 3359, ✉ doricarch@fullers.co.uk,
⊕ www.fullers.co.uk
⊕ 12-11 Mon-Sat; 12-10.30 Sun. *Children welcome*
Cask beers ✅ 9 (Fuller's, Butcombe, Harviestoun, Kelham Island, Timothy Taylor), **Other beers** 3 keg
⑩ Pub grub
Big screen sport

Housed in an unpromising 1960s office block overlooking Euston bus station, part of the ugly 1960s redevelopment of Euston station, the Doric Arch is a useful standby though it's fallen some way below its former glories. Once it was a free house known as the Head

Calthorpe Arms

Doric Arch

of Steam, with a wide selection of often rare cask ales, always including a mild. In 2005 it was bought by Fuller's, who announced they would maintain a generous guest beer policy while introducing some of their own brands. A few years on, besides the owning brewery's Discovery, ESB, London Pride and two often seasonal choices, the remaining four non-Fuller's beers are permanent tried and trusted favourites: Bitter & Twisted, Butcombe Bitter, Pale Rider and Taylor Landlord. Good beers all, but hardly rare in London, and not a mild in sight. Still, the collection of railway memorabilia and old stations signs remains, the raised platform at the back still surveys the comings and goings at the bus station, and drink befuddled customers are still challenged to remember the code for access to the toilets, protected by a combination lock to deter passers by. Food includes glazed ham, baked aubergine and hake and chips, and there's a children's menu. If you're puzzled by the pub's current name, see the entry for the Euston Tap below.

Insider tip! The most sought after seats are in a small cubby hole, appropriately reminiscent of an old fashioned train compartment.

≽ Euston ⊖ Euston, Euston Square ⨀ LCN+ 0, 6, 6A ⚑ Jubilee Walkway

EUSTON TAP ☆ 25
Bar, specialist
West Lodge, 190 Euston Road, NW1 2EF
☎ (020) 3137 8837, ⊕ www.eustontap.com, **fbk, tw** eustontap
⊙ 12-11 Mon-Sat; 12-10 Sun. Children until 8pm

Cask beers ✓ 8 (Marble, Thornbridge, unusual guests), **Other beers** 19 international keg, 80-100 bottles including many rarities ⊞ Pizzas to order in, ☷ Terrace overlooking Euston Square Gardens
Occasional meet the brewer events and tastings

When the southern terminus of the London and Birmingham Railway opened at Euston in 1837, it was equipped with a grand entrance through a 22m neo-Classical Doric arch, the largest ever built.

The arch was demolished in 1961 and the ensuing controversy helped prompt more respectful attitudes to urban heritage. Most of the masonry has since been located and may yet be restored when the station is rebuilt to accomodate the new high speed line to the north. Meanwhile two lodges that originally flanked the arch can still be admired on site, carved with sometimes aspirational destinations. Most people passing by on Euston Road might assume these structures are purely decorative, but in 2010 one of the most ambitious new beer venues yet opened in London poured its first pints in the unlikely location of the west lodge.

Venture through a side entrance and you'll find a small rectangular drinking area equipped with stools and shelves and a petite but stylish bar. Borrowing from the practice of some US beer bars, this has draught taps mounted on the copper bar back rather than the bar itself, with siphon taps for the cask ales and a multitude of keg lines topped with US-style tap handles, while crammed fridges flank the bar. A precarious spiral staircase winds to a mezzanine level where there's an equally small sofa-strewn lounge, while outside seating in Euston Square Gardens expands the accommodation.

I can't help being worried about that staircase, as few of the beers on offer weigh in at session strength. The regular cask beer is Thornbridge Old Swan, with a range of changing guests that favour other Thornbridge beers and those from BrewDog, Bristol, Dark Star, Marble, Ossett, Purity and Riverhead, including rarities, specials, and strong and dark options. These are eclipsed by 19 keg lines (a 20th tap dispenses keg cider) offering less familiar beers from Anchor and Sierra Nevada, oaked IPA from California's Stone, several

Euston Tap

German wheat beers, unfiltered Czech lager from Bernard, and small batch ales from tiny Prague micros Matuška and Kocour, hard to find even in their home territory. The lengthy bottled list will send beer geeks reaching for their notebooks – Port Old and Older Viscosity, Lost Abbey Angel's Share and numerous Mikkeller specials, one of which sells for £43.50 a bottle. Founders and Green Flash join Victory and Goose Island in the American listings, Cantillon provides top lambics, and there's a strong range of German bottles including unfiltered Kellerbier, Altbier and Kölsch. Quality New York-style pizzas are delivered in. The bar shares ownership with the Sheffield Tap on Sheffield station and Bloomsbury Bowling Lanes (above).

Insider tip! It's well worth following the bar on Twitter or Facebook to keep track of rare specials, themed events and beer launches.

≉ Euston ⊖ Euston, Euston Square ⊛ LCN+ 0, 6, 6A ♠♠ Jubilee Walkway

JEREMY BENTHAM
Traditional pub
31 University Street, WC1E 6JL
☎ (020) 7387 3033
⊕ 11.30-11 Mon-Fri; Closed Sat & Sun. *Children until early evening*
Cask beers ✔ 4 (Harveys, Ringwood, guests), **Other beers** Keg Budvar, **Also** 1 real cider, 50 whiskies
🍴 Pub grub, 🪑 Benches on street

Deep in university territory, this cosy pub offers Ringwood Best Bitter and Harveys Sussex Best, with Young's Bitter and Wychwood Brakspear Bitter on rotation, and guests drawn from the Punch Finest Cask range such as Adnams, Beartown, Brains or Sadlers. Home made lunches include popular burgers, beef and ale pie and veggie quesadillas. Unsurprisingly it's popular with academics: "See that regular over there," confided the landlord, "he works on the Large Hadron Collider at CERN." The pub was named in honour of London University co-founder and utilitarian philosopher Bentham, whose skeleton, stuffed with straw, dressed in its owner's clothes and topped with a wax head, is kept on public display at UCL in accordance with his will, and occasionally attends council meetings where it is listed as present but not voting. The pub does its bit in contributing to Bentham's greatest happiness principle.

≉ Euston ⊖ Euston Square, Warren Street ⊛ LCN+ 0, 6, 6A ♠♠ Jubilee Walkway

KING CHARLES I
Traditional pub
55-57 Northdown Street, N1 9BL
☎ (020) 7837 7758
⊕ 5-11 Mon-Thu; 5-1am Fri; 5-11 Sat; Closed Sun. *Children until 7pm*
Cask beers ✔ 4 (Brodie's, 3 unusual guests), **Other beers** 8 bottles, **Also** Malts
🍴 None but customers welcome to order takeaways, 🪑 Benches on street
Bar billiards, shove ha'penny, board games

This quirky little freehouse is decorated with tribal masks, stuffed animal heads and brewery mirrors, and furnished with comfortably worn stools and tables and a juke box. A Brodie's beer is always on, though the precise one varies; otherwise there are good choices from the likes of Adnams, B&T, Harviestoun, Otley or Thwaites. Some Brodie's bottles including an imperial stout can also be found, alongside Meantime, Stiegl and – perhaps surprisingly – Bosteels Deus champagne beer. Worth cracking open to celebrate finding such a gem so close to Kings Cross station!

≷ Kings Cross St Pancras ⊖ Kings Cross St Pancras ⬚ LCN+0, links to LCN+6, 16 ✸ Links to Jubilee Greenway, Jubilee Walkway

MABEL'S
Traditional pub
9 Mabledon Place, WC1H 9AZ
☏ (020) 7387 7739, ✉ mabels@shepherd-neame.co.uk, ⊕ www.shepherd-neame.co.uk
✪ 11-11 Mon-Wed; 11-midnight Thu-Sat; 12-10.30 Sun. *Children welcome if eating*
Cask beers ✔ 5 (Shepherd Neame), **Other beers** 4 bottles (Shepherd Neame)
⑪ Enhanced pub grub, ⊞ Tables on street
Big screen sport

A bright and unpretentious place set just back from the Euston Road, opposite the impressive 1997 British Library building and the Shaw Theatre, this is one of Faversham brewery Shepherd Neame's (p310) small estate of London pubs, and a cheerful environment in which to sample their beers. Bishop's Finger,

Mabel's

Kent's Best, Master Brew and Spitfire are always on while the fifth tap dispenses one of the quarterly seasonals; Whistable Organic Ale is among the bottles. Regular pub grub on the menu is enhanced by exotica like vegetable tagine and chicken balti. The main bar area has high tables and there's a charming, but inevitably popular, snug.

≷ Kings Cross St Pancras ⊖ Kings Cross St Pancras ⬚ LCN+0, 6 ✸ Jubilee Walkway

MUSEUM TAVERN
Traditional pub ☆
49 Great Russell Street, WC1B 3BA
☏ (020) 7242 8987
✪ 11-11.30 Mon-Thu; 11-midnight Fri & Sat; 12-10 Sun. *Children until early evening*
Cask beers ✔ 7 (Fuller's, Theakston, Timothy Taylor, Wells & Young's, 3 guests), **Other beers** 2 keg, 3 bottles
⑪ Pub grub and specials, ⊞ Tables on street
Monthly brewery beer tastings, occasional themed parties

Given its advantageous location right opposite the British Museum, this place doesn't have to try very hard but puts praiseworthy efforts into being a friendly and attractive venue in its own right, helped enormously by a mellowed heritage interior. In fact the pub was here first, opening as the Dog & Duck in the 18th century, but cannily rebranded when one of the capital's top attractions landed on its doorstep in 1823. The distinctive panelled ceiling, heavy wood bar back, counter and Watney's Imperial Stout mirror survive from a major refit in 1889. Amazingly considering its relatively small size, it was originally divided into five smaller areas, as evidenced by the various outside doors and labelling in the glass. Now a Punch Taylor Walker pub, it's a permanent outlet for Theakston Old Peculier, alongside Landlord, London Pride, Young's Gold and guests that tend to come from better known names like Adnams, Greene King, Sharp's or St Austell, occasionally spiced up by the likes of BrewDog. Preprinted standard menus outline classic pub grub – bangers, pies, fish & chips.

⊖ Tottenham Court Road ⬚ LCN+6A, 39 ✸ Jubilee Walkway

BOROUGH

You'll sometimes hear the stretch of the river Thames through central London called the "string of pearls" – the river traces the city's rich history through a dazzling succession of landmarks. The stroll down the south bank route of the Thames Path from Lambeth Bridge at least as far as Tower Bridge is an essential London experience.

Towards the downstream end of this strip, between Southwark Bridge and Tower Bridge and along Borough High Street, strolling beer lovers will find their own string of pearls: a dense concentration of must-visit outlets that between them offer London's ultimate pub crawl. This is the heart of historic Southwark, centred on the point where Watling Street, the Roman road linking the city to the Kent coast and via ferry to the mainland, made its crossing of the Thames.

In Tudor times Southwark hosted all the disreputable activities that the prosperous City banned, including theatregoing and brewing. Beer would have flowed here from countless house breweries. In later years major brewers like Barclay Perkins and Courage found their homes here.

With its long history as a travellers' rest and a centre of brewing and entertainment, the Borough is once again renowned for its fine ale. It even has a couple of – albeit tiny – breweries in Brew Wharf (p266) and Kernel (p273).

A major driver of the eating and drinking scene is Borough Market, which on early weekday mornings still fulfils its traditional function as a wholesale fruit and veg market, but on Thursday, Friday and Saturday daytimes mutates into London's leading speciality gourmet food market, with a host of traders, many selling wares direct from the farm or kitchen. It's an essential, if potentially wallet-challenging, stop for anyone interested in good food and indeed rare beers – see Utobeer below.

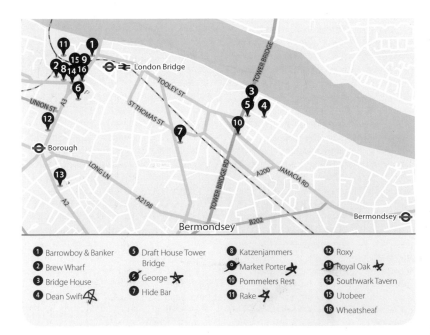

1. Barrowboy & Banker
2. Brew Wharf
3. Bridge House
4. Dean Swift
5. Draft House Tower Bridge
6. George
7. Hide Bar
8. Katzenjammers
9. Market Porter
10. Pommelers Rest
11. Rake
12. Roxy
13. Royal Oak
14. Southwark Tavern
15. Utobeer
16. Wheatsheaf

Barrowboy & Banker

BARROWBOY & BANKER
Contemporary pub
6-8 Borough High Street, SE1 9QQ
☎ (020) 7403 5415, ✉ barrow@fullers.co.uk,
⊕ www.fullers.co.uk
✪ 11-11 Mon-Fri; 12-11 Sat; 12-10.30 Sun.
Children until early evening
Cask beers ✔ 5 (Fuller's), **Other beers** 2 keg,
10 bottles (all Fuller's)
⊞ Pies and enhanced pub grub
Big screen sports, functions

If you can resist the temptation to read this
pub's name as a potentially scandalous
tabloid headline, it could stand as a motto for
the ideal British pub experience, where
people of all social origins mix comfortably
together, united in their appreciation of good
beer and good company ('Barrow Young
Person and Banker' would be more inclusive
but at the expense of alliteration). It's almost
immediately to the south of London Bridge
and right by the steps down to Glaziers Hall.
The barrow boys come from Borough Market
nearby; the bankers come from the City on
their way home via London Bridge, though
the building is also a former bank – in fact the
first branch of the National Westminster.

An early 1990s Fuller's conversion has
preserved the pillars, chandeliers, intriguing
standard lamps, marble, floor tiles and the
staircase that sweeps up to an attractive
gallery. There were more bankers than barrow
boys when I called, enjoying well served pints
of Chiswick, Discovery, ESB, London Pride and
Fuller's seasonals. A comprehensive range of

Fuller's bottles is also on offer including 1845,
Brewer's Reserve and Vintage Ale. The menu
offers pies, burgers, sausages, sandwiches and
platters, and you can even get married here.

⇌ London Bridge ⊖ London Bridge ⊗ CS4,
NCN2 ↗ Thames Path, Jubilee Greenway, Jubilee
Walkway

BREW WHARF
Bar, restaurant
14-16 Stoney Street, SE1 9AD
☎ (020) 7378 6601, ⊕ www.brewwharf.com
✪ 12-11 Mon-Sat; 12-4 Sun. *Children welcome*
Cask beers ✔ 2+ (own), **Other beers** 10 keg,
50 bottles
⊞ Gastro menu, some cooking with beer,
⊞ Front patio, ♿
*Seasonal events, beer festivals in neighbouring
Vinopolis*

Among Borough's attractions is Vinopolis, an
exhibition and 'tasting experience' in the
impressively chunky brick arches of a former
railway viaduct. As its name suggests, it's
primarily focused on wine, but among its
attached catering outlets is Brew Wharf, an
informal restaurant and bar with its own
microbrewery (p266), which sets out to take
beer "as seriously as wine". The two home
brews change constantly but tend to be
creative stuff: a chocolate milk stout and a
spiced brown ale when I last called in, and
hoppy blond ales often make an appearance.
Kegs include Brugse Zot, Camden Town and
Stiegl while the eclectic bottled list features

Kernel and Dark Star alongside Green Flash, Hopfenkönig, Nils Oscar, Rochefort and La Trappe. Meals, served in the bar or under enamel beer adverts in an adjoining arch, are well-prepared modern pub favourites at slightly upmarket prices – lamb shank, sausage and mash, pan fried cod, nut roast and more exotic options like taglioni nero with squid – with beer matching suggestions of course.

Insider tip! Look out for the chalked up Beer Prayer: "Our ales, which art in barrels..."

≥ London Bridge ⊖ London Bridge ♿ CS4, NCN3 ✦ Thames Path, Jubilee Greenway, Jubilee Walkway

Brew Wharf

BRIDGE HOUSE
Contemporary pub
218 Tower Bridge Road, SE1 2UP
📞 (020) 7407 5818
⚙ 12-11 Mon-Wed; 12-midnight Thu-Sat; 12-11 Sun. *Children until 8pm*
Cask beers ✔ 4 (3 Adnams, 1 Purity), **Other beers** 2-3 bottles (Adnams), 2 keg (German), **Also** Wines
🍴 Gastro-ish menu, 🪑 Two tables on street, ♿ *Monthly comedy night, occasional other live entertainment*

These days Adnams' pump clips are a relatively common sight on the capital's handpumps, but this is the only London pub actually owned by the well-loved Southwold independent. Appropriately given the brewery's maritime location on the Suffolk coast, the pub enjoys a prime waterside site on the southern approach to Tower Bridge. It's bright, cheerful and friendly with a mixed crowd. Food, served in the bar and in an upstairs dining room, is decent and good value – coconut and chilli skewers and air

dried ham compliment more traditional options like casserole and shepherd's pie. The cask ales live up to the pub's ambassadorial role, with the brewery's classic Bitter and Broadside supplemented by Explorer or a winter seasonal and a guest beer from Purity. Locher Weissbier, German Bitburger lager and a few Adnams bottled beers expand the offer – they briefly stocked the champagne-bottled Celebration beer in 2010.

Insider tip! The downstairs café-bar looks out at unexpected street level onto cobbled Horse Lane and is a pleasant place to sit if open.

≥ London Bridge ⊖ Tower Hill, London Bridge **DLR** Tower Gateway ♿ CS4, NCN4 ✦ Thames Path, Jubilee Greenway, Jubilee Walkway

DEAN SWIFT ☆ 25
Contemporary pub, specialist
32 Lafone Street, SE1 2LX
📞 (020) 7357 0748, ⊕ www.thedeanswift.com, tw DeanSwiftSe1
⚙ 12-midnight Mon-Thu; 12-1am Fri & Sat; 12-midnight Sun. *Children welcome*
Cask beers ✔ 4 (Sambrook's, unusual guests), **Other beers** 7 keg, 40 bottles
🍴 Gastro, pasta and cheese menu, ♿ No disabled toilet but all flat access
Sun quiz, tasting and meet the brewer evenings, themed beer events

The area around Butlers Wharf just downstream of Tower Bridge was one of the earliest riverfront zones to be regenerated, its red brick warehouses and industrial buildings – including the old Courage brewery right by the bridge – now converted to offices, shops, posh restaurants and sought after flats. Just around the corner from Shad Thames, with its distinctive aerial walkways, this 'Local Beer House', opened in 2010, is one of the most pleasant and inviting of the new pubs currently fermenting vibrantly in London's beer culture. It's a smallish place with a choice of seating and clean and elegant decor.

Wandle is the only regular cask; guests may well be from Redemption and other London breweries, alongside contributors from further afield like BrewDog, Fyne, Thornbridge or Purity. It's one of the few places you're likely to see rare caskings from nearby Kernel, and if

Dean Swift

not you can enjoy a good range of the highly rated brewery's bottled beers, leading a well chosen list that stretches to Brooklyn (East India Pale Ale), Dogfish Head, Harviestoun (including Ola Dubh whisky cask beers), Orval and Rochefort. Kegs include BrewDog Punk IPA, Maisels Weisse and an own label Belgian Pils sourced from Huyghe in East Flanders.

A tempting menu runs to venison braised in Kernel porter, spatchcock *poussin*, mussels and various pastas and risottos besides home-cooked snacks and beer and artisanal cheese tasting platters. For all the quality on offer, though, it's a relaxed, dressed down atmosphere and when there's a big match on the Dean proves it's still a Bermondsey local at heart by rolling down the big screen. The owners are in the process of refurbishing the Olde Red Cow at Smithfield (71 Long Lane, EC1A 1EJ) as a sister pub, which should be open by the time you read this.

Pub trivia: The name commemorates Irish satirist and political commentator Jonathan Swift: the fictitious title character of his most famous work, *Gulliver's Travels*, was a Bermondsey man.

≥ London Bridge ⊖ Tower Hill, London Bridge, Bermondsey **DLR** Tower Gateway ⮡ NCN4, links to LCN+22 ⮕ Thames Path, Jubilee Greenway, Jubilee Walkway

DRAFT HOUSE TOWER BRIDGE
Bar, specialist
206-208 Tower Bridge Road, SE1 2UP
📞 (020) 7378 9995, ✉ booktb@drafthouse.
co.uk, ⊕ www.drafthouse.co.uk
🕐 12-11 Mon-Sat; 12-10.30 Sun (may open earlier Sat & Sun for brunch). *Children welcome*
Cask beers ❷ 2-4 (Sambrook's, unusual guests), **Other beers** 21 keg, 100+ bottles, **Also** Malts
🍴 British/American pub grub
Quiz, meet the brewer and tasting events, visits to Sambrook's brewery, functions

Charlie McVeigh's small Draft House chain of specialist beer bars, currently three strong, is a new and welcome addition to the London beer scene, with a self proclaimed mission to "do for beer what our culture has done for food and wine over the past twenty years: namely, we take its provenance, cellaring and serving seriously." The implication that they're the first at this might sound just a little arrogant to the proprietors of some of the longer established places listed here, but Charlie is undoubtedly a pioneer in marketing a big range of international craft beer to the broader public using honest enthusiasm and sharp presentation rather than gimmickry. With its bright colours, pop culture posters, cheery diner style, well informed and welcoming staff and obvious eagerness to communicate, not to mention the Websters spelling of its name, the enterprise has drawn its inspiration from the other side of the Atlantic at least as much as from the native pub tradition, giving it a fresh approach which is clearly helping it win a new audience for good beer. So far this Tower Bridge branch, opened late in 2010, is the newest and most centrally located member of the family and the most likely to be stumbled across by innocent tourists – its siblings at Northcote (p196) and Westbridge (p197) are listed elsewhere.

Sambrook's beers are a fixture on the handpumps while other guest casks are normally sourced locally. Kegs include beers from Dublin's Porterhouse (p306), rarely seen outside their own pubs, alongside Meantime, Palm, Schremser and Stiegl, with changing guests from Germany, the USA and France, the last particularly welcome as it's extremely hard to find French craft beer in the UK. Sampling is facilitated since the chain bills itself as 'the home of the third', one of very few British retailers taking advantage of the legality of third pints (189ml) as an ideal tasting measure.

Beer in bottles stretches from Kernel a few hundred meters away to Robson's in KwaZuluNatal, and includes real lambics from Boon and Cantillon, decent Belgian abbey beers, and a strong US selection that stretches beyond Anchor, Brooklyn and Goose Island to Dogfish Head, Great Divide, Stone and Victory. Food can be eaten in the bar or the attached restaurant with its diner-style booths upholstered in green leather. Beer matching suggestions, some a little eccentric, are included on a menu that spans British traditional (potted meats, British cheeses, beer battered haddock, steaks) and American and international cuisine (croques, mussels, burgers, squid and imaginative veggie options). Quirky decorations such as oversized classic album covers and Ghostbusters wallpaper on the way down to the toilets complete an appealing picture.

Insider tip! A good-value fixed-price meal deal including thirds of beer matching each course was being trialled when I visited – check the website or call for details of hours of operation.

≥ London Bridge ⊖ Tower Hill, London Bridge **DLR** Tower Gateway ⊙⊙ CS4, NCN4 ⚡ Thames Path, Jubilee Greenway, Jubilee Walkway

GEORGE
Traditional pub ★
77 Borough High Street, SE1 1NH
📞 (020) 7407 2056, ⊕ www.nationaltrust.org.uk/main/w-georgeinn
⊙ 11-11 daily. *Children until 9pm in certain rooms only*
Cask beers ⊘ 6 (Greene King, occasional guests), **Other beers** 5 bottles
🍴 Enhanced pub grub, 🎪 Large courtyard,
♿ No disabled toilet but some flat access
Monthly acoustic music, occasional morris dancing and outdoor theatre, summer barbecues

London Bridge station is only the most recent expression of Southwark's longstanding role as a transport terminus. For centuries the Borough was the natural starting and finishing point for travellers south and east, dense with inns. The bigger establishments were arranged around courtyards off the High Street, many of which still exist today, including Talbot Yard, location of the Tabard where Geoffrey's Chaucer's fictitious pilgrims mustered in the *Canterbury Tales*. This was demolished in the 19th century, but another historic inn, the George, still

Draft House

George

commands the next yard north. Originally the George & Dragon, it's stood here since at least 1598, but what you see today is a mere 335 years old, dating from a rebuilding after a serious fire that consumed most of mediaeval Southwark. The distinctive wooden galleries would once have extended all round the yard, but one wing at least endures as London's only remaining example of a 17th century galleried coaching inn.

Even this fragment is surprisingly extensive and it's well worth exploring the various spaces including the upstairs panelled rooms if they're open. Admire the courtyard from one of the balconies and you'll be reliving an experience familiar to Samuel Pepys, Samuel Johnson and Charles Dickens. The most authentically fitted downstairs room is the first on the right as you enter the courtyard, where some of the woodwork may well date back to the 1676 rebuild. The pub is now owned by the National Trust who lease it to Greene King, and it's a fine setting in which to sample the brewer's wares. Abbot, IPA and London Glory are always available, alongside house brew George Inn Ale, actually a rebadged Morland Original Bitter. The guest may be a Greene King seasonal or something like Caledonian Deuchars IPA. The likes of Budvar and Vedett boost the choice in bottles. Don't expect to feast on larks, blackbirds and calf's head with oysters: food is standard pub grub.

Visitor's note: Look for the glassed off servery sporting a now disused Victorian cash register-style beer engine.

≋ London Bridge ⊖ London Bridge ⊕ CS4, NCN4 ∥ Thames Path, Jubilee Greenway, Jubilee Walkway

HIDE BAR
Bar
39-45 Bermondsey Street, SE1 3XF
📞 (020) 7403 6655, ⊕ www.thehidebar.com, **fbk, tw** HideBarLondon
🕙 5-1am Mon-Thu; 5-2am Fri & Sat; 3-11 Sun.
Children until early evening
Cask beer None, **Other beers** 3 keg (Meantime), 15 bottles, **Also** Malts and speciality spirits, cocktails, wines
🍴 Snacks, appetisers, sharing plates and hot specials, 🚻
Two tastings (wine, beer, spirits) a month, weekly vintage cocktail night

The first section of the extensive drinks list at this smallish, stylish but friendly and relaxed bar at the top of trendy Bermondsey Street details a range of cocktails prepared to order with due theatricality by the young, smart bar staff – call in on Thursday and you can imagine yourself in monochrome era Manhattan with an authentic vintage recipe fixed at the retro corner bar. But the next section on the list is beer. There's no cask, but there's no bland industrial lager either. The three kegs come from Meantime,

Katzenjammers

including their London Pale Ale, Helles lager and a changing seasonal. They're supplemented by 15 bottles: a mix of regulars and guests – Kernel pale ales and porters come from just round the corner, while Duvel, Schneider Weisse, Schlenkerla, Verhaege Duchesse de Bourgogne and Meantime's big bottles of IPA and Porter cover an impressive range of flavours. It's a laid back place, confident in its own quality, and when I visited, in a refreshing reversal of the situation in some of the more traditional pubs in this guide, I was one of only a handful of men in a space mainly occupied by women.

≋ London Bridge ⊖ London Bridge ⊕ CS4, NCN4 ●● Thames Path, Jubilee Greenway, Jubilee Walkway

KATZENJAMMERS
Bar
24 Southwark Street, SE1 1TY
☎ (020) 3417 0196
⊕ www.katzenjammers.co.uk
✿ 12-11 Mon-Sat; 12-10 Sun
Cask beers None, **Other beers** 8 German keg, 20+ German and some Belgian bottles, **Also** Schnapps
⊞ Bavarian-style menu, ⊞ Benches on street
Oompah band, seasonal events

The presence of the Hop Exchange, with its extensive collonaded façade along Southwark Street, is a reminder of how important a

brewing centre this area once was. Built in 1867 as a single market for the hop trade, it was once one of many similar commodity exchanges in London; it has outlived them all, though in a new guise as an events venue. The vaulted storage cellars may no longer be stacked with hop 'pockets' but since 2009 they've housed two bars, both under the same ownership, that amply showcase the principal use of the resinous plant: the Wheatsheaf (see below) and this German-themed joint.

As often with such places its attraction is partly explained by caricatures of hearty Bavarian partying facilitated by *Dirndl*-clad *Mädeln* bearing foaming *Krüge*. But it's also taken much greater trouble than some comparable venues to provide a respectable choice of authentic foaming substances. Keg wheat beers come from Paulaner and include their Hacker-Pschorr brand, rarely seen in London, and there's tasty Helles from Kaltenberg and Fischer's, in rather less Bavarian Dortmund. A decent range of bottles includes Früh Kölsch, Schlösser Altbier, Schlenkerla smoked beer and further wheaty choices. Food is predictably big on sausages and schnitzel, while vegetarian choices include *Käsespätzle*, the Fatherland's answer to macaroni cheese. Daytimes are quieter and better for beer sampling, but the plain benches are more atmospheric when packed by merry folk swaying to an oompah band that includes Queen covers in its repertoire.

Further info: If you like your Lederhosen well and truly slapped, then the best known venues in London are the two German-owned Bavarian Beerhouses (190 City Road, EC1V 2QH or 9 Crutched Friars, EC3N 2AU, ⊕ www.bavarian-beerhouse.com) but despite boasting the longest Oktoberfest celebrations in the UK and the only London menu, to our knowledge, to list curiously compelling cheesy snack *Obatzda,* their beer range is too limited to justify a full entry in this book.

⇌ London Bridge ⊖ London Bridge ⊶ CS4, 6, 7, NCN4 ⟋⟋ Jubilee Greenway, Jubilee Walkway, Thames Path

MARKET PORTER ☆ 25

Traditional pub, specialist
9 Stoney Street, SE1 9AA
📞 (020) 7407 2495, ⊕ www.markettaverns.
co.uk/The-Market-Porter
☼ 6am-8.30am, 11-11 Mon-Fri; 12-11 Sat;
12-10.30 Sun
Cask beers ✔ 12 (Harveys, 11 unusual guests),
Other beers 6 keg (BrewDog, Meantime)
🍴 Enhanced pub grub, ♿

Since long before the Borough became Beer Central, the massed handpumps of this old free house opposite Borough Market have been attracting a crowd that frequently spills out onto surrounding streets. Despite its new neighbours it's still an essential stop for anyone wanting a crash course in the variety on offer from contemporary British craft brewing. Aside from the permanent presence of Sussex Bitter, the policy is to buy in beers new to the pub wherever possible, sell them quickly and put something different on, sometimes as often as nine times a day, with around 50 different cask ales offered over the course of a typical week, though inevitably a few beers make return visits.

There's usually a variety of styles, including milds and other dark offerings, and occasional stronger stuff. As an example, beers from Angus, Byker, Boggart, Jarrow, Mighty Oak, Northumberland, Rudgate and Wolf were on when I called.

The advantage is that there's always something new to try, often from very small outfits that otherwise rarely appear in London. The disadvantage is that you never know what to expect, the experience can be a little

hit and miss and discoveries are unlikely to return. There's no list of what's on, so making a considered choice means perusing the pump clips, not always easy when the crowd at the bar is three deep, and the generally friendly staff are too rushed to advise.

The warm and woody main bar is short on furniture to provide the standing room necessary for busy times, with only a few small tables and old wooden barrels round the sides, but there are more tables in an extension behind.

The homely upstairs restaurant is usually an oasis of calm, offering the likes of steak and ale pie, smoked salmon, veggie pasta and mixed grill, while the downstairs food offerings are more of the pie and sandwich variety. The same company owns the Carpenters Arms (p98).

Insider tip! If you like the idea of sampling obscure microbrews as Radio 4's *Today* programme hits the airwaves, note the pub is one of the few in London that still makes use of its early morning market license.

⇌ London Bridge ⊖ London Bridge ⊶ CS4, 6, 7, NCN4 ⟋⟋ Jubilee Greenway, Jubilee Walkway, Thames Path

Market Porter

POMMELERS REST
Contemporary pub
196-198 Tower Bridge Road, SE1 2UN
☎ (020) 7378 1399
🌐 www.jdwetherspoon.co.uk
⊙ 7am-midnight Mon-Fri; 7am-1am Sat & Sun.
Children welcome daytime
Cask beers ✓ 10-12 (Greene King, Sambrook's, Fuller's, unusual guests), **Other beers** Usual Wetherspoon keg and bottles
🍽 Wetherspoon menu, ♿
Wetherspoon beer festivals and promotions

Opened in 1998 in a former hotel, this biggish place is one of London's better Wetherspoons and completes a trio of good beer options on the southern approach to Tower Bridge (see Bridge House and Draft House above). Aside from the regular Greene King options, the beer range can include a good showing from regional independents outside London like Hyde's in Manchester and Arkells in Swindon while Sambrook's is also regularly represented. It's a notably enthusiastic supporter of the twice yearly Wetherspoon beer festivals.

Pub trivia: The name recalls the historic connection of the area to the leather trade, also commemorated in nearby street names like Leathermarket Street and Tanner Street.

≋ London Bridge ⊖ Tower Hill, London Bridge **DLR** Tower Gateway ⊶ CS4, NCN4 ⚲ Thames Path, Jubilee Greenway, Jubilee Walkway

RAKE ☆ 25
Bar, specialist
14 Winchester Walk, SE1 9AG
☎ (020) 7407 0557, **tw** Rakebar
⊙ 12-11 Mon-Fri; 10-11 Sat; Closed Sun (except for special events). *Children on terrace only*
Cask beers ✓ 3 (Dark Star, unusual guests), **Other beers** 7 keg, 130 bottles, **Also** Real cider
🍽 Enhanced bar snacks only, 🌳 Front terrace, ♿
2 annual beer festivals, themed beer events and tastings

As attested by the various autographs on the wall, this tiny bar has become an essential stop on the international craft beer circuit since Richard Dinwoodie and Mike Hill of Utobeer (below), converted it from a greasy spoon café into the avant garde of a new wave of London beer bars in 2006. The cask handpumps dispense a changing Dark Star beer and guest choices from the more cutting edge micros including BrewDog, Bristol, Hardknott, Marble, Newmans (Celt Experience), Otley and Thornbridge. Keg taps include a pils that alternates Kaiserdom, Lindeboom and Veltins and guests that might come from Anchor, De Koninck, Schlenkerla or Stone.

Suppliers of bottled beers encompass beer geek favourites like Belgium's Alvinne, the Netherlands' Molen and Norway's Nøgne-Ø alongside local boy Kernel and top scoring Somerset brewer Moor. I spotted Cantillon Rosé de Gambrinus, Goose Island Bourbon County, Moylan's Imperial Stout and Rochefort 10 among the delights in the fridges. Regular tastings, often featuring rare beers, are held in an upstairs room (see 🌐 lovebeeratborough. ning.com) and other events include a Welsh beer festival in March.

The crowd is by no means entirely comprised of tickers huddled over tasting notes but includes market traders and shoppers – the pub shares its loo with the market – and discerning local workers. Though the pleasant wooden-decked and heated terrace helps, the restricted space – "the size of a minicab office" comments one reviewer – quickly becomes crowded. A US brewer wrote on the wall that it's the best pub in London – you may disagree but it's easily among the very top choices for serious beer lovers.

Insider tip! Visit mid afternoon on a non-market day to browse the list at leisure.

≋ London Bridge ⊖ London Bridge ⊶ CS4, 6, 7, NCN4 ⚲ Jubilee Greenway, Jubilee Walkway, Thames Path

Rake

Roxy

ROXY
Bar
128-132 Borough High Street, SE1 1LB
☎ (020) 7407 4057, ⊕ roxybarandscreen.com,
fbk, tw Roxy_Bar_Screen
✪ 5-1am Mon-Thu; 5-2am Fri; 1-2am Sat;
1-1am Sun
Cask beers None, **Other beers** 2 keg, 10
bottles, **Also** 160 spirits and liqueurs, cocktails
🍽 Diner / pub grub, 🪑 Tables on street, ♿
*Full programme of film, TV and sport screenings,
Wed comedy, monthly film quiz, occasional DJs,
cocktail hours*

The Roxy Bar & Screen is a picture house for
the widescreen TV generation, well targeted
at those who appreciate the communal
experience of the silver screen but are
reluctant to give up the comfort of their 5.1
surround sound-equipped living rooms. Poke
your head in and it looks like a rather hip and
smart bar, but behind a curtain at the back of
the long, narrow, mirrored and subtly lit space
is a screening room furnished not with tip-up
seats but sofas and cabaret-style tables. The
high end digital projector exhibits everything
from blockbusters and live sport to cult
movies and contemporary experimental
shorts. Unexpectedly, there are some
blockbusters and cult favourites of a different
kind behind the bar, programmed with the
collaboration of Utobeer (below). The beer list
changes every few months but on my visit
included Erdinger Dunkel, Coopers Sparkling
Ale and Goose Island Honkers Ale – a sign of
effort that only a few years ago would have
been considered completely unnecessary
somewhere like this. Food includes dishes like
cod loin, five spice pork belly and halloumi
and vegetable stack besides burgers and

pizzas. They should be up for a best
supporting Oscar at least.

🚆 London Bridge ⊖ Borough 🚲 CS4, 6, 7,
NCN4 🚶 Jubilee Greenway, Jubilee Walkway,
Thames Path

ROYAL OAK ☆ 25
Traditional pub
44 Tabard Street, SE1 4JU
☎ (020) 7357 7173
✪ 12-11 Mon-Sat; 12-9.30 Sun
Cask beers ✅ 6 (5 Harveys, 1 guest), **Other
beers** 12+ bottles (Harveys), **Also** 1 real cider
🍽 Pub grub
Functions

The Royal Oak is well loved with good reason
as it's pretty much the perfect traditional pub
– clean, bright and civilised but unpretentious
and friendly, with a genuine community feel,
a welcome lack of recorded music and
bleeping machines, in a Victorian building
with some surviving heritage features, and
offering an excellent range of top quality
beers. It's the only London pub tied to Lewes
brewer Harveys, one of England's most
respected surviving independent family
brewers. Its Sussex Bitter is an increasingly
common sight in discerning London pubs but
is by no means the brewery's only great beer,
as you'll discover here, where it's joined by
Armada, Mild, Pale Ale and seasonals and a
guest: Fuller's Gales' HSB when I called. Then
there's a comprehensive range of traditional
and unusual bottled specialities including
strong Elizabethan Ale and benchmark-setting
Imperial Russian Stout, also available to take
away. Good food includes sandwiches, pies,

Royal Oak

One of a string of pubs facing Borough Market, the Southwark Tavern is working hard to hold its own among the neighbouring beer champions. A Mitchells & Butlers Castle pub, it offers a friendly, youthful welcome with a neat range of cask ale on its scrubbed horseshoe bar – London Pale Ale and Doom Bar are the regulars but supplemented by interesting guests that might come from Leeds, Rudgate, Williams Brothers, Wychwood and the like. I found the rare cask version of Worthington White Shield here. As usual with the chain there's plenty of imported keg and bottled beer too – Chimay, Franziskaner, Innis & Gunn, Kozel and Sierra Nevada to name a few. The kitchen has a challenge given the garden of gourmet delights nearby – its offering is big on steaks, sausages, gammon hock, nut roast and the 'ultimate burger'.

Pub trivia: The cellar contains several brick booths arranged in a curve, labelled as cells to suggest a connection with the notorious Marshalsea prison, whose inmates were mainly debtors. "This is just a story we tell Americans," comments the barman wryly. In fact they're old storage areas: the first incarnation of the real Marshalsea stood more or less opposite on the other side of Borough High Street, while its successor, where Charles Dickens' father once languished, was a little further south, on a site now occupied by Southwark Local Studies Library. Of the original building, only a boundary wall survives.

≈ London Bridge ⊖ London Bridge ᗭᗠ CS4, 6, 7, NCN4 ✸ Jubilee Greenway, Jubilee Walkway, Thames Path

UTOBEER ☆ **25**
Shop
Borough Market, Borough High Street, SE1 1TL
☏ (020) 7378 9461, ⊕ www.utobeer.co.uk
✪ Closed Mon & Tue; 11-6 Wed & Thu; 10-6 Fri; 9-5 Sat
Cask beer None, **Other beers** 700+ international bottles, gift sets, **Also** Specialist ciders and spirits, crown cap fridge magnets
🍴 Extensive choice of specialist and gourmet food from surrounding stalls, ♿ No disabled toilet but flat access

For well over a decade Utobeer has flown the flag for fine beer among all the other fine food and drink at Borough Market, providing

hotpots and home cooked veggie options. The space around the island counter is divided in two, still distinguished by the greater amounts of soft furnishings on the 'saloon' side, with an old-style hatchway in the lobby once used for off sales. Check weekend opening times before setting out as they have a tendency to change.

Pub trivia: Tabard Street is the old route of the Kent Road, as followed by Chaucer's fictitious pilgrims, thus its current name which commemorates the now vanished inn where they assembled. See also under the George, above.

≈ London Bridge ⊖ Borough ᗭᗠ CS4, 6, 7, NCN4 ✸ Jubilee Greenway, Jubilee Walkway, Thames Path

SOUTHWARK TAVERN
Contemporary pub
22 Southwark Street, SE1 1TU
☏ (020) 7403 0257
⊕ www.thesouthwarktavern.co.uk
✪ 11-midnight Mon-Wed; 11-1am Thu & Fri; 10am-1am Sat; 11-midnight Sun. *Children until 5pm*
Cask beers ✔ 6 (Meantime, Sharp's, 4 unusual guests), **Other beers** 7 keg, 10 bottles
🍴 Enhanced pub grub, 🍺 Tables on street
Tue quiz, board games, themed seasonal events

one of London's and Britain's most reliable sources of the cream of international beer culture and helping broaden taste horizons among both drinkers and brewers, particularly since it's also spawned the Rake bar nearby (above) and branched into direct imports on its own account. Sharing the market's 'Drinks Cage' with three wine merchants, it may no longer offer quite the biggest range of bottled beers, nor the most keenly priced, but it certainly has the most well chosen, a selection that collectively demonstrates both the refined and complex heights beer can reach and the huge variety of tastes it offers and moods and occasions it partners.

In recent years the business has been a leading champion of US craft brewing in the UK and regularly stocks beers from Big Sky, Coronado, Dogfish Head, Eel River, Great Divide, Green Flash, Jolly Pumpkin, Left Hand, He'Brew (brewed at Olde Saratoga), Odell, Rogue, Stone, Tommyknocker and Victory. The Belgian list takes in acknowledged classics (all five regularly available Trappists, real lambics from Boon and Cantillon, St Bernardus and St Feuillien abbey beers) and exciting newcomers (Alvinne, Belgoo/Binchoise, Légendes, De Ranke, Rulles and Dutch cross-border interloper Scheldebrouwerij). The British choice favours BrewDog, Breconshire, Dark Star, Hardknott, Hepworth, Kernel, Moor, Otley, Whitstable and more, including some of the more experimental brews from Sharp's. The Dutch offerings go beyond La Trappe to IJ, Jopen, St Christoffel, Texels and other micros rarely seen in the UK, while from the rest of the world there's Carnegie Porter, Mikkeller, Nøgne-Ø, a big range of Schlenkerla and even stylishly

Southwark Tavern

presented Italian craft brews from Amarcord and Borgo. Easily enough to forgive them their painfully punning name.

≈ London Bridge ⊖ London Bridge ⚲ CS4, 6, 7, NC4 ⚑ Jubilee Greenway, Jubilee Walkway, Thames Path

WHEATSHEAF
Contemporary pub, specialist
24 Southwark Street, SE1 1TY
☏ (020) 7407 9934
✪ 11-11 Mon-Sat; 12-10 Sun. *Children until 6pm*
Cask beers ✔ 10 (Wells & Young's, 8 unusual guests), **Other beers** 2 keg, 3 bottles
🍴 Pub grub, ⊞ Benches on street
Darts, board games, big screen sport, occasional live music

The Wheatsheaf once stood between the Market Porter and the Southwark Tavern (above). Then came the Thameslink Project to improve the cross-city rail links from north to south, once known as Thameslink 2000, which gives an indication of its slow and tortuous progress. The old Wheatsheaf now stands boarded up in the shadow of a new viaduct which doesn't yet have agreed access to the existing rail network. In the meantime the former tenant has been rehoused in the basement of the Hop Exchange, as not only a surrogate Wheatsheaf but also the German-themed Katzenjammers beer cellar (above). The old pub was and is Young's property; the new is free of tie, operated by the small Red Car pubco, though still stocks Bitter and Special as well as house ale Nethergate Redcar Bitter. The other seven taps chase novelty by constantly dispensing new guest beers, including a healthy range of darker options. A snapshot might find beers from Cox & Holbrook, Mauldons, Mill Green, Titanic and Waveney. In a vaulted brick cellar strewn with brown sofas and decorated with a poignant photo collection comprising striking black and white portraits of the old place's former regulars, this is a relaxing and rewarding alternative local source of obscure cask ales. The Castle (p81) is a sister Red Car pub.

≈ London Bridge ⊖ London Bridge ⚲ CS4, 6, 7, NC4 ⚑ Jubilee Greenway, Jubilee Walkway, Thames Path

CITY

To the east of the central area, the 'square mile' of the City is the site of the original settlement that developed into the Roman provincial capital and gave its Celtic name, via Latin, to the entire metropolis. The City was once a true city in all its multifunctional aspects, while Westminster was just for kings, bishops and politicians. As the capital grew the City exerted an influence far beyond its own boundaries, once having the power to charge duties on goods from Staines to Gravesend. It still maintains an anomalous and rather undemocratic local authority. Though there are a few residential areas like the Barbican, most of the City is a business district, throbbing to the thrum of international capital on working days but curiously deserted at weekends except for explorers and tourists. City pubs are generally tailored to City workers, who often like real ale but seem content with a limited range of better known brands; they almost invariably close at weekends unless near to tourist honeypots or transport hubs.

BLACKFRIAR

Traditional pub ★
174 Queen Victoria Street, EC4V 4EG
☎ (020) 7236 5474, ⊕ www.nicholsonspubs.co.uk/theblackfriarblackfriarslondon
✪ 10.30-11 Mon-Sat; 12-10.30 Sun. *Children until 9pm*
Cask beers ✪ 8 (Fuller's, Sharp's, Timothy Taylor, guests), **Other beers** 2 bottles
🍽 Nicholson's menu, 🎪 Front terrace
Occasional tastings, functions

Some of the heritage pubs listed here were merely typical in their day and are remarkable primarily for their survival. The

Blackfriar in its current incarnation, however, has never been anything but extraordinary. The narrow wedge of a building, dating from 1875, was remodelled in 1905 into a unique British art nouveau extravaganza by architect H Fuller-Clark and artist Henry Poole, taking as its theme the Dominican friary that once stood in the area, which derives its name from the brothers' distinctive black cloaks. From the street the glittering mosaic pub name, statuary and plaques are intriguing enough, but inside is overwhelming. Under a series of broad arches, every surface is sumptuous, with layers of multicoloured

❶ Blackfriar   ❷ Cockpit   ❸ Crosse Keys   ❹ Old Doctor Butler's Head

Blackfriar

marble, stained glass, mirrors and richly polished wood, lavishly illustrated with imagined scenes of monastic life, most in dark and dramatic handmade bas relief. The former snack bar at the back of the saloon, in particular, is a richly carved grotto illustrating aphorisms like "haste is slow". It's all a marvellous challenge to the English reputation for reserve, but we can only speculate on what its supposed subjects the Dominicans, mendicant preachers who helped found the Inquisition, would make of it.

The Blackfriar is a frequent call on sightseeing tours of offbeat London but happily for us it's also now a much improved beer venue under the stewardship of Mitchells & Butlers' Nicholsons chain. Doom Bar, London Pride and Landlord are regulars while guests are drawn from the seasonal list and might include interesting stuff from Adnams, Black Horse, BrewDog, Kelham Island, Saltaire or Thornbridge. A comprehensive pub grub menu particularly focuses on pies, and there are free postcards too.

≠ Blackfriars ⊖ Blackfriars ☙ | CN+7, 38, link to NCN4 ✦ Jubilee Walkway, Thames Path, link to Jubilee Greenway

COCKPIT
Traditional pub
7 St Andrews Hill, EC4V 5BY
📞 (020) 7248 7315
✪ 11-11 Mon-Fri; 11-6 Sat; 12-7 Sun
Cask beers ✔ 5 (Adnams, Marston's, Wells & Young's, guests), **Also** 10 malts
🍴 Pub grub
Big screen news and sport, pub games

Besides public executions, popular entertainments in London a few centuries ago included watching two enraged cockerels tear each other to pieces with metal spurs and betting on the outcome. The purpose-built facilities used for the practice are recalled in the unusual design of this corner pub, with its recessed central pit and spectator galleries above, lit through now-listed leaded windows.

The idea that it was once actually used as a cockpit, as repeated in some tourist guides, is surely fanciful. There's more evidence to support its other claim to fame – that it stands on the site of the only property William Shakespeare ever owned in London, though the exact location isn't certain and it's unlikely the Bard himself ever lived there. Today it's a welcome City refuge for lovers of well-kept cask beer, with more of a local feel than many

Crosse Keys

in the area, and is also open weekend daytimes. Appropriately given their cockerel logo, it's a former Courage pub and though now owned by Enterprise stocks Wells & Young's revival of Courage Best and Directors, alongside Marston's Pedigree (a rarer sight in London than it once was), Adnams Bitter and a guest that might be from Banks's, Hook Norton, Timothy Taylor or Wychwood. Home-cooked food is of the doorstep sandwich and cottage pie variety. It's the closest listing in this guide to one of London's best known landmarks, Christopher Wren's masterpiece St Pauls Cathedral.

≈ Blackfriars ⊖ Blackfriars ⟳ LCN+7, 38, link to NCN4 ♦♦ Jubilee Walkway, Thames Path, link to Jubilee Greenway

CROSSE KEYS ☆ 25

Contemporary pub
9 Gracechurch Street, EC3V 0DR
☎ (020) 7623 4824
⊕ www.jdwetherspoon.co.uk
☼ 7am-11pm Mon-Thu; 7am-midnight Fri; 9-7 Sat; Closed Sun. *Children until early evening if eating*
Cask beers ✔ Up to 23 (Fuller's, Greene King, unusual guests), **Other beers** Usual Wetherspoon keg and bottles, **Also** 1-2 real ciders/perries
🍴 Wetherspoon menu, ♿
Wetherspoon beer festivals and promotions, meeting rooms

Though the good value prices, corporate menu, canned music ban, densely packed and numbered standard wooden tables and curry nights are present and correct, the Crosse Keys is most certainly not your average local Wetherspoon.

Two features in particular stand out: one is the building, a palatial banking hall that was once the London headquarters of HSBC. Massive pillars rise towards high skylights between the cool green and grey marble walls in the huge central bar, and a grand staircase rises to a balcony where there are more intimate spaces, some of which can be reserved for meetings including a fine boardroom. Mounted on the balcony are marble sculptures in Chinese style, reminding us this was originally the Hong Kong and Shanghai Bank, and there are other nods to the world's oldest civilisation if you look hard.

The second noteworthy feature is the beer. The pub prides itself on one of the widest cask ale choices in the chain, and is the only one to offer over 100 beers during Wetherspoon festivals. There are usually at least 16 listed on the TV monitors above the big island bar and regularly the full complement of 23 – a 24th handpump is reserved for cider. Fuller's London Pride and Greene King Abbot and IPA are the only regulars while the others plunder Spoons' lengthy guest ale list: as a sample, on a midweek night I spotted pumpclips from

Acorn, Arundel, Banks & Taylor, Batemans, Blindman, Exmoor, O'Hanlon's, Oxfordshire, Salopian, Three B's, Titanic, Tring, Vale and Wold Top, with a good mix of styles including milds and porters. Staff are friendly and helpful and beer quality high, though weekend hours are limited.

Pub trivia: The pub revives the name of a coaching inn that once stood on the site. The heraldic reference is to St Peter, doubtless inspired by neighbouring St Peter upon Cornhill church, one of Christopher Wren's post-Great Fire rebuilds which claims to stand on the site of the oldest Christian church in Britain.

⇌ Cannon Street, Liverpool Street ⊖ Bank ⊕ LCN+0, Strand, Limehouse, Southwark ⫻ Jubilee Walkway

OLD DOCTOR BUTLER'S HEAD
Traditional pub
2 Masons Avenue, EC2V 5BT
📞 (020) 7606 3504, ✉olddoctorbutlers@ shepherd-neame.co.uk, ⊕ www.shepherd-neame.co.uk
🕐 11-11 Mon-Fri; Closed Sat & Sun. *Children until early evening*
Cask beers ✔ 6 (Shepherd Neame), **Other beers** 2 bottles
🍴 Traditional English menu and pub grub,

🪑 Standing only
Big screen sport, functions

William Butler was a quack purveyor of medicinal ale who ingratiated himself with James I and was appointed court physician. Pubs selling his ale displayed his portrait, thus the name of this quaint, low beamed, wood panelled and gaslit (if the landlord can obtain the mantles) place hidden down an alley near Moorgate, now one of the few proper pubs in the area

It lays claim to being one of London's oldest pubs and traces its history back to 1610, though it's been much rebuilt and much of what you see today is younger than it looks – the left hand side is the oldest. Food is befittingly English including suet pudding and doorstep sandwiches, served in the bar or in the upstairs restaurant. Beer is well kept quality stuff from Shepherd Neame: Bishop's Finger, Kent's Best, Master Brew, Spitfire and a seasonal. Butler's infamously laxative brew – a strong ale infused with senna, oak, agrimony, maidenhair and scurvygrass – is, perhaps fortunately, no longer available.

⇌ Moorgate ⊖ Moorgate, Bank ⊕ LCN+ 0 and city links ⫻ Jubilee Walkway

Old Doctor Butler's Head

CLERKENWELL

Clerkenwell, named after the Clerk's (or Cleric's) Well in Farringdon Lane, was one of London's first suburbs. To the immediate north of the City, in medieval times it housed several important religious institutions including St Mary's Benedictine nunnery and the priory of the Knights Hospitallers of St John of Jerusalem, a monastic order that provided medical services during the Crusades. The priory gate still stands across St John's Lane, adjoining the offices of the order's modern manifestation St John Ambulance. In later centuries this was a fashionable residential area and a centre of printing, watch and clock making and brewing – the Cannon brewery on St John Street closed in 1955. It's also been a hotbed of radicals and revolutionaries with links to Chartism, socialism and communism: Vladimir Lenin published *Iskra* (The Spark) in 1902 from offices that are now the Marx Memorial Library on Clerkenwell Green, while the rather more cuddly but still left-leaning daily the *Guardian* was based on Farringdon Road until 2008. Step out of Farringdon station, currently being rebuilt for the new Crossrail link, and you should spot the pavement plaques of the Clerkenwell Historic Trail which will help you explore this fascinating area: many of our listings are on or near the route.

CROWN
Traditional pub
43 Clerkenwell Green, EC1R 0EG
☏ (020) 7253 4973
⊕ www.thecrowntavernec1.co.uk
☼ 12-midnight daily. *Children until 6pm (8pm Sat & Sun)*
Cask beers ✔ 6 (Fuller's, Timothy Taylor, 4 often unusual guests), **Other beers** 8 keg, 10 bottles, **Also** 10 malts, wines
⑪ Enhanced pub grub / gastro menu, ▥ Tables on square
Functions

The market where the Artful Dodger tutored Oliver Twist in the basics of street robbery is gone, but the ancient village centre of Clerkenwell Green, overlooked by medieval St John's Gate, is still an attractive and atmospheric public space. This big and well appointed pub, claiming a history from 1641 but rebuilt in 1815 and now a pleasant place of glittery wallpaper and handsome wood, is perfectly placed to take advantage of it. Visit the lovely Apollo room upstairs and you'll spot display cases housing empty bottles of

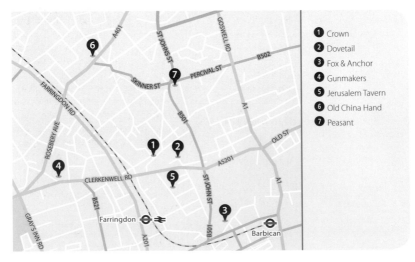

1. Crown
2. Dovetail
3. Fox & Anchor
4. Gunmakers
5. Jerusalem Tavern
6. Old China Hand
7. Peasant

Crown

classic world beers and books by the late Michael Jackson – the pub once vied with the White Horse in Fulham (p225) in offering a serious specialist beer list. Sadly the range is now much reduced but as a Mitchells & Butlers Castle pub there's still beery interest to be had. Besides cask London Pride and Landlord, the guest pumps rotate through up to 40 different beers a month, perhaps including the products of Adnams, Copper Dragon, Jersey, Saltaire or Williams Brothers. Duvel and Coopers Sparkling Ale are the pick of the bottled list. Food runs to pulled beef brisket cottage pie, mushroom spinach and chestnut risotto or grilled mackerel alongside sandwiches and burgers.

Pub trivia: It's claimed the young Joseph Stalin first met Vladimir Lenin under the Conspirators' Clock in the back room in 1903.

≋ Farringdon ⊖ Farringdon ⊶ LCN+7, 39 ⬳ Clerkenwell Historic Trail

DOVETAIL
Bar, specialist
9-10 Jerusalem Passage, EC1V 4JP
☎ (020) 7490 7321, ⊕ www.dovepubs.com
🕐 12-11 Mon-Sat; Closed Sun. *Children welcome*
Cask beer None, **Other beers** 14 keg,
90 bottles (Belgian)
🍴 Belgian and British pub grub, ⊞ A few tables on alley
Private tastings

The name of this intriguing alleyway just off Clerkenwell Green recalls the city where the Order of St John was founded, and the Dovetail claims to be built on stones brought back from Palestine. The bar is the little sister of the first rate Dove in Hackney (p126) but concentrates exclusively on Belgian beers: the smart pewter and marble bar counter is a rare outlet for draught Rodenbach alongside Chimay Triple, Brugse Zot and a guest that's sometimes Westmalle Dubbel. Bottled Trappists from Achel, Chimay, Orval, Rochefort and Westmalle lead a strong list that stretches to Boon Mariage Parfait Oude Geuze, De Koninck Triple, Van Steenberge Leute Bokbier and Verhaege Duchess de Bourgogne. As with the Dove, food has a Belgian twist with mussels, *carbonnade flamande, waterzooi* and veggie and meaty croquettes and sausages. Advertising enamels, green tiled tables, gothic chairs and poster-sized reproductions of one of Belgium's other famous cultural exports, Hergé's *Tintin* graphic novels, complete an attractive picture.

≋ Farringdon ⊖ Farringdon ⊶ LCN+7, 39 ⬳ Clerkenwell Historic Trail

FOX & ANCHOR
Traditional pub
115 Charterhouse Street, EC1M 6AA
☎ (020) 7250 1300, ⊕ www.foxandanchor.com
⊘ 7am-11pm Mon-Thu; 7am-midnight Fri;
8.30am-midnight Sat; 8.30am-10pm Sun.
Children until 7pm
Cask beers ✔ 6 (Nethergate, 5 sometimes
unusual guests), **Other beers** 4 keg, 20 bottles
(mainly British), **Also** Wines, specialist spirits
including 60 whiskies
⑪ Breakfast, traditional English/gastro menu,
🎏 Tables on street, ♿
Sun/Mon jazz duo, occasional big screen sport

"Pubs go posh", runs the headline of a
newspaper article on the reopening of this
historic pub in 2008, now framed and proudly
displayed on a wall full of media coverage.
And posh it is too, but still friendly and
welcoming thanks to attentive landlord Scott
and his staff. Dark polished wood and mirrors
dominate the main bar, with an original bar
back, tiling and floor mosaics, a sumptuous
pewter bar top and five sought after, and
bookable, booths in the 'Fox's Den' at the
back. It's just round the corner from the
Charterhouse, a former priory and later school
and almshouses, and right opposite historic
Smithfield meat market, thus the early
morning opening – although some of the
market traders might blink at the £16.50 price
tag on the premium breakfast. The beer is still
affordable, however, and the menu reasonably
priced considering the quality though,
perhaps inevitably given the location, not

Fox & Anchor

especially vegetarian friendly. Oysters,
imaginative salads, pies, daily roasts and
specials like smoked haddock and spinach
bake are typical, while traditional bar snacks
like pickled eggs and pork scratchings are all
home made.

The Fox & Anchor ale, a rebadged
Nethergate Three Point Eight, is the only
regular on the pumps, but there's usually
something from Adnams, Purity or Sharp's and
occasional appearances by the likes of
BrewDog. A porter or stout is invariably on
and strongly recommended to accompany
the oysters. The superior bottled range
includes specialities Chalky's Bark and Chalky's
Bite from Sharp's, Coniston Bluebird and
Robinson's Old Tom. There are six upmarket
bedrooms above.

Insider tip! Beers are served in pewter tankards
as a matter of course, but if you'd rather admire
the colour, glasses are available on request.

≋ Farringdon ⊖ Barbican, Farringdon 🚲
LCN+7, 39 ⚐ Clerkenwell Historic Trail

GUNMAKERS
Contemporary pub
13 Eyre Street Hill, EC1R 5ET
☎ (020) 7278 1022, ⊕ thegunmakers.co.uk,
tw thegunmakers
⊘ 11-11 Mon-Fri; Closed Sat & Sun – check
website for weekend hours. *Children welcome
daytime*
Cask beers ✔ 4 (Purity, Woodforde's, 2 unusual
guests), **Other beers** 2 keg, 1 bottle, **Also** Wines
⑪ French-influenced gastro menu

London historians might assume the
Gunmakers – just on the other side of
Farringdon Road and technically in Holborn
but very much Clerkenwell in terms of
proximity and spirit – took its name from the
original Maxim gun factory, makers of the
world's first machine guns, nearby. But in fact
this modest building was a gunmaker's studio
in 1840, and had already become a pub
several decades before Hiram Maxim
registered his first patents in 1883. In 2009 it
was taken on by former solicitor Jeff Bell, who
under the name of Stonch had been one of
the most widely read and respected of
pioneering British beer bloggers, and a

Gunmakers

critical but insightful chronicler of London drinking houses whose work partially inspired this book.

Given Jeff's record as an enthusiastic advocate of good beer and great pubs, you'd expect him to walk the walk and you won't be disappointed. Mad Goose and Woodforde's Wherry are the immaculately kept regulars, supplemented by guests that are often linked and themed – BrewDog, Dark Star, Harviestoun, Leeds and Thornbridge are favourites, with current offerings regularly tweeted. There's also Meantime Helles on keg and more handpumps may be installed. The place is muzak- and TV-free with more space than evident initially, particularly the pleasant glass ceilinged area at the back. A French chef provides good fresh food with a Gallic touch, such as steak *frites*, Toulouse sausages and veggie tagliatelle.

≹ Farringdon ⊖ Farringdon, Chancery Lane
🚲 LCN+7, 39 ⚓ Link to Clerkenwell Historic Trail

JERUSALEM TAVERN
Traditional pub
55 Britton Street, EC1M 5UQ
📞 (020) 7490 4281, ⊕ www.stpetersbrewery.
co.uk/London, **tw** jerusalemtavern
🕐 11-11 Mon-Fri; Closed Sat & Sun. *Children
lunchtime if eating*
Cask beers ✅ 6 (St Peter's), **Other beers** 2 keg,
17 bottles, gift packs, minikegs (St Peter's), **Also**
7 malts
🍽 Short enhanced pub grub menu, 🪑 Benches
on street

Its name another echo of the Knights of St John and their role in the Crusades, the original Jerusalem Tavern stood adjacent to the Priory gateway on Clerkewell Green. In 1996 the St Peter's Brewery revived the name for their first London pub nearby, still their only tied house aside from the bar at St Peter's Hall, the brewery's Suffolk base. This building dates from 1720 and was once used as a coffee house, but more recently it was a watchmaker's. The glass partition that separated the shop from the workshop still stands, forming a small separate seating area at the front decorated with tiles that are careful reproductions of the ones the builders discovered behind panelling here during the renovation. The homely area within is not much bigger, with a few tables in cubby holes and one on a curious elevated platform.

Six cask ales are served using a siphoning ale extractor system from fake barrel heads behind the bar: Best Bitter, Golden Ale and Mild are regulars, plus one of the fruit beers for which the brewery is known and two specials or seasonals. Then there's an ale on keg, an anonymous lager – actually Bitburger – and the full range of St Peter's bottled beers. The lunchtime menu is short but wholesome, and might include lamb and porter stew or spinach and goat's cheese slice. This unusual pub has won numerous awards and is understandably popular, so you'll need to time your visit to avoid the crowds.

≹ Farringdon ⊖ Farringdon 🚲 LCN+7, 39 ⚓
Clerkenwell Historic Trail

OLD CHINA HAND
Contemporary pub
8 Tysoe Street, EC1R 4RQ
☎ (020) 7278 7678, ⊕ clerkenwellbar.com
🕐 12-midnight Mon-Thu; 12-1.30am Fri & Sat;
12-11 Sun
Cask beers ✔ 3 (Bath, O'Hanlon's, 1 guest),
Other beers 6 keg, 40 bottles
🍴 Tapas-style menu, 🌳 Front terrace
*Ping pong, board games, occasional big screen
sport, occasional live music*

Favourably located on a small square just
across from regenerated Exmouth Market with
its specialist shops, and not far from the Royal
Ballet at Sadlers Wells, the Old China Hand
boasts it's a "pub that's a little different". The
long narrow space is candlelit and comfortable,
with oddities like a fairylit hammock and a ping
pong table. Once it was known as O'Hanlon's
after its then owners, who in 1996 launched a
microbrewery (not on site) which became a
success in its own right, migrating to Devon in
2000 (p304). The pub is no longer directly
linked to the brewery but still regularly stocks
its beer. The cask ales change but are often
from southwest England – as well as O'Hanlon's
and Bath you might see Stonehenge, Milk
Street or maybe Sambrook's from nearer by.
Bottled beers include choices from some of
these brewers as well as Meantime, La Trappe,
Corsican Pietra, Duvel-Moortgat and others,
while De Koninck, Sierra Nevada Pale and
Freedom Lager are on keg. A new food policy
was being introduced when I visited so ring or
check the website for the latest.

Peasant

Pub trivia: The Thames Water building round the
corner is sited at New River Head, the original
collection point for the 17th century watercourse
that brought fresh water from Hertfordshire to
London. The start of a signed trail all the way to
Hertford is nearby.

⇌ Farringdon ⊖ Angel, Farringdon 🚲 LCN+0,
7, 39 ✔✔ Clerkenwell Historic Trail, New River Walk

PEASANT
Gastropub
240 St John Street, EC1V 4PH
☎ (020) 7336 7726, ⊕ www.thepeasant.co.uk
🕐 12-11 Mon-Sat; 12-10.30 Sun. *Children
until 7pm*
Cask beers ✔ 4 (Crouch Vale, Nethergate,
Wells & Young's, 1 unusual guest), **Other beers**
5 keg, 12 bottles, **Also** Malts, wines, cigars
🍴 Serious gastro menu, 🌳 Benches on street,
rooftop terrace garden
*Twice yearly beer festivals, occasional big screen
sport*

This friendly gastropub halfway between
Smithfield and Angel maintains an imposing
Victorian presence on its crossroads site, with
big arched windows, huge mirrors, an open
fire, a chunky bar back and remnants of
original tiling, some of it sadly partially
obscured by a big screen. Tasty food
downstairs could include mussel, clam and
coley stew, wild boar sausages or vegetarian
haggis, while the upstairs restaurant is serious
stuff at serious prices. Bombardier, Brewer's
Gold and Truman's Runner are the regular
casks and a fourth handpump rotates the likes
of Cotleigh, Otley, Oxfordshire, Rudgate and
Skinners. Camden Town wheat beer is on keg;
a complementary bottled list, chosen by
knowledgeable manager Nick Rouse, has
nothing especially unusual for London but
there's no arguing with the quality of Little
Creatures, Brooklyn Black Chocolate Stout or
Rochefort 8. Beer festivals twice a year expand
the choice further.

Insider tip! They offer a feasting menu for large
groups which might comprise whole roast
suckling pig or giant pie, though there are also
veggie options.

⇌ Farringdon ⊖ Barbican, Farringdon 🚲
LCN+0, 7, 39 ✔✔ Link to New River Walk

COVENT GARDEN

On the West End's eastern fringe, Covent Garden is a fine example of the constant remaking and regeneration of London's urban fabric. From 1200 it was a market garden attached to Westminster Abbey and Convent, thus its original name Convent Garden, but following Henry VIII's anti-clerical land grab, it ended up in the hands of the Dukes of Bedford. In 1630 they commissioned Inigo Jones to build St Paul's church and three terraces around an Italianate piazza, and a few decades later a fruit and vegetable market started on one corner of this. The neoclassical market hall of 1830 eventually became London's principal wholesale greengrocery market.

When the market moved to Nine Elms in 1974, the whole area became the first major example of the sort of leisure and tourism-based regeneration now common in London. The piazza reopened in 1980 as home to craft and fashion shops, eateries and bars, its spaces enlivened by licensed street performers. Since then similar businesses have taken over the old warehouses and workshops that surrounded it, creating a new and distinctive quarter that's especially popular with younger visitors. The fascinating London Transport Museum also stands on the piazza.

BELGO CENTRAAL
Restaurant
50 Earlham Street, WC2H 9LJ
📞 (020) 7813 2233
🌐 www.belgo-restaurants.co.uk
🕐 12-11 Mon-Thu; 12-11.30 Fri & Sat; 12-10.30 Sun. *Children welcome*
Cask beer None, **Other beers** 6 keg, 75 bottles (Belgian), **Also** Genever
🍴 Belgian/international menu, ♿

When Québecois Denis Blais and Belgian André Plisnier founded the original Belgo, now Belgo Noord (p141), in Camden in 1992, the concept of a Belgian beer and food restaurant for London seemed far sighted. Today Blais and Plisnier are long gone and the chain is down to five London branches, part of the same group that owns Café Rouge. Sadly the concept has stagnated while the beer world has gone on developing around it, and Belgo now seems something of a caricature of itself. The cooking is fine, the venues friendly and fun, but even though there are still a good few very decent options on the beer lists, you get the impression they don't care about the beer that much – it's simply part of the 'Belgian' gimmick. And Belgo has lost the advantage of exclusivity – you'll find numerous other places in this book to enjoy quality Belgian beer.

Opened in 1998, this flagship West End branch is the biggest and probably the best Belgo. A clanky goods lift takes customers

❶ Belgo Centraal
❷ Belgo Kingsway
❸ Cross Keys
❹ Harp
❺ Lowlander
❻ Porterhouse
❼ Ship & Shovell

Belgo Centraal

down to a cavernous warehouse basement where the menu reflects the company strapline *'Moules – Frites – Bières'* with eight variations on mussels and chips, other Belgian dishes like *waterzooi*, *stoemp* and cheese croquettes, the odd bit of cooking with beer, and a few veggie options. Things get rapidly busy and noisy so booking is recommended particularly at peak times. The draught beers are variable, while the bottled beer list has some solid options including a comprehensive Trappist selection, Saison Dupont, Boon Oude Geuze and Mariage Parfait, St Bernardus Grottenbier and Rodenbach Grand Cru. You can sample the

full bottled range in the small standup bar on the ground floor in the evenings but if you just want a beer it's best to head for Belgo Kingsway nearby (below).

Insider tip! Look out for the bargain lunch deals and 'beat the clock' happy hours.

≋ Charing Cross ⊖ Covent Garden ⊶ LCN+ 6, 6a, links to St James's, City ⁄⁄ Jubilee Walkway

BELGO KINGSWAY
Bar, restaurant
67 Kingsway, WC2B 6TD
☎ (020) 7242 7489
⊕ www.belgo-restaurants.co.uk
⊕ 11-11 Mon-Wed; 11-midnight Thu; 11-1am Fri & Sat; 11-11 Sun. *Children welcome*
Cask beers None, **Other beers** 8 keg, 75 bottles (Belgian), **Also** Genever
⊕ Belgian/international menu, ⊠

Essentially unchanged from when it was one of Belgo's spinoff Bièrodrome bars, this place caters equally for drinkers as well as diners using two separate spaces and is a more practical choice than nearby Belgo Centraal (above) if you just want a beer. The list is a bit shorter but includes some similarly good stuff. Food is essentially the same as Centraal but served in less distinctive surroundings.

⊖ Holborn ⊶ LCN+ 6, 6a, links to St James's, City ⁄⁄ Jubilee Walkway

Belgo Kingsway

CROSS KEYS
Traditional pub
31 Endell Street, WC2H 9EB
☎ (020) 7836 5185
⊕ crosskeyscoventgarden.com
🕐 11-11 Mon-Sat; 12-10.30 Sun
Cask beers ✅ 4 (Brodie's, occasional guests),
Also 1 real cider
🍽 Sandwiches, pies, Sunday roast
Functions

The smaller of the two central London pubs
leased from Enterprise by the Brodie family and
selling their beers (see also the Old Coffee
House p108), this was built on Endell Street in
the 1840s and boasts an ornate baroque
façade made even more spectacular by the
addition of floral displays and foliage. The
relatively modest interior is dark and traditional,
lined with leather banquettes and crammed
with stuff, including various dangling brass and
copper objects, a display of Beatles
memorabilia and an Elvis autograph (bought
from a collector some years back – the
performers had no connection to the pub). Off
the area's tourist epicentre, it's a proper local
muzak-free pub serving what is still a
residential area. Beer highlights are Brodie's fine
Amarilla, IPA, English Best and seasonals, with
the occasional guest that might even be from
Ha'penny, all at good prices for the area.

➔ Covent Garden 🚲 LCN+ 6, 6a, links to St
James's, City 🚶 Jubilee Walkway

HARP ☆ **25**
Traditional pub
47 Chandos Place, WC2N 4HS
☎ (020) 7836 0291
⊕ harpcoventgarden.com, **fbk, tw** harppub
🕐 10.30am-11pm Mon; 10.30am-11.30pm Tue-
Sat; 12-10.30 Sun
Cask beers ✅ 8 (Sambrook's, unusual often
local guests), **Other beers** 6 bottles, **Also** 8 real
ciders, 2 real perries, 15 single malts, wines
🍽 Sausage baguettes, 🌳 Rear alleyway

Built as the Welsh Harp in the 1830s, this small
free house with a lovely stained glass frontage
is a magnet for beer lovers seeking out
probably the best choice of real ale in the
West End. Landlady Bridget Walsh, who took
over as tenant in 1993 and bought the
freehold a few years back, has created a

Harp

civilised but relaxed and very friendly venue,
music and TV-free and majoring on beautifully
kept cask beer from London and around.
   Sambrook's are a fixture but you're also
likely to encounter ever-rotating and often
rare offerings from Redemption,
Twickenham, Dark Star, Harveys and others,
including milds and other dark delights. The
characterful smallish main bar has bare
floorboards, chandeliers, standup tables and
stools, its walls crammed with mirrors and
faded period portraits and prints. Up the
rickety stairs is a more relaxed space with
pink walls, comfy chairs and houseplants, like
the guest lounge of a particularly nice old
B&B. Be warned the celebrated home-
cooked sausages often run out, though there
are plenty of other food options nearby.
Deservedly, the Harp became the first
London pub to win CAMRA's National Pub of
the Year award in 2010. It's a delightful
surprise to find a place as good as this a
stone's throw from Leicester Square, and just
round the corner from the National Gallery
and National Portrait Gallery.

Insider tip! Go through the unmarked door at
the back of the ground floor bar to emerge in a
hidden alleyway, where stands created from
wooden barrels give smokers somewhere to rest
their drinks.

🚆 Charing Cross ➔ Charing Cross, Leicester
Square 🚲 LCN+ 6, 6a, links to St James's, City
🚶 Jubilee Walkway, Thames Path

Lowlander

LOWLANDER
Bar, specialist
36 Drury Lane, WC2B 5RR
☎ (020) 7379 7446, ⊕ www.lowlander.com, **fbk**
✪ 11.30-11 Mon-Sat; 12-10.30 Sun. *Children welcome daytimes*
Cask beer None, **Other beers** 15 keg, 80+ bottles (mainly Belgian), **Also** Genever
🍴 Belgian/international menu, 🚻 Tables on street
Tutored tastings for groups, occasional microbrewery festivals

Opened in 2001 within sight of the impressive art deco Freemason's Hall, this conscientious bar styles itself a *grand café* in the Belgian tradition but if truth be told, though it's *grand* on welcome and enthusiasm for good beer, it's rather less *grand* in dimensions. And given its popularity, you're advised to visit off peak if you can. Downstairs most seating is on big benches, with some smaller sofas and tables; upstairs there's a small balcony which I can't help thinking must have been inspired by the one in the Paters Vaetje café across from Antwerp cathedral and is just as eagerly sought out by regulars.

At the outset the bar sourced beer across the Low Countries but the Dutch options

have dwindled with only La Trappe left. The Belgian choices include Brugse Zot, Van Eecke Watous Wit and Van Honsebrouck Kasteel Blond and Bruin among the kegs, and a solid list of bottles. The Troubadour beers, brewed at Proef, Saison Dupont, Verhaege Echte Kriek and Ellezelloise Hercule are among the highlights. Then there's the "hidden treasures" list of changing specials which on my last visit included Hanssens Oude Kriek and La Trappe Quadrupel. Food options naturally include mussels and options like asparagus risotto, pot roast or fish pie. Prices, inevitably round here, are a little high, but the place demonstrates attention to detail and a genuine commitment to beer education. Sadly a more ambitious sister venue in the City didn't survive the recession.

Insider tip! A helpful note on the menu explains that beers are served by default at 6-8°C but will be presented warmer on request.

⇌ Charing Cross ⊖ Covent Garden 🚲 LCN+ 6, 6a, links to St James's, City 🚶 Jubilee Walkway

PORTERHOUSE
Contemporary pub
21-22 Maiden Lane, WC2E 7NA
☎ (020) 7379 7917
⊕ www.porterhousebrewco.com
✪ 11-11 Mon-Wed; 11-11.30 Thu-Sat; 12-10.30 Sun
Cask beers ⬤ 1-2 (Porterhouse, occasional guests), **Other beers** 11 keg (Porterhouse and international), 85 bottles, **Also** Cocktails
🍴 Enhanced pub grub, 🚻 Front patio, ♿
Thu-Sat live bands and DJs, Sun early evening Irish music session, occasional beer festivals, seasonal parties

This vast converted warehouse has been serving up genuine Irish craft beer culture in London for well over a decade as the English outpost of a small microbrewery estate based near Dublin. The orange-lit and labyrinthine multi-level interior is decked out in spaceship-like post-industrial tubing with a massive beer bottle collection displayed on every spare surface. The one Porterhouse cask ale, TSB, is not always available but there's usually at least one beer on handpump, perhaps from Thwaites. At least half a dozen further own

Porterhouse

brands are available on keg, including porter, stout and red ale. The bottled range, catalogued in a thick menu, includes Anchor Steam, Früh Kölsch, Goose Island IPA, St Feuillien abbey beers, Rochefort 10 and Worthington White Shield besides mediocre lagers from exotic places. Food is pizza, burgers, steaks, fry-ups and salads. It's a brash, busy place that heats up still further when the live bands strike up; the booths in the basement are more restful, or try the Irish acoustic session early on Sunday evening.

Insider tip! Don't simply arrange to "meet in the Porterhouse" without specifying a place – you may very well never see each other again!

≋ Charing Cross ⊖ Covent Garden 🚲 LCN+ 6, 6a, links to St James's, City 🚶 Jubilee Walkway

SHIP & SHOVELL
Traditional pub
2-3 Craven Passage, WC2N 5PH
📞 (020) 7839 1311
🌐 www.hall-woodhouse.co.uk
🕐 11-11 Mon-Sat; Closed Sun. *Children only on Sat in designated bar*
Cask beers ✓ 3 (Badger), **Other beers**
3 bottles (Badger)
🍴 Sandwiches, pub grub, 🪑 Standing room outside
Darts, functions

Through the tunnel under the Charing Cross platforms and a few doors down from legendary gay disco Heaven, the Ship & Shovell is a pub of two halves. It's split between a pair of old buildings either side of a pedestrian walkway, and when things get busy during fine weather, as they often do, the staff have the unenviable job of keeping the right of way unobstructed by the merry throng. The north side is grander with glittering mirrors and a panelled front area; the south side, not always open, feels older but is actually newer, with a bright upstairs room, booths and a rear snug that might have once had a river view. This is a Badger pub, serving well presented First Gold, Tanglefoot and a seasonal or special, with a few bottled beers too, while the menu runs to beef lasagne or vegetable cobbler.

Pub trivia: The sign and the spelling now refer to Admiral Cloudesley Shovell, whose distinguished naval career ended as one of the 2,000 victims of the 1707 Scilly naval disaster when four large ships were wrecked on rocks. But it's more likely that the name was originally inspired by the workers who unloaded ships on the adjacent river wharves, leaving their shovels outside the pub door when they sought refreshment.

≋ Charing Cross ⊖ Charing Cross, Embankment 🚲 LCN+6, 6a, links to NCN4 🚶 Jubilee Greenway, Thames Path, links to Jubilee Walkway

Ship & Shovell

FITZROVIA

North of Soho and west of Bloomsbury lies an area developed from the late 18th century in smaller plots belonging to different landowners, and therefore less grand and more jumbled than its eastern neighbour. The term Fitzrovia is now in common use but it was originally a slightly disparaging nickname coined in the 1930s when the area was popular with artists and bohemians – George Orwell, Dylan Thomas, Augustus John, Quentin Crisp and many others lived here. Orwell and friends drank at the Fitzroy Tavern (16 Charlotte Street, W1T 2NA, now a Samuel Smith's pub and an essential stop on any literary pub tour but not selected for this guide), in turn named for landowner Charles FitzRoy – originally the Norman French term for the bastard son of a king. The legendary 100 Club, known for everything from trad jazz to punk, is on one edge in Oxford Street, and the psychedelic UFO Club, which nurtured the young Pink Floyd, stood on another edge in Tottenham Court Road. One of London's most distinctive modern landmarks, the 189m BT Tower, has dominated the skyline since 1966. Today the surrounding streets are home to various TV, media and advertising companies.

Meux's Horse Shoe brewery stood at Fitzrovia's southeast corner at the junction of Tottenham Court Road and Oxford Street from 1764. In one of the most notorious accidents in brewing history, in October 1814 one of the brewery's vast wooden tuns containing over half a million litres of maturing porter collapsed, flooding the slum housing across the road at St Giles and leaving nine people dead of injuries, drowning and alcohol poisoning. The firm, which successfully avoided paying compensation and even managed to reclaim the duty on the beer, became part of Ind Coope in 1961 and the Horse Shoe was closed in 1964.

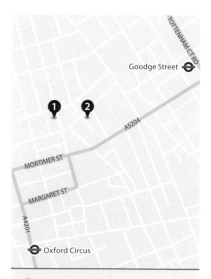

❶ Crown & Sceptre
❷ Green Man

CROWN & SCEPTRE

Contemporary pub
26-27 Foley Street, W1W 6DS
📞 (020) 7307 9971, 🌐 www.thecrownandsceptrew1.co.uk, **fbk**
🕐 12-11 Mon-Sat; 12-10.30 Sun. *Children until 6pm*
Cask beers ✓ 4+ (Purity, Sambrook's, 2 guests), **Other beers** 7 keg, 5 bottles, **Also** 1 real cider
🍴 Enhanced pub grub, 🪑 Tables on street until early evening, ♿
Food promotions

A grand old Victorian pub with high, elaborate ceilings and mosaic floors that's been rejigged to suit the designer label-clad media types who now frequent the area, this is now a fun if rather noisy place with retro standard lamps, mismatched sofas, a jazzy soundtrack and pictures of 60s icons like Dave Davies. As it's a Mitchells & Butlers Castle pub the beer range is improving, with Pure Ubu and Wandle as regular casks, Kelham Island Pale Rider frequently appearing and guests from a range

Crown & Sceptre

of breweries. Brooklyn Lager and Duvel provide other smart choices. Food when I checked was pub grub with an exotic touch but was due to go a little more upmarket.

Oxford Circus LCN+0 and links to Charing Cross, Marylebone

GREEN MAN
Contemporary pub, specialist
36 Riding House Street, W1W 7ES
 (020) 7580 9087
 www.thegreenmanw1.co.uk
 12-11 Mon-Sat; 12-10.30 Sun. *Children until 6pm*
Cask beers ✔ 3 (Purity, Sharp's, unusual guest), **Other beers** 2 keg, 5 bottles, **Also** Large range of real and bottled ciders and perries
 Nibbles, sandwiches, mains, prix fixe,
 Tables on street, No disabled toilet but all flat access
Fri DJs, Monthly comedy night, other occasional performances

Just off the main drag of Fitzrovia's media village, this offbeat, buzzy and very friendly street corner pub would be top of the list in a guide to London's Best Ciders and Perries, with over 40 examples on offer. Pleasingly they're complimented by a small but well chosen and carefully served beer selection, with cask regulars Pure Ubu and Doom Bar and a changing guest that's typically

something of the quality of Thornbridge Jaipur. Bottled Belgian fruit beers and draught German wheat beer extend the beer choice further. All are enjoyed to a hip soundtrack by a diverse and quite youngish crowd. The single ground floor drinking area is decorated with press cuttings, maps, graffiti art and surfer nicknacks, with a small, more loungey space tucked behind the bar, while the black painted upstairs room feels less frenetic when, as often, the place gets lively. Food is enhanced pub grub such as pork belly and veggie risotto.

Goodge Street, Oxford Circus LCN+ 0

Green Man

HOLBORN & 'LEGAL LONDON'

Holborn is the western fringe of the City, on the other side of the redacted river Fleet, which now runs in pipes under Farringdon Road, having carved a geography still obvious from the heights of Holborn Viaduct. The river in its steep valley likely explains the place name as 'hollow bourne' which is also used for the main east-west road, High Holborn. To the south the Knights Templar established their London base, the Temple, in the 12th century. They were eventually supplanted by lawyers, who built the sprawling complexes known as the Inns of Court, still housing the professional associations for barristers (the senior category of legal professionals in England and Wales). The Royal Courts of Justice have stood nearby on the Strand since 1882. Barristers are traditionally said to be 'called to the bar' of a court, but many of them are happy to called to the other kind of bar too, which explains the continued reputation of the area for quality hospitality.

In the 18th century the streets were packed with pubs and coffee houses frequented by influential characters, including some establishments that furnished other diversions: several gay brothels, known as 'molly houses' operated in the 1720s. The juicy gossip in the air attracted members of another profession with a reputation for hard drinking: journalism. Most national newspapers were once based on and around Fleet Street and the street's name is still a byword for the British press, though the hacks had largely departed by the end of the millennium.

Princess Louise (p84)

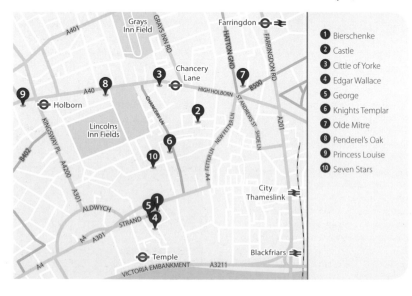

1. Bierschenke
2. Castle
3. Cittie of Yorke
4. Edgar Wallace
5. George
6. Knights Templar
7. Olde Mitre
8. Penderel's Oak
9. Princess Louise
10. Seven Stars

BIERSCHENKE
Bar
46 Essex Street, WC2R 3JF
☎ (020) 7936 2536, ⊕ www.bierschenke.co.uk
✪ 11.30-11 Mon-Fri; Closed Sat & Sun. *Children welcome at lunchtime*
Cask beer None, **Other beers** 9 German keg, 4 German bottles
⑪ German-style menu
Wed Oompah band, big screen sport, Oktoberfest and other seasonal events

Opened in 2010, this small cellar space is one of an increasing number of German-themed bars in the capital. It's a bright and slightly Spartan place that, like most similar establishments, works when full and raucous, but the beer will tempt at quieter times. König Ludwig Weissbier and fine Flensburger Pils are top options in bottle, while Köstritzer Schwarzbier is available on keg beside various examples of Pils, Helles and wheat beer. Sausages, schnitzels, pork knuckle and the like are on the menu.

⊖ Temple ⊙⊙ LCN+7, 39 ♦♦ Jubilee Walkway

CASTLE
Traditional pub
26 Furnival Street, EC4A 1JS
☎ (020) 7404 131
✪ 11-11 Mon-Fri; Closed Sat & Sun. *Children upstairs if eating*
Cask beers ✔ 8 (Nethergate, 7 unusual guests), **Other beers** 3 keg, **Also** Malts
⑪ Homemade pub grub and specials, toasted sandwiches, ♿ No disabled toilet but flat access
Darts, functions, occasional TV sport

This side street pub is a decent, uncomplicated place operated by small pubco Red Car, also responsible for the Wheatsheaf (p63). Nethergate's Red Car Ale is a fixture, but the rest of the cask ales in this free house are chosen by friendly landlord Lee to provide variety and a good balance of styles, including darker and stronger options. Bath, Dark Star, Mauldons, Triple fff, White Horse and York might appear alongside products from very small breweries that catch his eye. Home cooked grub is served until it runs out, after which they fire up the toasted sandwich maker, and there's a pretty upstairs

room, sometimes with other beers available, that offers full table service at lunchtime and overspill on busy evenings. The current building dates from 1901 but there are records of previous pubs back to the 16th century on this patch of land, which once formed part of an Inn of Court.

⊖ Chancery Lane ⊙⊙ LCN+7, 39 ♦♦ Jubilee Walkway

CITTIE OF YORKE
Traditional pub ★
22 High Holborn, WC1V 6BS
☎ (020) 7242 7670
✪ 12-11 Mon-Sat; Closed Sun. *Children during food service*
Cask beers ✔ 1 (Samuel Smith), **Other beers** 5 keg, 7 bottles (Samuel Smith)
⑪ Pub grub
Skittles

The building presents a handsome but relatively modest face to High Holborn – grey stone, wood panels and leaded windows – but head down the atmospheric stone-floored side corridor and through a luxuriously woody lounge with murals of writers and thinkers and you're in one of the most unusual and memorable pub interiors in Britain. Huge vats hang rather worryingly above a long, chunky bar counter, while the high, open half-timbered roof stretches loftily above. Numerous elaborately carved booths line the sides, like confessionals or, more likely, the booths once found in courtroom lobbies for lawyers to consult privately with their clients. A big triangular stove with Gothic detailing provides a handy surface for standing drinkers.

Cittie of Yorke

But don't be deceived into thinking you've stumbled into some miraculous survival of a Tudor banqueting hall – this is a vision of Old England as conceived in 1924. The only part that's as old as it looks is the cellar bar, in vaults that predate the current building. It's impressive nonetheless, and now Grade II* listed, an extraordinary environment in which to sample Samuel Smith's one cask beer, Old Brewery Bitter, and perhaps to explore their more extensive range of speciality bottles. Food is a 2010s vision of Old English pub grub, and canned music is appropriately absent. For a no less spectacular Sam's heritage pub that is more typical of vintage pub design, try the Princess Louise (below).

⊖ Holborn 🚲 LCN+7, 39 🚶 Jubilee Walkway

EDGAR WALLACE

Traditional pub
40 Essex Street, WC2R 3JF
📞 (020) 7353 3120
⚙ 11-11 Mon-Fri; Closed Sat & Sun
Cask beers ✔ 8 (Crouch Vale, Nethergate, 6 unusual guests), **Other beers** 1 keg
🍴 Sandwiches and pub grub
Functions

Behind the rather defensive exterior of the Edgar Wallace, at the end of an alley that twists round the Middle Temple, is a bright and welcoming single bar, undisturbed by piped music or TV. Its walls are clad promisingly in pump clips and, fascinatingly,

Edgar Wallace

in advertising from years gone by, proudly exhibiting now forbidden cigarette ads and tacky marketing junk for noxious sparkling perry Babycham, the height of 1970s sophistication. The pub was originally the Essex Head, after local landowner the Earl of Essex, but since 1977 has preferred to honour crime writer Edgar Wallace, author of the original treatment of *King Kong* and over 175 novels. Brother and sister John and Jackie took over as new landlords in 2010 but have no intention of changing the beer policy. The stylish metal pump handles always dispense Nethergate IPA, rebadged as EPA (Edgar's Pale Ale), and Brewers Gold. The rest might include beers from Ascot, Bank Top, Brodie's, Everards, Itchen Valley, O'Hanlon's, Rebellion or White Horse. Fish and chips, burgers, steaks and halloumi kebabs are on the menu.

Visitor's note: Used for lunchtime dining and otherwise as a function room, the pleasant upstairs space incorporates an extensive Edgar Wallace library.

⊖ Temple 🚲 LCN+7, 39 🚶 Jubilee Walkway

GEORGE

Traditional pub
213 Strand, WC2R 1AP
📞 (020) 7353 9638, 🌐 www.
capitalpubcompany.com/the-george
⚙ 11-11 Mon-Sat; 12-9 Sun. *Children until 9.30pm*
Cask beers ✔ 5 (Hogs Back, Sharp's, guests), **Other beers** 1 keg, 5 bottles
🍴 Pub grub, sandwiches, platters, ♿
Fri & Sat comedy, annual beer festivals, big screen sport, occasional quizzes and seasonal events, functions

Not far from the Law Courts and therefore a frequent destination for impromptu celebrations and sorrow drowning, the George bears a date of 1723 and with its elaborate half-timbered Tudor frontage looks olde worlde enough to get cameras snapping. In fact the current building is an elaborate 1890s pastiche, though there were previous Georges on this site, one of them a coffee house. Now part of the Capital pub chain, it takes care of its cask ales. There's always something from Hog's Back and something

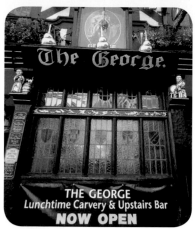

George

from Sharp's, but not always the ubiquitous Doom Bar. The rest rotate – Adnams, Black Sheep, Harveys, Hook Norton, Sambrook's and Twickenham might well put in appearances, while annual beer festivals focus on smaller brewers. Dishes like rabbit stew, vegetable lasagne, open sandwiches, pies and all day breakfasts will fortify you for the witness box.

Insider tip! Look for the elegant snug with red upholstered benches and an elaborate carved fireplace.

⊖ Temple ⊕ LCN+7, 39 ✚ Jubilee Walkway

KNIGHTS TEMPLAR
Contemporary pub
95 Chancery Lane, WC2A 1DT
☎ (020) 7831 2660
⊕ www.jdwetherspoon.co.uk
✪ 9am-midnight Mon-Fri; 9am-1am Sat; 9am-midnight Sun. *Children until early evening if eating*
Cask beers ✔ 8 (Greene King, Fuller's, unusual guests), **Other beers** Usual Wetherspoon keg and bottles, **Also** 2 real ciders/perries
⬓ Wetherspoon menu, ♿
Various small meetings

One of London's most impressive Wetherspoon conversions, this occupies a corner site at the south end of Chancery Lane. Formerly the Union Bank, it retains the opulent decoration of the main banking hall

with its slender black marble pillars reaching up to an airy ceiling. A mezzanine level is sometimes used for evening club and society meetings – as well as the local legal profession the pub is popular with students from nearby King's College and the London School of Economic & Political Science (LSE). A modern sculpture of a Knight Templar dominates the bar back, setting the theme for other Templar memorabilia scattered around. The space is refreshingly uncluttered with the normal Wetherspoon promotional materials, and even the toilets are impressive. Better still, this is one of the chain's most adventurous cask ale pubs, taking full advantage of the guest ales roster – Coach House, Evan Fvans and White Horse when I called.

Pub trivia: Most people today have probably heard of former local landowners the Templars through Dan Brown's bestselling potboiler *The Da Vinci Code*, and indeed the pub can be glimpsed in the film adaptation, but appropriately enough the order also helped invent the banking system.

⊖ Chancery Lane ⊕ LCN+ 6, 7 ✚ Jubilee Walkway

OLDE MITRE ☆ 25
Traditional pub ★
1 Ely Court, EC1N 6SJ
☎ (020) 7405 4751, ✉ enquiries@yeoldemitre.co.uk, ⊕ www.yeoldmitre.co.uk
✪ 11-11 Mon-Fri; Closed Sat & Sun
Cask beers ✔ 7 (Fuller's, 4 unusual guests), **Other beers** 5 international bottles, **Also** 5 international bottles
⬓ Sandwiches and snacks, ⊞ Only standing room in alley
Beer festival coinciding with GBBF

Hidden down a tiny dead end alley marked by an old fashioned lamp standard at the south end of Hatton Garden, centre of London's diamond trade, the Olde Mitre of all the pubs listed here is the one you're most likely to read about in tourist guides to London. They'll tell you about its antiquity, dating back to 1546, though what you see now is a combination of a 1757 rebuild, a 1781 extension and a Tudor-style interior refit from around 1930. They'll tell you about the surviving fragment of a cherry tree revealed behind glass near the entrance, which may have been danced around by Elizabeth I and once marked the boundary between Christopher Hatton's garden and the Bishop of Ely's – the pub was originally built on the latter's property for the benefit of his staff. They might even tell you the pub is really in Cambridgeshire, which is clearly nonsense, though the bishops did deny London's authority over their property and the pub's license was issued in Cambridgeshire until the 1950s.

What they probably won't tell you is that for some years the pub has been one of the most reliable sources of top quality cask ale in central London. It's now a Fuller's house but landlords Scotty and Kathy enjoy considerable freedom to order in from other breweries, and besides London Pride, Discovery and Gales' Seafarers you may well find beers from Cairngorm, Dark Star, Harviestoun, Leeds, Roosters, Rudgate, Saltaire and more. They get through 25 different Christmas beers in December and January, 25 different milds in May, and stage a mini festival of their own during the Great British Beer Festival, the only weekend in the year the pub opens. The various rooms on three levels easily get cramped and crowded, there's no TV or piped music and minimal food, but they've earned a string of awards for fine beer, and you don't need to leave London to enjoy it.

≋ Farringdon ⊖ Chancery Lane ⬲ LCN+7, 39
🚶 Link to Jubilee Walkway

Olde Mitre

PENDEREL'S OAK

Contemporary pub
286-288 High Holborn, WC1V 7HJ
📞 (020) 7242 5669
🌐 www.jdwetherspoon.co.uk
🕐 8am-11pm Mon-Wed; 8am-midnight Thu; 8am-1am Fri; 9am-1am Sat; 10-11 Sun. *Children until early evening if eating*
Cask beers ✔ 10 (Greene King, Marston's, unusual guests), **Other beers** Usual Wetherspoon keg and bottles, **Also** 2 real ciders/perries
🍴 Wetherspoon menu, 🪑 Tables on street, ♿ *Occasional events*

An enormous Wetherspoon on the ground floor of a 1960s office block on High Holborn, this is one of the chain's central London outlets particularly known for its adventurous guest beer policy – beer from, among others, Vale, BrewDog and Cotleigh was on offer when I called. Clever design has brought some intimacy to the large open space, pine furniture gives a Scandinavian feel and shelves full of law books remind you we're on the edge of London's legal quarter. A second large bar downstairs is officially a Lloyds No 1, with background music, occasional performances and fewer cask options.

⊖ Chancery Lane, Holborn ⬲ LCN+ 6, 7 🚶 Jubilee Walkway

PRINCESS LOUISE

Traditional pub ★
208-209 High Holborn, WC1V 7BW
📞 (020) 7405 8816
🕐 11.30-11 Mon-Fri; 12-11 Sat; 12-10.30 Sun
Cask beers ✔ 1 (Samuel Smith), **Other beers** 7 keg, 7 bottles (Samuel Smith)
🍴 Sandwiches and pub grub

Named after Queen Victoria's wayward fourth daughter, this splendid drinking palace just west of the main Holborn junction is one of London's pub heritage treasures. The elegant but relatively modest 1872 exterior conceals an impressive confection of mosaic tiles, mirrors, carved wood and glass, with an elaborate original bar back and moulded ceiling, all created during a radical remodelling in 1891. Timber and etched glass screens project from a horseshoe bar to divide the space into a number of smaller rooms,

Princess Louise

with connecting corridors down both sides. In fact the original partitioning was swept away in the 1960s and what we see today is the result of careful restoration by current owner Samuel Smith in 2008. Alongside the very different but equally impressive Cittie of Yorke (above), this is a great environment in which to sample the brewery's one cask beer and numerous own brewed keg and bottled specialities.

Visitor's note: Gentlemen should be sure to visit what are thought to be the second most sumptuous pub lavatories in the country.

⊖ Holborn ᧣ LCN+ 6, 7 ∥ Jubilee Walkway

SEVEN STARS
Traditional pub ☆
53-54 Carey Street, WC2A 2JB
☎ (020) 7242 8521
✪ 11-11 Mon-Fri; 12-11 Sat; 12-10.30 Sun
Cask beers ✔ 5 (Adnams, Dark Star, guests),
Other beers 2 keg, 2 bottles, **Also** Wines, cigars
🍽 Gastro menu

The landlady of this eccentric but quite charming pub in a 1680s building behind the Royal Courts of Justice is wonderfully named celebrity chef Roxy Beaujolais, author of *Home from the Inn Contented*. The long narrow main bar is the most intriguing of three rooms, with a big old Victorian bar back with 1880s advertising, a creaky sloping ceiling, small

glass cabinets of curiosities, posters for old movies with legal themes, portraits of judges, wooden toys, numerous cat-shaped decorations and a real cat, Thomas Paine, normally ensconced on one of the bar stools. Elsewhere there are art prints and photos of writers, including Bertolt Brecht. Chalked up food changes daily but is, as you'd expect, reliably inventive – steak tartare, chicken pies, muscles, bruschetta or veggie linguine, perhaps. There's a slight raffishly Parisian air about the place, like an eccentric old café in the Marais or Montmartre, but with good beer. The Adnams beers are Bitter and Broadside; the Dark Star rotates and the guests might also come from Dark Star or from Young's or Sambrook's. "We're about serious eating and drinking for grownups," commented one of the bar staff.

⊖ Chancery Lane ᧣ LCN+ 6, 7 ∥ Jubilee Walkway

Seven Stars

ISLINGTON (ANGEL)

When budding playwright Joe Orton and his troubled partner Kenneth Halliwell lived in Noel Road, Islington, in the early 1960s, carrying out the creative modifications to library books for which they were later jailed, the area was regarded as a sink of inner city poverty and decay. Only a few years later it was in the vanguard of the new pheonomenon of gentrification, and the seal was indelibly set on its left-leaning middle classness when Labour politician and local resident Tony Blair, architect of New Labour and future prime minister, made his infamous pact with rival Gordon Brown at an Upper Street restaurant in 1994. Originally a wayside village on the Great North Road and the drove route to Smithfield, it was famous in the 19th century for its music halls. Upper Street today is a lively and trendy strip, while nearby Chapel Market provides a glimpse of the old Islington.

The district is a sprawling place and the northern part of it is dealt with under Canonbury & Barnsbury (p144). This section includes the venues nearer to Angel tube, named after the Angel pub that once stood by the turnpike gate on the Great North Road, at the busy junction with City and Pentonville Roads.

CHARLES LAMB

Gastropub
16 Elia Street, N1 8DE
☎ (020) 7837 5040
🌐 www.thecharleslambpub.com
🕐 4-11 Mon & Tue; 12-11 Wed-Sat; 12-10.30 Sun. *Children Very welcome*
Cask beers ✦ 3 (Dark Star, Triple fff, 1 unusual often local guest), **Other beers** 5 keg (British and Belgian), 8 bottles, **Also** 1 real cider (summer), wines, malts

🍽 Changing gastro menu, snacks only on Sun,
🪑 Tables on street
Art exhibitions, seasonal events

This small and very welcoming street corner pub, tucked away among previously modest but now highly desirable streets near the Regent's Canal, gets pretty much everything right. A sympathetic 2005 refurbishment has preserved some pleasingly well-worn spaces

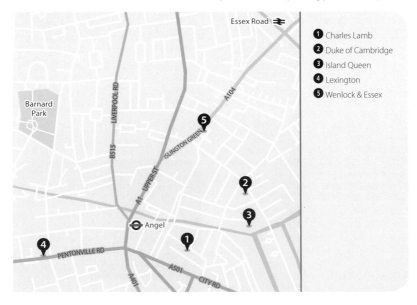

Essex Road ⇄

Barnard Park

❶ Charles Lamb
❷ Duke of Cambridge
❸ Island Queen
❹ Lexington
❺ Wenlock & Essex

❺
❷
❸
⊖ Angel
❶
❹
PENTONVILLE RD

LIVERPOOL RD
A104
B515
A1 – UPPER ST
ISLINGTON GREEN
A401
A501
CITY RD

Charles Lamb

in pastel green with original brown tiling – a main bar area where the pub's former name, the Prince Albert, is still visible on the bar back clock; a tiny snug commemorating its current namesake; and a bright additional room decorated with old London maps which, if you're like me, could keep you occupied for hours. The beer range isn't vast but is conscientiously selected on the basis that, as a sign says, "Good people drink good beer", and everything deserves its place.

Hophead and Alton's Pride are permanent on cask, while the guest is something special, usually dark in winter, often chosen in response to customer suggestions. Products from Bath, Brodie's, RCH, Redemption, Slater's and Thornbridge have all been stocked. Camden Town might appear on keg, while Kernel beers are among the bottles. The keenly priced French influenced menu has been widely praised – smoked trout pâté, lamb merguez sausages with Puy lentils, mushroom stroganoff and various fine soups might be on offer. The French flavour extends to a bilingual website (*"Pub londonien traditionnel à la cuisine familiale"*), a listing in *Les Routiers* and a big do for Bastille Day on 14 July. This is one of my personal favourite London pubs.

Pub trivia: Look for the biography of essayist Charles Lamb, who lived nearby in the 1790s. "'Tis

the privilege of friendship," he once wrote, "to talk nonsense and to have that nonsense respected" – a fine motto for a pub.

≈ Essex Road ⊖ Angel ⊙ CS12, LCN+16, Barbican link, Regent's Canal towpath ✈ Jubilee Greenway, New River Path

DUKE OF CAMBRIDGE
Gastropub
30 St Peters Street, N1 8JT
☎ (020) 7359 3066, ⊕ www.dukeorganic.co.uk
⊙ 12-11 Mon-Sat; 12-10.30 Sun. *Children very welcome*
Cask beers ✔ 4 (Pitfield, St Peter's, occasional organic guests), **Other beers** 2 British organic keg lagers, 10 organic bottles, **Also** Organic wines, 15 malts
⊕ Organic gastro menu, ⊞ Tables on street

Refurbished and relaunched by Geetie Singh in 1998 as Britain's first certified organic gastropub, the Cambridge is particularly noteworthy for our purposes as a regular stockist of beers from Pitfield, an early pioneer London microbrewer that's since relocated to rural Essex.

Session bitter Pitfield SB is brewed especially for the pub, then there's Eco Warrior, St Peter's Organic Ale and guests from Hepworth or Marble. Pitfield and Freedom, another brewery with a London origin, supply keg lagers, bottles and gift packs – historical

Island Queen

recreation Pitfield 1850 Porter is a particular find. The extensive if slightly pricey menu has numerous veggie options as well as ethically-sourced and free range meat and fish: choices change seasonally but may include asparagus and garlic risotto, sardines with lentils and braised radicchio, or lamb curry. The big main bar is a bit sparse and stripped, but there's a lovely conservatory at the side created from a formerly open yard.

⇌ Essex Road ⊖ Angel ⊙⊙ CS12, LCN+16, Barbican link, Regent's Canal towpath ⚓ Jubilee Greenway, New River Path

Duke of Cambridge

ISLAND QUEEN
Contemporary pub ☆
87 Noel Road, N1 8HD
📞 (020) 7354 8741
🌐 www.theislandqueenislington.co.uk, **fbk**
⊙ 12-11 Mon-Wed; 12-11.30 Thu; 12-midnight Fri & Sat; 12-11 Sun. *Children until 7pm*
Cask beers ✔ 4 (Sharp's, Timothy Taylor, 2 unusual guests), **Other beers** 9 keg, 5 bottles, **Also** Wines
🍴 Enhanced pub grub, 🪑 Front terrace, ♿
Tue quiz, seasonal parties, functions, TV sport

This cheerful place not far from the Regent's Canal is very Islington, but it's also an important heritage pub, built in 1851 and refitted in the 1880s and 1890s. Historic elements – the wood and glass frontage, remnants of porches, etched glass screens, mosaics, a curved island bar and a high embossed Lincrusta ceiling – have been incorporated in a more recent makeover to create an atmospheric series of spaces. A Mitchells & Butlers Castle pub, it offers Landlord and Doom Bar on cask, but with interesting guests that might be from Cropton, Saltaire, White Horse and others. Schneider Weisse is the pick of the kegs while Duvel and Budvar are in the fridges. An extensive menu might include veggie platters, steak and ale pie and pork belly.

Visitor's note: Don't miss the huge mirrors painted with foliage.

⇌ Essex Road ⊖ Angel ⊕ CS12, LCN+16, Barbican link, Regent's Canal towpath ⫽ Jubilee Greenway, New River Path

LEXINGTON

Bar
96-98 Pentonville Road, N1 9JB
☎ (020) 7837 5371
⊕ www.thelexington.co.uk, **fbk**
✪ 12-2am Mon-Thu; 12pm-4am Fri & Sat; 12-midnight Sun. *Children until 7pm if eating, downstairs only*
Cask beers ✔ 2 (Sambrook's or other London brewer), **Other beers** 1 keg (Brooklyn), 12 US bottles, **Also** 60 US whiskies
🍽 Pub grub and diner menu, 🪑 Tables on street *Mon pop quiz, Sun lounge DJ, live bands and DJs upstairs most nights, table football*

This substantial pub on the way to Kings Cross is a lively and rather cool American lounge decked out in a fantasy vision of Southern bordello baroque – red drapes, flock wallpaper, steers' skulls and wall mounted rifles. Upstairs is a popular indie music venue (admission payable) while downstairs hosts DJs and the weekly Rough Trade music quiz. Most impressive among the drink choices is an encyclopaedic list of specialist American whiskies, but there's also a decent range of imported craft beers from the likes of Flying Dog, Goose Island, Left Hand and Saranac (F X Matt), plus Sambrook's Junction and other London beers on cask. Food, unsurprisingly, includes gourmet burgers and fajitas. Proudly displayed on the wall is the quote "Beer is proof God loves us and wants us to be happy," which is usually spuriously attributed to Benjamin Franklin, who in fact said something

Lexington

similar about wine, but the Lexington goes one better by putting it into the mouth of Abraham Lincoln!

Insider tip! Look out for offers such as a 25% discount on weekday lunches and a 10% discount to all mailing list members.

⇌ Kings Cross, St Pancras ⊖ Angel 🚌 Penton Street (numerous Kings Cross, Angel) ⊕ LCN+ Finsbury - Holloway, link to LCN+16 ⫽ Links to New River Path, Jubilee Greenway

WENLOCK & ESSEX

Bar
18-26 Essex Road, N1 8LN
☎ (020) 7704 0871
⊕ www.wenlockandessex.com
✪ 10.30am-midnight Mon-Wed; 10.30am-12.30am Thu; 10.30am-2.30am Fri & Sat; 10.30am-midnight Sun. *Children welcome daytime*
Cask beers ✔ 2 (Camden Town, Wells & Young's), **Other beers** 6 keg, 8 bottles, **Also** Cocktails
🍽 Brunch, sandwiches, enhanced pub grub, 🪑 Tables on street, ♿
Fri & Sat dance club

Reopened in 2010 by the Barworks chain that also includes the Black Heart (p142), this is a much bigger, brasher place. Multi-coloured illuminated lettering and a big revolving door lure you into a fairground kitsch interior with red paint, bare bulbs and a neon sign inviting you to 'Satan's Circus' – actually a dance venue complete with a *Saturday Night Fever*-style lightbox floor. The big picture windows provide daytime people watching while in the evenings it's more of a loud party place. There's good beer to fuel the fun – Courage Directors and Camden Town bitter on cask, more Camden Town beers on keg and a handful of bottled choices that include Bath Wild Hare and Orval. Food is pie and mash, spinach and feta parcels, steaks, mussels and popular brunches and roasts. How well the novelty will wear remains to be seen but much respect for going beyond bland lager.

⇌ Essex Road ⊖ Angel 🚌 Essex Road (numerous from Angel) ⊕ LCN+ Angel - Hackney ⫽ New River Path, link to Jubilee Greenway

KENSINGTON, CHELSEA & EARL'S COURT

'Go West!' has been an enduring maxim of London's wealth so it's not surprising the strip just beyond Westminster contains some of the capital's most select areas. The manor originally belonged to the Vere family, Earls of Oxford, who literally held court at Earl's Court, today one of the less well-to-do parts of the district. Since 1937 it's housed the Earls Court Exhibition Centre, Inner London's biggest events venue.

Kensington proper, with its generously proportioned streets, houses and squares, has long been much posher. As a legacy of the 1851 Great Exhibition in Hyde Park, Exhibition Row in the east sports a string of prestigious national museums including the Natural History, the Science and the Victoria & Albert. Victoria had the area facing Kensington Gardens remade in Albert's memory after his death, commissioning the distinctive Albert Hall concert venue, now home of the Proms. West from here is Kensington High Street, perhaps London's most famous shopping street after Oxford Street and once home to several prestigious department stores – Kensington Roof Gardens remains as a reminder of their glory.

Chelsea, reaching towards the Thames in the south, attracted 19th century artists like J M W Turner and James McNeill Whistler. Some of these artists found inspiration in the local riverside scenery, as might you. Angry Young Men raged at the Royal Court Theatre on Sloane Square in the 1950s. In the late 1960s the Kings Road had strings of hippy boutiques and members of both the Beatles and the Rolling Stones living nearby; a few years later Vivienne Westwood's SEX became the crucible of punk rock. Anyone wearing bondage trousers here today is most likely a tourist paying their respects, or maybe a minor young royal on their way to a fancy dress party.

Courtfield

1 Anglesea Arms   2 Courtfield   3 Drayton Arms   4 Queens Head

ANGLESEA ARMS
Traditional pub
15 Selwood Terrace, SW7 3QJ
☎ (020) 7373 7960, ⊕ www.angleseaarms.com
✪ 11-11 Mon-Sat; 12-10.30 Sun. *Children until early evening*
Cask beers ✔ 6 (Adnams, Fuller's. Sambrook's, Sharp's, guests), **Other beers** 5 bottles, **Also** Wines
⑩ Upmarket pub grub, ▦ Front and side terraces
Twice yearly guest beer months, occasional big screen rugby, themed seasonal parties

Built in the 1820s on the site of a market garden and numbering Charles Dickens and D H Lawrence among its former neighbours, this elegant pub with extensive outdoor seating is now in the capable hands of the Capital Pub Company. Indoors it boasts imposing wood panelling and green leather benches, with decorations that reflect its rugby loyalties. Upmarket fresh homemade food might include wild boar sausages, monkfish or wild mushroom risotto. Adnams Bitter and Wandle Junction are always on, tap 3 rotates ESB and London Pride, tap 4 various Sharp's beers, tap 5 alternates Adnams Broadside and a Purity beer, while tap 6 might be something from Black Sheep, Marston's, Timothy Taylor or Twickenham. In March and October a constantly changing variety of beers is featured across all the cask lines and they take note of customer feedback when deciding which ones to invite back.

⊖ South Kensington ⮐ LCN+ Battersea to Bayswater, link to NCN4, LCN+5

COURTFIELD
Traditional pub
187 Earls Court Road, SW5 9AN
☎ (020) 7370 2626
✪ 8am-midnight Mon-Sat; 9am-11 Sun.
Children welcome before 7pm (later in restaurant)
Cask beers ✔ 6 (Fuller's, Theakston, Timothy Taylor, Wadworth, Wells & Young's, Wychwood), **Other beers** 3 keg
⑩ Pub grub, ▦ Tables on street

Right opposite Earl's Court tube, the Courtfield has been much improved recently as one of Punch's Taylor Walker pubs. Inside there's tiling and wood panelling to admire and a lengthy

pub grub menu to choose from; upstairs a more sophisticated menu is served in a tall windowed Victorian dining room. Beers don't change that often: the current lineup is London Pride, Old Peculier, Landlord, Wadworth 6X (less common in London than it once was), Young's Gold and Hobgoblin. A good place to find well-known real ale classics in top nick.

⊖ Earls Court ⮐ LCN+ Bayswater, Chelsea, Fulham

DRAYTON ARMS
Contemporary pub
153 Old Brompton Road, SW5 0LJ
☎ (020) 7835 2301
⊕ www.thedraytonarmssw5.co.uk
✪ 12-midnight Mon-Fri; 10-midnight Sat & Sun.
Children until 6pm
Cask beers ✔ 4 (Marston's, Sambrook's, Sharp's, 1 unusual guest), **Other beers** 9 keg, 4 bottles, **Also** 1 real cider, cocktails
⑩ Enhanced pub grub, ▦ Terrace on street, ♿
Mon quiz, Tue tastings, occasional sport, fringe theatre

The exterior, on a curve of Brompton Road, is worthy of more than a passing glance: elaborate *fin de siècle* terracotta and big arched windows with a hint of art nouveau about their decorated panes. Inside is characterful too, clearly aimed at the remaining Kensington bohos, with mismatched furniture and an open fire in a nice alcove, although I'm unconvinced by the

Anglesea Arms

Drayton Arms

shoe fetishist prints. Standard cask offerings are Wandle, Doom Bar and Draught Bass, with a guest from the unusual range regularly available in Mitchells & Butlers Castle pubs like this one. Keg Franziskaner wheat beer and Sierra Nevada Pale Ale, and White Shield and Duvel in bottles, supplement the cask choices, while the menu offers steaks, burgers, pies, veggie risotto and duck confit.

⊖ Gloucester Road, South Kensington ☍ LCN+ Bayswater, Chelsea, Fulham

QUEENS HEAD
Traditional pub
27 Tryon Street, SW3 3LG
☎ (020) 7589 0262
☻ 12-11 Mon-Thu; 12-midnight Fri & Sat; 12-11 Sun
Cask beers ✔ 2 (Fuller's, Sharp's)
⊞ Pub grub, ⊞ Tables on street
Tue quiz, Sat (fortnighty) karaoke, seasonal parties

London has what's almost certainly the biggest lesbian and gay population in Europe and one of the biggest, most vibrant and most visited gay scenes in the world, with hundreds of venues all over the capital, ranging from so-fashionable-it-hurts bars to so-sleazy-it-hurts dives. One thing gay London hasn't done so well, however, is beer – industrial lager and alcopops are the general rule. There are a handful of notable exceptions: none would qualify for a listing purely on its beer choice but I've included two of the best here to do justice to the range of London's drinking houses. The other is the King William IV (p150) and more information can be obtained from LAGRAD (Lesbian and Gay Real Ale Drinkers, p324). I hope that lesbian and gay readers, like me, will feel able to enjoy a beer in any place in this book. For more about the general gay scene in London, consult the copious free papers distributed in nearly all gay venues.

The Queens Head, tucked down a side street off the Kings Road, is remarkable not just as a gay pub serving real ale but as practically the only remaining genuine community pub in its area, welcoming to all customers, "like a family" as a regular told me. Serving cask beer is an inherent part of this: "We've always had ale," comments landlord Freddie. "It's part of the pub tradition." It's still divided into three separate spaces around an island bar, with traditional flock wallpaper, pub furniture and a huge mirrored screen. Food is basic honest stuff of the burgers, sandwiches, scampi and jackets variety; beer is well kept Doom Bar and London Pride, though occasionally veering towards the likes of Slater's Honey Bee or something from Brains.

⊖ Sloane Square ☍ Links to LCN+5

NOTTING HILL

Notting Hill, north of Kensington is another much changed area. Developed from the 1820s as a middle class suburb, after World War II it became notorious as an area of run down private flats and bedsits exploited by ruthless shark landlords like Peter Rachman, conditions that among other things fuelled the establishment of housing charity Shelter. An influx of Caribbean immigrants in the 1950s initially faced hostility and race riots but later helped establish a flourishing community as expressed by the famous Carnival on August bank holiday weekend, staged since 1965 and now one of the largest street festivals in Europe. The area has also been a longstanding home of alternative culture. In recent years the character has changed again as the big houses backing onto communal gardens – a key feature of the original development – attract the attention of gentrifiers. British prime minister David Cameron is an ex-resident and it's telling that most people today probably associate the place more with floppy haired Hugh Grant than the Carnival or 1970s counterculture, thanks to 1999 hit romcom *Notting Hill*, written by Richard Curtis, who lives locally. There's much of interest, notably Portobello Road with its brightly painted terraces, independent shops and street market, a huge attraction on Saturdays when the antique and second hand clothes dealers come out in force.

Duke of Wellington

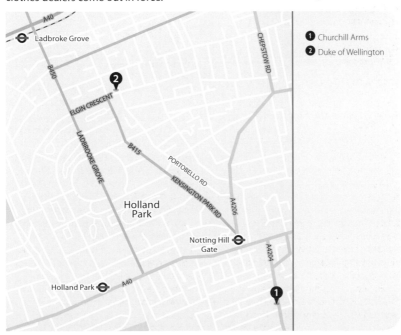

1 Churchill Arms
2 Duke of Wellington

Churchill Arms

CHURCHILL ARMS
Traditional pub ☆
119 Kensington Church Street, W8 7LN
☎ (020) 7727 4242, ✉ churchillarms@fullers.
co.uk, ⊕ www.fullers.co.uk
☼ 11-11 Mon-Wed; 11-midnight Thu-Sat;
12-10.30 Sun. *Children welcome*
Cask beers ✅ 5 (Fuller's), **Other beers** 2 keg,
6 bottles (Fuller's)
🍴 Thai menu, some British pub grub
Themed party nights

This remarkable pub is a local institution,
making a good job of keeping both the local
community and the tourists happy under
landlord Gerry O'Brien, who's been here since
the 1980s. Outside is an award-winning
cascade of foliage, particularly in spring.
Inside, the panelled walls, tiled fireplace and
stained glass were installed in a 1930 refit but
the surviving snob screens are even earlier.
The rambling place is cluttered with intriguing
junk – not just homages to Winston Churchill,
although these are plentiful, but other
political memorabilia besides chamber pots,
spoons, bottles, lamps and souvenirs of the
County Clare hurling team. Round the corner
in the conservatory, the attached Thai
restaurant is a lepidopterist's dream, draped in
trailing plants and decorated with stuffed
birds and butterflies in display cases. This is a
Fuller's house and a reliable source of
Chiswick, Discovery, ESB, London Pride and a
changing special or seasonal, with a few
bottles of interest too. Technically it's on the

Kensington side of Notting Hill Gate but
within easy reach of the tube station.

➴ Notting Hill Gate 🚲 LCN+ Chelsea, Kensal
Green, Paddington ⚓ Link to Jubilee Greenway

DUKE OF WELLINGTON
Traditional pub
179 Portobello Road, W11 2ED
☎ (020) 7727 6727
⊕ www.thedukeofwellingtonpub.com
☼ 11-midnight Mon-Sat; 12-11 Sun. *Children
welcome*
Cask beers ✅ 6 (Wells & Young's, occasional
guests), **Other beers** 5 keg, 1-2 bottles,
Also Wines
🍴 Enhanced pub grub, 🪑 Tables on street, ♿
Big screen sport

An imposing Young's pub in the bustling midst
of Portobello market, looking handsome
following a 2008 refurbishment, with a tall
wood bar back, a deeply decorated ceiling and
remains of old screens in the main bar. The big
and very popular dining area to one side serves
up the wholesome likes of beer battered fish
and chips, mushroom risotto and pies.
Bombardier, London Gold, Bitter and Special
line up on the bar alongside a Young's seasonal
and either another Wells & Young's brand or
Sambrook's. The perfect refresher after a
morning rummage for vintage clothing.

➴ Notting Hill Gate, Ladbroke Grove 🚲 LCN+
Kensal Green, Paddington

OLD STREET

Halfway along Old Street is a major roundabout and Underground station just about at the point where Hoxton, Islington, Shoreditch and Clerkenwell meet, with Moorfields Eye Hospital nearby. The area, with its numerous striking recent buildings, has been dubbed the 'Silicon Roundabout' thanks to the presence of over 80 high tech IT businesses. I admit I've used it as a bit of administrative convenience to cover two pubs within striking distance of the tube.

Further down City Road from the junction, you come to Chiswell Street, just on the City boundary, where Whitbread, one of the world's first purpose-built industrial breweries, operated between 1750 and 1976 – it's now a corporate events venue.

OLD FOUNTAIN
Traditional pub
3 Baldwin Street, EC1V 9NU
☎ (020) 7253 2970
🌐 www.oldfountain.co.uk, **tw** OldFountainAles
🕐 11-11 Mon-Fri; Closed Sat & Sun. *Children until early evening*
Cask beers ✅ 6 (Fuller's, 5 unusual guests),
Other beers 3 keg, 20 mainly British bottles,
Also 2 real ciders/perries
🍴 Pub grub and sandwiches, 🚏 Tables on street, roof terrace planned, ♿ No disabled toilet but level access
2 annual beer festivals

Between Baldwin Street and Peerless Street with entrances both sides, this beer haven of a free house has been in the Durrant family

since 1964. It's a smallish, friendly old pub with padded benches, stained glass, and a menu of pizzas, sandwiches and home cooked specials dished up from a separate servery. London Pride is the only regular cask; other brewers might include Ascot, Brodie's, Cottage, Crouch Vale, Dark Star, Moorhouse's, O'Hanlon's, Pitfield and York. A growing bottled list encompasses BrewDog, Kernel and Paulaner. Worth getting to know particularly given the uncertain future of the award-winning but threatened Wenlock Arms (below).

🚆 Old Street ⊖ Old Street 🚲 LCN+0, Dalston, City 🚶 Links to Jubilee Greenway, Jubilee Walkway

Old Fountain

❶ Old Fountain
❷ Wenlock Arms

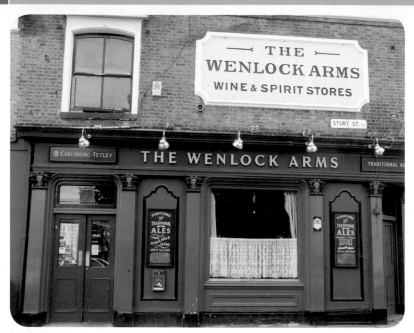

Wenlock Arms

WENLOCK ARMS
Traditional pub, specialist
26 Wenlock Road, N1 7TA
📞 (020) 7608 3406
🌐 www.wenlock-arms.co.uk
🕐 12-midnight Mon-Thu; 12-1am Fri & Sat;
12-midnight Sun. *Children until 9pm*
Cask beers ✅ 8 (Crouch Vale, Dark Star,
changing unusual guests), **Other beers** 1 keg,
5 bottles, **Also** 1 real cider
*Thu quiz, Fri trad jazz, Sat jazz/blues, darts, board
games*

This multi-award winning one-bar pub in
partly industrial backstreets off City Road is a
legend among discerning London drinkers. It
was originally a Courage pub despite standing
defiantly opposite the Wenlock Brewery,
which closed in the 1960s – the Wenlocks
were former landowners so the name
predates both businesses. Since 1994 it's been
operated as a serious real ale free house by
joint landlords Steve and Will. In 2010 came
the shocking news that it was likely to be sold
and demolished to make way for a new
development. The plans fell through, and at
the time of writing it's business as usual,
though Steve and Will are still keen to move

on and are actively looking to sell, so its future
is uncertain. And it has to be said their
tiredness shows, as the pub, never a beauty
contest winner, is now looking frayed and
worn and in need of a spruce up.

The beer is still great though: Brewer's
Gold, Hophead, and at least one mild, usually
Mighty Oak Oscar Wilde or Dark Star Over the
Moon, a pump that rotates between Adnams
Bitter and Harveys Sussex Best, plus guests
from the likes of Acorn, BrewDog,
Sawbridgeworth and many more, with
Budvar, Chimay and Paulaner in the fridge.
The 'Save the Wenlock' campaign has been
trying to find a buyer who will keep the place
going as a fine beer haven – hopefully they'll
be successful, but in the meantime check
before setting out.

Insider tip! Visit on a Friday night for a jazz trio
playing 20's and 30's classics, or on a Saturday for
a rotating list of jazz, blues and cockney bands.

🚆 Old Street ⊖ Old Street, Angel 🚌 Windsor
Terrace (numerous Angel, Old Street) 🚲
LCN+0, Angel-Barbican and Regents Canal
towpath ⏩ Jubilee Greenway

PADDINGTON & MARYLEBONE

Marylebone stretches north from the western section of Oxford Street to the 18th century turnpike of Marylebone Road. Once a rustic manor, its name means St Mary by the Bourne – the bourne being the Tyburn. Meandering Marylebone Lane follows its course. Once known for duelling on Marylebone Fields, it was developed in the 18th century as upmarket accommodation and hasn't much changed its use or its cachet, laid out with solid houses around grand squares.

The stretch of Oxford Street on its southern boundary is lined with famous department stores, while Edgware Road to the west, which follows the straight course of Roman Watling Street, is London's Middle Eastern quarter, with Lebanese restaurants and shisha cafés. Harley Street has exclusive private clinics while Marylebone High Street is lined with trendy shops and restaurants. Baker Street is best known for a fictitious resident, Arthur Conan Doyle's detective Sherlock Holmes.

Paddington to the northwest changed forever in 1838 when it became the London terminus of the Great Western Railway, built on land allegedly acquired for next to nothing from the Bishop of London, whose tenants were summarily evicted. The current station, built in 1854, is mainly the work of the great engineer Isambard Kingdom Brunel. It originally provided a vital interchange for goods traffic with the Grand Union and Regent's Canals nearby – the areas around the old canal basin are being redeveloped under the name Paddington Waterside.

Carpenters Arms

1. Carpenters Arms
2. Cleveland Arms
3. Mad Bishop & Bear
4. Metropolitan
5. Selfridges Food Hall

CARPENTERS ARMS
Traditional pub
12 Seymour Place, W1H 7NE
☎ (020) 7723 1050, ⊕ www.markettaverns.
co.uk/The-Carpenters-Arms/
✪ 11-11 Mon-Sat; 12-10.30 Sun. *Children until 7pm*
Cask beers ✪ 6 (Harveys, 5 unusual guests),
🍴 Tables on street
Tue poker, monthly quizzes and karaoke, darts, chess club, big screen sport, functions

Head off the main roads around busy Marble Arch to find this delightful free house, under the same management as the Market Porter (p59). The place retains the feel of a traditional local, with some preserved mosaics, tiling and pillars and a big wooden bar that splits it into two separate areas, with some cosy booths. Harveys Sussex Best is the only regular; guests aren't quite the same ever-changing mix as at the Borough pub but might include beers from Acorn, Cottage, Hogs Back, Kelburn, Loddon, Sambrook's, Windsor and Eton, York and more. A rare gem for the West End.

Visitor's note: The pub is only a short walk from Marble Arch and Speaker's Corner.

⊖ Marble Arch 🚲 CS9, 10, 11, LCN+0, 5, Hyde Park routes 🚶 Hyde Park paths linking to Jubilee Greenway

Mad Bishop & Bear

CLEVELAND ARMS
Traditional pub
28 Chilworth Street, W2 6DT
☎ (020) 7706 1759
✪ 11-11.30 Mon-Thu; 11-midnight Fri & Sat; 11-10.30 Sun. *Children welcome*
Cask beers ✪ 4 (Greene King, Harveys, Timothy Taylor, 1 unusual guest), **Other beers** 6 changing bottles
🍽 Good value pub grub, 🍴 Benches on street
Tue quiz, Wed curry club, weekend charity tombola

This cheery red half-panelled pub is a welcome slice of real life in the residential streets west of Paddington. Bargain priced food includes Thai curries, beef bourguignon and sausage and mash for around a fiver. Beer comprises three well kept regulars – Greene King IPA, Harveys Sussex Best and Taylor Landlord – plus a changing guest that might come from BrewDog, Hawkshead, Loddon, Nethergate, Rudgate, White Horse or Woodforde's among others. Interest is added by a vintage fruit machine, dried hops on top of the bar back, old train and bus signs, and extensive evidence of charity fundraising.

Insider tip! Walk right through the pool area to find a back door that looks out onto a cobbled mews.

≠ Paddington ⊖ Paddington 🚲 LCN+ Kensal Green, Kilburn, Marylebone, Kensington, Regents Canal towpath 🚶 Jubilee Greenway, Grand Union Canal Walk

MAD BISHOP & BEAR ☆ 25
Traditional pub
Upper Level Paddington Station, W2 1HB
☎ (020) 7402 2441, ✉ madbishopandbear@ fullers.co.uk, ⊕ www.fullers.co.uk
✪ 8am-11 Mon-Thu; 8am-11.30 Fri; 8am-11 Sat; 10-10.30 Sun. *Children welcome, with kids menu*
Cask beers ✪ 5 (Fuller's), Other beers 1 keg, 10 bottles
🍽 Breakfast, sandwiches, pub grub, ♿

Though it seems unlikely, one of the very best places in central London to sample Fuller's beers can be reached by climbing the escalators to the top floor of the Lawns, the food and shopping court that now occupies Paddington station's former front concourse.

The interior is surprisingly ornate with pillars, mirrors, a decorated ceiling and an impressive five tier chandelier. There are nooks and crannies to hide in and friendly and helpful staff. Although many of your fellow drinkers will be transient visitors keeping their eye on the live departure boards, you've a good excuse to linger. Chiswick, Discovery, ESB and London Pride are all present and correct on the pump clips while a Fuller's seasonal or a guest, maybe St Austell Tribute, adds an extra cask choice. And taking pride of place alongside the wines behind the bar is a wide range of the brewery's bottled beers, including 1845 and special editions like Vintage Ale, sometimes including older vintages, and Brewer's Reserve. Food starts with breakfast and continues with the likes of sandwiches, burgers, pasta, bangers and pies.

Metropolitan

Wooden Hand, with a 'Coming Soon' board positioned to lure the repeat visitor.

≈ Paddington ⊖ Paddington ⊕ LCN+ Kensal Green, Kilburn, Marylebone, Kensington, Regents Canal towpath ✦ Jubilee Greenway, Grand Union Canal Walk

≈ Marylebone ⊖ Baker Street ⊕ LCN+0, 50 ✦ Regents Park footpaths

METROPOLITAN
Contemporary pub
7 Station Approach, NW1 5LD
☎ (020) 7486 3489
⊕ www.jdwetherspoon.co.uk
◷ 9am-midnight Mon-Sat; 9am-11.30pm Sun.
Children until early evening
Cask beers ◉ 11 (Adnams, Greene King, Theakston, 6 unusual guests), **Other beers** Usual Wetherspoon keg and bottles, **Also** 3 real ciders/perries
⬛ Wetherspoon menu, ⬛
Wetherspoon beer festivals and promotions

Converted from offices in the huge 1920s London Transport block above Baker Street station, also home to Madame Tussauds, this is an enormous Wetherspoon curiously decorated with pillars and coats of arms in ceiling recesses. The big open space doesn't make this the cosiest drinking hole in the world, but being right on top of the station helps, and the beer range is several notches above the chain's average. Adnams Explorer, Greene King IPA and Abbot and Theakston Old Peculier are usually on, joined by several guests that might come from Acorn, Arkells, Arundel, Blindmans, Burton Bridge, Leeds or

SELFRIDGES FOOD HALL
Shop
400 Oxford Street, W1A 1AB
☎ 0800 123400, ⊕ www.selfridges.com
◷ 9.30-8 Mon-Wed; 9.30-9 Thu; 9.30-8 Fri; 9.30-6.15 Sat; 11.30-8 Sun
Cask beers None, **Other beers** 70 British and international bottles, **Also** Fine wines, specialist spirits, cigars
⬛ Gourmet fast food and specialist ingredients

Opened in 1909 by Wisconsin-born Henry Selfridge, this Oxford Street landmark is one of the best known department stores in the world. Its range of bottled beers is by no means the largest in London but is well chosen and since you might be visiting anyway is definitely worth a look, especially with all sorts of other tempting gourmet delights on offer around it. Given the iconic nature of the store it would be good to see a few more British selections but you will find Dark Star, O'Hanlon's, Meantime, Sharp's and Traquair alongside the likes of Cantillon, Goose Island, Schneider, Westmalle, Victory and other decent imports. Don't look for beers in the wine shop – they're in a chiller cabinet in the food hall at street level in the southwest corner of the building, close by the Orchard Street entrance.

⊖ Bond Street, Marble Arch ⊕ LCN+0, 39, 50

SHOREDITCH & HOXTON

Outside the City walls, Shoreditch preceded Southwark as a resort for less respectable activities, including theatre, and William Shakespeare first worked here when he came to London. The tradition continued with a cluster of Victorian music halls.

Hoxton was originally the western part of the parish. Elegant Hoxton Square was laid out in the 1680s to create a fashionable suburb but by the late 19th century most of the area was impoverished. To the north there are still areas of poor social housing, but in the past couple of decades the south of the whole district has become painfully trendy, with former industrial units remade as galleries and bars. More established cultural institutions include one of London's fascinating specialist museums, the Geffrye, exhibiting the history of England's domestic interiors.

Had I been writing this a decade ago I would happily have told you that Shoreditch was the place where Ralph Harwood perfected the brewing of porter, which was first served at the Blue Last in Curtain Road in 1730. More scrupulous beer historians have recently questioned this received wisdom, suggesting that porter probably evolved in several places, and is more likely to have been perfected at Humphrey Parsons' Red Lion brewery at what's now St Katharine's Dock.

Our definition of Hoxton and Shoreditch takes in a bit of Bethnal Green too, to encompass all of Zone 1 – for the rest of this area see under East London (p119) and the Pride of Spitalfields under Aldgate (p44).

BAR MUSIC HALL
Bar
134 Curtain Road, EC2A 3AR
☎ (020) 7729 7216
⊕ www.barmusichall.co.uk, **fbk**
🕐 11-midnight Mon-Wed; 11-1am Thu; 11-3am Fri & Sat; 11-10.30 Sun. *Children until 7pm*
Cask beer None, **Other beers** 10 keg, 6 bottles

(Duvel-Moortgat)
🍽 Upmarket diner menu, 🪑 Tables on street, ♿
Thu live bands, Fri & Sat DJs / Live bands, art fairs, jumble sales, big screen sport

This massive place is so far the only British tied house in the estate of Belgian 'new national' brewer Duvel-Moortgat (p293). An enormous

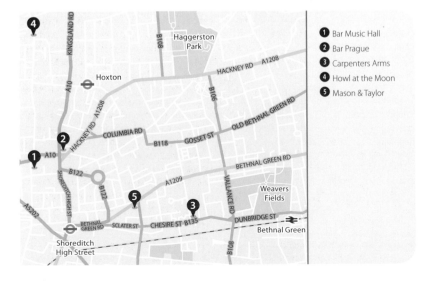

1 Bar Music Hall
2 Bar Prague
3 Carpenters Arms
4 Howl at the Moon
5 Mason & Taylor

Bar Music Hall

triangular island bar, suspended beamed ceiling, spangly lights and bead curtains give it a stylish look not dissimilar to some of the bigger contemporary bars in Duvel's home country, curious facts about which are listed on a wall display. A big range from the brewery and its various subsidiaries is available on keg including De Koninck, La Chouffe, filtered Duvel Groen, the Maredsous abbey beers and Bernard lager from the Czech Republic. Not surprisingly, Duvel itself leads the bottled beer range, alongside the bottle-conditioned versions of the Maredsous beers and wheat beer Vedett White. A varied menu isn't especially Belgian in style, though includes cheese and Duvel croquettes alongside burgers, pastas, steaks, deli sandwiches and a popular brunch. It's an unusual venue with lots going on besides eating and drinking, so call early if you want a quiet drink.

Pub trivia: Don't imagine you're walking in the footsteps of Marie Lloyd and Harry Lauder – the building was originally merely a warehouse, though it did once house contemporary company the Brick Lane Music Hall, now based in Silvertown.

🚆 Liverpool Street, Old Street ⊖ Old Street, Shoreditch High Street 🚲 Links to LCN+9, 10

BAR PRAGUE
Bar
6 Kingsland Road, E2 8DA
📞 (020) 7739 9110, ⊕ www.barprague.com
☼ 12-1.30am daily. *Children until early evening*
Cask beer None, **Other beers** 3 Czech keg, 8 Czech bottles, **Also** Czech schnapps and liqueurs
🍴 Bagels and sharing plates, ♿
Art exhibitions, occasional live bands and DJs

This comfy, chilled out, red painted Czech-owned bar feels more like one of the new breed of Czech *čajovny* (tea rooms) than a traditional Bohemian boozer. There's a hint of arty Shoreditch thrown in, too, with a gallery downstairs, but there's no doubting the quality of the beer. Draught options are blond and dark Budvar plus Staropramen, while the fridge offers less frequently encountered choices in bottle including Bohemia Regent Prezident, Krušovice, Žatec and Budvar. The selection could be broader still given the rich brewing heritage it draws on, and apparently once was, but Czech beers are sadly neglected by British importers. In the daytime the mixed collection of sofas and tables is a relaxing space, while evening gets more buzzy, attracting a youngish crowd.

🚆 Old Street, Liverpool Street ⊖ Old Street, Shoreditch High Street 🚲 Links to LCN+9, 10

CARPENTERS ARMS ☆ 25

Contemporary pub
73 Cheshire Street, E2 6EG
☎ (020) 7739 6342
⊕ www.carpentersarmsfreehouse.com
✪ 4-11.30 Mon; 12-11.30 Wed & Thu;
12-12.30am Fri & Sat; 12-11.30 Sun. *Children until 8.30pm*
Cask beers ✔ 3 (Adnams, Timothy Taylor, 1 unusual guest), **Other beers** 4 keg, 30+ bottles, **Also** Malts, wines
🍴 Pub grub/gastro menu, ⛱ Small beer garden

This pub, actually in Bethnal Green a little walk off the north end of Brick Lane, was the place gangland bosses Ronnie and Reggie Kray bought for their mother, thus the portrait of the notorious twins in Andy Warhol Marilyn guise on the wall. These days the pub pursues a more honest living as a reinvented East End boozer with good food, a great selection of beers and convivial company. Following a refit by current landlords Eric and Nigel, its small rooms are now simply but elegantly decked out in woody tones, enlivened by fresh flowers and displays of carpenter's tools, while a lovely little backyard boasts greenery and sculptures.

Carpenters Arms

Cask beers include Landlord and a changing Adnams beer – often a seasonal – and they're a regular stockist of the new Truman beers, rather pleasingly given their local connections, and Purity too. Kegs include Meantime London Pale Ale and a changing German guest, while the nicely chosen bottled list has more Meantime beers as well as Brooklyn Black Chocolate, Brugse Zot, Harviestoun whisky barrel aged Ola Dubh, Little Creatures, Orval and Schneider Weisse. The menu runs from home cooked pub grub like burgers and pies to oysters and snails, which I doubt were a familiar sight in Mrs Kray's kitchen, and there's a range of cheese boards and other grazing platters. Civilised but relaxed and welcoming, this is a real gem of a place.

🚄 Bethnal Green, Cambridge Heath ⊖ Bethnal Green, Shoreditch High Street 🚲 LCN+9, 39

HOWL AT THE MOON

Contemporary pub
178 Hoxton Street, N1 5LH
☎ (020) 3341 2525
⊕ howlatthemoonlondon.com
✪ 12-11 Mon-Thu; 12-1am Fri & Sat; 12-11 Sun. *Children welcome before 5.30pm*
Cask beers ✔ 4 (Dark Star, Pitfield, local guests), **Other beers** 4 keg, 7-8 bottles
🍴 Pizzas, sandwiches, soups lunchtime and evening, ⛱ Benches on street, ♿ No disabled toilet but flat access
Tue quiz, Fri DJs, Sat live bands, rugby team, board games

Lengthy Hoxton Street with its traditional market endures as a slice of the old East End: walk north along it and you'll leave most of the fashion victims and Hoxton fin haircuts behind. Just past the Community Garden with its incongruous clock, originally atop the Eastern Hospital at Homerton, is this pleasant pub, remade in 2009 in eclectic contemporary style but retaining a community focus. Some of the furniture may be made from railway sleepers, but it's still used as the headquarters of the Old Street Rugby Club.

A free house, it stocks Dark Star Hophead as a regular, while other taps dispense more from Dark Star or beers from Brodie's, Fuller's or Pitfield. Budvar, Brooklyn Lager and

Howl at the Moon

Coopers Sparkling Ale are in the fridge and there's a changing craft keg tap. Stone baked pizzas, sandwiches and soups constitute the menu and there are discounts for civil servants and students.

≷ Liverpool Street, Old Street ⊖ Hoxton, Old Street 🚌 St Leonards Hospital (243 Old Street, numerous Liverpool Street) 🚲 LCN+16, Grand Union Canal towpath 🚶 Jubilee Greenway

MASON & TAYLOR
Bar, specialist
51-55 Bethnal Green Road, E1 6LA
📞 (020) 7749 9670, 🌐 www.masonandtaylor. co.uk, **fbk, tw** masontaylore1
☼ 5-midnight Mon-Thu; 5-2am Fri; 12-2am Sat; 12-midnight Sun. *Children welcome*
Cask beers ✔ 3-4 (Dark Star, unusual guests), **Other beers** 8 keg, 40 bottles, **Also** 3-4 real ciders
🍴 'English tapas' plates and specials, 🪑 Benches on street, ♿
Fri & Sat DJs, seasonal beer festivals, meet the brewer evenings and tastings

Opened late in 2010, this is one of London's most ambitious new beer bars, from the people that brought you the Duke of Wellington (p94) and at least as alluring. Mason & Taylor – the co-owner is named Mason, while both the head chef and the bar manager, though no relation, are named Taylor – is a swishly designed place below a new residential building on Bethnal Green Road, with candlelit, sewing machine-style tables and picture windows on the ground floor and a cellar bar strewn with floppy sofas that takes on a more clubby vibe later.

Three handpumps dispense Dark Star Hophead and beers from the likes of Brodie's, Harveys, Golden Valley, Thornbridge and York, with a fourth cask on gravity at weekends. Kegs include Camden Town, Chimay Triple, Westmalle Dubbel and a changing US porter or stout. The tempting bottled range changes every two months and might well offer Kernel beers, Marble Chocolate, Acorn Gorlovka, Great Divide Titan IPA, Breconshire Golden Valley or a house porter commissioned from Brodie's. Seasonal beer festivals are planned to extend the range further. Food focuses on small plates, tapas style, like artichokes, ox tongue, Arbroath smokies, quail eggs or pear and walnut salads, except for Sundays when there's a roast. Just bubbling under my Top 25, partly as it's so new, it's a great expression of the current buzz around beer in London and definitely one to watch.

Insider tip! A rare bar that sells beer in third pints, so make sure you take advantage.

≷ Bethnal Green, Old Street ⊖ Shoreditch High Street 🚲 LCN+9

SOHO & LEICESTER SQUARE

Every city needs somewhere like raffish, disreputable, eccentric Soho, especially a city that can be as businesslike as London, and if you asked people to name their favourite central district, I'd be surprised if it didn't come top of the list. Henry VIII knew it as a hunting park and it's likely the name comes from a hunting call. Developed from the 1670s by aristrocratic landowners, it never became a fashionable suburb but instead an early manifestation of multicultural London.

Soho is also notorious for its associations with the sex industry, going back at least to the late 18th century. In the postwar period criminal gangs ruled but policing and licensing have cleaned things up, limiting the now regulated businesses to southern Soho, the closest thing London has to an official red light district. And Soho was a formative centre of British popular music, from trad jazz and beatnik clubs through the 2i's Coffee Bar in the rock 'n' roll era to 1960s R&B joints like the Flamingo and the Marquee. In recent years Old Compton Street has become the hub of London's biggest 'gay village', while Wardour Street is the traditional home of the British film industry, and advertising agencies pepper the area. While not as edgy or outrageous as it once was, Soho still breathes life, and people still live here.

On the western boundary is Regent Street, part of John Nash's never quite realised grand avenue from the river via Regents Park to Camden, with shopping nexus Oxford Circus in the northwest corner. Shaftesbury Avenue, built in the 1880s, rapidly became synonymous with London's Theatreland with at least six major commercial theatres and several more in surrounding streets. It ends at Piccadilly Circus, an enduring London rendezvous with its neon signs. To the south is London's Chinatown which developed from the 1970s around a cluster of restaurants. Beyond this is Leicester Square where the pleasant garden still recalls late 17th century elegance despite the cluster of huge cinemas and other commercial hubbub around it.

This area boasts several legendary pubs though their fame is mainly due not to their beer but to their characters, most of whom are long gone, so few of them feature here.

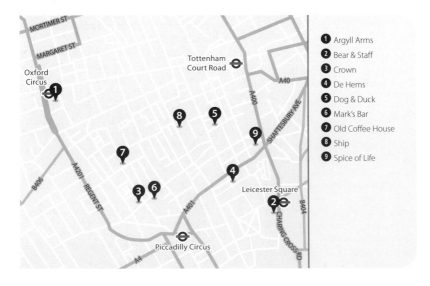

1 Argyll Arms
2 Bear & Staff
3 Crown
4 De Hems
5 Dog & Duck
6 Mark's Bar
7 Old Coffee House
8 Ship
9 Spice of Life

Argyll Arms

ARGYLL ARMS
Traditional pub ★
18 Argyll Street, W1F 7TP
☎ (020) 7734 6117, ⊕ www.nicholsonspubs.
co.uk/theargyllarmsoxfordcircuslondon/
☼ 10-11.30 Mon-Thu; 10am-midnight Fri & Sat;
10-11 Sun. *Children welcome until 8pm*
Cask beers ✅ 7-8 (Fuller's, Sharp's, Timothy
Taylor, unusual guests), **Other beers** 2 keg,
2 bottles
🍴 Pub grub, breakfasts, snacks and meals,
🚉 Front terrace
*Occasional Meet the Brewer events, Thu sausage
and ale night, functions*

Centrally located round the corner from
Oxford Circus, with tables set out on
pedestrianised Argyll Street, this cavernous
building has one of the best real ale ranges of
the numerous Mitchells & Butlers Nicholson's
pubs in the West End, on top of which it's a
pub heritage landmark. The northwest corner
of Soho on which it stands is the Argyll estate,
developed from 1706 by powerful Scottish
aristocrats the Dukes of Argyll, still among the
biggest private landowners in Britain today.
There's been a pub here since the creation of
Argyll Street in 1740, though the current
building dates from 1868. The richly decorated
ceiling is quite likely original, but the interior
was remodelled in the 1890s in the favourite
style of the period, with the drinking area
between a corridor and a long bar partitioned
into several smaller spaces with carved wood

and glass screens, dramatically enhanced by
ornate mirrors.

Besides Doom Bar, Landlord and Pride the
guests are drawn from Nicholson's seasonally
changing list of beers from well reputed
micros and independents such as Acorn,
Brains, Cropton, Hook Norton, Kelham Island,
Rudgate, Saltaire, Thornbridge, Thwaites,
White Horse, Williams Brothers and Wolf –
look for the booklets which include tasting
notes and food matching suggestions. If
you're not sure what to choose, ask for a taste
under the pub's 'Sip before you Sup' policy.
Erdinger Weissbier is on draught and the odd
bottle of Budvar or Sierra Nevada Pale Ale can
be spotted. As with most pubs in the chain
there's an extensive moderately priced all day
menu, from breakfast fry ups through soup
and sandwiches to pub grub mains such as
beef and ale pie, gourmet sausages. grilled
salmon and roasted vegetable risotto.

⊖ Oxford Circus 🚲 CS9, 10, 11, LCN+ 39, 50 🚲
Link to Jubilee Walkway

BEAR & STAFF
Traditional pub
10-12 Bear Street, WC2H 7AX
☎ (020) 7321 0814, ⊕ www.nicholsonspubs.
co.uk/thebearandstaffleicestersquarelondon/
☼ 10-11.30 Mon-Sat; 10-11 Sun. *Children
welcome anytime in the dining room and until
9pm downstairs*

Cask beers ❷ 6 (Fuller's, Sharp's, Timothy Taylor, guests), **Other beers** 3 bottles
🍴 Pub grub, breakfasts, snacks and meals
Thu sausage and ale night, functions

This smallish but cosy and welcoming pub, dating from 1714 and rebuilt in 1878, is conveniently sited just off Leicester.Square: a raised alcove decorated with old tobacco advertising is particularly inviting. The three guest beers are drawn from the Nicholson's list and the menu is standard for the chain (see Argyll Arms above) but with a slant towards pies. The name is drawn from the crest of the aristocratic Neville family, Earls of Warwick, key players in the Wars of the Roses. A more recent association is with former regular Charles Chaplin, to whom the upstairs bar is dedicated.

≋ Charing Cross ⊖ Leicester Square 🚲 LCN+ 6A, 39 ✹ Jubilee Walkway

CROWN
Traditional pub
64 Brewer Street, W1F 9TP
📞 (020) 7287 8420, ⊕ www.nicholsonspubs. co.uk/thecrownbrewerstreetlondon/
⊙ 10-11.30 Mon-Thu; 10-midnight Fri & Sat; 10-11 Sun. *Children in upstairs bar only*
Cask beers ❷ 5 (Fuller's, Sharp's, Timothy Taylor, guests), **Other beers** 3 bottles
🍴 Pub grub, breakfasts, snacks and meals
Thu pie and ale night, functions

Brewer Street is an appropriate address at which to enjoy a beer, though the breweries that gave the thoroughfare its name are long gone. Thomas Ayres' Brewery, later the Starkey Brewery, operated from 1664-1829 on the site where the art deco Lex Garage now stands. Davis's brewery was built next to it in 1671 "to the great annoyance of the neighbourhood" but had shut down by 1745. The Crown has a different claim to fame: its construction as an extension of an adjoining hotel in 1935 entailed the controversial demolition of Hickford's Rooms, once a major concert venue where the precocious 9-year-old Wolfgang Amadeus Mozart performed in 1765. It's now a moderately sized and pleasant Nicholson's pub decorated with discreetly pink wallpaper, offering interesting guests from the pub chain's list alongside their standard menu (see

Argyll Arms above). There's a more secluded area at the back and the elegant Mozart Bar upstairs. Mark's Bar (see below) is next door.

⊖ Piccadilly Circus 🚲 CS9, 10, 11, LCN+ 39, 50 ✹ Link to Jubilee Walkway

DE HEMS
Bar
11 Macclesfield Street, W1D 5BW
📞 (020) 7437 2494, ⊕ www.nicholsonspubs. co.uk/dehemsdutchcafebarsoholondon/
⊙ 10-midnight Mon-Thu; 10-12.30am Fri & Sat; 10-11 Sun. *Children until 7pm*
Cask beer None, **Other beers** 7 keg, 12 bottles, **Also** Genever
🍴 Dutch snacks, breakfasts, Dutch/British pub grub, ♿
Occasional Dutch events and DJs

De Hems is just about what you'd expect to get if you crossed a central London pub with the more boisterous kind of urban Dutch *bruin café*, though it's not quite cramped and cluttered enough to achieve that state of sociable cosiness Dutch speakers call *gezelligheid*. Captain De Hem was a retired Dutch sailor who ran the pub, then called the Macclesfield, as an oyster bar in the early 1900s, and during World War II the place was used as an unofficial headquarters of the exiled Dutch resistance. Renamed De Hems in 1959, it was soon attracting beat scene stalwarts like Georgie Fame, Alan Price and Rolling Stones manager Andrew Loog Oldham. Now surrounded by London's Chinatown, it retains its expat custom and you may occasionally encounter bouts of arm swaying and communal singing in the guttural mother tongue.

It's now part of the Nicholson's chain but has wisely not been standardised, keeping its bilingual signing and menu of authentically unhealthy street food such as *bitterballen* (meatballs), *frikandellen* (sausages) and *patatje oorlog* (chips with satay sauce) – a bit like an expat Scottish bar selling deep fried pizza. More Brit-friendly varieties of pub grub can also be obtained. Unsurprisingly keg pils leads the draught beer offering, though the Limburg-brewed house brand, Lindeboom, is rarely seen in the UK. It's supported by a variety of other specialist beers, mainly from

Dog & Duck

Belgium and Germany, such as Leffe and Franziskaner Weissbier on tap, bottled Delirium Tremens, Duvel and all three Chimays. Sadly missing are the products of Netherlands craft brewers, with the exception of the top quality La Trappe Trappist ales.

Insider tip! If you want a quiet time, try the more chilled upstairs room on a midweek afternoon, and take care to avoid national festivals like Koninginnedag (Queen's Day) on 30 April when the place bursts at the seams.

⊖ Piccadilly Circus 🚴 LCN+ 6A, 39 🚶 Link to Jubilee Walkway

DOG & DUCK
Traditional pub ★
18 Bateman Street, W1D 3AJ
📞 (020) 7494 0697, ⊕ www.nicholsonspubs.co.uk/thedogandducksoholondon/
🕐 10-11 daily. *Children until 9pm*
Cask beers ✔ 6 (Fuller's, Timothy Taylor, guests)
🍴 Pub grub, breakfasts, snacks and meals
Thu sausage and ale night, functions

This small and delightful street corner pub is adored by heritage buffs for its preserved wall tiling and advertising mirrors from an 1897 rebuild, and its 1930s wooden bar, and proudly numbers Dante Gabriel Rossetti and George Orwell among former regulars. The latter is commemorated by the pleasant

Orwell Bar upstairs which has a good view of the bustling streets below. But it owes its more recent celebrity to being the place Madonna recommended for the quality of its Timothy Taylor's Landlord in a 2005 interview with Jonathan Ross. Landlord is still on sale in top condition, alongside London Pride and four changing cask beers from the Nicholson's list, while food is from a pub grub menu typical for the chain (see Argyll Arms above). Fame hasn't spoiled its local, lived-in feel, though it can easily get packed.

Pub trivia: Look for the depictions of a dog and duck in carved and painted stone high up on the exterior and in a mosaic by the Frith Street entrance. The name is a hunting reference, a reminder of Soho's past.

⊖ Tottenham Court Road 🚴 LCN+ 6A, 39 🚶 Link to Jubilee Walkway

MARK'S BAR (HIX)
Bar
66-70 Brewer Street, W1F 9UP
📞 (020) 7292 3518, ⊕ www.marksbar.co.uk
🕐 12-midnight Mon-Sat; 12-11.30 Sun. *Children until 5pm*
Cask beer None, **Other beers** 6 bottles, **Also** Cocktails, specialist spirits, wines
🍴 Hand made bar snacks, full Modern British menu from upstairs restaurant, ♿
Bar billiards (organised competition Sun)

Mark's Bar

Almost hidden among the long list of classic and original cocktails, rare malts and artisanal spirits at Mark's is a short but well chosen selection of British craft beers. It includes two choices commissioned by owner Mark Hix from the well regarded Dorset independent brewery Palmer – an IPA and an Oyster Ale – plus Sharp's tasty Chalky's Bite and beers from Harviestoun and St Peter's. These can be enjoyed with top notch British cooking upstairs in the upmarket Hix restaurant, or in this swish but relatively informal Manhattan-style basement bar with its Dunhill furniture, tin ceiling tiles and laboratory glass in which exotic ingredients slowly infuse on a low, glossy bar top. A bar billiards table strikes an incongruous note – Mark himself referees regular tournaments.

Chosen as London's best bar by *Time Out* in 2010, it's predictably popular with a well heeled creative crowd and doesn't accept bookings, so hopeful customers are turned away when full. It's perhaps one of the more unlikely entries in this book, but included as an example of a promising trend that could be taken a lot further – surely the West End has room for at least one luxurious and fashionable bar where fine beer outnumbers the wines and cocktails on the drinks list. And if you baulk at the prices, there's always the Crown next door (see above).

Visitor's note: Under the terms of the license you're required to eat, so a bowl of Twiglets is automatically served and added to your bill if you just order a drink, but the ever-changing, hand-cooked bar snacks, caviar aside, are surprisingly keenly priced. Also worth considering are the pre- and post-theatre deals in the upstairs restaurant.

⊖ Piccadilly Circus ⊙⊛ CS9, 10, 11, LCN+ 39, 50
🚶 Link to Jubilee Walkway

OLD COFFEE HOUSE
Traditional pub
49 Beak Street, W1F 9SF
📞 (020) 7437 2197
🕐 11-11 Mon-Sat; 12-10.30 Sun. *Children welcome upstairs lunchtimes*
Cask beers ✔ 5 (Brodie's, local guests)
🍴 Basic pub lunches
Functions

This corner site did indeed once host a genuine Coffee House, one of an extinct species of catering establishments much favoured by London's literary and political classes in the 17th and 18th centuries. The current 1850s building is now simply a pub, one of the more straightforward and unpretentious boozers in Soho, with a decently sized single bar. It's one of two West End pubs run by Brodie's – the Cross Keys (p75) is more of a local and rather better looking – and comes with their customary bric-a-brac such as old musical instruments, kitchen utensils, stuffed animals and, for some unexplained reason, a signed photo of rock band Kiss.

The brewery's Olde Ardour, English Best and IPA are regularly available at good value prices for the area, usually with another Brodie's beer and something from another small London brewer – Redemption Pale when I called. The function room upstairs opens for unreconstructed pub grub at lunchtimes, which is probably now the best time to ask for a cup of coffee.

⊖ Oxford Circus, Piccadilly Circus ♿ CS9, 10, 11, LCN+ 39, 50 ♙♙ Link to Jubilee Walkway

SHIP
Traditional pub
116 Wardour Street, W1F 0TT
☎ (020) 7437 8446, ✉ ship.soho@fullers.co.uk,
⊕ www.fullers.co.uk
✪ 12-11 Mon-Sat; Closed Sun
Cask beers ✪ 3 (Fuller's), **Other beers** 1-2 bottles
⊞ Home cooked traditional lunches,
⊟ Standing room In alley outside
Occasional theme and party nights

Fuller's beers aren't hard to find in central London but this small pub on the corner of prettily tiled blind alley Flaxman Court has a deserved reputation for presenting them at their absolute peak. Discovery, ESB and London Pride are the regulars (sadly no Chiswick Bitter), served from an imposing wooden bar in a traditional long and narrow drinking area with lovely engraved glass windows. The vast stack of CDs behind the bar testifies to the range of music played at manageable volume to a loyal and relatively youngish crowd: 90s indie and Led Zeppelin when I called. Simple freshly made comfort food is served on weekday lunchtimes: the fish finger sandwiches are particularly favoured.

⊖ Tottenham Court Road ♿ LCN+ 6A, 39 ♙♙ Link to Jubilee Walkway

SPICE OF LIFE
Traditional pub
6 Moor Street, W1D 5NA
☎ (020) 7437 7013
⊕ www.spiceoflifesoho.com, **fbk**
✪ 10-11 Mon-Sat; 12-10.30 Sun
Cask beers ✪ 4 (McMullen), **Other beers** 2 keg; 3 bottles, **Also** Wines
⊞ Enhanced pub grub and brunches, ⬚
Daily live music downstairs

Well located on a wedge-shaped site next to the Palace Theatre on Cambridge Circus, this is easily the most interesting of the two West End pubs tied to Hertfordshire brewer McMullen (the other is the Nags Head, 10 James Street, WC2E 8BT). It's a popular meeting place as well as an entertainment destination in its own right: the comfortable basement room with its nightly programme is recognised as one of London's best small music venues. The current pub was built as The Cantons in 1898 – the name is still visible in the stonework – and started promoting music in the 1960s, with Bob Dylan, Paul Simon and the Sex Pistols among its featured artists. But even if you're not bound for a gig, it's worth pondering the choice of Mac's beers from a red leather bench in the large but comfortable single bar upstairs. Cask Ale, Country Bitter and the historic AK light mild are on handpump alongside one of the brewery's seasonals while Stronghart and Hertford Castle are in bottle along with a few imported specialities. The menu kicks off with breakfast and brunch and moves on to pub grub with an exotic touch, categorised as 'bites' of bar (soup, small snacks), light (salads, sandwiches, quesadilla) and bigger (sausages, veggieburger, köfte) varieties.

⊖ Leicester Square ♿ LCN+ 6A, 39 ♙♙ Link to Jubilee Walkway

Spice of Life

SOUTHBANK

Like most of London's riverside, the strip directly across from the Strand and Westminster was once heavily industrialised. Things began to change from 1922 when the London County Council moved to its fine new County Hall on the downstream side of Westminster Bridge. The Red Lion brewery operated slightly futher downriver from 1837 to 1924, its buildings crowned with a giant lion made of an artificial ceramic material called Coade stone. In 1951 the area, now largely derelict through disuse or bomb damage, became the centrepiece of the Festival of Britain, a 'tonic' for a nation slowly recovering from war. The Royal Festival Hall, on the brewery site, is a surviving building from the time and became the nucleus of a new cultural centre including the Queen Elizabeth Hall, Hayward Gallery, Purcell Room, Jubilee Gardens and National Film Theatre, much of it built in the brutalist architecture of the time, the complex soon acquiring the name South Bank.

The various institutions, and the reach of the term, have since expanded. The National Theatre on the other side of Waterloo Bridge was added in 1976, County Hall now houses a hotel and exhibitions, while the overgrown ferris wheel that is the London Eye has dominated the riverfront since 1999. The chain of attractions now continues downstream along the Thames Path, including Coin Street Community Gardens, and the revamped OXO Tower with its great views from the 8th floor brasserie, which sells a few good bottled beers (⊕ www.harveynichols.com/oxo-tower-london).

We've taken a liberal view of the area, including Bankside where the Tate Britain art gallery occupies a massive former power station and the rebuilt Shakespeare's Globe theatre pulls the crowds. Zeitgeist in Lambeth stretches the definition a little far but it didn't fit in anywhere else. The Southbank lost its intervening space in a recent rebranding, but the brewery's old lion still stands proudly, now guarding the steps from County Hall to Westminster Bridge.

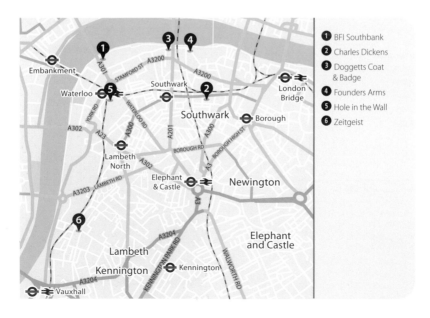

❶ BFI Southbank
❷ Charles Dickens
❸ Doggetts Coat & Badge
❹ Founders Arms
❺ Hole in the Wall
❻ Zeitgeist

BFI SOUTHBANK (RIVERFRONT)

Bar, restaurant
Belvedere Road, SE1 8XT
☎ (020) 7401 9000
⊕ www.bfi.org.uk/southbank
☼ 9am-11pm Mon-Sat; 10-11 Sun. *Children very welcome*
Cask beers ✅ 3 (Sharp's, occasional guests), **Other beers** 5 keg, 6-8 bottles, **Also** Wines
🍴 Gastro-style British food, savouries, bar menu + sit-down restaurant, cakes, 🌞 Riverfront terrace, ♿
Occasional live piano, arthouse and archive film and TV screenings

BFI Southbank, formerly the National Film Theatre, opened in its current site under Waterloo Bridge in 1957. Its setting right on the riverside, with a popular second hand book market on its doorstep, has long assured its bars and restaurants passing trade, but they haven't always made the best of the opportunity. Current caterers Benugo are doing much better than their predecessors at creating places you'd want to visit even if you weren't here to watch a rediscovered gem of 1960s television or something long and perplexing with subtitles. Some prefer the loungey Benugo Bar deep inside the building but I'll plump for the lively Riverfront, with its splendid outdoor terrace (deckchairs in summer).

It's also got the best beer selection, with cask Doom Bar, Cornish Coaster and another Sharp's beer, keg craft lagers, and Duvel, Chimay and Coopers Sparkling Ale in the fridge. A bar menu includes cakes, breakfasts, burgers and sandwiches, while the restaurant opposite might have mussels, roast squash or duck leg. And with four screens and a free video-on-demand digital médiathèque drawing on a prodigious archive, the film programme is one of the best you'll find.

� Waterloo ⊖ Waterloo 🚲 NCN4, LCN+6 🚶 Jubilee Greenway, Jubilee Walkway, Thames Path

CHARLES DICKENS

Traditional pub
160 Union Street, SE1 0LH
☎ (020) 7401 3744
⊕ www.thecharlesdickens.co.uk
☼ 12-11 Mon-Sat; 12-9 Sun. *Children until 7pm*

Cask beers ✅ 6 (unusual guests), **Other beers** 1 keg, 1-2 bottles
🍴 Pub grub, 🌞 Beer garden
Wed quiz, big screen sport, functions

A warm and welcome bolthole set some way back from the river in the rapidly changing area between Blackfriars and Southwark bridges, this is a reliable source of interesting micro-brews relatively close to the Tate Modern. Cask ales change constantly, with a bias towards southwest England and more local brewers: Butcombe, Cottage, Downton, Hogs Back, Mighty Oak, Nelson, Skinners, Twickenham, Whitstable and Wickwar may well appear. Food is well-priced, home made fare like meat or veggie sausage and mash, pork hock, fishcakes, pies and ploughman's. It's pleasantly and comfortably furnished in traditional style and decorated with numerous prints related to the author whose name it has borrowed. May close earlier than stated on quiet Sundays.

≈ Waterloo ⊖ Borough, Southwark 🚲 NCN4, CS5, 6, 7, LCN+2, 23 🚶 Jubilee Greenway, Jubilee Walkway, Thames Path

DOGGETTS COAT & BADGE

Traditional pub
1 Blackfriars Bridge, SE1 9UD
☎ (020) 7633 9081
⊕ www.doggettscoatandbadge.co.uk
☼ 10-11 Mon-Wed; 10am-midnight Thu-Sat; 10-11 Sun. *Children until 9pm*
Cask beers ✅ 10 (Fuller's, Sharp's, unusual guests), **Other beers** 3 keg, 6 bottles
🍴 Breakfast, sandwiches and pub grub, 🌞 Front terrace, beer garden, ♿
Meet the brewer nights, food tastings

Charles Dickens

Doggetts Coat & Badge

Forget the yearly petty tussle at Putney between two obscure universities – the oldest boat race on the Thames and indeed in the world is Doggetts Coat & Badge, held in late July, when six apprentice watermen labour from London Bridge to Cadogan Pier, 7,400m (4 miles 5 furlongs) upstream. Established in 1715 by successful comic actor Thomas Doggett, it's been financed by his legacy ever since – the prize is a traditional red waterman's coat with silver badge. The pub named after it, right on the river at Blackfriars Bridge, is in an uninviting 1970s building still wondering if its architectural style is ever going to mellow. Inside is much more pleasant, if clearly faked up, and also massive, extending to four floors and a terrace with ever more impressive views, though the upper floors are rarely all in use and often reserved for private functions. It's an improving member of Mitchells & Butlers Nicholson's chain with an excellent choice of cask ale: Doom Bar and London Pride are regular, Taylor Landlord recurring, and the rest tend to come from well regarded micros including Ascot, BrewDog, Downton, Ringwood and Thornbridge. Meantime Chocolate and Sierra Nevada Pale Ale might be found in the fridge, food is the usual wide Nicholson's menu, with quarterly tasting evenings to help develop new dishes, and red coats are not obligatory.

≈ Blackfriars ⊖ Blackfriars, Southwark ᐊᕱᐅ NCN4, CS5, 6, 7, LCN+2, 23 ✹ Jubilee Greenway, Jubilee Walkway, Thames Path

FOUNDERS ARMS
Contemporary pub
52 Hopton Street, SE1 9JH
📞 (020) 7928 1899
🌐 www.foundersarms.co.uk, **tw** FoundersArms
⚙ 10-11 Mon-Thu; 10am-midnight Fri; 9am-midnight Sat; 9am-11 Sun. *Children welcome*
Cask beers ✔ 4 (Wells & Young's), **Other beers** 3 keg, 7 bottles, **Also** Wines, malts
🍴 Enhanced pub grub/gastro, 🌣 Large riverside terrace, ♿

This dumpy, angular building may not be an architectural masterpiece, but even when it was opened by the Dean of St Paul's in 1979 it enjoyed a favoured location, just downstream of Blackfriars Bridge looking straight across at Wren's iconic dome. Since then the Tate Modern, the Bankside Gallery, Shakespeare's Globe and the Millennium footbridge have opened on this stretch of the Thames Path and the Founders' value has rocketed. There's a lot to enjoy besides the views and the convenience though. Bombardier, Bitter, Special and a Wells & Young's seasonal are reliably served on cask, with bottled specialities including Special London Ale and Double Chocolate Stout, plus Negra Modelo and keg Hoegaarden. A varied food offer includes beef, mushroom and Young's ale pie, sea bass, sweet potato curry, brunches and a burger named after Tower 42, formerly the NatWest tower, another landmark visible from the extensive riverside terrace.

Visitor's note: For the most spectacular view of the pub, approach from Southwark Bridge at night, when flaming lanterns illuminate the terrace.

≈ Blackfriars ⊖ Blackfriars, Southwark ᐊᕱᐅ NCN4, CS5, 6, 7, LCN+2, 23 ✹ Jubilee Greenway, Jubilee Walkway, Thames Path

HOLE IN THE WALL
Traditional pub
5 Mepham Street, SE1 8SQ
📞 (020) 7928 6196
⚙ 11-11 Mon-Thu; 11-11.30 Fri & Sat; 12-10.30 Sun. *Children welcome*
Cask beers 7 (see below), **Other beers** 3 bottles, **Also** 1 real cider
🍴 Basic pub grub, 🌣 Small rear patio
Occasional live music, big screen sport

Half hidden in railway arches opposite Waterloo station's Victory Arch, this little place has been serving well informed travellers for decades, offering much better beers than anywhere actually on the station. They don't go for in for lots of changing guests: instead expect to find well-served pints of Adnams Bitter, Bass from Marston's, Greene King IPA, Hogs Back TEA, Young's Bitter and any two of Greene King Old Speckled Hen or Abbot, Sambrook's Wandle and Wychwood Hobgoblin, plus surprisingly good Grolsch Weizen in the fridge. Simple, cheap food like casseroles, burgers, pasta and nachos is also on sale. Don't expect luxury – the place is very frayed at the edges, like a rundown clubhouse, with a cabin-like front bar decorated with rugby shirts, a more cavernous main bar with big screens and a tiny yard at the back for smokers. The wall mounted copy of Abba's 'Waterloo' single is a nice touch. Also handy for the BFI Imax, the Old and Young Vic theatres and the Southbank complex.

≈ Waterloo ⊖ Waterloo ᗑ NCN4, LCN 16 ⚤ Jubilee Greenway, Jubilee Walkway, Thames Path

ZEITGEIST

Bar
49-51 Black Prince Road, SE11 6AB
☎ (020) 7840 0426, ⊕ zeitgeist-london.com
✪ 12-midnight Mon & Tue; 12-12.30am Wed & Thu; 12pm-1.30am Fri & Sat; 12-11 Sun.
Children welcome
Cask beer None, **Other beers** 13 keg, 30 bottled (German), **Also** Schnapps
⑩ German menu, 🍺 Beer garden
Occasional themed events and music, Bundesliga big screen TV

Just back from Albert Embankment near Lambeth Bridge is the historic heart of Lambeth. Edward the Black Prince, Duke of Cornwall, once had a palace near here and much of the land is still ultimately owned by the current Duke – Prince Charles. Lambeth Walk, leading north towards Waterloo, gave its name to a dance but there's little to detain you now. The Archbishop of Canterbury has his London residence at Lambeth Palace and right by it, opposite the bridge, is the quirky Museum of Garden History, in the former church where landscape gardening pioneers

the Tradescants are buried. Just to the south, a patch of green marks the site of once world famous Vauxhall Pleasure Gardens.

At the end of the 19th century this was a gathering place for music hall artists and Charles Chaplin may well have known the Jolly Gardeners from the days when his father played piano here. In 2008 the pub, by then decaying, was given a makeover by new German owners and turned into a decent German beer bar, mercifully free of accordions and fake Bavarian kitsch. The Victorian shell is obvious from the big and heavy island bar and the high ceilings; the current decor is rather sombre with lots of stools and giant high banquettes but the atmosphere is friendly and cheerful. German expats come to watch the *Bundesliga* and to sample beer options that are in excess of what they'd expect at home, where a limited choice of the local style is the norm. The keg taps dispense wheat beers, *Kölsch* and pale and dark lagers from brewers all over Germany such as Bitburger, DAB, Gaffel, Krombacher, Paulaner, Rothaus, Schwaben-Bräu and Weihenstephaner, alongside interesting and well priced bottles from Dinkelacker, Flensburger, König Ludwig, Maisels, Schlenkerla, Schneider, Wernesgrüner and more. The menu includes numerous German specialities like *Leberkäse*, *falscher Hase*, *Schweinebraten* and *Käsespätzle*, with soups, salads and of course enough sausages and schnitzels to fuel another World Cup win.

≈ Vauxhall ⊖ Vauxhall ᗑ LCN+2, 3, link to NCN4 ⚤ Jubilee Greenway, Jubilee Walkway, Thames Path

Founders Arms

WESTMINSTER, VICTORIA & PIMLICO

London's function as England's power base developed on Thorney Island, a marshy promontory between two channels of the Tyburn where it joined the Thames. Westminster Abbey had been founded here by the 960s. By 1050 it had been joined by the Palace of Westminster, the principal residence of the English royals and later the regular meeting place of what became England's Parliament. Westminster Hall, the largest hall in Europe when built in 1097, is the oldest surviving part; the familiar Gothic Revival complex that surrounds it, generally known as the Houses of Parliament, was purpose built as a centre of government between 1840 and 1860. If you can cope with the queues and security, it's well worth visiting.

From traffic choked Parliament Square the big government departments spread north along Whitehall to Trafalgar Square and southwest towards Victoria. To the west the chain of Royal Parks begins with pretty St James's Park; on the other side of this is Buckingham Palace, official home of British monarchs from Victoria onwards. The station named after her is now a busy transport hub but head south and you're in the quieter streets of puzzlingly named Pimlico, another characterful suburb once associated with genteel eccentricity, with the Tate Britain nearby.

BUCKINGHAM ARMS
Traditional pub
62 Petty France, SW1H 9EU
☎ (020) 7222 3386, ⊕ www.youngs.co.uk
🕐 11-11 Mon-Fri; 12-6 summer Sat & Sun; 12-5 winter Sat; Closed winter Sun. *Children until 5pm*
Cask beers ✅ 5 (Wells & Young's, 2 guests including Sambrook's), **Other beers** 6 bottles
🍴 Pub grub, sandwiches, hot specials, 🛇
Monthly quiz, occasional big screen sport

Petty France – from 'petit France' or 'Little France' – takes it names from a past community

of Huguenot refugees, but is probably best known as the location of the office where emergency passports were issued.

The Buckingham Arms, a fine Victorian local further down the street is one of only two London pubs listed in every single edition of the *Good Beer Guide* (see also the Star below). In 2002 the passport office moved to new and more efficient facilities in Victoria but the pub continues to hit the *Good Beer Guide* standards and is now looking even more handsome after a recent refit, with a skylight picking out the plain wood and the mirrored

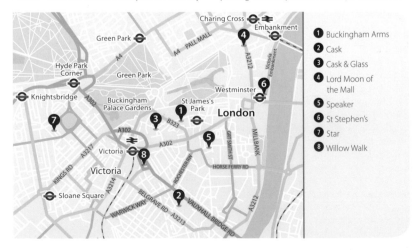

1. Buckingham Arms
2. Cask
3. Cask & Glass
4. Lord Moon of the Mall
5. Speaker
6. St Stephen's
7. Star
8. Willow Walk

Buckingham Arms

bar back. Bombardier, Bitter and Special are supplemented by guests that may well come from Sambrook's or St Austell. London Gold and Special London Ale are among the bottled choices, while food might include bangers and mash, spaghetti bolognaise or sweet potato curry.

Insider tip! We like the side corridor that's been cleverly converted into an unusual additional drinking space.

≈ Victoria ⊖ St James's Park ⊙ LCN+ Waterloo, Chelsea and links to Royal Parks routes ❦ Links to Jubilee Walkway

CASK ☆ 25

Bar, specialist
6 Charlwood Street, SW1V 2EE
((020) 7630 7225
⊕ www.caskpubandkitchen.com, **fbk**, tw CASK_PUB_SW1
⊙ 4-11 Mon; 12-11 Tue-Sat; 12-10.30 Sun.
Children until early evening
Cask beers ⊘ 10 (BrewDog, Dark Star, Thornbridge, unusual guests), **Other beers** 8 keg, 400 bottled beers incluing many rarities ⊡ Enhanced pub grub, sandwiches and grazing platters, ⊞ Tables on street
Monthly meet the brewer evenings, brewer themed nights, beer launches

Once a decaying street corner local on the corner of a housing block, abandoned without hope by its owners Greene King, this has been transformed on a free-of-tie lease into one of the very best of London's new generation of specialist beer bars. It boasts what's likely London's widest choice for sit down drinking, served in a cheerful and modern, if slightly basic, space. Given some of the rare treats on offer, don't be surprised to spot dedicated geeks, but the friendly welcome, good advice and decent food – grazing platters, game pie, sausages, steaks, risotto, burgers – has persuaded a loyal coterie of discerning but less obsessive locals to frequent the place too.

The eponymous casks constantly change but always offer a spread of styles including dark and strong options and unusual specialities. Unsurprisingly BrewDog, Dark Star and Thornbridge are regularly represented but there are many others including brewers rarely seen in London, like Dancing Duck, Derby, Falstaff and Five Towns, and more familiar names like Crouch Vale, Mighty Oak, Otley, Saltaire, Whim and Wolf. Kegs are from Brugse Zot, Moravka and Rothaus with guest imports from the likes of adventurous German micro Braustelle, itinerant Danish iconoclast Mikkeller and US craft brewers. The vast bottled list is a treasurehouse, with lots from Mikkeller and De Molen alongside Italian brewer Borgo, several obscure Germans and a very strong representation from French-speaking Belgium. Naturally there are good lambics and Trappists – even ultra-rare Westvleteren, at a price – and a good US list that stretches to specials from Stone, rarities from Lost Abbey/Port and the delightful big bottles from Jolly Pumpkin. If you really want to spend some money they have BrewDog's silly gravity beers at up to £60 a

330ml bottle, but thankfully most are at much more affordable prices.

It's well worth keeping track of the events diary for Meet the Brewer evenings and themed events where one brewery takes over most of the lines, often with rarities on offer. An instant gem of London's specialist beer scene, and handy for the Tate Britain too.

Insider tip! You don't have to cram it all in at once – there are take home containers for draught and if you buy six bottles to take away you get the cheapest one free.

⇌ Victoria ⊖ Pimlico, Victoria ⊘ NCN4 ⚏ Links to Thames Path

CASK & GLASS
Traditional pub
39-41 Palace Street, SW1E 5HN
📞 (020) 7834 7630, ✉ cask&glass@shepherd-neame.co.uk, 🌐 www.shepherd-neame.co.uk
🕐 11-11 Mon-Fri; 12-8 Sat; Closed Sun
Cask beers ✅ 4 (Shepherd Neame), **Other beers** 3 bottles
🍴 Toasted sandwiches, 🎪 Front terrace

One of the first pubs Faversham brewer Shepherd Neame bought in London, this is also one of the claimants to the title of the capital's smallest pub. It's very homely, with a

Cask & Glass

foliage-draped frontage, brown padded benches, an original fireplace, aged dark wood, a display case of clay pipes and walls crammed with caricatures. "Guaranteed Malt and Hops Only" reads the vintage lightbox above the bar. Top quality Kent's Best, Master Brew and Spitfire are the regular cask ales, with a Shep's seasonal too, and 1698 and Whistable Bay in bottles. It's relatively close to Victoria station, Buckingham Palace and Green Park and sometimes attracts politicians, but don't let that put you off.

⇌ Victoria ⊖ St James's Park, Victoria ⊘ LCN+ Waterloo, Chelsea and links to Royal Parks routes ⚏ Links to Jubilee Walkway, Jubilee Greenway, Princess Diana Memorial Walk

LORD MOON OF THE MALL
Contemporary pub
16-18 Whitehall, SW1A 2DY
📞 (020) 7839 7701
🌐 www.jdwetherspoon.co.uk
🕐 9am-11pm Mon & Tue; 9am-11.30pm Wed & Thu; 9am-midnight Fri & Sat; 9am-11pm Sun.
Children until early evening if eating
Cask beers ✅ 11 (Fuller's, Greene King, 9 unusual guests), **Other beers** Usual Wetherspoon keg and bottles, **Also** 1 real cider
🍴 Wetherspoon menu, ♿
Wetherspoon beer festivals and promotions

Another Wetherspoon bank conversion, this doesn't quite reach the heights of the Crosse Keys (p66) in decor or beer choice, but its reliable cellaring of a bigger-than-usual range of cask beers is especially noteworthy given its location, right by Trafalgar Square and well placed for the National Gallery, Green Park and the Cabinet War Rooms. London Pride and Greene King Abbot and IPA are the regulars but others could come from Brains, Cains, Conwy, Cotleigh, Hook Norton, Saltaire, Springhead and Wold Top. It's the usual Wetherspoon open plan setup but look for a few more booths at the back, and note points of interest like the statues in niches and the high vaulted ceiling.

⇌ Charing Cross ⊖ Charing Cross, Westminster ⊘ LCN+ Marylebone, Vauxhall Bridge ⚏ Jubilee Walkway, links to Thames Path, Jubilee Greenway

Lord Moon of the Mall

SPEAKER

Traditional pub
46 Great Peter Street, SW1P 2HA
☎ (020) 7222 1749, ⊕ www.pleisure.com/pubs-the-speaker.html, **fbk**
🕑 12-11 Mon-Fri; Closed Sat & Sun
Cask beers ✔ 4 (Shepherd Neame, Wells & Young's, 2 unusual guests), **Other beers** 1 keg (Urquell), 1-2 bottles
🍴 Sandwiches, home made specials and pub grub
Regular themed beer events

The Speaker has one of the most important and challenging jobs in the House of Commons, chairing the debates. Though speakers are MPs elected by their colleagues, their role is strictly non-political and impartial – appropriate, perhaps, for a pub within heckling distance of Parliament. Appreciators of good beer should be unwaveringly partial to this fine place, though, part of a small Brighton-based pubco that describes itself as "a big fan of traditional cask ale." Bitter and Spitfire are regulars, while guests come from the likes of Hogs Back, RCH and Twickenham. Themed fortnights see all the pumps rapidly rotate through a long list of beers from very small breweries, perhaps seasonal beers or something more imaginative. They've been known to hold fortnights of 'Embarrassing ales you would not ask your granny to order' for example – the last one featured beers from Bowman, Fuzzy Duck, Hornbeam, Houston and Tirril, all names hardly seen in London

pubs. Food, very good value for the area, includes sandwiches, jackets, hot specials and home made pâté, enjoyed in an atmosphere of civilised conversation unhindered by background music and games machines. There's a fine collection of political caricatures on the walls – impartial, of course.

⇌ Victoria ⊖ St James's Park 🚲 LCN+ links Waterloo, Chelsea, Charing Cross and NCN4 🚶 Links to Jubilee Greenway, Jubilee Walkway, Thames Path

ST STEPHEN'S

Traditional pub ☆
10 Bridge Street, SW1A 2JR
☎ (020) 7295 2286, ✉ ststephenstavern.london@hall-woodhouse.co.uk,
⊕ www.hall-woodhouse.co.uk
🕑 10-11.30 Mon-Thu; 10am-midnight Fri; 10-11.30 Sat; 10.30-10.30 Sun. *Children welcome weekend daytime*
Cask beers ✔ 3 (Badger), **Other beers** 5 bottles (Badger)
🍴 Pub grub until, 🪑 Benches on street, ♿ *Functions*

On the immediate approach to Westminster Bridge the St Stephen's Tavern, built in 1875, takes it name from the iconic Gothic Revival St Stephen's Tower directly opposite, known to most of us by the name of the bell it houses, Big Ben. Standing on parliamentary

St Stephen's

land and inevitably busy with tourists and visitors to the place across the road, it's well worth investigating partly for its lofty rooms and impressive Victorian bar fittings, giving it an elegance that well matches its setting – exotic etched mirrors and glass, a coffered ceiling, and upholstered leather benches in House of Lords green. Dorset brewer Hall & Woodhouse restored the pub sensitively in 2003 and it now showcases their beers: First Gold and Tanglefoot are regulars and there's a changing seasonal. Food includes salads, sandwiches, burgers and Our Famous Sussex Smokey, a smoked fish crumble.

Star

Insider tip! The mezzanine upstairs may be quieter than downstairs, with some cosy booths.

⊖ Westminster ⬭ NCN4, LCN+ Marylebone, Vauxhall Bridge ✸ Jubilee Greenway, Jubilee Walkway, Thames Path

STAR
Traditional pub
6 Belgrave Mews West, SW1X 8HT
☏ (020) 7235 3019, ✉startavern@fullers.co.uk,
⊕ www.fullers.co.uk
✪ 11-11 Mon-Fri; 12-11 Sat; 12-10.30 Sun.
Children welcome
Cask beers ✔ 5 (Fuller's), **Other beers** 1 keg, 2 bottles (Fuller's), **Also** 30+ whiskies
⑪ Enhanced pub grub
Functions

Tucked away in elegant Belgravia, west of Buckingham Palace, down an alley that runs between the Austrian and German embassies, the Star Tavern is the other London pub to have appeared in every edition of the *Good Beer Guide* (see also Buckingham Arms above). From its modest size it was probably intended for domestic staff in the big houses hereabouts, and is still a relaxed and informal place centred on an old horseshoe bar, shabbily genteel but spotlessly clean. It once had a more wicked reputation as a criminal rendezvous – the Great Train Robbery was planned here and stars like Peter O'Toole and Diana Dors would come to rub shoulders with gang bosses. These days it's an honest purveyor of fine beer, a Fuller's house that offers Chiswick, Discovery, ESB and London Pride alongside a changing seasonal, and a few bottles that include Golden Pride

and 1845. Food is typified by pies, pork belly, roasted aubergine, steaks and home made pork scratchings.

⇌ Victoria ⊖ Hyde Park Corner, Knightsbridge ⬭ LCN+5 ✸ Links to Hyde Park and Jubilee Greenway

WILLOW WALK
Contemporary pub
25 Wilton Road, SW1V 1LW
☏ (020) 7828 2953
⊕ www.jdwetherspoon.co.uk
✪ 7am-midnight Mon-Sat; 7am-11.30pm Sun.
Children until early evening if eating
Cask beers ✔ 9 (Fuller's, Greene King, Wells & Young's, unusual guests), **Other beers** Usual Wetherspoon keg and bottles, **Also** 3 real ciders/perries
⑪ Wetherspoon menu, ♿
Wetherspoon beer festivals and promotions

Top recommendation for a good range of beer near busy Victoria station, this Wetherspoons occupies the ground floor of a modern office block in the wedge between Wilton Road and Vauxhall Bridge Road. It's a bit like a pub in a corridor, with entrances at both ends, but it's a reliable source of well kept and interesting guest cask beers alongside the likes of Abbot, IPA, London Pride and Director's, and often features milds and dark beers. Banks & Taylor, Box Steam, Brentwood, Brewster's, Cottage and Nethergate might well be spotted on the pump clips. The window tables are the best seats in the house.

⇌ Victoria ⊖ Victoria ⬭ LCN+ link to LCN5, Strand, Chelsea ✸ Link to Jubilee Greenway

EAST LONDON

EAST LONDON

East London in this book covers all the E postcodes outside the central area, and the rest of London east of these and north of the Thames to the Essex boundary.

The east was historically London's workhorse: the City of London refused to allow noxious industries within its walls, so all the slaughterhouses, soap and paint factories, cloth dyers and chemical works, not to mention breweries, spilled eastward down the Thames, joined by a rapidly growing army of labourers to work it all. In the 19th century the population was swelled further by people displaced by the redevelopment of central London slum housing, and successive waves of refugees and economic migrants. French Protestant Huguenots, Irish weavers, Chinese seamen and East European Jews helped create a multicultural community here long before the term was coined. This was the gorblimey East End of Cockney legend, replete with jellied eels, rhyming slang and knees ups in the corner boozer – as well as some of the densest and poorest housing in the developed world. It was lubricated by ales from Truman in Brick Lane, Charrington on Mile End Road, Taylor Walker in Limehouse and Whitbread on the edge of the City.

Times change and that East End is now gone. The Jewish community moved north and west, while many of the Cockneys were relocated to new towns outside London. Postwar immigration and the redevelopment of the old docks brought waves of newcomers: Bangladeshi refugees settled around Brick Lane from the 1970s, while the creation of a major new European business district on the Isle of Dogs attracted a new middle class. Bohemians, hippies and other alternative and artistic types have long clustered here, from squatting punks to the New British Artists that colonised the last redoubts of working class central London around Hoxton and Shoreditch in the 1990s (p100). Most of the places listed below have been reinvented to meet the demands of the newer and better off inhabitants, but some remnants of the past remain.

More widely, East London is home to some of London's most extensive green spaces including Victoria Park (Eleanor Arms, p135), the Lee Valley Park (Anchor & Hope, p137), Epping Forest (Kings Head, p137) and the developing Thames Chase Community Forest straddling the far eastern boundary (Thatched House, p138). As I write, it stands on the edge of yet another transformation with the vast Queen Elizabeth Olympic Park at Stratford set to become a whole new urban quarter as one of the legacies of London's hosting the 2012 Olympic and Paralympic Games.

< **King Edward VII (p136)**

BETHNAL GREEN & MILE END

Today Bethnal Green is the deep East End, but the gardens around the library and the tube station were once part of a real village green. The green stands on the junction of Cambridge Heath Road and Roman Road, the latter the ancient route east from London to Colchester. That route was realigned south in 1110 to a new bridge across the river Lee; its junction with Grove Road was named Mile End as it was a mile from Aldgate, and the road became Mile End Road.

The area was heavily bombed in World War II – 173 people sheltering in Bethnal Green tube died in 1943 when the station took a direct hit – and Mile End Park was subsequently created from a chain of bomb damaged industrial sites.

The western part of Bethnal Green falls within our definition of Central London and is covered under Shoreditch (p100) and Aldgate (p43).

CAMEL

Contemporary pub
277 Globe Road, E2 0JD
📞 (020) 8983 9888, **fbk**
🕐 4-11 Mon-Thu & Sat; 11-11 Fri; 11-10.30 Sun.
Children welcome
Cask beers ✔ 3 (Sambrook's, Crouch Vale),
Other beers 5 keg, 3-4 bottles, **Also** Wines
🍴 Upmarket pie and mash, 🪑 Benches on street
Monthly quiz, occasional live music, board games

Camel

On a quiet residential street just around the corner from the historic centre of Bethnal Green and the V&A Museum of Childhood, the comfortable Camel is the East End reinvented. The single fairly small narrow bar with its plain wooden tables, bare floorboards, extreme floral wallpaper and globular designer lampshades is regularly packed with a youngish crowd tucking into the Cockney staple of pie, mash and mushy peas, though the pies are as likely to be filled with goat's cheese and butternut squash as minced beef and onions and don't leave you much change out of a tenner. When I visited the cask beer offer had stabilised on Sambrook's Wandle and Junction and Crouch End Brewer's Gold, but might evolve further. Kegs include Licher Weizen and two beers

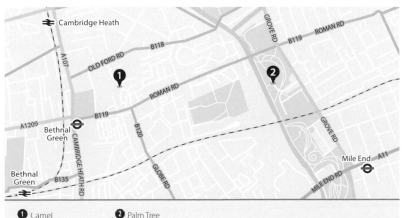

❶ Camel   ❷ Palm Tree

from Freedom brewery, once based in London, while Sierra Nevada Pale Ale and (sweetened) Boon Kriek are in the fridges. Luvverly.

Pub trivia: As evidenced by the photos on the walls, the pub has long been a rendezvous for coach trips to the Kent coast. The tradition is continued by the present management, who encourage participants to wear full 1940s dress.

⇌ Cambridge Heath ⊖ Bethnal Green ⊙ Links to NCN1 and LCN+ Mile End Road, Vallance Road ⫽ Links to Regents Canal, Mile End Park

PALM TREE
Traditional pub ☆
127 Grove Road, E3 5RP
☎ (020) 8980 2918
⊙ 12.30-10.30 daily
Cask beers ✔ 2 (unusual guests), **Other beers** 2-3 bottles
⑪ Simple food during events, occasional sandwiches, ⊞ Terrace, surrounding park
Fri-Sun Jazz / pop trio, quiz, darts

ANCHOR BREWERY

The Anchor brewery opened in 1757 on Mile End Road between Whitechapel and Stepney Green, co-founded by Robert Westfield who'd brewed in the area since 1738. The Charrington family eventually achieved full ownership of the business which was the second biggest brewery in London by 1808, and in the 1870s expanded operations to Burton on Trent. In 1967 Charrington merged with Bass of Burton and Mitchells & Butlers of Birmingham to form Bass Charrington, one of the Big Six national brewers of the era, ending its London operations in 1975. Part of the site is occupied by the Anchor shopping centre; Adams House and Charrington House on the corner of Cephas Avenue are all that remain of the original brewery buildings. The Bass legacy has since been divided up by multinational brewers Anheuser-Busch InBev and MolsonCoors.

Palm Tree

This characterful East End boozer was originally surrounded by houses of similar age, but the Blitz and 1960s planning have left it curiously marooned in the middle of Mile End Park, right by the Regents Canal, and a short walk from the landmark Green Bridge. The orange-lit interior, with two completely separate bars, one of which boasts a striking curved bar counter, is very much as it must have been in the 1930s. Landlord Alf has run the place for 34 years – the distinctive foil wallpaper was picked out by his wife when they first took over in 1977. A classic easy listening soundtrack is substituted on weekend evenings with live performance from what's unkindly described on one website as "an old man jazz trio". The East End Fives dartboard with its 9-foot (2.74m) oche is another surviving curiosity. Once a Truman pub, it's now free of tie: the beer choice might not be huge but is more than made up for by the quality and the unique location. Two well-kept cask ales are sourced far and wide – Harviestoun, Mauldons, Oxford and Sharp's might be on, while Sambrook's and Welton's provide local colour and Mann's and Newcastle browns are fridge fixtures. We suspect the three palm trees to the north of the pub postdate its naming, but they're a nice touch nonetheless, especially when covered in snow.

Pub trivia: The picture gallery repays examination: old East End scenes, caricatures of sports personalities of yesteryear, and an array of minor and not-so-minor celebrities above the curved bar, all of whom Alf insists enjoyed a pint here, including Frank Sinatra when he was playing the now-vanished Mile End Arena.

⊖ Mile End ⊙ NCN1 ⫽ Jubilee Greenway

DOCKLANDS

The direct route to the sea provided by the Thames is one of the keys to London's historic trading supremacy, and the 19th century saw the creation of major dock complexes to furnish this trade. The Port of London became the biggest and busiest port yet known, at the very hub of the world's biggest and most profitable empire.

Even as that empire fell apart after World War II, the docks continued to prosper, but with the development of containerisation the Port of London declined rapidly – all the docks had closed by 1981. The government of the day created the London Docklands Development Corporation, giving it powers to override local planning rules and offer tax breaks. The LDDC's most visible legacy is on the Isle of Dogs, the area within the oxbow meander of the Thames between Limehouse and Leamouth. Here private developers have turned the old West India Docks into a high rise business district clustered around the 235m Canary Wharf tower (officially 1 Canada Square), like a little piece of a North American big city downtown parachuted into east London. It's easily explored on the Docklands Light Railway which threads scenically between the towers and over the old docks, but descend to ground level to appreciate the scale of it, as well as some surprisingly pleasant public gardens.

GUN

Gastropub
27 Coldharbour, E14 9NS
☎ (020) 7215 5222, ⊕ www.thegundocklands.com, **tw** thegundocklands
☼ 11-midnight Mon-Sat; 11-11 Sun. *Children welcome*
Cask beers ✔ 3 (Adnams, Fuller's, 1 guest), **Other beers** 2 bottles, **Also** 150 wines, malts, cocktails
▥ Upmarket pub grub/gastro menu,
▦ Riverside and side terraces, ♿
Mon quiz, functions

The two pubs on the Isle of Dogs listed here – the other is the North Pole below – each tell their own story about the huge changes to the area over the past few decades. The Gun stands on Coldharbour, a street immediately parallel to the Thames in the northeast corner of the Isle that counts Admiral Nelson among its former residents. Cut off by the construction of the West India Docks, it's now an enclave of historic housing squeezed between the locks that link the dock complex to the river, and its character, river views and

❶ The Gun
❷ North Pole
❸ Town of Ramsgate
❹ Waitrose Canary Warf

proximity to Canary Wharf have made it one of the most desirable addresses in east London. The pub, a former dockers' local that traces its history to 1720, got a posh gastro makeover in 2004 following a serious fire, with several heritage features preserved including a fine bar back with tiling details. Smartly dressed waiters dish up oysters and pheasant on crisp white tablecloths in the front bar – some main courses on the award-winning menu reach north of £25 (booking advisable), though you can also get macaroni cheese or a sausage roll at the bar for around a fiver. There are several more drinking areas round the back, including a lovely dark red painted room with club armchairs and books and a riverside terrace, with breathtaking views across the

Gun

Thames to the Greenwich peninsula. From here you can admire Norman Foster's landmark 1999 Millennium Dome (O_2) directly opposite, and ponder the strange history of Docklands over a well-kept cask ale. London Pride and Adnams Bitter are regulars while the third pump might dispense an Adnams or Greene King seasonal. Meantime London Pale and Kostritzer Schwarzbier are in bottle.

Insider tip! In the summer, food options expand with an outdoor Portugese grill on the terrace.

DLR Blackwall 🚲 LCN Canning Town, Island Gardens 🚶 Lea Valley Path

NORTH POLE
Traditional pub
74 Manilla Street, E14 8LG
☎ (020) 7987 5443
🕐 11-11 Mon-Fri; closed Sat & Sun. *Children welcome daytime*
Cask beers ✓ 3 (Fuller's, Timothy Taylor, 1 guest)
🍴 Fast food and sandwiches, 🏡 Rear patio
Pool

Take the pedestrian route over the dock from the impressive glass canopy of Canary Wharf tube, cross Marsh Wall, go down a short flight of steps and you're in a different world of modest cottages and social housing – the Isle of Dogs once had the highest concentration of council housing in England. Unlike the gastrofied Gun (above), the green painted North Pole, surrounded by floral planters on its small wedge of a corner site, remains unaltered from the days when this was one of the world's busiest ports, with the same half panelling and traditional red settles, though the customers have changed. Landlord John, an Islander who took on the pub in 1981 after he lost his job at the docks, says only a tiny handful of regulars now live locally; the majority are workers at Canary Wharf with insider knowledge about a drinking house of authenticity and character, in contrast to the upmarket chain bars closer to the office. London Pride and Taylor Landlord are regulars while the guest is likely something from the Marston's group – Wychwood Hobgoblin when I called – or Sharp's Doom Bar. Nothing unusual, but well served in an environment that's remarkable for the area, winning it a Best London Pub award from fancyapint.com in 2009. Catch it while it lasts.

Insider tip! In warm weather, the garden is a delightful sun trap.

🚇 Canary Wharf **DLR** South Quay 🚲 NCN1 🚶 Thames Path

TOWN OF RAMSGATE
Traditional pub
62 Wapping High Street, E1W 2PN
☎ (020) 7481 8000
🕐 11-11 Mon-Sat; 12-10.30 Sun. *Children welcome*

Cask beers ✅ 4 (Fuller's, Sharp's, Wells & Young's, 1 guest), **Other beers** 2 keg, 2 bottles 🍴 Pub grub and specials, ☂ Rear riverside patio, ♿ No disabled toilets but flat access
Mon quiz, Tue food promotions

Wapping, the stretch of the north bank immediately east of the Pool of London, was until 1830 the site of Execution Dock, where the Admiralty hanged pirates and other maritime miscreants on the foreshore. Wapping boasts two historic riverfront pubs reached down cobbled streets past old warehouses – the Prospect of Whitby at 57 Wapping Wall, and the Town of Ramsgate, which is a little less quaint but also less touristy, more welcoming and much more beer friendly. It's allegedly the place where 'Hanging Judge' George Jeffreys was arrested in 1688 while attempting to flee the country following the overthrow of James II. Today this Enterprise tenancy is a single long and narrow wood panelled bar with some cosy booths and a rear terrace backing straight on to the river, with views across to Rotherhithe and its distinctive church. The gigantic old fashioned cash register in one corner is for decoration only: landlords Jan and Peter use a more recent model to add up the bill for solid classics like Young's Bitter, London Pride and Doom Bar. The guest tap tends towards best bitters from better-known breweries like Adnams, Batemans, Black Sheep, Ringwood or Skinners. Food is quality home cooked pub grub – bangers and mash, pies, ploughman's, burgers and sandwiches.

Visitor's note: The alley to the side of the pub leads to the ancient riverside access point of Wapping Old Stairs, where Jeffreys made the mistake of coming ashore for a pint.

⇌ Wapping 🚲 LCN+ Limehouse, Shoreditch, Tower ⏸ Thames Path

WAITROSE CANARY WHARF
Shop
Canada Place, E14 5EW
☎ (020) 7719 0300, ⊕ www.waitrose.com
🕐 7.30am-9pm Mon-Fri, 8.30-8 Sat; 12-6 Sun
Cask beer None, **Other beers** 100 bottles, beer gift packs, **Also** Full range of wines and spirits 🍴 Quality fast food to eat in, comprehensive supermarket range to take away, ♿

Waitrose Canary Warf

Perhaps surprisingly, the business district of Canary Wharf has also become a popular shopping destination, with a complex network of malls threading American-style through the basements of the office blocks. Sadly chain bars and eateries dominate the catering trade and those wishing to sit down with a nice pint are advised to veer away to the North Pole or the Gun (above). For take away beer, though, this big supermarket at the eastern end of the shopping complex is surprisingly rewarding. Waitrose is the upmarket grocery subsidiary of department store chain the John Lewis Partnership, one of the Britain's most successful workers' cooperatives. It's easily the best national supermarket for specialist beer, and this is one of its flagship stores. Many of the better distributed British bottle-conditioned ales are offered here at keen prices – Fuller's 1845 and Vintage Ale, Hog's Back TEA, Hook Norton Double Stout, Hop Back Summer Lightning, Meantime IPA and London Porter, St Austell Admiral's Ale, Wychwood Brakspear Triple – alongside quality West St Mungo Lager from Glasgow. Decent imported stuff includes Belgian 'champagne beer' Bosteels Deus, Budvar Dark, Nils Oscar God Lager from Sweden and decent own brand pale and dark Weissbier from Arcobräu in Bavaria. Check the website above for other branches.

⊖ Canary Wharf **DLR** Canary Wharf 🚲 Links to NCN1 and LCN+ Canning Town ⏸ Links to Thames Path, Lea Valley Path

HACKNEY

Once a one street Middlesex village popular with the Tudor gentry, Hackney succumbed to London's outward development with the arrival of the railway in 1850, though fragments of the past survive in the 13th-century church tower and the part-16th-century manor house of Sutton Place, now owned by the National Trust. In the 20th century it became one of London's poorest and most diverse communities, as well as a refuge for bohemians, squatters and alternative lifestylers attracted by the neglected local housing stock. Its cultural vibrancy helped drive the creation in the late 20th century of a Cultural Quarter centred on the Town Hall square, including a library, museum, the failed Ocean music venue, now being turned into a cinema, and the famous Hackney Empire, a surviving giant of the music hall era.

DOVE ☆ 25

Contemporary pub, bar
24-28 Broadway Market, E8 4QJ
☎ (020) 7275 7617, ⊕ www.dovepubs.com
⏱ 12-11 Mon-Thu; 12-midnight Fri & Sat; 12-11 Sun. *Children until 6pm*
Cask beers ✓ 6 (Brains, Crouch Vale, Timothy Taylor, 3 unusual guests), **Other beers** 9 keg, 100 bottles (Belgian), **Also** Wines, genever ⊞ Belgian and British pub grub, ⊞ Tables on street, small balcony
Wed & Sun jazz, annual Belgian beer festival, beer tastings, seasonal events

Broadway Market is another East End place with a story to tell about social change, and has become something of a local battleground for the gentrification debate. It's sited on an old drovers' route from Hackney, once used by farmers taking livestock to the City of London, and the street market and shops grew up in the mid-19th century to serve their needs. By the turn of the millennium the old community had moved on and the street had fallen into decline. Then, following a locally organised campaign and some deft public realm work by Hackney council, it was reinvented as one of the area's trendiest destinations, with the shops and Saturday market traders now selling handicrafts, organic foods and designer clothes.

   With its extensive specialist beer selection, good food and quirky but relaxed vibe, the Dove sits well here, but in fact its makeover from a Victorian boozer called the Goring Arms dates from the 1990s, long before the street's recent facelift. The place is bigger inside than it looks outside, unfolding as a series of eclectically decorated and often

crowded rooms, some with aged dark wood panelling and tiling, some brighter with odd pictures and bizarrely framed mirrors, and a cute little outdoor balcony at the back. The ceiling painting in the front bar – a pastiche of Michelangelo's *Creation* incorporating two glasses of Leffe at the crucial point – signals the national loyalties of the beer offer; indeed this is probably the nicest place to enjoy a

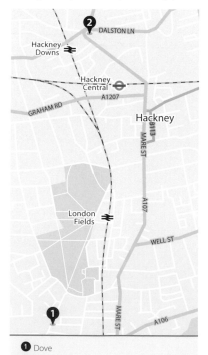

❶ Dove
❷ Pembury Tavern

Dove

good range of Belgian beers in London. Kegs including Palm Spéciale, Halve Maan Brugse Zot and Huyghe Delirium Tremens are complemented by an impressive list of bottles that taps five Trappist breweries, proper lambics from Boon and Mort Subite, and serious abbey beers from Slaghmuylder and St Feuillien. Pleasingly served alongside these are a solid range of British cask ales: Flowers IPA, Brewers Gold and Landlord are joined by guests likely to come from Dark Star, Mighty Oak or Salopian. The kitchen serves up Belgian classics – *carbonnade flamande* made with beer, fish soup *waterzooi*, mussels and chips – and international dishes like *kleftiko*, Thai curry and vegetarian cassoulet. Piped music and big screen TV are decidedly absent. The same company owns Dovetail in Clerkenwell (p69).

Visitor's note: Look out for the peculiar Leffe corner, an enclave of elaborately carved church-style Gothic pews.

≈ London Fields ⊖ Hackney Central, Shoreditch High Street ➡ Broadway Market (236 Canonbury - Hackney, 394 Shoreditch - Hackney) 🚲 LCN+16, Regents Canal towpath, links to CS1 ✈ Jubilee Greenway, London Fields paths

---

PEMBURY TAVERN
Contemporary pub
90 Amhurst Road, E8 1JH
☎ (020) 8986 8597
🌐 www.individualpubs.co.uk/pembury
⊙ 12-midnight Mon-Thu; 12-1am Fri & Sat; 12-11 Sun. *Children until 9pm*
Cask beers ✔ 8-10 (Milton, 1-2 unusual guests), **Other beers** 1 keg (Moravka),

13 bottles (Belgian, German), Also 15 malts
🍴 Pizzas, pub grub/gastro specials, 🪑 Benches on street in summer, ♿
3 beer festivals annually, occasional art fairs and live music, board games, bar billiards, pool

This big and imposing pub dominating the busy junction of Amhurst Road and Dalston Lane by Hackney Downs station was reopened in 2006 by the Individual Pubs Company after several years of dereliction following a fire. The pubco is linked to the Milton microbrewery on the outskirts of Cambridge (p302) so it's no surprise to see the long line of 16 handpumps on the bulky bar counter mainly dispensing selections from that company's extensive range of Classically named beers. The full compliment of pumps is only deployed during beer festivals when they're supplemented by additional beers on stillage, though a respectable nine or ten beers plus a cider are regularly on offer, always including Minotaur mild, golden session bitter Dionysus, pale and dark best bitters Sparta and Pegasus and dark strong ale Nero. The rest is made up of other Milton beers and guests from micros like Banks & Taylor, Hereford or Saltaire. Bottles include gems like Augustiner Hell, Orval, Schneider Weisse, Van Eecke Poperings Hommelbier and Verhaege Duchesse de Bourgogne. The interior is large and open with big chunky tables and a few more intimate enclosed spaces. With the basic but comfortable air of a community arts centre, despite the Cambridge connection it's Hackney through and through.

≈ Hackney Downs ⊖ Hackney Central 🚲 LCN+ Hackney, Shoreditch

LEYTON, LEYTONSTONE & WALTHAMSTOW

Among the outer reaches of the East End, Leyton and Walthamstow are strung out along the A112, which meanders north from Stratford along the east side of the Lee valley. Walthamstow in particular was an important village which still retains its historic centre (see Nags Head below) but the whole area was overwhelmed by terraced suburbia in the wake of the railways from the 1870s. Walthamstow has a proper old London outdoor market, dating from the 1880s. The town has recently developed a vibrant arts scene, coordinated through the E17 Art Trail. Leytonstone was the birthplace in 1899 of film director Alfred Hitchcock, whose work is celebrated in murals in the tube station. It's also right on the edge of the lower reaches of Epping Forest, which begins just on the other side of the ghastly Green Man roundabout at the end of the High Road. For more on the Forest see Kings Head (p137).

BIRKBECK TAVERN
Traditional pub
45 Langthorne Road, E11 4HL
☎ (020) 8539 2584
✪ 11-11 Mon-Thu; 11-midnight Fri & Sat; 12-11 Sun. *Children until 8pm*
Cask beers ✓ 4 (house beer, 3 unusual guests)
🍽 Rolls and sandwiches only, 🍺 Beer garden,
♿ No disabled toilet but all level access

Monthly folk club, home brewing meetings, functions, darts, pool, pub games, barbecues, charity nights

This local on a terraced back street south of Leyton station and the A12 is a long time real ale stalwart: landlady Kathy has worked here for two decades and she and her husband Richard now own the business. Inside it's a welcoming but functional drinking hole with

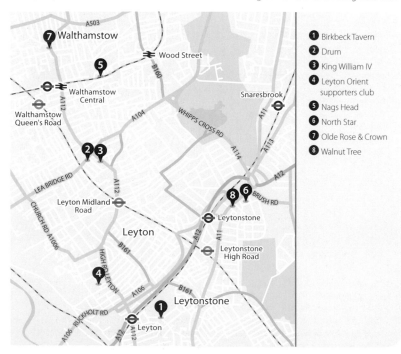

Map legend:
1. Birkbeck Tavern
2. Drum
3. King William IV
4. Leyton Orient supporters club
5. Nags Head
6. North Star
7. Olde Rose & Crown
8. Walnut Tree

a minimal food offer, and refreshingly brightly lit, with remnants of its original Victorian design. One side has a more public bar feel with a pool table; the other, bigger side is carpeted and includes what would have been a grand entrance with a fireplace and imposing staircase leading to the function room. A lovely garden at the back has flower beds and old chimney pots used as planters. It's a genuine free house, and draught ales include house bitter Rita's Special, its source a well kept secret but apparently "within the M25". Well-kept guests might come from Brentford, Brewster's, Cottage, Cotleigh, Mighty Oak, Slater's or Welton's and there's a try before you buy policy. A short walk from Leyton station and not far from the northeast corner of the Olympic Park (p134).

Insider tip! The pub is popular with the more discerning fans of nearby Leyton Orient FC and can get busy on match days, also welcoming well-behaved away supporters.

⊖ Leyton 🚲 LCN+ Leytonstone, Stratford

DRUM

Traditional pub
557-559 Lea Bridge Road, E10 7EQ
☎ (020) 8539 9845
🌐 www.jdwetherspoon.co.uk
✪ 9am-midnight Mon-Thu; 9am-1am Fri & Sat; 9am-midnight Sun. *Children welcome daytime if eating*
Cask beers ✔ 6-9 (Greene King, Brentwood, Nethergate, unusual guests), **Other beers** Usual Wetherspoon keg and bottles, **Also** 1 real cider/perry
🍴 Wetherspoon menu, 🏠 Side patio, ♿
Wed quiz, Wetherspoon beer festivals and promotions, occasional mini beer festivals featuring particular brewers

So named as it was once decorated by drums hanging from the ceiling, this became one of the first Wetherspoon pubs in 1986 and has survived as a rare small pub in the company's estate. Inside it still feels something like the Victorian corner boozer it once was, with what look like original tiled panels, some cosy and intimate spaces and a pleasant conservatory. Its commitment as a community pub is underlined by a friendly welcome and regular customer liaison meetings. There's an

Drum

exemplary cask ale policy supporting local brewers like Brentwood and Redemption, with the local CAMRA branch advising on what to stock. If you're impressed by the scale of the bigger Wetherspoon conversions while being underwhelmed by the atmosphere, you'll find the Drum an interesting comparison. At Leyton Green near the main A104/A112 junction on bus routes between Leyton and Walthamstow.

🚃 Stratford **DLR** Stratford ⊖ Leyton, Leyton Midland Road, Stratford 🚌 Leyton Green (69, 97 Leyton, Walthamstow Central; 257 Stratford) 🚲 LCN+ Walthamstow, Stratford

KING WILLIAM IV ☆ 25

Traditional pub, brewpub
816 High Road, E10 6AE
☎ (020) 8556 2460
✪ 11am-midnight Mon-Thu; 11-1am Fri & Sat; 11-midnight Sun. *Children until 9pm*
Cask beers ✔ 12-20 (Brodie's), **Other beers** 20-30 bottles (Brodie's), **Also** 1-2 real ciders/perries
🍴 Good value pub grub, 🏠 Tables on street, rear patio
Monthly jazz and music jam nights, darts, bar billiards, big screen sport, beer festivals

The biggest of three London pubs long owned by the Brodie family, and now the location of an extraordinarily prolific brewery in an outhouse across the side yard (p267).

King William IV

The building is a sprawling landmark on a site long associated with the licensed trade, though its present appearance dates from an 1891 reconstruction. A quirkily traditional interior is liberally dotted with the old musical instruments, copper kitchen equipment and other curiosities that characterise Brodie decor: a full sized vintage petrol pump, a sousaphone and several large and impressive engraved mirrors are among the more prominent exhibits. A big front bar is all deep red with banquettes lining the walls while through an arch is a more relaxing back room with an open fire and a bar billiards table. Food is simple but decent and good value: snacks, deli sandwiches, shepherd's pie, fish and chips, macaroni cheese.

At least 12 beers are on draught at once, sometimes 16, with an ambition to reach 20. It's quite likely all of them will be brewed in house by the inventive siblings Lizzie and James Brodie, in which case they'll be on sale at the uniform price of £1.99 a pint, though pump clips from the likes of Dark Star and Redemption occasionally interrupt the massed ranks of Brodiedom. English Best and IPA are the only regulars; the rest often include dark beers, especially in winter, and other specialities, like Amarilla, Mild, Olde Ardour, Red and Superior Porter. Even more own brands are available bottle conditioned, singly or in gift boxes, for consumption on or off the premises, including bottled variants of the draughts. Amazingly still more appear for the intermittent beer festivals. If you plan on working your way through the lot, you might find the upstairs eight bedroom hotel a welcome convenience.

Insider tip! Watch out for the occasional strong specialities, on sale for the same price as everything else. There can't be many places in the world where you can buy a 12.1% ABV Imperial stout at £1 a half pint, but do treat it with the respect it deserves!

⇌ Stratford **DLR** Stratford ⊖ Leyton, Leyton Midland Road, Stratford 🚋 Leyton Green (69, 97 Leyton, Walthamstow Central; 257 Stratford) 🚲 LCN+ Walthamstow, Stratford

LEYTON ORIENT SUPPORTERS CLUB
Social club
Matchroom Stadium, Oliver Road, E10 5NF
📞 (020) 8988 8288
🌐 www.orientsupporters.org
⚙ Times vary: see below
Cask beers ✔ 7 (Mighty Oak, 5 unusual guests), **Other beers** 2 bottles, **Also** 4 real ciders/perries, 8 malts
🎟 Filled rolls on match days only, 🚉 Standing room on terrace, ♿
Football matches, annual beer festival, fan events, quizzes, occasional big screen TV

Leyton Orient may currently only play in League One, in fact the third rung of English football, but its supporters' club has worked its way into the Premier League of beer venues. It all started in 1996 with one cask on the bar at the suggestion of a member, which proved so successful more were added, despite the challenges of a working in a Portakabin where the only way of keeping the beer cool was wet towels. Following a redevelopment of the Matchroom Stadium in 2006 the supporters gained their own purpose-built clubroom, a basic but large and comfortable space with a refrigerated beer store, from where friendly secretary and bar manager Mike Childs and his fellow volunteers dispense a great choice of beers. Maldon Gold and Oscar Wilde mild are always on, while the changing guests might include others from Mighty Oak alongside Burton Bridge, Goachers, Milk Street, O'Hanlon's, Oakham, Northumberland, Whitstable and more, all at keen prices.

Planning a visit requires reference to the O's' fixture calendar. The bar is open for 'Ale Nights' the Thursday before home matches (6-11pm), and immediately before and after the matches themselves, as well as for occasional special events and screenings of big international games: check the website or ring to confirm. Then there's the annual Piglet Beer Festival in early March where up to 30 beers are on offer. It's a members' club but drinkers carrying CAMRA membership cards or guides are welcome, as are well-behaved away supporters on match days. Lauded with numerous CAMRA national and regional Club of the Year awards which are proudly displayed beside the footie memorabilia, it's one of the most delightfully unexpected entries in this guide.

Insider tip! At the risk of stating the obvious, if you're here for the beer, go on an Ale Night – a relaxed contrast to the frenetic circumstances of match days.

Θ Leyton ⬳ LCN+ Walthamstow, Leytonstone, Stratford

NAGS HEAD
Contemporary pub
9 Orford Road, E17 9LP
☎ (020) 8520 9709
⊕ www.thenagsheade17.com
⊙ 4-11 Mon-Thu; 2-11 Fri; 12-11 Sat; 12-10.30 Sun. *Children outside only*
Cask beers ✔ 6 (Crouch Vale, Mighty Oak, St Austell, Timothy Taylor, 2 guests), **Other beers** 3 keg, 10 bottles (mainly Belgian fruits), **Also** Wines
🍴 Large beer garden
Weekly life drawing, belly dancing and pilates

classes, Sun pm jazz, book clubs, monthly wine tastings, occasional beer festivals

Just east of busy Hoe Street, and seemingly a world away, is the little-known, though now thoroughly gentrified, historic centre of Walthamstow Village, where St Mary's church, the 15th-century half-timbered Ancient House and the Vestry House museum form a picturesque cluster offset by a Victorian post box. A string of specialist restaurants on Orford Road is topped by this lovely pub, with a distinctive but tasteful and homely interior dating from a 2002 makeover: pine chairs, brown vinyl pouffes and towelling tablecloths. Wine is a feature, with regular tastings, but beer is certainly not forgotten: this is one of London's rare regular mild stockists, with Mighty Oak's delicious Oscar Wilde usually available, alongside Tribute, Brewers Gold, Landlord and guests that might come from Nethergate or Wychwood among others. Most of the Belgian bottles in the fridge are of the sweetened fruit variety but you might also spot De Koninck and Duvel, with Budvar, Leffe and Hoegaarden on keg. A bottled house beer brewed by Nethergate is named The Itinerant in honour of a visiting local cat. Felines are additionally honoured in the decoration and by events: they ran a cat-themed beer festival in 2010 and held a cat marriage to coincide with 2011's Royal Wedding. The pub's function as a community

Nags Head

centre is demonstrated by a busy diary of classes and other activities in the upstairs room. Perhaps surprisingly, there's no food other than bar snacks, but there are all those neighbouring restaurants and, as landlady Flossie puts it with refreshing honesty, "we're publicans, not restaurateurs."

Insider tip! In fine weather the pretty back garden is the favoured spot.

≋ Walthamstow Central ⊖ Walthamstow Central ⊟ W12 ⊚ LCN+9, links to Leyton, Stratford

North Star

NORTH STAR
Traditional pub
24 Browning Road, E11 3AR
☎ (020) 8989 5777
⊛ 4-11 Mon-Fri; 12-11 Sat; 12-10.30 Sun.
Children welcome daytime
Cask beers ✔ 5 (guests), **Other beers** 2 bottles
▥ Terrace and beer garden
Live music twice monthly, charity nights, darts, big screen sport

It's always reassuring when as a researcher you announce to bar staff that you're compiling a guide to London's best beer pubs and the eavesdropping regulars chorus enthusiastically that you've come to the right place. This unpretentious but thoroughly amenable and welcoming local hidden away in a Leytonstone backstreet, not far from the Green Man roundabout and part of Epping Forest, was the location of one such incident during the writing of this book. It's a traditional half-panelled place split into a

comfortable area with stools, benches and tables and a more functional one with dartboard and big screen. It boasts a good reputation for live music with outdoor gigs in the small but pretty beer garden in summer and a top quality jukebox the rest of the time. The rotating cask beers aren't particularly rare – Adnams Broadside, Caledonian Deuchars IPA, Hop Back GFB, Sharp's Doom Bar, and Taylor Landlord are regular visitors but they're in immaculate condition, and slightly more exotic choices from Otter or Wye Valley put in appearances too. They're also enthusiastic fundraisers with three events a year.

⊖ Leytonstone ⊚ LCN+ Wanstead, Redbridge, Stratford ⚏ Epping Forest Centenary Walk

OLDE ROSE & CROWN
Traditional pub
53-55 Hoe Street, E17 4SA
☎ (020) 8509 3880, ⊕ www.
yeolderoseandcrowntheatrepub.co.uk
⊛ 10-11 Mon-Thu; 10-midnight Fri & Sat; 12-11 Sun (no alcohol before 12pm). *Children very welcome*
Cask beers ✔ 3-6 (Adnams, Fuller's, Sharp's, Woodforde's, unusual guests), **Also** 2-3 ciders/ perries, malts
▥ Sandwiches, jacket potatos, homemade specials, ▥ Tables on street, ▤
Monthly open mic, film quiz, 78 records night, weekly folk club, fringe theatre, art gallery, functions, vintage clothing sales, pool and pub games

While I'm grateful for the more thoroughly preserved Victorian pubs listed in this book, there's a special delight in spotting surviving fragments of pub heritage in unexpected

Olde Rose & Crown

Walnut Tree

places. In this imposing street corner building at the northern end of Walthamstow's main street, you'll be intrigued by a small and oddly enclosed area to the right of the bar, where an impressive mosaic floor announces the pub's name. This was originally an entrance set back from the street, until someone claimed the space by building an off license in front of it that later became part of the drinking area. Other relics such as tiling, wall decorations and the remains of screens dot the fabric, sympathetically preserved in a 2008 refit under current landlords, Joanna and Panikos. They've turned it into a real community resource: a packed programme of quizzes, performances and DJs who work exclusively from 78s is complimented by full scale theatre shows, vintage clothing sales and art exhibitions. Food is simple but freshly cooked, including jacket potatoes, sandwiches, salads and hot specials. While Doom Bar, London Pride, Wherry and Adnams beers regularly recur on the bar, other casks might come from Coach House, Crouch Vale, Little Valley, Mauldons, Milestone or RCH, often with a darker beer and a good mix of gravities. One of those places that might persuade you to move house.

Insider tip! We like the raised space around the baby grand piano.

🚃 Walthamstow Central ⊖ Walthamstow Central 🚲 LCN+9, links to Leyton, Stratford

WALNUT TREE
Contemporary pub
857-861 High Street, E11 1HH
📞 (020) 8539 2526
🌐 www.jdwetherspoon.co.uk
🕗 8am-midnight Mon-Thu; 8am-1am Fri-Sun.
Children welcome daytime if eating
Cask beers ✅ 8-10 (Greene King, Wells & Young's, unusual guests), **Other beers** Usual Wetherspoon keg and bottles, **Also** 3 ciders/ perries
🍴 Wetherspoon menu, ☎ Side terrace, ♿
Wetherspoon beer festivals and promotions

In many respects this biggish pub on Leytonstone High Street is a standard issue Wetherspoon – a 1997 shop conversion with the usual mix of booths and high and low tables, including some along the large windowed glass front which are excellent for people watching. One distinctive feature is the unusual bronze walnut tree sculpture that illustrates the pub's name, while possibly also reminding drinkers of the proximity of Epping Forest. Another is the well chosen range of cask beers. The management are particularly keen on unusual guests, which might come from Nethergate or Cotleigh, and make an effort to obtain Greene King's strong Abbot Reserve when they can. They also aim for a good mix of dark and light, weak and strong, and operate a 'nominate a guest' policy. Worth a look.

⊖ Leytonstone 🚲 LCN+ Wanstead, Redbridge, Stratford 🚶 Epping Forest Centenary Walk

AROUND THE OLYMPIC PARK

Stratford, an historic market town at the point where the Roman road to Colchester crossed the river Lee, is the main gateway to the Olympic Park. This culturally diverse and economically deprived part of London is being transformed almost beyond recognition in preparation for the Olympic and Paralympic Games in 2012. Stratford International station, on the high speed line between St Pancras and the mainland, is already open, though only domestic high speed services to Kent currently stop there. Another new development adjacent to it, Stratford City, includes a massive shopping centre. The town is also home to the Discover national children's storytelling centre. This section also includes some other locations around the Olympic site.

BLACK LION
Traditional pub
59-61 High Street, E13 0AD
☎ (020) 8472 2351
⊕ www.blacklionplaistow.co.uk
✪ 11-11 Mon-Sat; 12-10.30 Sun. *Children welcome*
Cask beers ✪ 3-4 (Wells & Young's, guests)
🍴 Basic pub grub and sandwiches, 🍺 Beer garden
Big screen sport, functions

Traditionally boxing was, alongside football, one of the most important sports in East End culture, and for some East Enders a route out of poverty. The West Ham Boys Amateur Boxing Club, established in 1922, is one of the surviving centres of the sport, turning out a string of champions like Terry Spinks and

Nigel Benn. The club – which is currently fighting off the threat of redevelopment – stands in the precincts of this fascinating pub on Plaistow High Street. Despite numerous accretions it's still obvious this is an old roadside hostelry surviving from more rustic times, a sprawling place with a collection of outhouses and former stable blocks around an extensive courtyard that now provides an attractive beer garden. Parts are at least 500 years old though it was rebuilt as a coaching inn in 1747 and got a new frontage in 1875. Staff too tend to longevity – legendary barmaid Millie Morris worked here from 1929 to 1997.

There's a narrow, low-beamed main bar, and a separate, rather hidden quiet room, including a lovely bay window seat, that you

❶ Black Lion   ❸ Goldengrove
❷ Eleanor Arms   ❹ King Edward VII

either have to go outside or walk behind the counter to reach. This was once a popular drinking den for West Ham players whose Upton Park ground is only 15 minutes walk away. The pub gets busy on match days with (generally well-behaved) fans, some of whom have been known to confuse the cockerel logo dating from its days as a Courage house with the emblem of a rival North London team. Now a free house, it stocks Wells & Young's revival of Courage Best as a regular, alongside guests that might come from smaller brewers like Mighty Oak, Red Squirrel, Slater's or Welton's alongside bigger names like Adnams, Brains, St Austell or Theakstons. Food is basic pub grub of the sort that might help you refuel after 12 rounds in the ring or two halves on the pitch. It's a little way from the Olympic Park but well placed for the Greenway walking and cycling route along the Northern Outfall Sewer that leads straight to the Park's main southern entrance.

⊖ Plaistow ⮎ LCN+ Stratford, Upton Park, Greenway ⫽ Link to Capital Ring, Jubilee Greenway

ELEANOR ARMS
Traditional pub
460 Old Ford Road, E3 5JP
☎ (020) 8980 6992, ⊕ www.eleanorarms.co.uk, **tw** frankiepub
◷ 4-11 Mon; 12-11 Tue-Sat; 12-10.30 Sun
Cask beers ✓ 4 (Shepherd Neame, occasional guest), **Other beers** 8 bottles (Shepherd Neame)
🍴 Filled baguettes, 🌳 Beer garden, ♿
Monthly quizzes, jazz jams, open mic nights, occasional live bands, board games, shove ha'penny, pool, occasional big screen sport

Opened by Queen Victoria in 1845 as the first purpose-built major public park in London, Victoria Park was an early victory in the campaign for green refuges amid the polluted urban landscape. Currently in the throes of £4.5million restoration, the 'People's Park' is still a well used gem of a place. Its eastern edge is a stone's throw from the Olympic Park and it'll be used for some 2012 events, big screen relays and cycle parking. Cross the Hertford Union canal on the park's southern edge to reach Old Ford Road where the Eleanor Arms is one of the most inviting pubs in the area.

LONDON 2012 OLYMPICS

The Olympic and Paralympic Games are coming to Britain in 2012 on condition that they deliver something more than just a big sports event, including the regeneration of a massive 2.5 square kilometre expanse of formerly derelict and partly contaminated post-industrial land between Stratford, Hackney and Leyton. This site, now renamed the Queen Elizabeth Olympic Park to mark the Queen's Diamond Jubilee, will be the hub of the Games in August 2012. Several landmark venues such as the main Olympic Stadium and architecturally innovative Aquatics Centre and Velodrome are located here as well as the athletes' village and media centre. Afterwards it will be transformed into a whole new district on a scale which, as Mayor Boris Johnson has pointed out, hasn't been seen in London since Georgian times, including 11,000 new homes, a university and a major new landscaped urban park. The river Lee splits into various natural and artificial channels through the site, known as the Bow Back Rivers, and the landscaping will make full use of these, turning dirty drains into attractive water features.

For a closer look, visit the View Tube by Pudding Mill Lane DLR station (⊕ www.theviewtube.co.uk), walk or cycle along the western perimeter on the Capital Ring and Lea Valley Path, book one of the free bus tours of the site itself (☎ 0300 2012 001), or join a (paid-for) guided walk of the area. Note that events are also taking place at other London venues including Greenwich (p178) and Hyde Park (Carpenters Arms p98, Star p118), and outside London – for more on this and everything else to do with the Games, visit ⊕ www.

Once a Fuller's house, it was one of a batch in London bought by Kent brewer Shepherd Neame (p310) in the late 1980s and is a great showcase for their beers – Kent's Best is a regular, Master Brew and Bishop's Finger are usually on and the quartet is completed by a seasonal. An extensive range of Shep's bottled beers is also on offer including bottle conditioned 1698 and the tasty organic beer Whitstable Bay. Music loving landlords Frankie and Lesley have decorated the place with classic rock posters, old advertising and quirky art and strewn it with a comfortable mix of tables and sofas to create a welcoming community space.

⊖ Bow Road, Bethnal Green **DLR** Bow Church 🚍 Old Ford Road (8 Bethnal Green - Bow Church) 🚲 NCN1, LCN+16, Regents and Hertford Union towpaths, Hackney Parks Olympic Greenway 🚶 Jubilee Greenway, Regents Canal towpath, link to Capital Ring and Lea Valley Path, Victoria Park paths

GOLDENGROVE
Contemporary pub
146-148 The Grove, E15 1NS
🔖 (020) 8519 0750, ⊕ www.jdwetherspoon.co.uk
☸ 7am-midnight daily. *Children welcome daytime if eating*
Cask beers ✔ 7 (Greene King, Wells & Young's, guests), **Other beers** Usual Wetherspoon keg and bottles, **Also** 1 real cider / perry
🍽 Wetherspoon menu, 🌳 Rear patio, ♿

Just on the edge of Stratford's town centre, this plain but popular community Wetherspoon's offers a range of well-kept cask beers that's more adventurous than average: I spotted Thornbridge, Cotleigh and Maxim. The most sought-after tables are in the booths down the left hand side of the otherwise slightly cramped space. It's just round the corner from Stratford Cultural Quarter with its famous Theatre Royal – wall displays in the pub give some history – and the name is a reference to the work of the eccentric pioneering modernist poet Gerard Manley Hopkins who was born in the town in 1844.

🚆 Maryland ⊖ Stratford **DLR** Stratford 🚲 NCN 1, LCN+ 16, Limehouse Cut and Epping Forest Greenways 🚶 Capital Ring, Jubilee Greenway, Lea Valley Walk

KING EDWARD VII
Traditional pub
47 Broadway, E15 4BQ
🔖 (020) 8534 2313, ⊕ www.kingeddie.co.uk
☸ 12-11 Mon-Wed; 12-midnight Thu-Sat; 12-11.30 Sun
Cask beers ✔ 4 (Nethergate house beer, Wells & Young's, Sharp's, 1 guest), **Other beers** 5 bottles, **Also** Specialist whisky and vodka, wines
🍽 Pub grub/gastro menu, 🌳 Rear patio
Thu open mike, Sun quiz

There are few distinctive buildings besides the huge 1830s St John's church on Stratford town centre's Broadway, but one of them is the Grade II listed King Edward VII, a wide, squat green-painted Victorian structure squeezed incongruously between two taller blocks. The low-ceilinged front bar inside, with its beams and engraved glass alcoves, still retains a rustic atmosphere appropriate to a former Essex market town. Behind it is an airy dining room with skylights, and down a tiled corridor at the side a saloon bar replete with leather armchairs. A decent menu features game and seafood with a good few veggie options, enjoyed while restrained Motown hits play in the background. The beer choice isn't huge but it's in good nick: the house beer from Nethergate (a rebadged Three Point Nine) is a decent session bitter and guests can include Cottage and Hook Norton. Bottle

King Edward VII

conditioned ales and specialities like Innis & Gunn occasionally appear. Reckoned by many to be the best pub in Stratford, it can get busy, so consider booking a table if you want to eat.

Pub trivia: The pub was originally named the King of Prussia but patriotically renamed during World War I – look for the profile of Edward VII etched into one of the windows.

≋ Stratford ⊖ Stratford **DLR** Stratford ⮱ NCN 1, LCN+ 16, Limehouse Cut and Epping Forest Greenways ⫽ Capital Ring, Jubilee Greenway, Lea Valley Walk

OTHER LOCATIONS

CHINGFORD

KINGS HEAD
Contemporary pub
2B Kings Head Hill, E4 7EA
☎ (020) 8529 6283
⊙ 12-11 Mon-Wed; 12-midnight Thu-Sat; 12-11 Sun. *Children 14+ welcome if eating*
Cask beers ✔ 6 (Adnams, Fuller's, Greene King, Timothy Taylor, 2 guests), **Also** Wines
⊕ Pub grub, ⊞ Beer garden backing onto forest, ♿
Tue grill night, Wed & Sun quiz, Thu curry night

Epping Forest on the eastern slope of the Lee Valley was a prize jewel in the 19th-century struggle of local people and conservationists to save as much of London's countryside as possible for public enjoyment as the city expanded – the patchwork texture of today's capital, with its substantial tracts of green space, is their legacy.

Designated a royal hunting forest in the 12th century, the forest was already much reduced in 1878 when a parliamentary Act protected the remaining open space and passed it into the care of the City of London, which still administers it today. Many of the best known visitor honeypots are outside the London boundary, but the green wedge drives deep into east London, and forest lands include not only woodlands of ancient pollarded trees but parkland and heath.

Chingford is one of the forest's gateway towns but the pubs near the tube station and better known monuments like Queen Elizabeth's Hunting Lodge are disappointing. Much better is this old place on the summit of a hill named after it, which backs onto a finger of forest land. It now boasts with some justification that it's the best real ale pub in the area – besides Greene King IPA, Taylor Landlord and London Pride the knowledgeable bar staff might be serving Acorn, Brains, Copper Dragon, Thwaites, White Shield or Wolf, with suggestions invited from drinkers. Inside it's quite big with various drinking and dining spaces, a bit too much like a furniture showroom but comfortable enough as a rendezvous after a woodland stroll. See under Leyton (p128) for southern access points to the forest.

Visitor's note: Before you go through the front door, look left to admire the commanding view over the Lee Valley.

≋ Chingford, Walthamstow Central ⊖ Walthamstow Central, Walthamstow Queens Road ⧫ Kings Head Hill (97 Walthamstow, 313, 379 Chingford) ⮱ Link to NCN1 ⫽ Link to London Loop and Epping Forest Centenary Walk

CLAPTON

ANCHOR & HOPE
Traditional pub
15 High Hill Ferry, E5 9HG
☎ (020) 8806 1730, ⊕ www.fullers.co.uk
⊙ 1-11 Mon-Thu; 12-11 Fri & Sat; 12-10.30 Sun.
Children welcome
Cask beers ✔ 3 (Fuller's), **Other beers** 5-6 bottles (Fuller's)
⊕ Filled rolls, ⊞ Benches overlooking river
Occasional quizzes, film nights, live music, barbecues in summer

From the lovely formal gardens of Springfield Park in Clapton you descend sharply through a wildflower meadow to meet the broad floor of the Lee Valley and the wide open wetlands of Walthamstow marshes, where aviation pioneer A V Roe flew the first all-British aircraft in 1909, stretching out beyond the busy marina on the River Lee Navigation. The marshes are part of the Lee Valley Park, a magnificent chain of green spaces linking Ware in Hertfordshire to the Lee's confluence with the Thames near Blackwall, set aside for recreation and conservation by Act of Parliament thanks to local campaigning in the 1960s. Just to the south, the High Hill Ferry once plied across the river, and its ferry house remains as this small, unspoilt and irregularly shaped corner pub. Former landlord Les Heath dispensed over 9 million pints here during a tenure of more than half a century until his death in 2003. When he arrived the beer was supplied by now defunct Ipswich brewer Tolly Cobbold's Walthamstow subsidiary and the pub is still known locally as the Tolly House although Fuller's griffin has long stood astride the sign. Wisely the current owners have changed little since Ted departed: it's still a basic boozer with a lino floor, open fire and three excellently kept cask beers including Pride, ESB and a seasonal, with 1845 among the bottles in the fridge. The quality of the beer is assisted by the short length of the pipes from the small cellar, which is cooled by the proximity of the river. It's a relatively short walk from Stoke Newington (p158) on the Capital Ring, and popular with walkers and cyclists enjoying the towpath and marshes.

Visitor's note: If exploring the surroundings, don't be surprised to see orthodox Hasidic Jews wandering the streets and park in traditional dress, especially on Saturdays. The area is home to the biggest community of Hasidim outside Israel and New York City.

≋ Clapton ⊟ Mount Pleasant Lane (393 Stoke Newington – Clapton) ⌖ NCN1, Lee Navigation towpath and Lee Valley Olympic Greenways ✦✦ Capital Ring, Lea Valley Path

Anchor & Hope

UPMINSTER

THATCHED HOUSE
Contemporary pub, restaurant
St Marys Lane, Upminster, RM14 3LT
☎ (01708) 641408, ⊕ www.vintageinn.co.uk
✪ 12-11 Mon-Sat; 12-10.30 Sun. *Children very welcome*
Cask beers ✔ 4 (Adnams, Fuller's, Greene King, 1 guest), **Other beers** 2-3 keg, **Also** Wines
⑪ Upmarket pub grub, ▦ Rear patio, ♿
Wed steak night, Fri fish night

Sadly now sporting a solidly tiled roof, but still in an impressively rustic setting, the Thatched House is perched on London's eastern edge in Thames Chase Community Forest, an expansive near-100 square kilometre tract of country parks, woodlands and previously derelict green belt land that's become one of the success stories of London's urban fringe. Buses are sparse, with none on Sundays, and it's a stretch of the legs through outer suburbia from Upminster station – a more inviting way of approaching it is on foot or by bike along the lane from the innovative Forest Visitor Centre, a quarter of an hour's walk away, though there's also a sizable car park. Inside it's quite posh but cosy, like the lobby of a decent country hotel. Diners get the biggest space with a view through big windows to open ground at the back, but the bar area is pleasant too, with an open fire and luxurious armchairs. Food is country cooking, with forest mushroom gratin, hunter's chicken or beef and ale pie, and it's inevitably popular for Sunday roasts. It's one of Mitchells & Butlers Vintage Inns pubs and though the regular beers are a well served but unsurprising trio of London Pride, Greene King IPA and Adnams Bitter, the guest might stretch to Williams Brothers' Fraoch Heather Ale or Thornbridge Jaipur.

Further info: Detailed information and maps of the Community Forest can be found at ⊕ www. thameschase.org.uk

≋ Upminster ✆ Upminster ⊟ Pond Walk (346 then 750m walk), Winchester Avenue (347, hourly, not Sun) ⌖ Thames Chase routes ✦✦ On paths from Upminster Park to Thames Chase Visitor Centre

NORTH LONDON

North London in this book includes all the N and NW postcodes outside the central area, and points north to the boundary of Hertfordshire.

London sprawled ever further northwards throughout the 19th century, swallowing wayside villages as new horse-drawn bus services along the numerous north-south roads, soon followed by railways, widened opportunities for commuting. North London always had a more mixed residential complexion than the proletarian east. Parts of it were just as poor, receiving their share of former slum dwellers displaced by the new rail terminals and other major works in the central area. Before Camden dressed its children in black and Islington gave the world New Labour, there were large parts of both boroughs where even the police feared to tread.

Today there are still plenty of earthier districts where unregenerated 1960s council estates sprout abruptly beside gentrified Victorian streets, but interspersed between these are the leafier suburbs, often occupying the numerous hills where the air was fresher and established village centres provided attractive nuclei for the burgeoning terraced houses. Hampstead, with its magnificent Heath, is the most famous example of the boho-posh London village, with neighbouring Highgate not far behind. Our survey extends to Barnet and Enfield, important historic towns in their own right but now part of the outer reaches of Greater London – between them lies some fine greenbelt countryside in Watling Chase Community Forest.

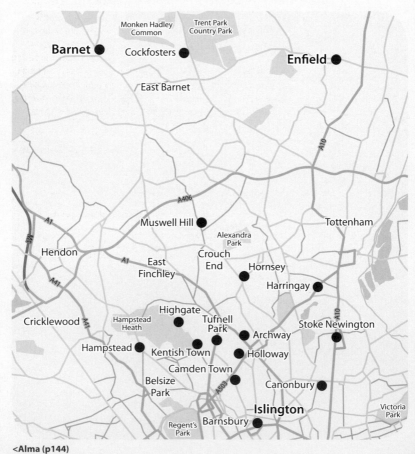

<Alma (p144)

CAMDEN TOWN

Camden Town is now one of London's top alternative tourist attractions, with tens of thousands of visitors pouring into the area every weekend, attracted by the vast acres of market stalls and shops stocking youth fashions, art, crafts and music.

Of the markets, only Inverness Street is truly historic – the rest date back no further than 1972, when a small weekend craft market opened in a former timber yard at Camden Lock. Business exploded in the post-punk 1980s and the association with youth and music culture was further underlined when MTV took over the TV-am studios as its UK headquarters. The other big attractions in the area are Regent's Park, one of London's loveliest Royal Parks, to the southwest and, within it, ZSL (Zoological Society of London), still known to everyone but the brand police simply as London Zoo. Really good beer outlets are sadly still rare but the growing interest among informed younger drinkers has driven some recent improvements. The smart new Camden Town Brewery (p268) is actually technically in Kentish Town (p154).

BELGO NOORD

Restaurant, bar
72-73 Chalk Farm Road, NW1 8AN
☎ (020) 7267 0718
⊕ www.belgo-restaurants.co.uk, **fbk**
⊙ 12-11 Mon-Fri; 12-11.30 Sat; 12-10.30 Sun.
Children welcome
Cask beer None, **Other beers** 4 keg, 65+
Belgian bottles, **Also** Genever
🍴 Belgian/international menu

This is the original Belgo, opened in 1992, but despite a redesign incorporating arched ceilings and a stylish bar, it's now probably the least amenable branch of the Belgian-themed mussels, chips and beer chain. Food and beer follow the Belgo Centraal model (p73) and though the draughts are limited there are some undisputed high scorers in bottles including Orval, Rochefort, Saison Dupont, Rodenbach Grand Cru, Boon Oude Geuze and Mariage Parfait and St Bernardus Grottenbier. It's mainly operated as a dining destination, though a small upstairs bar is open from 5pm on Friday and Saturday for those who just want to drink.

⊖ Chalk Farm 🚲 LCN+ 6A, Swiss Cottage 🚶 Jubilee Greenway

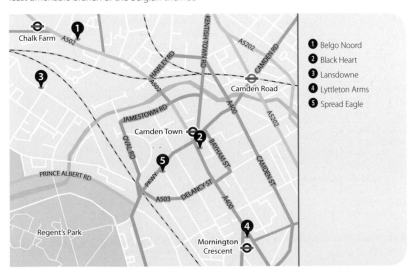

1 Belgo Noord
2 Black Heart
3 Lansdowne
4 Lyttleton Arms
5 Spread Eagle

BLACK HEART

Bar
3 Greenland Place, NW1 0AP
📞 (020) 7428 9730, 🌐 www.ourblackheart.com,
fbk, tw Theblack_heart
🕐 12-midnight Mon-Thu; 12-1am Fri & Sat;
12-midnight Sun. *Children until early evening*
Cask beers ✅ 2 (Camden Town, Wells &
Young's), **Other beers** 5 keg, 8 bottles, **Also**
Specialist spirits, wines
🍕 Pizzas and snacks, ♿
Tue & Wed comedy, Thu-Sat DJs, functions

Very close to Camden Town tube but hidden
in an alley between Camden High Street and
Bayham Street, the Black Heart isn't made
easier to spot on a dark night by the model
black heart that serves as a pub sign. It's part
of the small and youthful Barworks chain,
which makes a point of offering decent beer
to its funky partying clientele. The chain also
includes the brash Wenlock & Essex (p89) but
the Black Heart is much smaller, friendlier and
more intimate, despite the matt black interior
and the choice collection of Catholic tat and
skulls deployed ironically by way of
decoration. In a welcome move, Wells
Bombardier has recently been displaced on
cask by Camden Town products; more of the
local brewer's beers are on keg alongside
Paulaner lager and Erdinger wheat beer and a
small but well chosen bottled range that
stretches to Anchor Liberty Ale from San
Francisco. Upstairs events include a club night
by the name of 'Eat Your Own Sick'. I have to
say I'd prefer one of the authentic American
pizzas washed down with a pint of locally
brewed cask ale.

🚇 Camden Town 🚲 LCN+ 6A, Swiss Cottage
♦ Jubilee Greenway

LANSDOWNE

Gastropub
90 Gloucester Avenue, NW1 8HX
📞 (020) 7483 0409
🌐 www.thelansdownepub.co.uk
🕐 12-11 Mon-Fri; 10am-11 Sat; 10am-10.30 Sun.
Children welcome
Cask beers ✅ 2 (Adnams, Wells & Young's),
Other beers 3 bottles, **Also** Wines
🍕 Pizzas and gastro menu, 🚲 Tables on
street, ♿
Regular wine matching dinners

Among the residential streets of Primrose Hill
on the other side of the railway lines from
Camden's main drag, and not far from both
the hill itself and the English Folk Dance and
Song Society's headquarters at Cecil Sharp
House, this veteran gastropub, opened in its
current guise in 1992, is a classic of its genre.
The cream-coloured exterior still carries
Charrington lettered tiling.

Downstairs has big wooden tables for
drinking or grazing on quality pizzas, while
the delightfully elegant upstairs restaurant
(booking advisable) offers a serious menu that
might include cornfed chicken, bacon and
mushroom pie, lamb steak with tapenade and
celeriac mash or spiced potatoes with black
beans and coriander salsa. While decidedly
gastro it's also still a pub, and manager Megan
told me cheerfully that "dogs, drunkards and
kids are welcome so long as they behave
themselves." Bombardier is the regular but the
Adnams beers rotate with the Southwold
brewer's rich Old Ale on offer when I visited.
The tenants are currently in the process of
buying the freehold and plan to increase the
beer range in future.

🚇 Chalk Farm 🚲 LCN+ link to Swiss Cottage,
Kentish Town ♦ Links to Belsize Walk and
Jubilee Greenway

LYTTLETON ARMS

Contemporary pub
1 Camden High Street, NW1 7JE
📞 (020) 7387 2749
🌐 www.thelyttletonarmscamden.co.uk
🕐 11-midnight daily. *Children until 8pm (earlier
if major event nearby)*

Lyttleton Arms

Cask beers ✅ 4-5 (unusual guests), **Other beers** 6 keg, **Also** 1 real cider
🍴 Enhanced pub grub/gastro menu, 🪑 Tables on street, ♿
Fri & Sat DJs, Sun quiz, occasional live music and comedy, tasting evenings, board games, functions

In yet more evidence of the growing interest in quality beer among a younger generation of London drinkers, when Mitchells & Butlers overhauled the Southampton Arms opposite Mornington Crescent tube in 2010, they set out to attract a more vibrant customer base partly by improving the range of beers. This big, brash pub, renamed in honour of the late jazz trumpeter and radio presenter Humphrey Lyttleton, does good trade from its neighbours, the trendy Koko music venue, current incarnation of the Camden Palace, and the old Black Cat cigarette factory, now renamed Greater London House and home to numerous media and creative firms. In pride of place on the bar are four changing guest ales, often inventive and unusual creations from brewers like Castle Rock, Copper Dragon, Saltaire or Williams Brothers – Cropton's Yorkshire-brewed cask version of Michigan micro North Peak's Vicious American Wheat was on offer when I called, served up by staff whom manager Ian assures me are thoroughly trained in beer appreciation. A range of international kegs includes imported Brooklyn Lager while Duvel and Sierra Nevada Pale Ale are the pick of the bottled range. Characterful food options might include beef brisket, vegetable tart or pigeon. The brown leather furniture, retro standard lamps and toy panthers might be a little too self consciously quirky for some tastes and the music would be way too loud for Humph, but this is still a welcome new arrival.

⊖ Mornington Crescent 🚲 LCN+ 6A, link to 6
🚶 Links to Belsize Walk and Jubilee Greenway

SPREAD EAGLE
Traditional pub
141 Albert Street, NW1 7NB
📞 (020) 7267 1410, ✉ spreadeagle.camden@youngs.co.uk, 🌐 www.youngs.co.uk
🕐 11-11 Mon-Thu, 11-midnight Fri & Sat; 12-11.30 Sun. *Children until 8pm*

Spread Eagle

Cask beers ✅ 5 (Wells & Young's, occasional guests)
🍴 Enhanced pub grub, 🪑 Tables on street
Tue quiz, occasional DJs

The Spread Eagle would be a modest gem wherever it was located but as one of only a tiny handful of traditional pubs left among the boom box bars of style conscious Camden it's especially worthy of note – a fact that hasn't escaped the locals who regularly pack it out at weekends. It's a pleasant and civilised wood-panelled place with a choice of stools, high and low tables and comfy booths, dividing neatly into front and rear spaces. As a Young's house it serves top rate Bitter, Special and Bombardier as regulars, with seasonals and specials from the Wells & Young's range and Sambrook's featuring periodically. There's also a small collection of bottles including Young's Special London Ale, while pies, bangers and veggie curries typify the food menu. In a small concession to Camden culture, DJ Wheelybag spins rockabilly tunes on a monthly basis.

Insider tip! There are two options for best seats in the house – the cushions on the front bay window which are perfect for people watching, or the secluded sofas under the stairs.

⊖ Camden Road, Camden Town 🚲 LCN+ 6A, Swiss Cottage 🚶 Jubilee Greenway, Belsize Walk

CANONBURY & BARNSBURY

This section covers the northern part of London N1 and nearby bits of N5; more southerly outlets, closer to Angel and other Zone 1 stations, are dealt with under Islington (p86) and Old Street (p95) in the Central London chapter.

The backbone of the area is the Great North Road – Upper Street and Holloway Road – with Barnsbury in the west and Canonbury in the east. The former was once a Georgian semi-rural retreat and still maintains some impressive terraces. The latter, built on land owned by the canons of St Bartholemew's priory, was a 19th century development that fell on poorer times but has since been partially gentrified. The open space of Highbury Fields is just to the north and the course of the New River can be traced via a series of linear gardens (see also Three Compasses p163). Both Evelyn Waugh and keen pubgoer George Orwell once lived in Canonbury Square.

ALMA
Gastropub
59 Newington Green Road, N1 4QU
📞 (020) 7359 4536
🌐 www.thealma-n1.co.uk, **fbk**
⏰ 5-11 Mon-Wed; 11.30-11 Thu;
11.30-midnight Fri & Sat; 11.30-10.30 Sun.
Children until 9.30pm
Cask beers ✅ 2 (usually Redemption, 1 unusual/local guest), **Other beers** 3 bottles (New Zealand), **Also** Wines
🍴 Gastro menu, 🚪 Rear patio
Occasional quizzes, seasonal themed nights, tastings, board games

The fact that this bow fronted, atmospheric pub is run by New Zealander Kirsty Valentine

explains the curious presence of iconic kiwi foodstuffs like Wattie's tomato sauce and Minties, not to mention Speight's and Monteith's bottled beers, behind its lovely old horseshoe bar. Otherwise it's a fine North London gastropub, all deep red decor, worn wooden tables and elaborately inscribed chalkboards, with a cluster of sofas under a decorated ceiling at the back. An imaginative menu might include pan-fried swordfish, aubergine parmigiana or Barnsley lamb chop. The cask range is relatively small but a commitment to local producers means Redemption beers are regularly available, though the choice changes to suit seasonal

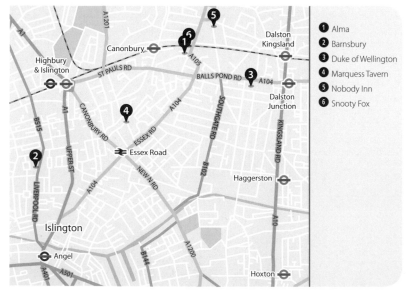

1. Alma
2. Barnsbury
3. Duke of Wellington
4. Marquess Tavern
5. Nobody Inn
6. Snooty Fox

Barnsbury

promotions. The back yard is very pleasant and the piano occasionally springs into action.

Insider tip! Check out the summer 'Picnic in the Park' service offering your choice of food from the menu packed up and ready to go with plates and cutlery.

⊖ Angel, Canonbury 🚇 Beresford Road (numerous from Angel) 🚲 LCN+ Kings Cross, Stoke Newington ⁄⁄ New River Path

BARNSBURY
Contemporary pub, specialist
209 Liverpool Road, N1 1LX
📞 (020) 7607 5519, ⊕ www.thebarnsbury.
co.uk, **tw** thebarnsburypub
⚙ 11-11 Mon-Sat; 11-10.30 Sun. *Children very welcome*
Cask beers 4-6 (St Austell or Triple fff, unusual guests), **Other beers** 3 keg, 10 bottles, **Also** Wines, malts
⑩ Upmarket pub grub, 🏠 Rear patio
Occasional themed nights and big screen sport

Islington's beer culture climbed a couple of notches in summer 2010 when new owners refurbished this pub not far off Upper Street and instituted a policy of rotating real ales from small independent breweries supplemented by a range of imported bottles. They've been counting the various cask beers served since – the total should be well into triple figures by the time you read this, triggering a donation to charity. Alton's Pride and Tribute regularly recur but others could

come from Acorn, Elgoods, Loddon, Oakham, Stonehenge, Tring or Wolf, and if you're unsure which to choose, tasting samples are gladly offered. The bottles are also set to vary but when I called they included luscious Brooklyn Black Chocolate Stout, Achouffe McChouffe and Schneider Weisse. Food runs from decent bar snacks like quality Scotch eggs and sausage rolls to pan fried duck breast and wild mushroom risotto, served under wine glass chandeliers in the clean, bright space around the horseshoe bar at the front or in the separate rear dining area. The top choice in the area for its interesting range.

Insider tip! The Mediterranean style patio at the back is a delight in fine weather.

⊖ Angel, Highbury & Islington 🚇 Islington Town Hall (numerous from Angel) 🚲 LCN+ Clerkenwell, Holloway, Hackney, link to LCN+16 ⁄⁄ Link to Jubilee Greenway

DUKE OF WELLINGTON
Contemporary pub
119 Balls Pond Road, N1 4BL
📞 (020) 7275 7640
⊕ www.thedukeofwellingtonn1.com, **fbk**,
tw TheDukeN1
⚙ 3-midnight Mon-Wed; 3-1am Thu & Fri; 11-1am Sat; 12-11.30 Sun. *Children until 8pm*
Cask beers ✅ 4 (Sambrook's, 3 unusual guests), **Other beers** 3 keg, **Also** Wines
⑩ Gastro/enhanced pub grub, 🏠 Tables on street, ♿

2 annual beer festivals, monthly film club, dinner club, games night, Mon table tennis, Thu eclectic DJ, big screen sport

A big roadside pub that though officially in Islington is practically in Dalston, the Duke of Wellington has stood here since 1842 though the current building shows signs of later Victorian refurbishment. It received a contemporary makeover in 2008 that polished its heart as a comfortable, sprawling community boozer. It now hosts a packed programme of events that includes beer festivals in January and autumn where up to 30 beers are on offer thanks to temporary stillages, expanding on a more modest everyday range that always features Sambrook's Wandle plus guests that might come from Ascot, Brodie's, Oxford or Skinners. The main drinking area retains its handsome island bar, etched glass, tiled fireplace and pillars while one of the mosaic-floored porches has been converted into a tiny snug. The screening room at the back, where the entertainment choices run from Premier League football to Ingmar Bergman, is more chilled with sofas and cushions. The menu tempts with Saturday brunches and options like potted shrimp, goat's cheese and leek pastry, warm salads, wild boar sausage and bream. The place works hard to get maximum returns from an Enterprise tenancy, making full use of the direct delivery scheme – it'll be interesting to see what the proprietors achieve in their free-of-tie second venue, the very different but at least as interesting Mason & Taylor in Shoreditch (p103).

Insider tip! Card-carrying CAMRA members should remember to ask for a discount on cask beer.

⊖ Dalston Kingsland, Dalston Junction ⊗⊚ LCN+ Stoke Newington, Shoreditch, Islington

MARQUESS TAVERN

Gastropub
32 Canonbury Street, N1 2TB
☎ (020) 7394 2975
⊕ www.marquesstavern.co.uk, **fbk**
🕐 5-11 Mon-Thu; 4-midnight Fri; 12-midnight Sat; 12-10.30 Sun. *Children welcome*
Cask beers ✔ 3 (Wells & Young's, occasional guests), **Other beers** 20-25 bottles, **Also** Malts, wines including English
🍽 Gastro menu, ⛱ Small front terrace
Tue quiz, Thu film night

The reinvention of this elegant Young's house as an award-winning gastropub with a solid beer focus a few years back was overseen by beer and wine writer Fiona Beckett and her son Will, authors of CAMRA's *An Appetite for Ale*. The Becketts have moved on but the current owners have changed little, retaining the classic bottled beer list and the menu's focus on seasonal ingredients. The stripped wood bar and outdoor tables are a pleasant environment while the dining room, with its mirrors, pilasters, skylight and decorated ceiling, is a

Marquess Tavern

stunning space. Don't expect cheap pub grub – the kitchen is renowned for its range of steaks alongside choices like Guinness battered haddock, salt baked beetroot and pheasant breast. Bitter, Special and a Young's seasonal or a guest that might be St Austell Tribute are on offer from the handpumps, while the aforementioned bottled list includes Coopers Sparkling Ale, Westmalle, the bone dry north German pilsner Jever, Williams Brothers Fraoch Heather Ale and Coniston Bluebird. My only niggle was the background music, which was a tad too loud on my visit.

Pub trivia: The New River used to run through the strip of public gardens right beside the pub.

⇌ Highbury & Islington ⊖ Angel, Highbury & Islington 🚌 Essex Road (271 Highbury, numerous Angel) ⊗⊚ LCN+ Camden, Hackney, Dalston, Islington, links to CS12 ⊘ New River Path

NORTH LONDON

Snooty Fox

NOBODY INN
Contemporary pub
92 Mildmay Park, N1 4PR
☎ (020) 7249 6430, **tw** nobodyn1
🕐 12-11 Mon-Wed; 12-midnight Thu-Sat; 12-11
Sun. *Children lunchtime if eating*
Cask beers ✔ 4 (St Austell or Sharp's, 3 often
local guests), **Other beers** 2 keg (Camden
Town), 8 bottles, **Also** Occasional real cider
🍴 Thai menu
*Meet the Brewer events, Fri film nights, Thu quiz,
big screen sport, pool, board games*

The name might make you wince, but this
characterful community pub on a corner of
Newington Green is more likely to make you
smile. It's an old place with a high decorated
ceiling that's taken on a pleasantly shambolic
new image, with art on the walls and a corner
occupied by an old fashioned red phone box
filled with balloons. Big screen sport often
dominates one side but the L-shaped bar
provides plenty of opportunity to escape it.
Tribute or Doom Bar is usually available, while
the guest cask beers might come from local
brewers Camden Town or Redemption as well
as perhaps Brains, Dark Star or Skinners. Fuller's
1845 and Duvel are the pick of the bottles. Thai
kitchen the Black Orchid (see also John Baird
p164) shares the premises, providing a full
menu including an express set lunch at £6.

⊖ Angel, Canonbury 🚆 Newington Green
(numerous, Angel) 🚲 Links to LCN+ Stoke
Newington, Dalston, Shoreditch, Finsbury Park,
Islington

SNOOTY FOX
Contemporary pub
75 Grosvenor Avenue, N5 2NN
☎ (020) 7354 0094
🕐 4-11 Mon-Thu; 4-1am Fri; 12-1am Sat;
12-10.30 Sun. *Children until 9pm*
Cask beers ✔ 3 (St Austell, Redemption,
1 unusual/local guest), **Also** 1 real cider
🍴 Imaginative pub grub, 🌳 Front terrace
*Tue quiz, Sat DJs, twice montly live jazz, monthly
ukelele open mic, two annual beer festivals,
jukebox, board games*

A modern, comfortable and not at all snooty
Enterprise tenancy just across from
Canonbury Overground station, this is a very
musical Fox, with a great collection of classic
rock and pop pics and a well-stocked jukebox,
and there can't be many pubs that boast a
monthly ukelele open mic night. Food might
include herb crusted salmon or halloumi
kebabs. They're also working hard on their
beer, supporting local breweries like
Sambrook's and Redemption and sourcing
others from further afield from the likes of
Exmoor, Otter, Nelson, Nethergate and
Westerham through the SIBA Direct Delivery
Scheme. Imaginatively themed beer festivals
boost the range – a recent Hit the North
festival saw Northern soul DJs providing a
classy accompaniment to the consumption
of 16 beers from the North of England. Keep
the faith!

⊖ Canonbury 🚲 LCN+ Kings Cross, Stoke
Newington 🚶 New River Path

MPSTEAD

Hampstead is the archetypal London village, and one of its most desirable residential areas. Although it has a history of radicalism and bohemianism which became particularly multicoloured in the late 1960s, it now has the highest concentration of millionaires in the UK. Once an obscure hamlet on the sandy ridge that stretches across this part of London, it came to prominence thanks to the numerous springs that emerge from the gravelly slopes. The rich and fashionable first arrived to take the waters in the 1700s; the wells later declined but the village's function as a resort for day tripping Londoners grew, particularly when the railway arrived in 1850. One of the major attractions was the open space of Hampstead Heath. Much of it was preserved as public open space in 1871 following decades of struggle between local people and landowners and is now managed mainly by the City of London.

There's so much of interest in Hampstead I couldn't hope to outline here, including its literary, artistic and radical connections – John Keats, Lord Byron, Sigmund Freud, Henry Moore, Glenda Jackson, architect Ernő Goldfinger and Ian Dury are among the names linked to the place. Strolling the well-preserved winding streets is a pleasure in itself, while the Heath, with its iconic views of central London from Parliament Hill and Kenwood, is not to be missed. And you won't have to go thirsty.

1 Czechoslovak National House
2 Holly Bush
3 Horseshoe
4 King William IV
5 Spaniards Inn

CZECHOSLOVAK NATIONAL HOUSE

Social club
74 West End Lane, NW6 2LX
☎ (020) 7372 1193
⊕ www.czechandslovakclub.co.uk
✆ Closed Mon; 5-11 Tue-Fri; 12-11 Sat; 12-10.30 Sun. *Children welcome*
Cask beer None, **Other beers** 2 keg (Budvar, Pilsner Urquell), 2 bottles, **Also** Czech and Slovak aperitifs and spirits
🍴 Czech/Slovak snacks and full meals,
🌳 Terrace, large beer garden, ♿
Czech TV

Not in Hampstead proper but in its less elevated and much earthier western annexe, this outpost of Czech and Slovak culture traces its history to the beginning of World War II when a club for exiled Czechoslovak service personnel fighting with the British forces was established in Holborn. It moved to its present location after the war, attracting those fleeing the pro-Soviet regime after 1948 and waves of migrants in recent decades. It's still much as it was in the 1950s, an old-style social club in a villa near West Hampstead's stations, but now open to everyone and something of an underused gem. Four rooms on the ground floor comprise a small bar, two other drinking rooms, one with a pool table, and a restaurant where the typical pub grub

Holly Bush

of the now divorced republics is the order of the day – *halušky*, schnitzels, potato pancakes and dumplings, *gulaš* and cheese fritters. Beer is of course an essential, with keg golden lagers from both Pilsner Urquell (Plzeňský Prazdroj) and Budweiser Budvar (Budějovický Budvar) in top condition, alongside bottles of Budvar Dark and Slovak beer Zlatý Bažant (Golden Pheasant, now a Heineken brand). It's a limited selection and it would be nice to see some of the smaller Czech brewers represented: house manager Václav says they tried Bernard but it didn't sell quickly enough. Nevertheless it's a delight to sample these justly famous brands in such a unique venue, under portraits of first Czechoslovak president Tomáš Masaryk and leader of the Velvet Revolution Václav Havel, and art nouveau posters by Alphonse Mucha.

Insider tip! On warm days try the sizeable beer garden, laid out Central European style with communal benches under a canvas shelter.

≈ West Hampstead ⊖ West Hampstead ⚲ Links to CS11, LCN+50

HOLLY BUSH
Traditional pub ☆
22 Holly Mount, NW3 6SG
☎ (020) 7435 2892, ✉ hollybush@fullers.co.uk,
⊕ www.fullers.co.uk
☼ 12-11 daily. *Children welcome daytime*
Cask beers ✔ 5 (Fuller's, Harveys), **Other beers**
6 bottles (Fuller's), **Also** Malts, wines
🍴 Gastro menu, 🪑 Tables on street
Functions

There was some anxiety among Hampstead's chatterati early in 2010 when this popular local institution, for a decades a free house and once famous for banning traffic wardens, was sold to Fuller's. Those concerns appear to have been soothed: the Chiswick brewer has retained the popular Harveys Sussex Best and occasional rotating guests while introducing its own range of Pride, ESB and Gales' Seafarer's, alongside a wide range of its excellent bottled beers. The historic interior of the pub has been left wisely untouched, though the previously banned traffic wardens now seem as welcome as anyone else. In an idyllic location half hidden on a pretty alleyway between Holly Hill and Heath Street, it's been licensed since 1802, hosted the first public meeting to conserve the Heath in 1829, and counts John Constable and Michael Faraday among former customers. It retains numerous features from Victorian refits, including bar counter and bar back and the remains of screens and panelling, while the patterned wallpaper looks like it's accumulated nicotine since at least a century before the smoking ban. A warren of rooms includes the highly prized 'Tavern Bar' snug to the right, a dining area at the back and an airy 'coffee room' to the left with an ornate fireplace, originally an alcohol-free zone. Food is upmarket and might include foie gras, cheese soufflé, Gressingham Duck or beef and ale pie.

⊖ Hampstead ⚲ Link to LCN+50, Hampstead Heath cycle routes ✦ Belsize Walk, Hampstead Heath footpaths

Horseshoe

HORSESHOE ☆ 25

Contemporary pub, specialist
28 Heath Street, NW3 6TE
☎ (020) 7431 6206, **fbk**
✪ 10-11 Mon-Thu; 10-midnight Fri & Sat;
10-10.30 Sun. *Children welcome*
Cask beers ✓ 3 (Camden Town, 1 unusual/
local guest), **Other beers** 5 keg (Camden Town,
Stiegl), 12 bottles, **Also** Wines
🍴 Gastro menu, 🪑 Benches on street
Fringe theatre

This corner pub and upstairs theatre, built in
the 1880s under the name Three Horseshoes
as part of a major redevelopment of central
Hampstead, is almost unrecognisable after a
thoroughgoing refurbishment in 2006
following a spell as a Wetherspoon. It's an
open, bright space with large windows,
stretches of whitewashed brickwork, refectory
tables and an open kitchen. The American
brewpub influence is not accidental as this is
the tap for the cosmopolitan-styled Camden
Town brewery, which started life in the cellar
though now has bigger premises in Kentish
Town (p268). The cask choice includes the
excellent own-brand Pale Ale and Bitter and a
guest from other London producers or like-
minded brewers elsewhere like Roosters,
supplemented by Camden's keg beers and a
wheat beer and lager from Stiegl in Austria.
A dozen or so international craft-brewed
bottles include nothing especially rare and
surprising but plenty of solid stuff from
Australians Coopers and Little Creatures,
Americans Anchor and Goose Island and
London's own Meantime.

It's a buzzy place, also admired by its
generally youngish clientele for its stylish
menu, which might include scallops, black
pudding, bean and roast garlic soup, hake,
pheasant or octopus, plus some lovely
desserts – booking is advisable. The
Pentameters theatre above has been under
the same management since the heady and
rather smoky days of 1968, when it was well
known for improvised poetry and jazz events,
and still retains something of the ethos of
those times.

Insider tip! Sometimes busy in the evenings but
perfect to linger after lunch, which includes
good-value set menus.

⊖ Hampstead, Hampstead Heath 🚲 Link to
LCN+50, Hampstead Heath cycle routes 🚶
Belsize Walk, Hampstead Heath footpaths

KING WILLIAM IV

Traditional pub
77 Hampstead High Street, NW3 1RE
☎ (020) 7435 5747
🌐 www.kingwilliamhampstead.co.uk, **fbk**
✪ 11-11 Mon-Thu; 11-midnight Fri-Sun
Cask beers ✓ 3 (Fuller's, Theakston, Wells &
Young's)
🍴 Enhanced pub grub, 🪑 Tables on street, beer
garden
*Mon quiz, occasional karaoke and live music,
functions, big screen sport*

Well placed just a short distance from
Hampstead tube, the 'pink Willie', as it's
affectionately known to some of its

customers, was a gay-friendly pub in freethinking Hampstead back in the 1930s, long before male gay sex was first decriminalised in the UK. These days, with its discreet rainbow flag tucked in the corner of the pub sign, pretty front courtyard, friendly welcome and tasteful interior, it's the sort of gay pub you could happily take your elderly aunt to. If she enjoys a pint of real ale, so much the better – alongside the Queens Head in Chelsea (p92) it's one of the few gay pubs to offer a range of cask beers, with London Pride and Directors always on and even Theakston Mild regularly available. Food includes steaks, pasta, burgers, sharing plates and smoked salmon.

⊖ Hampstead, Hampstead Heath ⬲ Link to LCN+50, Hampstead Heath cycle routes ⬩⬩ Belsize Walk, Hampstead Heath footpaths

SPANIARDS INN
Traditional pub
Spaniards Road, NW3 7JJ
📞 (020) 8731 8406
🌐 www.thespaniardshampstead.co.uk, **fbk**
✪ 12-11 daily. *Children welcome*
Cask beers ✔ Up to 6 (Adnams, Fuller's, Harveys, Timothy Taylor, guests), **Other beers** 9 keg, 7 bottles, **Also** 1 real cider, wines 🍴 Gastro/enhanced pub grub, 🎪 Large beer garden
Functions

The Spaniards is known to historians and aficionados of Hampstead lore as one of the locality's most legendary buildings, alleged bolthole of highwayman Dick Turpin and name checked by Charles Dickens in *Pickwick Papers*, and to drivers as one of its most irritating width restrictions. The pub and the old toll house opposite form a wonderfully car-hostile pinch point on Spaniards Road, adding to the already remarkably bucolic surroundings of Sandy Heath and Kenwood. Part of it dates from 1585, with some dark, low-ceilinged rooms and a particularly interesting upstairs function room, though with numerous later additions such as the white weatherboarded Edwardian extension, which now accommodates the main bar. Dispensed from here are a range of better known real ales – Landlord, Adnams Bitter,

Doom Bar, London Pride – alongside guests from the likes of Harveys or White Horse, sourced through owners Mitchells & Butlers. There's also an impressive range of international keg beers including Brooklyn Lager, Bavarian Franziskaner Weissbier, Küppers Kölsch from Cologne and Kozel from the Czech Republic, while bottled choices, though not as exotic as they once were, include bottle conditioned classic White Shield, Chimay Trappists and Innis & Gunn. Food is substantial British fare – potted pork, mushrooms baked with Stilton, smoked trout, glazed salmon and cottage pie. The enormous garden sports a wooden pergola and an outdoor bar in summer, and the welcome extended to dog walkers includes a Doggie Wash facility.

Insider tip! Yes, it's the perfect place to break a walk on the Heath or a visit to Kenwood on a fine weekend afternoon, but everyone else knows this too. The place still charms in winter, on rainy days or midweek and you'll have more space to yourself.

⊖ Hampstead 🚌 Spaniards Inn (210 Jack Straws Castle, 5 mins from Hampstead tube) ⬲ Hampstead Heath, Spaniards Road cycle routes ⬩⬩ Hampstead Heath footpaths

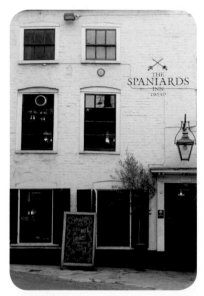

Spaniards Inn

HIGHGATE & ARCHWAY

On the other side of the Heath from Hampstead and almost as posh, Highgate is synonymous with its famous cemetery, one of a number of grand necropoli opened around London from the 1830s. Karl Marx heads a starry cast of inmates that includes Douglas Adams, George Eliot, Malcolm McLaren, Henry Moore and Max Wall. Originally a village atop a challenging hill on the Great North Road from central London, it was redeveloped as an elegant Georgian suburb, and poet Samuel Taylor Coleridge became a well-known resident. The road was moved to a less arduous alignment along a cutting at the side of the hill in 1896, leaving the village centre as a pretty enclave, now popular with celebrities. Highgate Woods, a miraculously preserved patch of ancient woodland managed by the City of London, is nearby.

The arched road bridge carrying Hornsey Lane across the diverted road cutting gave its name to Archway, at the bottom of the hill to the south. A much less glamorous area, it's dominated by the 1963 Archway Tower, surely one of the least pleasant environments in London and currently slated for redevelopment.

CHARLOTTE DESPARD
Contemporary pub
17-19 Archway Road, N19 3TX
☎ (020) 7272 7872, ⊕ www.
thecharlottedespard.co.uk, **fbk, tw** bongoworm
🕔 5-1am Mon; 12-1am Tue-Sat; 12-midnight
Sun. *Children until 10pm*
Cask beers ✔ 4 (Sambrook's, Timothy Taylor, 2 unusual/local guests), **Other beers** 1 keg, 20 bottles, **Also** Wines
🍴 Enhanced pub grub
Tue quiz, Fri/Sat DJs and/or live music including rock, funk, jazz, ska, art exhibitions, board games, table football, big screen football

Just round the corner from the tangle of traffic around Archway tube, this smallish and very welcoming local has a developing beer focus. The handpump count has recently doubled to accommodate guests from local brewers and some of the more interesting micros across Britain, while the changing bottled range covers the UK, Austria, Belgium, France, and the USA – beers from Kernel, Chimay and Austria's Schloss Eggenberg were among the highlights when I looked in. Straightforward, well-made food includes burgers, chicken dishes, quality cheeses,

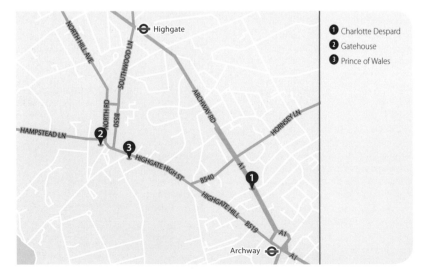

❶ Charlotte Despard
❷ Gatehouse
❸ Prince of Wales

Gatehouse

veggie pasta and fish finger sandwiches, with children's portions available. Stripped pine, wooden tables and sofas create a relaxing atmosphere in which to enjoy newspapers, free WiFi and great beer.

Pub trivia: Back in the 1980s, when it was called the Dog, the pub was one of the very earliest Wetherspoon pubs and the emerging pubco had its corporate headquarters upstairs.

⊖ Archway ᘓ Link to LCN+14

GATEHOUSE
Traditional pub
1 North Road, N6 4BD
☎ (020) 8340 8054
⊕ www.jdwetherspoon.co.uk
✿ 8am-11pm Mon & Tue; 8am-11.30pm Wed & Thu; 8am-midnight Fri & Sat; 8am-10.30pm Sun. *Children until early evening if eating*
Cask beers ✔ 8-10 (Greene King, Fuller's, unusual guests), **Other beers** Usual Wetherspoon keg and bottles, **Also** At least 1 real cider/perry
⏗ Wetherspoon menu, ⛭ Beer garden, ♿
Fringe theatre

Situated on a prominent corner at the top of pretty Highgate Village, this place claims to have been licensed since 1337. An ancient boundary ran through the building – at one point it was only half in London. An upstairs auditorium added in the 1890s is now home to one of London's most respected fringe theatres, while the current Tudor look dates from a 1905 renovation. Downstairs you may not at first spot that the pub is now part of the Wetherspoon chain, as the normal house style has been given a more discreet upmarket look in keeping with the building's heritage and the local demographic. Food

and drink are the pubco's usual offerings, with a particularly good selection of guests beers, perhaps from Nethergate, Salopian or Thwaites, including numerous seasonals.

Insider tip! The pub operates a 'Suggest a Guest' scheme so might be able to stock your favourite.

⊖ Highgate ☒ Highgate Village (numerous from Archway) ᘓ LCN+6A, link to Parkland walk ⚑ Link to Capital Ring, Parkland Walk, Hampstead Heath paths

PRINCE OF WALES
Traditional pub
53 Highgate High Street, N6 5JX
☎ (020) 8340 0445
✿ 12-11 Mon-Wed; 12-midnight Thu-Sat; 12-11 Sun. *Children until 10pm*
Cask beers ✔ 4 (Butcombe, 3 unusual guests)
⏗ Thai menu, ⛭ Small terrace on square
Tue quiz

This small, square one-bar pub in Highgate Village is of most interest to beer lovers for its regularly changing top quality guest cask beers from the likes of Arundel, Brains, Caledonian, Moorhouse's, Lancaster and Titanic. Otherwise it's renowned for its weekly quiz, known as one of the most challenging in London and taken very seriously by its regular entrants – you can even buy a quiz book based on it.

Insider tip! Walk right through the pub from the high street to discover a small but delightful terrace looking out onto attractive Pond Square.

⊖ Highgate ☒ Highgate Village (numerous from Archway) ᘓ LCN+6A, link to Parkland walk ⚑ Link to Capital Ring, Parkland Walk, Hampstead Heath paths

KENTISH TOWN & TUFNELL PARK

Kentish Town and Tufnell Park straddle the main routes north from the West End and Camden Town and were inevitably in the line of fire for ribbon development in the mid-19th century, particularly after the railways sliced through the area. Kentish Town has played an important role in rock music culture: the Tally Ho pub in Fortress Road, demolished in 2006, was credited as the birthplace of pub rock, a predecessor of punk, and art deco former cinema the London Forum has been a major rock venue from its days as the Town and Country Club in the 1980s.

Tufnell Park, with its rows of solid Victorian terraces, became comedy shorthand for 'shabby genteel', a reputation challenged in 1910 by the gruesome case of American dentist Dr Crippen, of Hilldrop Crescent, who murdered and dismembered his wife and was caught while attempting to flee across the Atlantic thanks to the recent invention of wireless telegraphy.

The Camden Town brewery is actually in Kentish Town, in the arches underneath Kentish Town West Overground – see p268.

DARTMOUTH ARMS
Contemporary pub
35 York Rise, NW5 1SP
☎ (020) 7485 3267, ⊕ faucetinn.com
🕐 11-11 Mon-Thu; 11-midnight Fri;
10-midnight Sat; 10-10.30 Sun. *Children welcome*
Cask beers ✅ 3 (Westerham, guests), **Other beers** 3 keg, 1-2 bottles, **Also** Wines
🍴 'English style tapas' and upmarket pub grub
Tue fortnightly quiz, monthly acoustic music, board games, functions, occasional big screen sport

Dartmouth Park, developed in the 1870s on ground owned by the Earl of Dartmouth on the lower southern slopes of Highgate Hill, is now something of a London village in its own right. A cluster of interesting little shops on York Rise, which follows the course of the buried river Fleet, forms something of a centre and includes this pleasant grey-green and pink floral wallpaper bedecked community gastropub, which advertises "Real beer, real food, a real fire and the best wines known to man." I can testify it delivers on at least the first

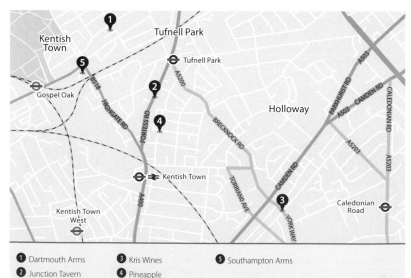

❶ Dartmouth Arms   ❸ Kris Wines   ❺ Southampton Arms
❷ Junction Tavern   ❹ Pineapple

Junction Tavern

three. In late 2010 it was acquired by the small Faucet Inn chain based in Westerham, Kent, and well-kept beers from the Westerham brewery always include Finchcocks Original, plus guests that might come from Adnams or Thwaites. Franziskaner Weissbier on keg and bottled Budvar widen the serious beer choice a little; real ciders and perries might reappear by the time you read this. Interesting food at reasonable prices includes 'English style tapas', sharing platters and mains such as sausages made with Westerham ale and caramelised shallot tatin. Regular football screenings demonstrate an earthier side to the place.

⊖ Gospel Oak, Tufnell Park ⧀ Link to LCN+6A, Hampstead Heath routes ⫸ Hampstead Heath footpaths

JUNCTION TAVERN
Gastropub
101 Fortress Road, NW5 1AG
☎ (020) 7485 9400
⊕ www.junctiontavern.co.uk
☼ 12-11 Mon-Sat; 12-10.30 Sun. *Children until 7pm*
Cask beers ✅ 4 (guests, often Sambrook's), **Other beers** 2 keg, 2 bottles, **Also** Wines and sherries
🍴 Gastro menu, 🌳 Beer garden
Mon quiz, twice yearly beer festivals, occasional beer theme months

The interior of this biggish street corner building is a mixture of traditional pub and posh restaurant, with a slight Scottish baronial

feel to the rear bar with its carved bar back, decorated ceiling and elaborate fireplace. The light front space is given over to candlelit dining, suggesting that food leads here. An imaginative menu that might include treacle and whisky cured salmon, slow roast pork belly or vegetarian pan fried polenta has won numerous plaudits from foodies and you'll likely need to book to bag a front table, though the full menu is available throughout. Beer is by no means forgotten: cask ales from Sambrook's, Caledonian, Exmoor, Harveys, Jennings, Sharp's and Wychwood are regularly spotted. A beer festival every three months extends to over 30 ales, often encompassing names rare in London such as Anglo Dutch, Concrete Cow, Green Jack, Marston Manor and Pictish, bringing it recognition as a local CAMRA Pub of the Year.

⇌ Kentish Town ⊖ Kentish Town, Tufnell Park 🚌 Lady Somerset Road (134 Kentish Town, Tufnell Park) ⧀ Links to LCN+14 and Hampstead Heath routes

KRIS WINES ☆ 25
Shop
394 York Way, N7 9LW
☎ (020) 7607 4871, ⊕ www.kriswines.com
☼ 2-11 Mon-Sat; 2-10 Sun
Cask beer None, **Other beers** 750 bottles, **Also** Small batch ciders and perries, wines

Krishna 'Kris' Menan is not the only owner of a neighbourhood off license (liquor store) to move beyond canned lager and cigarette papers towards speciality beer, but he's taken it further than most. Despite its name, his small shop stocks what may be the biggest and most comprehensive collection of international craft beers in London, with around 750 different lines. The range is meticulously researched through online rating sites and beer reviewers, so it's a great place to look for rarities beloved of beer geeks, with cult figures like the Netherlands' De Molen, Belgium's Alvinne and Struise, Denmark's Mikkeller, Italy's Baladin and del Borgo, California's Port/Lost Abbey and Stone and Scotland's BrewDog all present and correct when I called in, though Kris stresses many of these are hard to source and stocks can't be guaranteed.

Particularly well represented are: British bottle conditioned beers from small producers like Bartrams, Country Life, Felstar, Hopshackle, King, Moor and Pitfield as well as local lads Brodie's, Kernel and Sambrook's; a good Belgian range including top lambics from Cantillon, Girardin, Hanssens and Oud Beersel and some rare Wallonian ales; plenty of interesting Germans from Beck-Bräu (the Bavarian craft brewery, not the huge AB-InBev subsidiary in Bremen), Greifenklau, Hüber, St Georgen and Würzburger; numerous Americans rare in Britain including Eel River, Founders, Green Flash, Moylans, Southern Tier and Tommyknocker; and a welcome range of Dutch microbrews including Emelisse, 't IJ and Klein Duimpje. Inevitably it's cramped, and though generally organised by country you need to look carefully to spot everything. It's not especially handy for tube or train, but with a range like this a bus from Camden or Kings Cross is easily justified. Kris apologises he's not yet been able to source beers from Westvleteren, the Trappist brewery that deliberately limits production and refuses to distribute, but he'll keep trying.

🚅 Kentish Town, Kings Cross, St Pancras 🚇 Caledonian Road, Camden, Camden Road Kentish Town 🚌 York Way (390 Kings Cross, Tufnell Park, 29, 253 Camden Town) 🚲 LCN+ 6, 14, local link to LCN+7

PINEAPPLE
Traditional pub ☆
51 Leverton Street, NW5 2NX
📞 (020) 7284 4631
⏰ 12-11 Mon-Sat; 12-10.30 Sun. *Children until 7pm*
Cask beers ✅ 5 (Marston's Bass, unusual/local guests), **Other beers** 3 keg
🍴 Thai menu, 🍺 Beer garden
Mon quiz, Tue live acoustic music, twice yearly beer festivals

This handsome and welcoming local pub is only a short stroll from Kentish Town tube but seems a world away in its quiet and attractive terraced street. The pub was saved from closure thanks to a campaign by local people and CAMRA in the early 2000s and has since justified the effort. A pleasant mix of seating is arranged around a small central bar dominated by a big Bass mirror, and there's Bass itself on the bar, although the etched glass windows indicates this was once an Ind Coope house. Also on offer is a rotating range of "anything and everything", but nearly always including a local beer that might come from Camden Town, Redemption or Sambrook's. There's more space along to the back, past an impressive red marble fireplace and old settles to an elegant conservatory decorated with illustrations of wild birds, looking out onto a pleasant beer garden where spring and autumn festivals extend the range towards 35 cask ales. Food is an extensive choice of Thai dishes. The name may seem unlikely for a backstreet North London pub but, as a traditional symbol of hospitality, it's more than apt.

Pineapple

Southampton Arms

Insider tip! Try a Thai lunch for a fiver on weekdays.

⇌ Kentish Town ⊖ Kentish Town ⊙⃗ Link to LCN+14

SOUTHAMPTON ARMS ☆ **25**
Contemporary pub, specialist
139 Highgate Road, NW5 1LE
☎ 07958 780073
⊕ www.thesouthamptonarms.co.uk
tw SouthamptonNW5
✪ 12-midnight Mon-Sat; 12-11.30 Sun. *Children welcome daytime*
Cask beers ✓ 10 (unusual/local guests), **Other beers** 2 keg (Camden Town), **Also** 8 real ciders/perries
⊡ Substantial cheese and meat snacks, ▥ Beer garden
Mon quiz, Wed & Sun live piano

Transformed late in 2009 from a decaying old boozer into one of London's essential beer destinations, this smallish but impressive purveyor of 'Ale, Cider and Meat' rewards a stretch of the legs from Kentish Town tube or a shorter stroll from Gospel Oak Overground. The long single bar has bare floorboards, old church furniture, white-tiled walls and yellowed portraits, looking thrown together but probably thought about very carefully, with a slight hint of butcher's shop appropriate to the food offering – high quality pork pies, scotch eggs, sausage rolls and cheese baps. It's oddly pleasing that the refurb didn't extend to getting rid of the

outdoor toilet block, past which is an attractive sheltered yard. As far as they are aware, say the owners, it's the only dedicated ale and cider house in London to sell only beers and ciders from small independent producers.

The range constantly rotates, with only the two Camden Town keg beers a fixture, but there's always a mild and a porter or stout and a tendency towards the local. On my visit beers from Brodie's, Bristol, Dowbridge, Moor, RCH, Sambrook's, St Peter's, Thornbridge and Tring were on the pumps, and past visitors have included Crouch Vale, Empire, Raw and Whitstable; there are sometimes themed ranges from specific brewers like Manchester's marvellous Marble. Eight ciders or perries will please orchard lovers. Most promisingly the place is attracting a youngish crowd with a fair share of arty and creative types: I rubbed shoulders with the Mighty Boosh's Julian Barrett and Rich Fulcher. The former's character Howard Moon would be impressed with the stack of classy jazz vinyl behind the bar.

Insider tip! Visit on a Wednesday or Sunday to check out the piano recitals if you don't mind a crowd, but try to visit in the afternoon if you want a seat.

⊖ Gospel Oak, Kentish Town ☒ Lady Somerset Road (214, C2 Kentish Town/Highgate) ⊙⃗ LCN+6A, links to Hampstead Heath routes ⁄⁄ Links to Hampstead Heath paths, Belsize Walk

STOKE NEWINGTON

When the foundations for the terraced housing running east of Stoke Newington High Street towards Clapton were dug in the late 1870s, the work unearthed the remains of a 200,000-year-old flint axe factory, one of the most important paleolithic sites in the UK. Another hilltop site colonised by better-off Georgians as a country retreat close to London, Stoke Newington was the place where Daniel Defoe wrote *Robinson Crusoe* and Edgar Allen Poe received his early education. The area once boasted extensive parkland estates, fragments of which survive as the delightfully overgrown Victorian cemetery of Abney Park and fine green Clissold Park. The historic village centre near the latter in Church Street has a lovely old church now overshadowed by its stern successor, built in 1858 by George Gilbert Scott as suburbanisation set in. Today the centre of gravity has switched to the junction of Church Street and the main A10 road, which follows the route of Roman Ermine Street. Local prosperity faded rapidly after World War II but after the 1970s, when it was home to the Angry Brigade bombing gang, Stokey became one of the early targets of gentrification, developing a crop of specialist shops and a reputation for arty alternative lifestyles. Some of that atmosphere survives today.

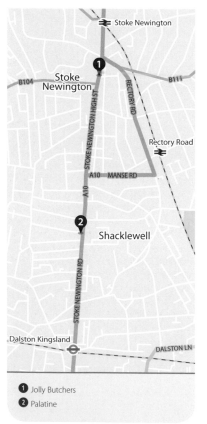

JOLLY BUTCHERS
Gastropub, specialist
204 Stoke Newington High Street, N16 7HU
☎ (020) 7249 9471, ⊕ www.jollybutchers.co.uk,
fbk, **tw** jollybutchers
✿ 4-midnight Mon-Fri; 12-1am Sat; 12-11 Sun.
Children welcome
Cask beers ● 7 (Crouch Vale, Dark Star, Redemption, Thornbridge, unusual/local guests), **Other beers** 10 keg, 16-20 bottles, **Also** 2 real ciders/perries, wines
⊞ Gastro/enhanced pub grub, ⊞ Benches on street, ⬛
Local beer weeks

Not so long ago this was a fearsome place where customers entertained themselves by throwing bottles at the bar. The current owner even confesses he felt nervous about making site visits during the sale negotiations. But the 2010 conversion into a specialist beer bar and gastropub has proved a great success. Most readers of this book will be more than satisfied with the beer offer, which almost always include something from all four of the highly achieving small breweries listed above. Small London breweries are regularly supported and unique specials and collaboration brews are sometimes launched here. It's one of the few outlets to stock cask beers from Kernel when available alongside the more familiar

❶ Jolly Butchers
❷ Palatine

Jolly Butchers

Brodie's, Camden Town and Redemption.
Camden Town, Meantime and at least two
from BrewDog are among the keg choices.
The selection of bottled beers starts at Kernel
and BrewDog and goes international with
Brooklyn (the lovely East India Pale Ale as well
as the lager), Goose Island and rarely seen
Dutch craft brewer Texels.

A shortish menu foregrounds cheese and
beer pairings in which beer writer Pete Brown
had a hand – farmhouse Brie and De Koninck,
for example – while extending to goats
cheese and pomegranate salad, Erdinger-
battered coley fillet and chips or Cumberland
sausage with home made sauerkraut and
mash. The decor repays study – all purple and
dark green, with art wallpaper featuring
women's faces, remnants of wall mosaics and
original stained glass in the huge arch
windows, and lampshades that look like they
were designed by Jean Cocteau. And most of
the regulars now look more likely to be
throwing empty tins of organic baby food in
the recycling than glasses at the bar. Just
bubbling under my Top 25, it's well worth
investigating.

≋ Stoke Newington ⊖ Dalston ◻ Stoke
Newington station (numerous, Dalston) ⊙◎
LCN+ Stamford Hill, Dalston, Lee Valley, Clapton
⫽ Capital Ring

PALATINE
Bar
97 Stoke Newington Road, N16 8BX
☎ 07887 776788, ⊕ www.thepalatine.net
☸ 5-midnight Mon-Thu; 5-2am Fri & Sat;
5-midnight Sun. *Children until 9pm*
Cask beers ✔ 3 (Brodie's, Ha'penny), **Other
beers** 1 keg, 4-5 bottles
🍽 Bar snacks and sharing plates, ♿
DJ Fri, live bands and karaoke, board games

Where Stoke Newington merges with Dalston,
on a strip of the A10 famed for its Turkish
Cypriot *ocakbaşı* restaurants, the Palatine is
another recent makeover with more than a
passing interest in beer. A loungey, laid-back
space full of floppy sofas and art prints, it has
a smart grey marble bar that's one of the few
in London regularly to dispense beers from
the tiny Ha'penny brewery (p272), who supply
the house ale as well as other beers. Brodie's
beers are also regularly featured and Kernel
might appear on cask as well as in bottle.
Erdinger wheat beer is on keg. A downstairs
dancefloor rocks weekly to DJs and the
occasional live band, while food is limited to
cheeseboards and pies. One to watch.

≋ Stoke Newington ⊖ Dalston ◻ Princess May
Road (numerous Stoke Newington, Dalston) ⊙◎
LCN routes Stoke Newington, Shoreditch,
Finsbury Park, Hackney

BARNET

OLDE MITRE
Traditional pub
58 High Street, Barnet, EN5 5SJ
📞 (020) 8449 6582
🕑 12-midnight Mon-Thu; 12-1am Fri & Sat;
12-midnight Sun. *Children welcome daytime*
Cask beers ✅ 6 (Adnams, Timothy Taylor,
guests), **Also** 1 real cider
🍴 Pub grub, 🌳 Beer garden and terrace
Functions

Now one of London's most northerly
outposts, Barnet (sometimes called High or
Chipping Barnet to distinguish it from
neighbouring suburbs) is a historic market
town, the venue for a celebrated horse fair
that's commemorated in Cockney rhyming
slang's 'Barnet fair' for 'hair'. Since it's astride a
route that for centuries was the Great North
Road from London to York and Edinburgh, it
has a history of catering to travellers and is
equipped with some fine old inns to serve the
coaches that once trundled through up to
150 times a day. Ye Olde Mitre Inn, as it styles
itself on the pub sign, is one example, created
in 1633 from three neighbouring pubs,
though it's much altered and a third its
original size. Today it's a lovely beer house and
community pub, with a motley collection of
furniture in a selection of pleasant spaces,
including a low ceilinged front bar, an
atmospheric room in a former stables off the

Olde Mitre

rear courtyard and a garden overlooked by
flats. The beer pumps make enthusiastic use
of Punch's Finest Cask list, dispensing choices
that might come from Bath, Daleside, Exmoor,
Leeds (delicious dark mild Midnight Bell when
I called), Wychwood or York alongside
Landlord and Adnams Bitter. Take home
containers are available for draught beers and
decently-priced pub grub is served.

➔ High Barnet 🚲 Links to Dollis Valley cycle
paths 🚶 London Loop, Dollis Valley walk

COCKFOSTERS

COCK & DRAGON
Contemporary pub, restaurant
14 Chalk Lane, Barnet, EN4 9HU
📞 (020) 8449 7160
🌐 www.cockanddragon-cockfosters.co.uk
🕑 11-11 Mon-Thu; 11-11.30 Fri & Sat; 11-10.30
Sun. *Children welcome*
Cask beers ✅ 3 (Greene King, 1 guest), **Other
beers** 2 keg, 6 bottles including Asian lagers
🍴 Pub grub and Thai lunches, 🌳 Extensive
garden and terrace
*Curry offer night Mon, Stir fry offer night Tue,
functions*

Cockfosters, at the end of the Piccadilly Line,
really feels like the edge of London. The built
up area ends abruptly just a little to the north
of the tube station, where the capital's
development was stopped in its tracks by
World War II and the subsequent introduction
of the Green Belt, leaving a fascinating
patchwork of 1930s commuter suburbia,
green space and countryside. Once part of
the royal hunting park of Enfield Chase, the
area later became a country estate, Trent Park,
now a large public park and a campus of
Middlesex University. This magnificent
pavilion-like hostelry was built in the late
1790s as part of a small village that developed
on the edge of the estate. It's a mix of
destination pub and Thai restaurant, with a
decor to match: traditional pub furniture and
wooden partitions are juxtaposed curiously
with Thai carvings and Buddhist imagery.
There's a restaurant at the back but the menu
is also available from the large bar at the front
or on the extensive outdoor terrace. Beer
choice is relatively limited but well kept:

Greene King Abbot and IPA with Sharp's Doom Bar the guest from cask when I visited, supplemented by several oriental lagers – Singha, Chang – alongside Liefmans Kriek and Budvar in bottle. The pub is right on the London Loop and an ideal stopping point for walks in Trent Park or east towards Barnet via Monken Hadley Common.

⊖ Cockfosters 🚲 Trent Park routes 🚶 London Loop, Pymmes Brook Trail

ENFIELD

WONDER
Traditional pub
1 Batley Road, Enfield, EN2 0JG
📞 (020) 8363 0202
🕐 11-11 Mon-Thu; 11-midnight Fri & Sat;
12-11 Sun
Cask beers ✔ 4 (McMullen), **Other beers**
4 bottles
🍺 Front terrace
Sat & Sun piano singalongs and jazz, darts, pub games

The real wonder of the Wonder is that it has survived intact and unspoilt as an old fashioned and ultra-traditional local boozer in the well-off suburbs north of Enfield Town, a last tranche of housing before the metropolis gives way to the Green Belt. The plain, lino-floored and half-panelled public bar is equipped with a piano around which customers are invited to join in Cockney singsongs on a regular basis. The cosy and comparatively luxurious carpeted saloon with its open fire has a house-proud front parlour feel. The walls are crammed with community history in the form of photographs of joyous nights past. There's no food other than basic bar snacks and no TV – it's a self-proclaimed football-free zone, though the sport formed the major topic of conversation among my fellow drinkers in the public bar when I visited. It's also an opportunity to try the beers from Hertford brewer McMullen at their best – AK, Cask Ale, Country Bitter and seasonals. In bottle are some classic old time beers including McMullen's Hertford Castle pale ale, AB InBev's Gold Label barley wine and Manns Brown. It's a trek from central London to Gordon Hill but worth it to get an idea of

what the best sort of neighbourhood London pub looked and felt like in the days when the Beatles were still together.

Insider tip! While indoors is strictly over-18s, there's some outdoor seating looking out onto lovely St Michael's Green with its children's play area.

≋ Gordon Hill 🚌 Lavender Hill (191 Enfield Town) 🚲 Link to NCN12 🚶 Links to London Loop, Hertfordshire Chain Walk, New River Path

Salisbury Hotel

HARRINGAY

SALISBURY HOTEL
Traditional pub ★
1 Grand Parade, Green Lanes, N4 1JX
📞 (020) 8800 9617
🕐 5-midnight Mon-Thu; 5-2am Fri; 12-2am Sat;
12-11.30 Sun. *Children welcome*
Cask beers ✔ 4 (3 Fuller's, 1 unusual guest),
Other beers 8 keg, 6 bottles, **Also** Malts, wines
🍴 Pub grub, 🍺 Only porch smoking area, ♿
Mon quiz, Wed poker, Thu Lindy Hop dance class, occasional Fri/Sat bands/DJs, functions, board games

The old drove road known as Green Lanes is one of London's longest streets, snaking all the way from Islington to Enfield through surroundings which now largely belie its name. When the stretch through Harringay was developed in the 1890s this was one of London's most vibrant suburbs, prompting brick manufacturer John Cathles Hill to top the row of terraced mansions known as Grand Parade with an ambitious pub-restaurant-hotel that is still one of the capital's most spectacular hostelries. The three storey hulk ringed with black larvikite pillars and surmounted by a crown still dominates the street from its corner site. Enter through the right hand porch as the posh people once did and you walk over a mosaic of the pub's name into a grand corridor with carved wood, mirrors, sought-after private booths and more mosaics underfoot. To the left are partitioned front and back drinking areas, also richly decorated and replete with pillars and pilasters around a big island bar, and further back is the old billiards room, now used for functions and events. The tiled marble floor dates from a careful restoration in 2003.

These are remarkable surroundings in which to enjoy Fuller's cask ales – regulars Pride, Gales' Seafarers and a seasonal – plus a rotating guest (the excellent Butcombe Bitter when I called), alongside a wide range of quality keg beers including two lagers from the rarely seen Litovel, from Moravia in the Czech Republic, and a wheat beer and Festbier from Rothaus. Food is decent pub grub including pizzas, fish, burgers and both meat and veggie pies. The hotel upstairs, incidentally, is no longer in use.

Pub trivia: Easy to miss but speaking most eloquently of the care that went into creating the pub are several original mirrors etched with art nouveau designs and hand painted with rustic scenes.

Harringay Green Lanes, Manor House, Turnpike Lane Green Lanes St Annes Road (29, 141 Harringay Green Lanes, Manor House, Turnpike Lane)

HOLLOWAY

CORONET
Contemporary pub
338-346 Holloway Road, N7 6NJ
(020) 7609 5014
www.jdwetherspoon.co.uk
8am-11pm Mon-Sat; 8am-10.30pm Sun.
Children until early evening if eating

Coronet

Cask beers 10 (Greene King, Marston's, unusual guests), **Other beers** Usual Wetherspoon keg and bottles, **Also** 2 real cides/perries
Wetherspoon menu, Small rear patio, Wetherspoon beer festivals and promotions

Right on the Holloway Road, London's major northern artery, just south of the Nags Head junction, the Coronet must be one of the most spectacular of all Wetherspoon conversions. The building is immediately recognisable as a former cinema: it was opened as the Savoy in 1940 but was known by its current name when the final reel ended in 1983. The foyer and stalls have been knocked through to create a very large pub, broken up with different seating areas, booths and a raised dais centred on a sculpture of a film projector, while preserving a sense of space. Many features of the original have survived intact including some impressive decorative panels. The circle is still visible, though sadly unused except to display huge stills from classic movies, and you walk under the proscenium arch where the screen used to be to access the small outdoor smoking area. Fortunately it's also one of the company's more imaginative real ale outlets: guests might come from the likes of Burton Bridge, Exmoor, Holdens, Mordue, Oakham or Thornbridge.

Holloway Road, Upper Holloway Holloway Road Tollington Road (numerous along Holloway Road) Links to CS12, LCN+14, Highbury and Crouch End

NORTH NINETEEN
Contemporary pub
194-196 Sussex Way, N19 4HZ
☎ (020) 7281 2786, ✉ info@northnineteen.
co.uk, ⊕ www.northnineteen.co.uk,
tw North_Nineteen
☼ 1-midnight Mon-Thu; 12-1am Fri & Sat;
12-midnight Sun. *Children until 10pm*
Cask beers ✔ 9 (Fuller's, Timothy Taylor,
Skinners, unusual guests), **Also** Wines, 30 malts
🍴 Steakhouse menu, 🌳 Terrace, beer garden
*Tue open mic night, Thu darts, occasional
karaoke, live bands and tastings, functions*

Tucked away in a residential street parallel to
Hornsey Road in Upper Holloway, this
characterful and friendly street corner pub is a
boon to local residents and well worth
seeking out for everyone else. Unusually for a
modern makeover it preserves a traditional
two-bar layout. The main bar has a games
area off to one side with sofas and swirly dark
blue wallpaper, while round the corner is a
second room used for regular open mic
nights and functions, quirkily decorated with
art, books, and a professional drawing board
used as a notice board. An outdoor terrace
alongside the quiet street is also attractive.
Food has recently taken a very meaty turn
with a steak house menu – steaks are huge
but there are tasty veggie dishes too. Beers
are well chosen guests from the Enterprise list
and always include dark options –
Nethergate's lovely Old Growler porter when I
visited, and Batemans seasonal Rosey Nosey.

⇌ Finsbury Park ⊖ Caledonian Road, Holloway
Road, Upper Holloway 🚌 Hornsey Road Hanley
Road (91 Caledonian Road), Holloway Road
Alexander Road (43, 271 Holloway Road) 🚲
CS12, links to Highbury, LCN+14

North Nineteen

Three Compasses

HORNSEY

THREE COMPASSES
Contemporary pub
62 High Street, N8 7NX
☎ (020) 8340 2729
⊕ www.threecompasses.com
☼ 11-11 Mon-Thu; 11-midnight Fri & Sat; 12-11
Sun. *Over 14s up to 9pm*
Cask beers ✔ 6 (Fuller's, Redemption, Timothy
Taylor, unusual guests), **Other beers** 3-4
bottles, **Also** Wines, cocktails
🍴 Enhanced pub grub, ♿
*Mon quiz, Tue pool league, Thu poker, board
games, pool, darts, occasional parties, theme
nights and big screen sports*

Actor Bob Hoskins' old manor of Hornsey was
once a country village between Muswell Hill
and Green Lanes. It's now on the divide
between the impoverished social housing of
Tottenham and Harringay and the affluence
on the slopes of the lofty hill. On the former
village street stands the Three Compasses.
This sizeable and recently restored late
Victorian pub was originally a coaching inn
with grounds that extended to the New River,
a 17th century artificial watercourse built to
bring water from wells near Hertford into
London. Sadly the pub no longer has outdoor
seating but it's working hard to serve its
community, with a chalkboard outside
highlighting the many reasons to call in. Not
least among these is the well kept choice of
ale, always including London Pride, Taylor
Landlord and Redemption Pale alongside

John Baird

three guests from the likes of Cottage, Hook Norton or Nethergate. The menu offers a thoughtful and varied interpretation of pub grub – salads, pies, pasta, stews, hot sandwiches – with lots of vegetarian options and also gluten free and other special diet choices. There's plenty of comfortable seating in a relaxed and informal environment, with a rear space used for pool, sport screenings and offbeat events that might include a celebration of Elvis Presley's birthday.

Insider tip! Try some of the beer and food matching recommendations outlined on the menu.

≥ Hornsey ⊖ Turnpike Lane ➡ Hornsey Myddleton Road (144 Turnpike Lane) ⟡ NCN7, CS12 ✦✦ New River Path

MUSWELL HILL

JOHN BAIRD
Contemporary pub, restaurant
122 Fortis Green Road, N10 3HN
☎ (020) 8444 8830
⊕ www.johnbaird-muswellhill.co.uk
🕐 11-11 Mon-Wed; 11-midnight Thu-Sat; 11-11 Sun. *Children until early evening*
Cask beers ✔ 7 (Wells & Young's, Sharp's, Wychwood, Hook Norton, guests), **Other beers** 1 keg (Budvar), 5 bottles, **Also** 2 real ciders/perries
🍴 Thai menu, 🌳 Beer garden, ♿
Thu & Sun quiz, 2 annual beer festivals, big screen sport

Well located on the edge of the trendy Muswell Hill, this pleasant pub is a good choice for a beer after indulging yourself in the local specialist shops or exploring the Parkland Walk to nearby Alexandra Palace Park and its 'palace' – actually an 1870s leisure and entertainment centre. Ally Pally, as it's affectionately known, was the venue for the first official Great British Beer Festival in 1977, but it's rather more famous as the site from which the world's first high definition public television service was transmitted by the BBC in the 1930s, and the pub's name honours Scottish television pioneer John Logie Baird (1888-1946), whose experimental systems were tested there. It's a redbrick corner building with a pleasant, modern interior a little dominated by big screens showing sport, and an attractive garden. Guest beers tend to come from better known breweries like Adnams, Black Sheep, Wells & Young's and Wychwood, but they're well kept by an enthusiastic landlord who also organises two festivals a year where the choice increases significantly. At the back is a full scale Thai restaurant, the Black Orchid, though the food is available throughout. The restaurant has another branch behind the Nobody Inn (p147).

≥ Hornsey ⊖ East Finchley, Turnpike Lane ➡ Muswell Hill Road (102, 234 East Finchley), Muswell Hill Broadway (144 Turnpike Lane, Hornsey) ⟡ Parkland Walk ✦✦ Parkland Walk

SOUTHEAST LONDON

SOUTHEAST LONDON

This section covers the SE postcodes outside the central area and further south and southeast to Bromley and Croydon. South London, and Southeast London in particular, is often portrayed as the wrong side of town, the poor relation, somehow less London than the north bank. After all, the Tube hardly ventures there, and the Borough is only a borough, not a city like the City or Westminster, even though it's had a cathedral since 1909. These ideas are more likely promulgated by north Londoners; south Londoners in their turn, and I declare an interest here, will assure you heartily that their side of the river is the most vibrant, exciting and historic, in a determined attempt to shake the chip from their shoulders.

The truth is that the centres of government and international finance, the world famous shopping and entertainment destinations and most of the principal museums, educational and cultural institutions are not in South London. The Borough did indeed grow up to service the City, and flourished on the fact that it wasn't governed by the City's rules. Southeast London is mainly residential and light industrial, but includes several intriguing centres, much of London's best green space and countryside, and, in Greenwich, a place everyone should visit at least once in their lives.

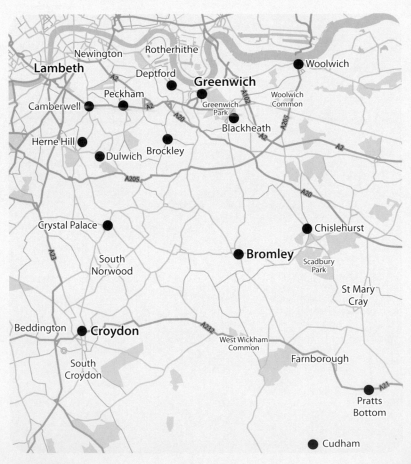

< **Bear (p172)**

BLACKHEATH

The modern A2 follows the route of old Roman Watling Street from London to Dover, ultimately leading, as all roads naturally do, to Rome. Past Deptford it rises steeply to cross a broad expanse of acid grassland known as Blackheath, some say as victims of the Black Death were buried here, but the derivation is more likely simply from 'bleak heath', which suits it well. A fashionable Georgian rural retreat grew up on a corner of this airy place, and many of its handsome terraces still stand today on the rim of the Heath, which was protected as a Metropolitan Common in 1871. The expanse of grass and scrub, popular with kite flyers and famed for its November fireworks, now forms an extensive green space together with adjacent Greenwich Park. Unsurpringly these picturesque qualities have made Blackheath one of the most desirable and expensive locations in southeast London. It's also home to a celebrated classical music venue, Blackheath Halls, now owned by Trinity College.

PRINCESS OF WALES

Traditional pub
1a Montpelier Row, SE3 0RL
📞 (020) 8852 5784
🌐 www.princessofwalespub.co.uk
🕐 12-11 Mon-Sat; 12-10.30 Sun. *Children welcome*
Cask beers ✅ 6 (Fuller's, Sharp's, 4 guests), **Other beers** 7 keg, 3 bottles, **Also** 1 real cider, wines
🍴 Pub grub, 🪑 Front terrace, large beer garden, ♿
Tue quiz, Wed beer night, monthly beer festivals in summer, board games

In a commanding position overlooking the Heath, this big but friendly pub has been refreshing those enjoying the open air for at least two centuries. It's now one of Mitchells & Butlers' Castle pubs and has significantly improved its beer offer, which may soon extend to eight handpumps. Pride and Doom Bar are regulars, while the changing guests – a new one every day – often come from Yorkshire breweries, reflecting the regional origins of the current manager. Copper Dragon, Cropton, Kelham Island and Timothy Taylor might be spotted, and Lancaster sneaks in somehow, alongside offerings from Sambrook's or White Horse. In summer stillages go up on a monthly basis, with as many as 40 beers available over a weekend. Czech lagers and keg selections from the nearby Meantime brewery widen

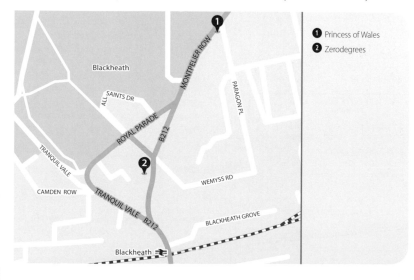

❶ Princess of Wales
❷ Zerodegrees

Princess of Wales

the choice, while food is big on pies, burgers and exotica like crab and wasabi cakes. Several varied spaces inside include a wood panelled games room with a Blackheath Hockey Club display and a bright and cheery conservatory. Needless to say, on sunny summer weekends it heaves.

Visitor's note: Although it's out of use during quiet times, the big old bar at the front is a sight to behold – all green painted glass, mirrors and black pilasters spiralled with gold.

⇄ Blackheath 🚲 LCN+ Lewisham, Eltham, links to Greenwich 🚶 Blackheath and Greenwich Park paths, link to Jubilee Greenway, Thames Path

ZERODEGREES

Bar, brewpub
29-31 Montpelier Vale, SE3 0TJ
📞 (020) 8852 5619, 🌐 www.zerodegrees.co.uk
🕐 12-midnight Mon-Sat; 12-11.30 Sun. *Children in restaurant*
Cask beer 6 (own), **Other beers** minicasks
🍽 Pizzas and Italian/American brewpub grub,
🌳 Front terrace
Sun DJs, big screen sport, brewery tours

From the outside this stylish brewpub doesn't look out of place in a row of old buildings overlooking a grassy triangle of heath, but

inside it's a different story: the walls are painted in abstract designs while steel staircases snake up past the gleaming brewhouse to a mezzanine floor. It opened in 2001 as one of the first British beer venues more obviously inspired by the US craft brewing scene than the native pub tradition. The fresh, unfiltered beers are served under air pressure. A pils, a pale ale, a black lager and a wheat beer are always on while the brewer experiments with the remaining two lines: an interesting spiced 'dry wheat beer' and an export stout were on when I visited (for more information about the brewery see p284). As often on the other side of the Atlantic, proper stonebaked pizzas take pride of place on the menu, which also includes pasta, mussels and sausage and mash, available in the bar with the big screen TV or in a recessed restaurant space with friendly table service.

The name refers to the proximity of the Greenwich Meridian at 0° longitude, but has been retained for subsequent daughter venues in Bristol, Cardiff and Reading.

⇄ Blackheath 🚲 LCN+ Lewisham, Eltham, local links to Greenwich 🚶 Blackheath and Greenwich Park paths, link to Jubilee Greenway, Thames Path

BROMLEY

Before the railway turned it into deep surburbia, Bromley was an important Kent market town on the road from London to Hastings and an official residence of the Bishop of Rochester, whose palace still stands and is used as a civic centre. Its most famous son is H G Wells, born above his father's shop in the High Street, though he disliked the place, labelling it a "morbid sprawl of population". More recently, David Bowie grew up here, running an arts lab in nearby Beckenham during the formative years of his career. The gutting of the historic town centre to build the Glades Shopping Centre in 1991 hasn't helped, but there are some pleasant parks and gardens, two theatres and a good few remaining historic buildings to engage you in addition to the beer outlets below.

BELGO BROMLEY
Bar, restaurant
242 The Glades Shopping Centre, BR1 1DN
☎ (020) 8466 8522
🌐 www.belgo-restaurants.co.uk
🕐 12-11 Mon-Sat; 12-10.30 Sun. *Children welcome*
Cask beer None, **Other beers** 4-5 keg, 50 bottles (mainly Belgian), **Also** Genever
🍽 Belgian/international menu, 🏠 Front terrace overlooking park, ♿

A Belgo in a shopping mall doesn't sound promising, but this is actually one of the more attractive branches of the chain. It's helped by a surprisingly pleasant setting, at the back of the Glades Shopping Centre looking out at leafy Queen's Garden. Until 2010 this was the Abbaye, part of another Belgian theme bar chain; it's now a bit less cosy and more boldly branded but straightforward for a Belgo, with a single grey-green room divided into bar and restaurant halves and an outdoor terrace onto the park. Beer and food menus are standard Belgo (see Belgo Centraal p73), with mussels and chips to the fore, beer-themed mains and bar snacks for those just wanting something to soak up the beer.

There are limited interesting draught options, but bottles still include some strong choices like trappists Achel and Orval, abbey beers St Feuillien and Maredsous, and specialities like Halve Maan Brugse Zot and St Bernardus Grottenbier. It's a bit cheaper and notably friendlier than more central branches.

🚉 Bromley North, Bromley South 🚲 LCN+27, LCN+ Crystal Palace, Lewisham, Mottingham

Bromley

① Belgo Bromley
② Bitter End
③ Red Lion

Bitter End

BITTER END
Shop
139 Masons Hill, BR2 9HW
📞 (020) 8466 6083, 🌐 www.thebitterend.biz
🕐 12-9 Mon-Sat; 12-2, 7-9 Sun
Cask beers ✅ 5-7 (usually Harveys, Timothy Taylor, unusual guests), **Other beers** 160 bottles, up to 200 bulk cask beers to order, **Also** 10 real ciders/perries
Tastings organised for external events

Co-licensees Nigel and John weren't the first to think of adding value to a local off license by selling cask beer to carry out, but their enterprise has been among the most enduring: the stillage first went up in this corner offie just outside Bromley town centre back in 1983. In recent years they've added a second business, BeerBarrels2u, which specialises in online sales of a choice of 200 beers in minipins and polypins for home delivery. In the shop, draught beer is available in more modest quantities of 4½ and 9 pints, and at something approaching half the price, pint for pint, you'd pay in a pub. Available beers constantly rotate but regularly include brews from Adnams, Dark Star, Harveys, Sharp's and Timothy Taylor, and tastings can be organised for parties and events. The bottled range has built up nicely too, and now stretches to over 150, including British bottle-conditioned ales from Royal Tunbridge Wells, St Austell and Dark Star, lesser known Belgians like Troubadour, Arend and Van Eecke, and American entrants from the likes of Dogfish Head. The website boasts of a beer festival in a shop, and it's not far wrong.

🚃 Bromley South 🚲 LCN+27, LCN+ Crystal Palace, Lewisham, Mottingham

RED LION
Traditional pub
10 North Road, BR1 3LG
📞 (020) 8460 2691
🕐 11-11 Mon-Sat; 11-midnight Sun
Cask beers ✅ 5 (Greene King, 3 guests)
🍴 Good value pub grub, 🏠 Front terrace
Darts, big screen sport

The pleasant Victorian residential area northeast of Bromley town centre manages to sustain several pubs, of which this is the most interesting for beer fans. Run by the same landlords, Chris and Siobhan, since 1992, it's a proper old local with a history going back to the 17th century, though was rebuilt from the ground up in 1890 by Whitbread. Much of the tiling from this period has survived, particularly in the front bar, a pleasant space with an open fire and lots of books where the TV sport is not too intrusive. For a while it was owned by Beards of Sussex, who styled the current bar back, and is now Greene King, though with considerable leeway to order guests – beers from Beartown, BrewDog, Cains, Harviestoun, Old Mill, Orkney, Stonehenge and White Horse regularly appear alongside IPA and Abbot. Simple pub grub includes traditional salads, chilli con carne, omelettes and more exotic choices like red Thai vegetable curry.

🚃 Bromley North 🚲 LCN+27, LCN+ Lewisham, Woolwich, links to Crystal Palace

Red Lion

CAMBERWELL, DULWICH & PECKHAM

Camberwell still stands on its village green, now a public park, on the highway from the ancient Thames crossing at Vauxhall southeast towards Kent. A mildly bohemian air and an alternative arts and music scene has been fed by the presence since 1898 of Camberwell College of Arts, which might also explain why the place lent its name to the Camberwell Carrot, a giant cannabis cigarette in cult film *Withnail and I*.

Peckham, just east of Camberwell, was the destination of Britain's first omnibus service, started by Thomas Tilling in 1850 to connect it with Oxford Street. Back then it was still a rural village, but the bus and later the train saw the last fields covered with houses and light industry by the end of the 19th century. Thankfully the open space of Peckham Rye, where the eight year old William Blake had his vision of angels in an oak tree, was preserved as an urban common and park. Today Peckham combines grand houses and gentrified streets with serious pockets of deprivation.

Dulwich Village to the south is one of the most fascinating and picturesque but least visited of London's villages, and in Dulwich Picture Gallery boasts one of the capital's true hidden gems. Once a minor hamlet attached to Camberwell, it grew when the land, which had been grabbed by Henry VIII on the dissolution of Bermondsey Abbey, was sold in 1605 to superstar actor Edward Alleyn. He founded Dulwich College and two other schools, gifting the entire estate to the College. The landowner's strict controls on development account for the well integrated and rustic appearance of Dulwich today – the last farm only closed in the 20th century.

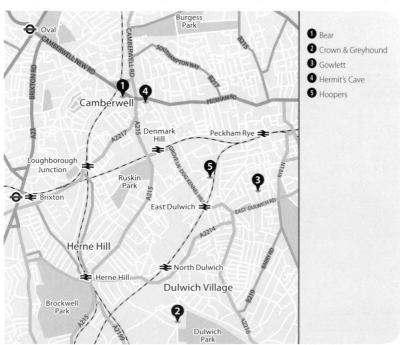

1 Bear
2 Crown & Greyhound
3 Gowlett
4 Hermit's Cave
5 Hoopers

BEAR

Gastropub
296a Camberwell New Road, SE5 0RP
☎ (020) 7274 7037, ⊕ www.thebear-freehouse.
co.uk, **tw** bearfreehouse
⊙ 12-11 Mon-Thu; 12-midnight Fri & Sat;
12-10.30 Sun. *Children until 7pm*
Cask beers ✓ 2 (unusual/local guests), **Other
beers** 2 keg, 4 bottles, **Also** Wines
⑪ Gastro menu, ⊞ Beer garden, front terrace,
⚿ No disabled toilet but ramped access
Tue quiz, occasional live music

This handsome and intriguingly decorated
gastropub and genuine free house may
currently only boast two cask pumps, but is
committed to ensuring they dispense
interesting and often local beers. Dark Star,
Meantime, Red Squirrel, Tring and
Twickenham are among the suppliers,
alongside Acorn, Oakham, Roosters, Slater's,
Teignworthy and Wye Valley from further
afield, with the likes of Chimay and Duvel in
bottles. An interesting menu might include
artichoke and spinach gratin, pheasant breast
or squid and mussel stew, and the Sunday
lunch has been commended in the Observer
Best Food awards. The wood panelling, bare
bricks, surviving stained glass and decorative
touches like old clocks and a mosaic of the
pub's name in cork create a relaxed
environment to enjoy it all.

Bear

Insider tip! The proximity of the College of Arts
and Kings College and Maudsley hospitals is
reflected in the discounts offered to card-
carrying students and NHS staff.

⊖ Oval 🚌 Sacred Heart School (numerous from
Oval) 🚲 LCN+ Bermondsey, Herne Hill,
Lambeth

CROWN & GREYHOUND

Traditional pub
73 Dulwich Village, SE21 7BJ
☎ (020) 8299 4976
⊕ www.thecrownandgreyhound.co.uk
⊙ 11-11 Mon-Thu; 11-midnight Fri & Sat;
11-10.30 Sun. *Children very welcome*
Cask beers ✓ 4 (Fuller's, Harveys, Sharp's, 1
unusual guest), **Other beers** 10 keg, 5 bottles,
Also 2-3 real ciders/perries, wines
⑪ Enhanced pub grub/gastro menu, ⊞ Beer
garden, front terrace, ⚿
*Sun quiz, Thu wine club, chess club, life drawing
classes, monthly vintage fashion sale, functions,
board games*

Famously the only pub in Dulwich Village, the
Crown & Greyhound is known locally as the
Dog but its full name tells a story of the
erosion of surface class distinctions in British
society. The site was originally occupied by
the Crown, intended for servants and
labourers, while their employers used another
pub called the Greyhound. Both were
demolished in 1900 and replaced by the
current large building, with
compartmentalised bars typical of the time
that continued to separate the classes for
some decades. These days the only distinction
is age – the pub generally goes out of its way
to be family friendly, particularly at weekends,
but reserves the former billiard room on the
left as an adults only space.

It's a Mitchells & Butlers Castle pub with a
decent beer offer – regulars Doom Bar,
London Pride and Sussex Best are joined by
what's often a more unusual pick from the
pubco's guest list, Saltaire Triple Chocoholic
on my visit. The kegs include two German
wheat beers and local Meantime Pale Ale,
while Chimay and Vedett White are among
the bottles. Roasted root risotto, steaks, duck,
sausages and the like are served in the bars or
restaurant area at prices labourers and
servants might baulk at slightly, but there's a

Crown & Geyhound

good value prix fixe deal on weekdays. There's much to admire in the stained and etched glass panels, carved and polished wood, elaborate ceiling and cheery conservatory.

≥ North Dulwich 🚉 Dulwich Village (P4 North Dulwich) 🚲 LCN+ 23, 25 🚶 Green Chain Walk

GOWLETT
Contemporary pub
62 Gowlett Road, SE15 4HY
📞 (020) 7635 7048, 🌐 www.thegowlett.com
🕐 12-midnight Mon-Thu; 12-1am Fri & Sat; 12-11.30 Sun. *Children welcome*
Cask beers ✅ 4 (Fuller's, 3 guests), **Other beers** 2 bottles
🍕 Pizzas, 🪑 Rear patio, ♿
Thu DIY 7" DJ, Sun DJs, annual beer festival, pool, board games

This comfortably made over Victorian community pub in a mildly gentrified bit of Peckham, not far from Rye Common and trendy Bellenden Road, has bounced in and out of the *Good Beer Guide* over the years, once even winning local CAMRA Pub of the Year, and is currently upping its game on beer choice. Regular London Pride is usually joined by Punch Finest Cask choices from Batemans, BrewDog, Hogs Back, Hop Back and Titanic, and the annual beer festival has been reinstated, with 16 beers and four ciders on

offer thanks to a stillage on the patio, and live bands and other events too. Food is proper pizzas, locals are invited to bring their vintage 7" singles to play on Thursdays, and the regular DJ spins funk, soul and chill – the latter condition also encouraged by the sloppy sofas and laid-back vibe.

≥ East Dulwich, Peckham Rye 🚉 Oakhurst Grove (37 Peckham Rye, 484 East Dulwich) 🚲 Links to LCN+22, 25

HERMIT'S CAVE
Traditional pub
28 Camberwell Church Street, SE5 8QU
📞 (020) 7703 3188
🕐 12-midnight Mon-Wed; 12-2am Thu-Sat; 12-midnight Sun. *Children welcome daytime*
Cask beers ✅ 4 (Brodie's, Daleside, 2 guests), **Other beers** 3 keg, **Also** 3 real ciders/perries
Big screen sport

This small, oddly-angled corner pub within a stone's throw of the Green is a Camberwell institution.

It's been through several incarnations over the years: the current version is decked out in cheeky pink and green, with all sorts of old junk – mannequins, tobacco boxes, vintage radios, a stuffed moose head – offsetting the heritage woodwork and elaborate marbled and mirrored fireplace in which an open fire regularly burns. It's an Enterprise pub with one free-of-tie pump, which dispenses house beer Loddon Gravesend Shrimpers. The others include at least one Brodie's, which might well be a mild, but other breweries like Adnams could appear. The big screen TV is equipped for Sky Sports 3D so don't be surprised to find the place full of people sporting funny glasses.

≈ Denmark Hill ⊖ Oval 🚌 Camberwell Green (various, Oval or Elephant and Castle) 🚲 LCN+23

HOOPERS ☆ 25

Contemporary pub, specialist
28 Ivanhoe Road, SE5 8DH
📞 (020) 7733 4797, 🌐 www.hoopersbar.co.uk
🕐 5.30-11 Mon & Tue; 5.30-11.30 Wed;
5.30-midnight Thu; 5-midnight Fri;
12.30-midnight Sat; 1-11 Sun. *Children until 9pm*
Cask beers ✓ 4 (unusual guests), **Other beers** 2 keg, 40+ mainly Belgian and German bottles, **Also** 2 real ciders/perries
🔟 Check website or phone, 🎏 Tables on street
Thu quiz, monthly comedy, quarterly beer festivals, meet the brewer evenings, regular live music, big screen sport, functions

Hidden in the hilly residential streets between Camberwell and East Dulwich, this welcoming and pleasant free house is well worth the effort to find. The flatiron building has been refitted in clean, bright style, but retains its original porches and a more traditionally decorated and furnished small snug.

A serious commitment to speciality beer starts with the four handpumps dispensing a changing selection of interesting guests: Ascot, Brodie's, Dark Star, Otley and Skinner's beers might appear alongside those of brewers rarely seen in London, like Newmans of Caerphilly or Toad of Doncaster. Adnams and Harveys seasonals are featured and Redemption might become a regular. Quarterly beer festivals, usually showcasing local brewers, and other beer events expand the cask choice still further.

The bottled range is half Belgian, including Orval, Rodenbach, St Bernardus and Van Eecke, but also visits the Netherlands (Texels), Britain (Meantime, Otley) and Germany (Früh,

Hoopers

Schneider, Schlenkerla, Weihestephaner), this last country's representation expanding considerably in the autumn when a comprehensive range of Oktoberfestbieren is on offer. On top of this Hoopers is one of very few other outlets for beers from Blackheath brewpub Zerodegrees (p284), offered alongside genuine Czech lager from Žatec.

Among all the zythological glories, though, it still finds the heart to be a proper community local, with a wide range of activities. At the time of writing they were "between chefs" so check beforehand if you want to eat, and note that B&B accomodation is available for those who wish to explore at maximum leisure.

Pub trivia: The collection of breweriana extends well beyond the usual vintage enamel signs. Check out the display case commemorating several famous names now defunct or fallen from grace, including Bass, Courage, Fremlins, Flowers and Gales. There's even a working original illuminated bar mount for notorious keg bitter Watneys Red Barrel, not that it's likely to induce glowing nostalgia in beer lovers of a certain age.

≈ East Dulwich 🚲 Local links to East Dulwich, Peckham, LCN+23

CROYDON

Of all the significant market towns swallowed by outer London, Croydon seems to me to have best retained its self sufficiency, although it's had its application for formal city status turned down several times on the grounds that it's not distinct enough from the surrounding metropolis. It was already the biggest town in Surrey before being incorporated officially into London in 1964. Today it boasts a bigger population than Hull or Coventry, numerous arts venues including the famous Fairfield Halls, several major employers, a destination shopping centre and a prime position on the rail and road routes between London, Gatwick Airport and Brighton. Croydon Palace was once the residence of the Archbishop of Canterbury and this and a few other medieval buildings still stand among the less attractive legacy of 1960s redevelopment. It was the site of London's first passenger airport, which closed in 1959, and is so far the only part of London where trams have returned to the streets. At the weekend many of its town centre bars are popular with the sort of younger drinkers that dress minimally even in sub-zero temperatures, but the list below will direct you to more relaxing company.

CLARET

Traditional pub, bar
4a Bingham Corner, CR0 7AA
☎ (020) 8656 7452
🕙 11.30-11.30 Mon-Wed; 11.30-midnight Thu; 11.30-12.30am Fri & Sat; 12-11.30 Sun
Cask beers ✅ 6 (Palmers, 5 unusual guests),
Also 2 real ciders, malts
🍴 Filled rolls Sat only
Beer festivals twice yearly, big screen sport

The name and the storefront site, some distance from the town centre but almost next door to a tram stop, give the impression of a 1980s wine bar, as indeed this once was. But for many years now it's been one of Croydon's most reliable outlets for an interesting range of cask ales. The long single space inside is mock Tudor with beams and roughly surfaced walls, brewery signs and mirrors and a proud display of CAMRA awards. Palmers IPA from Bridport, Dorset, is the longstanding house beer and there's a certificate on display marking the 750,000th pint sold. Guests in this genuine free house

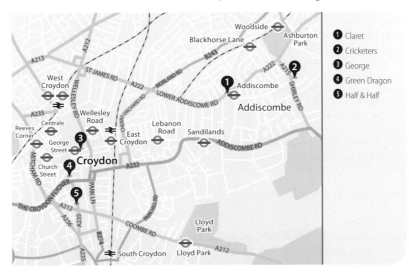

1 Claret
2 Cricketers
3 George
4 Green Dragon
5 Half & Half

come from all over with a slight bias towards southeast England – Ascot, Dark Star, Dorking, Mole, Salopian and Westerham are among the breweries regularly supported, and the choice climbs above 20 during the spring and autumn beer festivals. The same owners run a sister venue in Cheam, also called the Claret, but with a narrower choice of beers (33 The Broadway, SM3 8BL).

🚃 Addiscombe 🚲 Links to NCN21, LCN+ Croydon

CRICKETERS
Traditional pub
47 Shirley Road, CR0 7ER
📞 (020) 8662 1921
⌚ 11-11 daily. *Children until 7pm*
Cask beers ✓ 5-6 (Dark Star, Harveys, 4 unusual guests), **Other beers** 1 bottle,
Also Occasional real cider
🍴 Good value pub grub, 🌳 Rear patio and beer garden
Quarterly themed beer weekends, monthly live music and quiz, darts, pub games

A big, unpretentious, bright and blokeish Enterprise tenancy in Croydon's eastern reaches not far from the Claret (above), this is worth visiting for the friendly welcome and the well chosen selection of beers sourced through the SIBA Direct Delivery Scheme. Dark Star Hophead and Harveys Sussex Best are regulars, supplemented by guests that might come from Adnams, Exmoor, Harviestoun, Hogs Back, Hop Back, Moorhouse, Purple Moose, Palmers, Triple fff or Twickenham, to name a few from the pump clip display. Frequent beer festivals offering up to 15 choices are usually regionally themed – Scottish beers or Cumbrian beers, for example. Food stretches from cheeseburger and chips to Burmese curry and rice and is keenly priced, with Sunday lunch only £6. A retro video games console provides additional diversion.

Insider tip! We appreciated the more refined area at the back, with an open fire and bookshelves.

🚃 Addiscombe, Blackhorse Lane 🚲 NCN21, NCN+ Croydon 🚶 Link to Waterlink Way

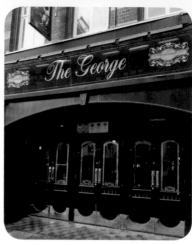

George

GEORGE
Contemporary pub
17-21 George Street, CR0 1LA
📞 (020) 8649 9077
🌐 www.jdwetherspoon.co.uk
⌚ 7am-midnight Mon-Thu; 7am-1.30am Fri & Sat; 7am-midnight Sun. *Children until early evening if eating*
Cask beers ✓ 10 (Greene King, Fuller's, 6 unusual guests), **Other beers** Usual Wetherspoon keg and bottles, **Also** 3 real ciders/perries
🍴 Wetherspoon menu until 10pm, ♿
Wetherspoon beer festivals and promotions

It's no surprise to see door supervisors in action on weekend evenings at this big Wetherspoon in the heart of central Croydon, as it inevitably picks up some of the young circuit drinking trade, but there's plenty of space for everyone – a good thing as the pub makes the best of the guest list. Two Thornbridge beers were on offer when I visited, alongside offerings from Brentwood, Brewster's, Dark Star and Mordue. Beers from Bath, Leeds, Limestone, Oakham, Rudgate or Triple fff may also be spotted. The interior decor is typical of a Wetherspoon shop conversion, with some sought-after booths towards the back.

Insider tip! There are two bars – check out both for the full range of beers on offer.

≋ East Croydon, West Croydon ☒ George Street
♻ LCN+ Croydon routes ✸ Vanguard Way,
Wandle Trail

GREEN DRAGON
Contemporary pub
58-60 High Street, CR0 1NA
☎ (020) 8667 0684
⊕ www.greendragoncroydon.co.uk
✪ 10am-midnight Mon-Thu; 10am-1am Fri &
Sat; 12-10.30 Sun. *Children very welcome*
Cask beers ✪ 7 (Dark Star, Hogs Back, unusual
guests), **Other beers** 2 keg (Belgian), **Also** 1 real
cider, wines
⑩ Breakfasts, pub grub, ♿
*Tue live music, comedy, Wed swing dance class,
Sat DJ, Sun live jazz, big screen sport, book swap,
art exhibitions, board games, pool, table football,
functions*

Regenerated from a Hog's Head in 2006, this
big and distinctive pub is now widely praised
as arguably the best in the town centre and
has proved something of a pioneer in
demonstrating you can be youthful, lively and
hip while still placing fine beer at the centre
of things. Indeed the word BEER appears in
large letters above the bar, heading up a list
that regularly features Dark Star – Hophead is
a regular, and numerous other beers from the
brewery appear too. The guests might come
from Allgates, Atlas, Hogs Back, Otter,
Twickenham or Westerham. Food starts with
breakfast and goes on to sandwiches, wraps,
pies and sharing plates. There's plenty to do

Green Dragon

besides drink, with quality live jazz, DJs and
numerous games, and a pleasant little area
under an arch where you can relax with one
of the books on offer.

≋ East Croydon, West Croydon ☒ George Street
♻ LCN+ Croydon routes ✸ Vanguard Way,
Wandle Trail

HALF & HALF
Bar
282 High Street, CR0 1NG
☎ (020) 8726 0080, ⊕ www.halfandhalf.uk.com
✪ 12-midnight Mon-Sat; 3-11 Sun
Cask beers ✪ 2 (Dark Star), **Other beers** 5 keg,
20 bottles, **Also** Wines, malts and vodkas
Occasional live music, quarterly tastings

A little further south along the High Street
than most circuit drinkers are prepared to
venture, this stylish little place is a welcome
retreat. The address formerly housed
international beer bar Beer Circus, but that
business prematurely closed in 2008. The Half
& Half doesn't attempt to offer anything like
the range of its predecessor, but it still has
some interesting stuff packed into a relatively
small space. It's credited with inventing the
practice of mixing light and dark Budweiser
Budvar, thus the name, and the specially
designed three way bar font used to
accomplish this feat – similar devices have
since appeared in a few other London bars,
no doubt to the puzzlement of Czech visitors.
Cask beers always include Dark Star Hophead,
with other Dark Star brands rotating on the
second pump. The best choices from the
bottled list are Belgian, including St Bernardus
Wit, Westmalle Tripel and the interesting
Belgoo beers brewed at Binchoise. Extensive
bar snacks of the premium nut, olive and
cracker variety make up for the lack of a
kitchen, and the restrained trancey music
might encourage some serious relaxation on
the floppy sofas downstairs.

Insider tip! Call in between Monday and
Thursday and get 20% off everything.

≋ East Croydon, South Croydon ☒ George Street
♻ LCN+ Croydon routes ✸ Vanguard Way,
Wandle Trail

GREENWICH & DEPTFORD

Once they've ticked off the must-sees in central London, the tourists normally head next to Maritime Greenwich, and with good reason. Not for nothing is it designated a World Heritage Site by UNESCO. Inigo Jones' pioneering neo-Classical Queen's House became the nucleus around which Christopher Wren and Nicholas Hawksmoor remodelled the site into what's still one of the most spectacular pieces of landscape and architectural planning in the world. The view sweeps from the Royal Observatory at the top of the hill, where the Prime Meridian of 0° longitude has been fixed by international agreement since 1884, past the Queen's House, now framed by collonades and the wings of the National Maritime Museum, and between the astonishing symmetrical domes of the Royal Naval College to the widening river.

The College is now part of the University of Greenwich and Trinity College of Music. Greenwich Park is hosting the London 2012 equestrian events. Other local attractions include the preserved Cutty Sark tea clipper (currently being restored and due to reopen in 2012), Hawksmoor's imposing St Alfege's church, various markets and the offbeat Fan Museum. Despite the busy one way system the town centre retains the atmosphere of a Georgian seaside town. The area is home to the Meantime brewery (p275), and two of their pubs are listed below.

Deptford is the poor relation, but is rich in heritage of its own, due in part to the former naval dockyards and victualling yards on Deptford Strand. Playwright Christopher Marlowe was murdered here in dodgy circumstances in 1593, while St Pauls Church has been labelled the most important Baroque church north of the Alps. Russian Tsar Pyotr I – Peter the Great – lived in diarist John Evelyn's house in 1697 while on a fact finding mission and worked incognito in the shipyard, annoying Evelyn by wrecking his prized garden hedges during a drunken carouse. We hope you'll appreciate the local hospitality as much as Pyotr did but are rather better behaved.

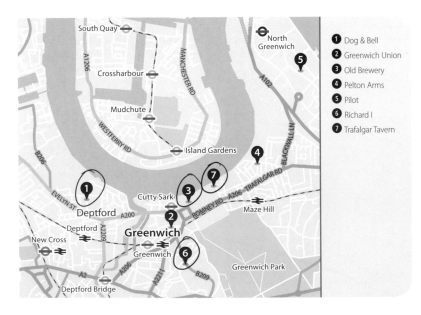

Dog & Bell

DOG & BELL ☆ 25
Traditional pub
116 Prince Street, SE8 3JD
☎ (020) 8692 5664
🕓 12-11.30 daily. *Children over 12 until 7pm only*
Cask beers ✅ 5-6 (Fuller's, 3-4 unusual guests),
Other beers 40-50 Belgian and German bottles,
Also 20 malts
🍴 Pub grub, 🍺 Beer garden, ♿
*Sun quiz, annual pickles festival, bar billiards,
darts, backgammon, board games, art
exhibitions*

One of London's pub gems, the Dog was
opened in 1823 and rebuilt in the late 1860s
Once tied to the now closed Wenlock brewery
of Islington, later to Bass and briefly to Fuller's
in the late 1970s, it's now free of tie but
continues to feature the Chiswick brewery's
ESB and London Pride. Current owners Charlie
and Eileen Gallagher arrived in 1988 and have
significantly expanded both its size and its
reputation, doing a magnificent job of
keeping it contemporary, comfortable and
welcoming to a diverse crowd while ensuring
it remains at heart a genuine community local
with an always reliable range of quality beers.

Guest ales are likely to come from Acorn,
Dark Star, Kelham Island, Nethergate,
Teignworthy, Westerham or Wolf, usually
including a range of strengths and colours. An
excellent list of Belgian beers includes craft
brewed treasures such as De Ranke, Dolle,

Dupont, Ellezelloise, Orval and St Bernardus
and genuine lambics from Cantillon and
Hanssens, with a couple of German bottles
too. Food is home-cooked and well-priced –
baguettes, fish dishes, shepherd's pie and
veggie specials – while the pickles festival in
early December must be unique in the capital.
A pleasant shaded yard decked with colourful
planters supplements the homely interior.

Visitor's note: The quiz, set by a rotating band of
volunteers, has the reputation of being one of
the toughest in London.

🚂 Deptford ⊖ Canada Water, Surrey Quays **DLR**
Cutty Sark 🚌 Abinger Grove (188 Canada Water,
Surrey Quays, Cutty Sark) 🚲 NCN1, 21, LCN+
New Cross 🚶 Jubilee Greenway, Thames Path,
Waterlink Way

GREENWICH UNION
Contemporary pub
56 Royal Hill, SE10 8RT
☎ (020) 8692 6258, 🌐 www.greenwichunion.
com, **fbk**, **tw** GreenwichUnion
🕓 12-11 Mon-Sat; 11.30-10.30 Sun. *Children
until 9pm*
Cask beers ✅ 3 (Dark Star, Meantime,
Sambrook's), **Other beers** 12-14 keg (Meantime
and others), 50+ bottles
🍴 Enhanced pub grub menu, 🍺 Beer garden
Board games

Opened in 2001 as Meantime's (p275) first
pub, the Union has recently been upstaged
by its owner's impressive Old Brewery (below),
but manager Daniel is fighting back by
offering a slightly bigger and smarter range of
beer and the short climb up Royal Hill is still
very much worthwhile. A friendly place with a
good sense of humour, it has bare wood, old
barrels, comfy chairs and a lovely rear terrace.

Greenwich Union

Old Brewery

The cask range has settled to Meantime's own London Pale Ale plus Hophead and Junction; there are many more own beers on keg including regulars Helles, London Lager, Stout, Wheat Beer and the alternative version of LPA which invites an interesting direct comparison to its cask counterpart. Specials and seasonals are supplemented by imports including a Pils and a Weissbier from Schönram in Bavaria. The bottled list encompasses several more own brands plus a solid Belgian range – real lambics from Boon and Cantillon, including the delicious Rosé de Gambrinus, Trappists from Chimay, Orval, Rochefort and Westmalle, and Liefmans Goudenband. Then there's quality German Altbier and Kölsch, a good choice from Anchor of San Francisco including Old Foghorn barley wine, and Sam Smith's Taddy Porter and Imperial Stout. Food is upmarket freshly made pub grub – smoked haddock parcels, butternut squash and leek dumplings, beef onion and Meantime stout pie, chargrilled steaks and a mouthwatering specialist cheeseboard. Right next door to another classic Greenwich pub, the Richard I (below), the Union marches on.

Insider tip! Two or more people can investigate the 5-course tasting menu, each course with a beer recommendation (£25 per person, beers not included).

⇌ Greenwich **DLR** Greenwich 🚌 Ashburnham Grove (numerous, Greenwich) 🚲 Links to Greenwich and Lewisham ⚡ Links to Jubilee Greenway, Thames Path, Waterlink Way

OLD BREWERY ☆ 25

Bar, restaurant, specialist
Pepys Building, Old Royal Naval College, SE10 9LM
📞 (020) 3327 1280, ⊕ www.oldbrewerygreenwich.com, **fbk**, **tw** OldBrewery
🕙 11-11 Mon-Sat; 11-10.30 Sun. *Children welcome*
Cask beers ✅ 3 (Meantime, 2 unusual/local guests), **Other beers** 11 keg (Meantime and others), 40+ bottles, **Also** Wines
🍴 Enhanced pub grub/gastro menu, 🪑 Front patio, ♿
Brewery tours, occasional live music, Mon-Wed food promotions

When the Royal Naval Hospital opened in 1712 as a hostel for veterans, in common with similar institutions of the day it included a brewery. Since 2010 it's had one again, though we can only guess what 18th century brewsters would make of the gleaming state-of-the-art microbrewery that now towers over diners in the stylish main space of Meantime's showcase venue. From 1873 the surrounding complex, at the heart of the World Heritage Site, was used as the Royal Naval College, but over the past decade or so it's been converted to universities and public buildings.

In such a setting you need to do something special and the Old Brewery rises to the challenge, ably assisted by efficient, knowledgable and friendly staff. As well as the microbrewery there's an impressive feature created from beer bottles and a large mural explaining the brewing process. Through the red curtains from the restaurant is a smallish but tasteful bar while outside is an extensive courtyard with shaded tables, inevitably popular in good weather. Food options might include duck egg on toast, roast ray wing or Galloway veal rib, all naturally provided with beer matching suggestions. Meantime London Pale Ale is regular on cask; the others when I visited were Dark Star Hophead and Sambrook's Junction but may rotate. Kegs are mainly regulars – a Kellerbier brewed in-house, Helles, London Stout and Wheat Beer, two Meantime guests and seasonals (house-brewed Hospital Porter on my visit), two from Schönramer and a Belgian or other imported guest. Besides more Meantime beers the bottle fridges boast an array of textbook classics – Anchor Steam and Old Foghorn, Cantillon Gueuze, Coopers Sparkling Ale, Goose Island IPA, Orval, Schneider Aventinus, Westmalle Dubbel – extensively described and helpfully classified in the substantial beer menu. Don't expect knock down prices in a location like this, but it's not exorbitant and the spectacular setting gives all this fine beer the respect it deserves.

⇌ Greenwich, Maze Hill **DLR** Cutty Sark ⮬ NCN1 and Greenwich Park links, link to NCN21 ⫽ Thames Path, Jubilee Greenway, link to Waterlink Way

PELTON ARMS
Traditional pub
23-25 Pelton Road, SE10 9PQ
☎ (020) 8858 0572
⊕ www.peltonarmspub.com
✪ 3.30-midnight Mon; 11-midnight Tue-Thu; 11am-1am Fri; 10am-1am Sat; 10-11 Sun. *Children until 6.30pm*
Cask beers ✔ 5-9 (Greene King, Wells & Young's, unusual guests)
⑪ Sandwiches, salads, pub grub, ⛱ Beer garden, ♿
Mon darts, Tue quiz, Wed knitting night, Thu open mic, Sat live bands, Sun acoustic night, monthly DIY DJ, bar billiards, occasional big screen sport

Follow the Thames Path downstream from the World Heritage Site and turn off into a side street of modest Victorian terraces to reach this top class local, enthusiastically run since 2009 by diamond geezer Geoff Keen. Inside

it's a curious but very comfortable cross between a traditional pub, complete with St George's Cross bunting, and a kitschy living room with retro standard lamps. The beer garden has a pleasant sheltered area with its own big screen. Bombardier and Greene King IPA are regulars but the rest of the extensive real ale selection plunders the Punch Finest Cask list – Batemans, Beartown, BrewDog, Leeds or Hydes beers might well find their way to the bar. Food is wholesome, well-priced stuff, from fish and chips, whitebait and pints of prawns to salads and Thai curry. They're big on events including regular live bands, Cockney knees-ups with the Pearly Queen of Greenwich, who uses the pub as her base...and knitting nights, would you Adam and Eve it?

Visitor's note: Forgot to pop out to the shops before you went for a pint? No problem, as the pub includes its own convenience store.

⇌ Maze Hill **DLR** Cutty Sark 🚌 Tyler Street (numerous, Greenwich) ⮬ NCN1 ⫽ Thames Path, Jubilee Greenway

PILOT
Traditional pub
68 River Way, SE10 0BE
☎ (020) 8858 5910, ✉ thepilot.greenwich@fullers.co.uk, ⊕ www.fullers.co.uk
✪ 11-11 Mon-Sat; 12-10.30 Sun. *Children until 9pm*

Pelton Arms

Cask beers ✓ 5-6 (Fuller's, occasional guests), Other beers 6 bottles (Fuller's)
🍴 Fish specialities and enhanced pub grub, cheese, 🍺 Beer garden, tables on street, ♿
Tue quiz and chip shop night, Sun acoustic jam, occasional tasting events, board games

The Greewich peninsula, in the right shoulder of the Thames meander that encloses the Isle of Dogs, was until relatively recently an industrial zone, with traffic on its way to the Blackwall Tunnel roaring past wharves and a massive gasworks. Curiously placed amid all this was a row of cottages and a pub dating from 1801, called the Pilot Inn – not, as many imagine, in reference to the river pilots who guided shipping, but because the houses and pub were built to serve a tidal watermill in which then Prime Minister William Pitt the Younger – the pilot of the nation – was a major investor. The location is now, if anything, even more curious. Immediately to the north are car parks surrounding Norman Foster's landmark O₂, formerly known as the Millennium Dome and now a successful entertainment complex which will be an Olympic venue in 2012. All around it a major new residential development is sprouting up.

For years a smallish free house, the Pilot became a Fuller's pub in 2002 and has swelled considerably with comfortable rooms across two levels and an extensive beer garden with crazy paving and an entertaining water feature. The oldest part by the main bar is also

the nicest and if you look carefully you can work out where the joins are. A good range of the brewery's beers is on offer – Chiswick, Discovery, ESB and London Pride as well as seasonals and occasional guests of the Adnams, Harveys or Timothy Taylor variety. Bottles stretch to limited edition specialities like Brewer's Reserve and Vintage Ale. The menu headlines on fish, usually sourced from New Billingsgate Market round the corner, but with other options including pies, burgers and butties, and an impressive selection of 40 different cheeses offered as tasting plates. Friendly manager Louis confesses they usually recommend wine to accompany these, but the connoisseur will opt for a Vintage Ale.

➤ Maze Hill ⊖ North Greenwich **DLR** Cutty Sark 🚌 Boord Street (188 Maze Hill, Cutty Sark, North Greenwich) 🚲 NCN1, LCN+ Greenwich, Woolwich 🚶 Thames Path, Jubilee Greenway

RICHARD I
Traditional pub
52-54 Royal Hill, SE10 8RT
📞 (020) 8692 2996, 🌐 www.richardthefirst.co.uk, **fbk, tw** Richard1stTolly
🕐 11-11 Mon-Sat; 12-10.30 Sun. *Children until 8pm*
Cask beers ✓ 4 (Wells & Young's, occasional guests), **Other beers** 6 bottles
🍴 Enhanced pub grub, 🍺 Front terrace, beer garden
Sun quiz, occasional charity nights, morris and molly dancers, summer barbecues

Two adjoining bow windowed Georgian cottages were at some stage fused together to create the public and saloon bars of this classic pub, now a Young's house but still known locally as Tolly's from the days when one side was tied to now defunct Tolly Cobbold's Walthamstow subsidiary (see also Anchor & Hope p137). Nowadays both sides are equally comfortable and display evocative photos of locals' outings to Derby Day or the Kent hop fields in the 1950s. Bitter, Special and a Young's seasonal are on handpump, alongside a fourth beer that could be Bombardier, Courage Best or Sharp's Doom Bar, while Special London Ale and Double Chocolate Stout are among the bottles. Vegetable crumble, venison casserole, roast chicken and sausage and mash typify the

Pilot

Richard I

food menu. The back garden is similarly proportioned to and at least as lovely as the Greenwich Union's next door (above).

Pub trivia: Molly dancing, if you must know, generally takes place on Plough Monday, the first Monday after 6th January and the traditional start to the agricultural year. A bit like morris dancing with added cross dressing, these days it's likely to involve women – including, apparently, bearded ladies – as well as men.

🚆 Greenwich **DLR** Greenwich 🚌 Ashburnham Grove (numerous, Greenwich) 🚲 Links to Greenwich and Lewisham 🚶 Links to Jubilee Greenway, Thames Path, Waterlink Way

TRAFALGAR TAVERN
Traditional pub
Park Row, SE10 9NW
📞 (020) 8858 2909
🌐 www.trafalgartavern.co.uk
🕐 12-11 Mon-Thu; 12-midnight Fri & Sat; 12-10.30 Sun. *Children until early evening*
Cask beers ✔ 6 (Adnams, Sharp's, 1 unusual guest), **Other beers** 3 keg, 8 bottles (Palm, Duvel-Moortgat), **Also** Malts, wines
🍴 Enhanced pub grub, 🪑 Tables on Thames Path
Sun open mic, functions

Built in 1837 and now Grade I listed, this huge cream-painted riverfront pile just downstream of the Royal Naval College is as much a piece of Greenwich heritage as its illustrious neighbour. Numerous 19th century politicians and writers including William Gladstone and Charles Dickens were fans of the pub's renowned whitebait dinners, and Dickens set the wedding breakfast in *Our Mutual Friend* in the downstairs bar. It's now run by Greenwich Inc, who own several catering venues in the area, and whitebait is still on the menu but breadcrumbed rather than simply floured – bar manager Brendan told me that the traditional method freaked too many customers out. Alternatively you might choose salads, swordfish, burgers or Ploughman's from the bar menu or sit down to smoked haddock or ricotta and spinach dumplings in the adjoining restaurant.

Traditional ale is very much part of the offer – Doom Bar and Adnams Bitter are regulars, other Adnams and Sharp's brands and seasonals are featured, and the changing guest might come from Slater's or Vale. They're also keen on Brabant brewer Palm and feature several of their beers including keg Palm Spéciale and Steenbrugge Blond; Belgian options in bottle include Duvel and Maredsous. The pub retains its grandiose, period feel with dark wood, decorated ceilings and those magnificent original bay windows that afford a spectacular view of the river. Upstairs a chandelier-draped ballroom is regularly hired for events and functions. Of course it's a tourist magnet, and gets very, very busy in summer, when drinkers spill past the recently installed statue of Nelson and down the Thames Path, but considering they could sell practically anything here it's great to see them selling something good.

🚆 Maze Hill **DLR** Cutty Sark 🚲 NCN1 and Greenwich Park links 🚶 Thames Path, Jubilee Greenway

HERNE HILL

Herne Hill, west of Dulwich, was simply a term for a geographical feature until the railway turned it into a place and the local countryside into housing. The hill itself is now occupied by Brockwell Park, one of London's loveliest, which separates Herne Hill from Brixton. Once it was the private estate of the mansion that's still perched on the summit, now used as a park café.

COMMERCIAL

Contemporary pub
212 Railton Road, SE24 0JT
📞 (020) 7733 8783
🌐 www.thecommercialhotelhernehill.co.uk
🕐 12-midnight Mon-Thu; 12-1am Fri & Sat; 12-midnight Sun
Cask beers ✅ 4 (Fuller's, Sharp's, unusual guests), **Other beers** 8 keg, 6 bottles, **Also** 1+ real cider, wines
🍽 Gastro-ish menu, 🌳 Beer garden, ♿
Mon quiz, Tue wine club, Wed stitch & bitch

Commercial

The immediate surroundings of Herne Hill station have recently been turned into a pleasant public space, and are well complemented by this big and busy but rather charming reinvented pub, a Mitchells & Butlers Castle pub attracting a mixed but generally youthful crowd. In the main space there's a lovely old bar back with etched glass and wooden furniture; at the back, sofas sprawl under a skylight and a Japanese mural. London Pride and Doom Bar are the regulars, assisted by more unusual options from brewers like Copper Dragon, Kelham Island, Otley, Leeds, Rudgate or White Horse to lubricate the Wednesday night stitching and bitching. Numerous imported kegs include Sierra Nevada Pale Ale, with Worthington White Shield and Duvel the pick of the bottles. Prix fixe deals up the value of the menu which could include black pudding, salmon or beer battered fish.

🚆 Herne Hill ⊖ Brixton 🚌 Herne Hill (3, 196 Brixton) 🚲 LCN+25 🚶 Brockwell Park paths and links to Dulwich Park

❶ Commercial   ❷ Florence   ❸ Prince Regent

FLORENCE

Contemporary pub, brewpub
131-133 Dulwich Road, SE24 0NG
📞 (020) 7326 4987, ⊕ www.florencehernehill.
com, **fbk, tw** theflorencepub
⏰ 11-midnight Mon-Thu; 11-1am Fri & Sat;
11-midnight Sun. *Children very welcome until
8pm*
Cask beers ✅ 3 (Florence, guests), **Other beers**
6 keg, 10 bottles
🍴 Eclectic UK/US pub grub, 🍺 Extensive beer
garden, ♿
*Themed seasonal events, children's playroom,
table football, occasional Meat Wagon visits*

Part of the Capital Pub Company but unique
in the chain for offering its own brewed cask
beer since an extensive refit in 2007 (see
p270), the generously proportioned Florence
is perfectly placed round the corner from the
station and right opposite Brockwell Park. It's a
natural destination for families enjoying the
green space, and even provides a kid's
playroom across the other side of the pretty
garden with its palm trees in illuminated pots.
And it's a stop on the rounds of the Meat
Wagon, an itinerant pop-up food seller
reputed to do the best burgers in London. If
the Wagon isn't around, the pub's own menu
offers dahl, venison lasagne, roast pumpkin
curry and burgers of its own, either in the bar
or the sit-down restaurant. House brewed
Beaver, Bonobo and Weasel are the regulars,
with Wells & Young's brands or Sharp's Doom
Bar usually occupying the fourth pump.
Bottles stretch to Duvel and Little Creatures,
and there are Meantime keg taps plus a half
and half dispenser for Budvar blond and dark
(see Half & Half p177).

🚆 Herne Hill ⊖ Brixton 🚌 Herne Hill (3, 196
Brixton) 🚲 LCN+25 🚶 Brockwell Park paths
and links to Dulwich Park

Florence

Prince Regent

PRINCE REGENT

Gastropub
69 Dulwich Road, SE24 0NJ
📞 (020) 7274 1567
⊕ www.theprinceregent.co.uk
⏰ 12-11 Mon-Wed; 12-midnight Thu-Sat;
12-10.30 Sun. *Children welcome*
Cask beers ✅ 4 (Black Sheep, guests), **Other
beers** 3 keg, 7 bottles, **Also** Wines
🍴 Brunch, bistro menu, 🍺 Front terrace, ♿
Mon meal deal, Tue quiz, functions

This handsome gastropub right opposite the
well-loved Brockwell Park Lido has an
imposing façade with a bust of its namesake
in a niche, though the extravagant Prince
might well have preferred its more
flamboyant near neighbour the Florence
(above). Inside it's staid but friendly, with
smart wood, etched glass and crisply aproned
waiters, and a great view of the street and
park from its big windows. Food is good
quality, well cooked generally no nonsense –
Irish stew, fish pie, pan-fried bream and
veggie sausage and mash, for example, with a
popular brunch. Black Sheep Bitter is the
regular cask, with well-kept guests from the
Punch Finest Cask Range such as Harviestoun,
Hobsons, Sharp's or Thwaites. Budvar, Chimay
Bleu and Sierra Nevada Pale are the pick of
the bottles.

Insider tip! The popular Monday meal deal
offers two courses from a prix fixe menu for £11
(booking advisable).

🚆 Herne Hill ⊖ Brixton 🚌 Herne Hill (3, 196
Brixton) 🚲 LCN+25 🚶 Brockwell Park paths
and links to Dulwich Park

BROCKLEY

MR LAWRENCE WINE MERCHANT / BAR

Shop, bar
391 Brockley Road, SE4 2PH
☎ (020) 8692 1550
🌐 www.mrlawrencewinemerchant.co.uk
⚙ Shop 12-9 daily; Bar 12-11 Mon-Sat; 12-10.30 Sun
Cask beer None, **Other beers** 300+ bottles in shop. 25-30 in bar, **Also** Specialist ciders and spirits, wines
🎁 Shop: artisanal chocolate. Bar: cassoulet and sharing plates, 🍹 Rear patio in bar
Occasional tastings

Graham Lawrence opened a wine bar in residential Brockley, on the hilly ridge southwest of Deptford, in 1992, and later began importing exclusive wines and ciders from small French producers. To help expand his import trade he opened an off license next door which is managed by his sister Linda. In the past five years both businesses have extended their policy of supporting quality artisanal producers from wine to beer, evolving a mouthwatering list that crams the shelves of the smallish but intriguing shop and lures beer hunters considerable distances. Rather than one or two beers each from numerous breweries, Linda tends to stock a comprehensive range from brewers she likes and is particularly keen to support local talent. So you should find several each from Dark Star, Gadds', Kernel, Meantime, Nelson, Pitfield, Sambrook's and Westerham alongside similarly wide representation from BrewDog, Durham and St Austell. International offerings come from Anchor, Anker (Gouden Carolus), Boon, Coopers, Goose Island, Paulaner, Schneider, Schlenkerla and St Bernardus with Trappists from Achel, Orval, La Trappe and Westmalle. Polypins are also available to order. Next door in the wine bar there's no draught beer, but there is a limited range of bottles, including from Boon, Kernel, Meantime and Pitfield, and a pleasant drinking environment in which to appreciate them, with comfy armchairs and old wooden tables. They used to do full three course dining but have streamlined to tasting plates and a nightly cassoulet: "I've got to the stage in my life," Graham told me, "where work is to be enjoyed, not worried about."

≋ Crofton Park ⊖ Brockley, New Cross 🚌 Crofton Park Station (171, 172 New Cross, Brockley) 🚲 NCN+ Forest Hill, Peckham 🚶 Link to Green Chain Walk

CHISELHURST

RAMBLERS REST
Traditional pub
Mill Place, Chislehurst, BR7 5HD

Mr Lawrence Wine Merchant / Bar

Ramblers Rest

☎ (020) 8467 1734
☼ 11.30-11 Mon-Sat; 12-10.30 Sun. *Children welcome*
Cask beers ✔ 5 (Fuller's, Wells & Young's, Wychwood or Sharp's), **Also** Malts
🍽 Good value pub grub and sandwiches, 🍺 Beer garden, adjacent common
Monthly quiz

The name suggests London's outer rural fringe and the pub's setting looks as rustic as the hunting prints that decorate the walls. The white weatherboarded building sits picturesquely at the bottom of a dip in an open green on Chislehurst Common. The mainly wooded common is one of those precious oases of suburban green space preserved by local campaigning in the late 19th century, and now managed by a board of conservators. As well as the common and the pretty village centre with its pond, nearby attractions include the so-called Chislehurst Caves, actually a complex of mining tunnels dating from medieval times. Inside the pub there's barely space for two people to stand between the bar and the front door, but there's spreading room each side, including a pleasant area on a lower level that looks like it's been knocked through into a neighbouring cottage. Cask ales are well-known brands – London Pride, Bombardier, Courage Best, Young's Bitter and a pump that alternates Doom Bar and Brakspear Bitter – but they're well maintained and there's good

value pub grub on offer too. Urban ramblers could indeed rest here as numerous footpaths connect it to two of the capital's green walking routes but everyone can take advantage of the fact that the place has won awards for its warm welcome.

≋ Chislehurst 🚲 Links to LCN+ Bromley, Orpington 🚶 Chislehurst Common paths linking to Green Chain Walk, London Loop

CRYSTAL PALACE

GRAPE & GRAIN
Contemporary pub
Anerley Hill, SE19 2TF
☎ (020) 8778 4109
🌐 www.thegrapeandgrainse19.co.uk
☼ 12-11 Mon-Thu; 12-midnight Fri & Sat; 12-10.30 Sun. *Children until 6pm*
Cask beers ✔ 8-10 (1 Purity, unusual/local guests), **Other beers** 4 keg, 5-6 bottles, **Also** Wine
🍽 Enhanced pub grub, 🍺 Front terrace, 🎵
Mon jazz big band, Thu quiz, Sun afternoon live jazz, monthly open mic and book club, twice yearly beer festivals, bar billiards, board games, big screen sport

Victorian Britain celebrated its burgeoning might in 1851 with the Great Exhibition in Hyde Park, centred on a vast 92,000 m² cast iron and glass exhibition hall soon dubbed the Crystal Palace. Later this wonder was moved piece by piece to a fashionable suburb atop Sydenham Hill. Here it commanded the slopes of a new park with wondrous water features and anatomically incorrect model dinosaurs, complete with its own railway station on a scale fit for a Queen and Empress. In 1936 the Palace was destroyed in a devastating fire, leaving only its name firmly attached to the suburb. Apart from the beloved dinosaurs, most of the park's original features have also vanished, but it's still worth visiting. The mammoth staircase once surmounted by the palace ends in a big open space, like a grand arch framing an empty stage. Downhill from here is the National Sports Centre, which is being refurbished as a London 2012 training venue.

The Grape & Grain is an old hilltop roadhouse at the junction on the park's

Blacksmiths Arms

northwest corner, formerly known, unsurprisingly, as the Crystal Palace Tavern among other names. Refurbished and much improved by new management in 2009, it makes a point of stocking a large range of unusual beers from small and independent breweries, with eight beers of varied colours and strengths on handpump and two on gravity. The choice may have increased to a dozen by the time you read this, and is upped to 30 at the twice yearly festivals. Pure Gold is the house ale; other breweries regularly supported include Brewster's, Hogs Back, Kent, Loddon, Leeds, Mordue, RCH, Thornbridge and Westerham. Meantime and Licher beers from Germany are on keg and a few better-known specialist imports are in the fridge. Food includes numerous veggie options – falafel burger, grilled halloumi, vegetable tempura – as well as sausages, baked ham and mussels. It's a pleasant wood-panelled space with an impressive art nouveau fireplace at one end, though a little cavernous if quiet, and bubbling under my Top 25.

Insider tip! Card-carrying CAMRA members get a discount on ales and food.

⚡ Crystal Palace ⊖ Crystal Palace 🚲 LCN+23
🚶 Capital Ring, Green Chain Walk

CUDHAM

BLACKSMITHS ARMS
Traditional pub
Cudham Lane South, Cudham, TN14 7QB
📞 (01959) 572678
🌐 www.theblacksmithsarms.co.uk
🕐 11-11 Mon-Sat; 12-11 Sun. *Children welcome*
Cask beers ✅ 4 (Adnams, Harveys, Wells & Young's, Hogs Back or Sharp's)
🍴 Enhanced pub grub, 🌳 Large beer garden
Occasional quiz and karaoke, bat and trap, Tue fish night, Fri steak night

Besides urban green spaces, London's patchwork encompasses genuine countryside, with the boundary stretching in the southeast all the way to the chalk hills of the North Downs, part of the same ridge that also forms the White Cliffs of Dover. The borough of Bromley is London's greenest, with 77 square km – over half its area – of open land protected as part of the capital's Green Belt, including a corner of the Kent Downs Area of Oustanding Natural Beauty. You don't have to go far out of suburban Orpington to find yourself in a very different landscape of rolling fields and chalk slopes, peaceful woodlands, narrow lanes winding between ancient hedgerows...and country pubs.

One great example is the Blacksmiths, a lovely old whitewashed building in the village of Cudham, which also boasts a church dating partly from Saxon times. In this rustic setting perched above a dramatic glacial valley, it's hard to believe you're still in London. The pub is the birthplace of music hall star Little Tich and among the commemorative plates and flying ducks on the walls of the L-shaped drinking area is a pair of his trademark elongated boots.

There's an inviting snug round the open fireplace, while the revived Courage Best is dispensed from a bar surmounted by a vintage Courage lightbox. Other beers are Adnams Bitter, Sussex Best and a fourth pump that alternates Sharp's Doom Bar or Hogs Back TEA. Traditional pub grub – jackets, lasagne, ploughman's – is supplemented by a chalkboard of freshly cooked specials that might include venison casserole or king scallops.

Buses out here are hourly and don't run on Sundays – walkers may well prefer to approach via Bromley's network of signed circular walks, which links the place to the Bulls Head at Pratts Bottom (below) and the North Downs Way National Trail.

Insider tip! Visit in summer to appreciate landlady Joyce's pride and joy, a huge garden, which has several times won Bromley's Best Pub Garden award. It includes an elaborate heated smokers' hut and a playing area for bat and trap, a curious relative of cricket unique to rural Kent, of which Cudham is historically a part.

⇌ Orpington 🚌 Cudham (R5, R10 Orpington NSn) 🚴 Numerous country lanes 🚶 Berry's Green Circular Walk linking to North Downs Way, Cudham Circular Walk

PRATTS BOTTOM

BULLS HEAD
Traditional pub
Rushmore Hill, Pratts Bottom, BR6 7NQ
📞 (01689) 852553
🌐 www.thebullsheadpub.net
🕐 11-11 Mon-Thu; 11-midnight Fri; 11-11 Sat; 12-10.30 Sun. *Children welcome*
Cask beers ✅ 5 (Fuller's, Sharp's, Wells & Young's, 2 guests), **Other beers** 2 bottles

🍴 Pub grub, 🏡 Large beer garden

Fortnightly quiz, live bands, monthly jam night, karaoke, film nights, big screen sports, Tue & Fri darts, board games, bat and trap, fundraising events

A short walk from Knockholt station, one stop from Orpington and with frequent trains to central London, Pratts Bottom (stop giggling at the back) is another of those Can't-Believe-It's-London villages so plentiful in the borough of Bromley. The Bulls Head, a 400-year-old collection of cottages and barns reinvented as a coaching inn behind a rather forbidding late Victorian black façade, commands the pretty village green where, according to landlord Vernon, everyone says hello to each other. The pub is a centre of local social life with a busy events programme promoted through a newsletter and a lively website, but its low-beamed labyrinth of rooms is also very welcoming to visitors. Quality classic cask ales are a major feature, accounting for half the beer sales: Courage Best, London Pride and Doom Bar might be joined by beers from Hop Back or McMullen. Food could include honey glazed ham and eggs, soufflé omelettes or beer battered cod. Enjoy the outdoor life in the big

Bulls Head

Rose's

garden or ask for information about circular walks: it's possible to walk from here to the Blacksmiths Arms at Cudham (above) or to Charles Darwin's house at Down along footpaths and lanes.

Visitor's note: Look out for the Curmudgeons' Corner.

⇌ Knockholt ⊟ Pratts Bottom (402 Bromley not Sun, R5, R10 Orpington not Sun) 🚲 LCN+27 ✈ Green Street Green Circular Walk, linking to Cudham Circular Walk

WOOLWICH

ROSE'S
Traditional pub
49 Hare Street, SE18 6NE
📞 (020) 8854 1538
⊘ 11-11 Mon-Sat; 12-6 Sun. *Children until 7pm*
Cask beers ✅ 3-6 (Fuller's, unusual guests),
Other beers 5 bottles
🍴 Possibly rolls at lunchtime, Sunday roasts
Darts, crib, occasional big screen sport

Woolwich, downstream of Greenwich, grew when Henry VIII established a dockyard here to build his ego-flattering flagship *Henri Grâce à Dieu*. It's now best known for the Royal Arsenal, established in 1671, which grew into a vast complex supplying Britain's armed forces. Workers there formed a football club in 1886 which, as Arsenal FC, moved across the river to Highbury in 1913 and is now one of the most successful English teams.

The site was finally demilitarised in 1994

and has since been impressively redeveloped for residential and other uses, including Firepower (the Royal Artillery museum), and a big new Young's pub, the Dial Arch (not yet visited). The Royal Artillery Barracks on the other side of town, with its seemingly endless façade, will be used in 2012 for Olympic and Paralympic shooting and archery events.

Woolwich is one terminal of the Woolwich Free Ferry, which gives you an excellent view of the iconic Thames Barrier, the world's second largest movable flood barrier, just upriver at Charlton and also worth a visit.

On the edge of the town centre, Rose's was originally known as the Prince Albert but succumbed to local usage by adopting its nickname, acquired during the tenure of a former landlady, as its official title. As a longstanding real ale free house and frequent *Good Beer Guide* entry, it prompted concern when slated for closure in 2007, but the sale fell through and in the event it was only shut for a day while new management took over.

Little has changed – it's a traditional place with a panelled ceiling, padded benches, an impressive mural of shipping on the river, and a vivarium inhabited by two sleepy iguanas. All six pumps only come into use while busy: London Pride is a regular and Cottage, Green Jack, Hereford, Inveralmond, Nelson, Welton's and Westerham are among the favoured contributors of guest beers. Take note of the notice on the bar: "Prices may vary according to customer attitude."

⇌ Woolwich Arsenal **DLR** Woolwich Arsenal 🚲

SOUTHWEST LONDON

SOUTHWEST LONDON

In this book southwest London covers all the SW postcodes outside the central area and south of the Thames, and the districts south and southwest of these to Richmond, Kingston and New Malden. This is potentially slightly confusing as there are also SW postcodes to the north of the Thames, but these are included under West London.

The southwest doesn't have quite the same stigma as the southeast. Its dense inner city areas tend to be recognised as vibrantly multicultural, most notably Brixton, or comfortably gentrified, like Clapham and Wandsworth. Following the Thames upriver you pass a line of ever leafier and more genteel suburbs – Putney, Barnes, Richmond, Kingston – while Wimbledon Common and Richmond Park together form the capital's largest expanse of open space.

Earl Ferrers (p218)

< **Belgo Clapham (p195)**

BARNES

Hampstead may be the most celebrated of London's 'villages' but Barnes is a strong challenger for village atmosphere, with its elegant streets lined with specialist shops, Georgian terraces along the river and pretty houses clustered round a pond. Since 1995 its major attraction has been the Wildfowl and Wetlands Trust's successful London Wetland Centre, a watery wildlife haven created out of old reservoirs in a bend of the Thames. But it's also rich in musical connections: Gustav Holst lived here, Marc Bolan died here and stars from the Beatles and Rolling Stones to Madonna and Mel C recorded at Olympic Studios on Church Road.

Red Lion

RED LION
Contemporary pub
2 Castelnau, SW13 9RU
📞 (020) 8748 2984, ✉ redlionbarnes@fullers.
co.uk, 🌐 www.fullers.co.uk, **tw** RedLionBarnes
✪ 11-11.30pm Mon-Sat; 12-11 Sun. *Children welcome daytime*
Cask beers ✔ 4 (Fuller's), **Other beers** 2 keg, 4 bottles (Fuller's), **Also** Wines
🍽 Gastro menu, 🚬 Sheltered non-smoking terrace, beer garden, ♿
Functions
Numerous Olympic recording artists popped out between takes for a quick pint at the Red Lion, including Jimi Hendrix who allegedly wrote two songs in the pub while working on

Are You Experienced in 1967. It lost its megastar customers when the studio closed in 2009 but is still a great place to enjoy Fuller's beers at their best, right by the drive to the Wetlands Centre. The handsome 1830s building had its interior controversially 'knocked through' in 2003 but the resulting L-shaped space still feels like two distinct areas – a smart, pastel-shaded front section and a more clubby rear section with moulded wood and stained glass. At the back is a sizeable terrace and garden, part of which is sheltered and non-smoking, which hosts barbeques in the summer. There's a real fire, gentle background music and free WiFi.

❶ Red Lion   ❷ Sun Inn

Red Lion

Angus McKean, who manages the pub with his partner Claire Morgan, is a chef by training so the food is serious but straightforward; his determination that the beer too should be top notch has won him a Master Cellarman award from the brewery. Fuller's Chiswick, Pride and ESB are permanent as well as a seasonal and keg London Porter. Surprisingly, a couple of Boon (sweetened) fruit lambics from Belgium are also on offer following a suggestion by a CAMRA member.

Pub trivia: Look hard at the wooden fixtures at the back and you'll see motifs of crabs, seahorses and scallops – apparently a previous landlord bought them as a job lot from a demolished seaman's mission in Grimsby.

≋ Barnes Bridge 🚌 Barnes Red Lion (209 Barnes Bridge, Hammersmith; others Hammersmith, Wandsworth) 🚲 NCN4, LCN+ Hammersmith, Barnes ⠕ Thames Path, Beverley Brook Walk

SUN INN
Contemporary pub
7 Church Road, SW13 9HE
📞 (020) 8876 5256
🌐 www.thesuninnbarnes.co.uk
🕐 11-11 (midnight Thu-Sat). *Children welcome daytime*
Cask beers ✔ 4 (Fuller's, Sharp's, 2 unusual guests), **Other beers** 10 keg, 7-8 bottles,

Also Occasional real cider
🍴 Enhanced pub grub, 🌳 Beer garden/patio, ♿ *Mon quiz, Wed wine club, occasional live music*

One of the buildings contributing to the picturesque quality of Barnes Green is this pretty whitewashed pub overlooking the pond. Inside it's something of a labyrinth, with at least seven distinct spaces round an island bar, and a homely, ramshackle mix of chairs and tables, sofas and cushions which gives it a slightly hippyish feel underlined on my visit by the dreamy indie music on the speakers. There's a front yard, a sheltered side terrace, a bowling green and even a flower stall.

It's a Mitchells & Butlers Castle pub that now boasts over 20 specialist beers in various forms including four cask ales from rotating suppliers, bottles including Duvel and Erdinger, and keg taps dispensing Meantime London Pale, Paulaner Helles and Sierra Nevada Pale Ale among others. Food is gastro-ish pub grub at fair prices.

Visitor's note: Walk past the bar and look for the alcove popular with daytime laptop tappers.

≋ Barnes Bridge 🚲 NCN4, LCN+ Hammersmith, Barnes ⠕ Thames Path, Beverley Brook Walk

BATTERSEA & CLAPHAM

The original village of Battersea, as the ending of its name indicates, was on an island at the mouth of the now-covered Falconbrook river. Local place names like Lavender Hill recall a more rustic age – lavender really was gathered on the hill.

Clapham, to the southeast of Battersea, showed up as a small village in the Domesday survey and started to grow in the 1660s as refugees from the Plague and the Great Fire relocated there. Later it was a fashionable Georgian retreat.

The area today is an intriguing mix. Some of the housing around the common is posh and sedate. Clapham Junction bustles with shoppers and audiences for Battersea Arts Centre, also host to CAMRA's Battersea Beer Festival. The Victorian streets house young professional families, with shops to match. Swathes of postwar social housing are being regenerated; among these flourishes Sambrook's Brewery (p279).

BELGO CLAPHAM
Bar, restaurant
48 Clapham High Street, SW4 7UR
☎ (020) 7720 1118
⊕ www.belgo-restaurants.co.uk
🕐 12–midnight (1am Thu, 2am Fri & Sat); 12pm–12.30am Sun. *Children welcome*
Cask beers None, **Other beers** 10 keg (Belgian, Czech, German), 60 bottles (Belgian), Also Genever
🍽 Belgian/international menu, 🍺 Terrace on street, ♿

This branch of the Belgo chain was originally branded a Bièrodrome so is at least as much a bar as a restaurant. Beer and food options and general approach are in line with the rest of the chain (see Belgo Centraal p73) though there are no real lambics. A draught De Koninck was disappointingly stale so best stick to the bottles, which include eight Trappists, Maredsous and St Feuillien abbey beers and strong stalwart Bush (Scaldis). The bar has long benches under an interesting

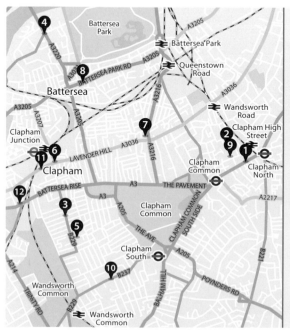

1 Belgo Clapham
2 Bread & Roses
3 Draft House Northcote
4 Draft House Westbridge
5 Eagle
6 Falcon
7 Ink Rooms
8 Lighthouse
9 Manor Arms
10 Nightingale
11 Project Orange
12 Roundhouse

arched roof; the slightly cramped restaurant area has a big, angled picture window onto the street corner and outside seating on a pleasant terrace.

⇌ Clapham High Street ⊖ Clapham North 🚲 CS7, LCN+ 5 ❧ Clapham Common paths

BREAD & ROSES
Contemporary pub
68 Clapham Manor Road, SW4 6DZ
☎ (020) 7498 1779
🌐 www.breadandrosespub.com
⊕ 4.30-11 (midnight Fri & Sat); 12-11 Sat; 12-10.30 Sun. *Children welcome daytime*
Cask beers ✔ 3 (Sharp's, 2 guests), **Other beers** 4 keg, 8 bottles
🍽 Spanish tapas, 🪑 Front and rear terraces, ♿ *Monthly quiz, Fri live bands or comedy, Sat DJs, big screen sports, table football, board games, functions*

Since the 1990s this pub in a quiet street has been operated by the Battersea and Wandsworth Trades Council through its trading arm, the Workers Beer Company, well known for raising money for social causes by providing volunteer-run bars at major events such as music festivals. The pub has a reputation as a radical rendezvous and quotes above the bar the James Oppenheim lyric from which it takes its name, commemorating the demands of striking women textile workers in Lawrence, Massachusetts, in 1912 for both bread and roses too. But don't expect to get deluged by handbills as it's also a bright, modern community space that welcomes everyone. Local lads study the football in the pleasant rear lounge, with a big screen on one wall and a trade union banner on the other. The beer is decent though not especially unusual by today's standards: Doom Bar and guests from the likes of Purity and Hogs Back, alongside bottles such as Brooklyn Lager, Budvar, Vedett White and Anchor Steam. Food is traditional Spanish tapas supplied by a local restaurant.

⇌ Clapham High Street ⊖ Clapham Common, Clapham North 🚲 Link to LCN+ Lambeth – Clapham, CS7, LCN+ 5

DRAFT HOUSE NORTHCOTE ☆ 25
Bar, specialist
94 Northcote Road, SW11 6QW
☎ (020) 7924 1814, ✉ northcote@drafthouse.co.uk, 🌐 www.drafthouse.co.uk
⊕ 12-11 Mon-Fri 10-11 Sat; 10-10.30 Sun. *Children welcome*
Cask beers ✔ 3 (1 Sambrook's, unusual/local guests), **Other beers** 15 keg, 55 bottles, **Also** Malts
🍽 British/US pub grub, 🪑 Tables on street, ♿ *Functions*

Draft House Northcote

Opened in 2009 as the second member of the Draft House family (see Draft House Tower Bridge, p55), this specialist beer bar fits right in to the strip of independent restaurants, foodie-oriented specialist shops and upmarket chains that is Northcote Road. It's a clean, modern space where cheerful bright green stools around a big wooden bar facilitate informal drinking, with a sit-down restaurant area at the back serving the chain's mix of upmarket diner and gastro cooking. Classy pop and soul plays quietly, with the musical theme echoed by the band posters and framed *New Musical Express* covers, though among them are some beery references, such as a long list of hop varieties on one poster. Sambrook's Wandle is a regular; the other two cask ales are often local. The extensive lists of keg and bottled beers pursue similar lines to the other Draft Houses: on my visit the guests included unfiltered Austrian Stiegl lager, Left Hand Juju Ginger and Schremser rye beer, all available in thirds of course, while the bottled list highlighted the classic strong version of Carnegie Porter from Sweden, and 750ml bottles of Duvel-Moortgat Maredsous abbey beer to share. All the Draft Houses do their job well but this one is marginally my favourite.

Insider tip! To get you started the beer list includes several themed 'pints of thirds', including ales, dark beers and 'the unusual', making connections across national brewing styles.

≈ Clapham Junction ⊖ Clapham Junction, Clapham South 🚌 Salcott Road (319 Clapham Junction, Streatham) 🚲 Local routes Battersea, Balham, Clapham ⁄⁄ Link to Capital Ring

DRAFT HOUSE WESTBRIDGE
Bar, specialist
74-76 Battersea Bridge Road, SW11 3AG
☎ (020) 7228 6482, ✉ westbridge@drafthouse.
co.uk, ⊕ www.drafthouse.co.uk
🕑 12-11 Mon-Thu; 12-midnight Fri;
11-midnight Sat; 11-10.30 Sun. *Children welcome*
Cask beers ✅ 3 (1 Sambrook's, unusual/local guests), **Other beers** 15 keg, 55 bottles, **Also** Malts
🍽 British/US pub grub, 🌳 Sheltered front terrace, ♿
Organised tours of Sambrook's brewery, functions

Draft House Westbridge

An exciting new force on the London beer scene arrived with the opening of this place in 2007 as the first of what's now a trio of Draft Houses (see Draft House Tower Bridge, p55). In a decently-sized, rounded-corner building, it has a pleasant front bar with big wooden tables, an outdoor terrace, a red ceilinged, candlelit restaurant area at the back and the Battersea Party Rooms available for private hire upstairs. Wall decorations include Iggy Pop, Rolling Stones and film posters, old Guinness ads and He-Man and the Masters of the Universe wallpaper on the way down to the toilets. On offer is a similar food menu and a similarly wide and well chosen range of local and international beers as the other branches, with a slightly higher turnover in cask beers. When I called they were dispensing two dark beers, Powerhouse Porter and Lees Chocoholic, besides Wandle, with Great Divide Yeti Imperial Stout and classic Mexican dark lager Negra Modelo among the bottles. Tower Bridge has the prize site and Northcote the buzz, but Westbridge offers much to keep the beer lover occupied.

≈ Battersea Park, Queenstown Road 🚌 Parkgate Road (49, 319 Clapham Junction) 🚲 Local routes Battersea Park, Wandsworth, link to NCN4 ⁄⁄ Thames Path

EAGLE
Traditional pub
104 Chatham Road, SW11 6HG
☎ (020) 7228 2328
🌐 www.theeaglealehouse.co.uk, **fbk**
⊙ 2-11 Mon-Fri; 12-11 Sat; 12-10.30 Sun.
Children welcome daytime
Cask beers ✅ 4-8 (Westerham, unusual guests), **Also** Malts
🍴 Only during events, 🪑 Beer garden
Beer festivals (May, August), major big screen sports events, occasional live music, board games, butchery courses on Sussex farm

Just off the southern stretch of trendy Northcote Road and round the corner from the library, the Eagle Ale House is a long established real ale stalwart and a local gem, defiantly maintaining the best kind of traditional pub atmosphere in an area overburdened by gastro makeovers and middle market chains. The well-worn interior is a pleasingly jumbled mix of benches and high tables for vertical drinking, and cosy cubby holes replete with clubby red leather armchairs and dusty books – it's believed the real life model for Sherlock Holmes' fictitious nemesis Moriarty drank here and you can just about imagine the arch fiend plotting his misdeeds in the snug. Football and rugby also jostle for priority and the big screen rolls down for major fixtures, while the sense of community is obvious from the photos and thank you letters from charities on the walls. The pub is tied to Enterprise but licensees Dave and Simon make full use of SIBA's Direct Delivery Scheme, with a changing range of interesting ales, usually including a mild or other dark beer and often but not always local. Westerham is regularly favoured; Dark Star, Downton, Keystone, Pilgrim, Potbelly, Surrey Hills and Tintagel might appear alongside bigger names like Harveys, Sharp's and St Austell. Beer festivals on the bank holiday weekends at the end of May and August push the choice still further.

Further info: A field near Blackboys in Sussex is rented by the pub and used for camping trips and butchery courses, the latter under the headline 'Come Swine With Me'.

≈ ⊖ Clapham Junction 🚌 Darley Road (319 Clapham Junction, Streatham) 🚲 Local routes Battersea, Balham, Clapham ⚑ Link to Capital Ring

FALCON
Traditional pub ★
2 St Johns Hill, SW11 1RU
☎ (020) 7228 2076, 🌐 www.nicholsonspubs.co.uk/thefalconclaphamjunctionlondon
⊙ 10-11.30 (midnight Thu-Sat); 10-11 Sun.
Children until 7pm
Cask beers ✅ 16-18 (Harveys, Fuller's, unusual guests), **Other beers** 2 keg, 5 bottles, **Also** 10 malts, wines
🍴 Pub grub, breakfasts, snacks and meals, ♿
Four beer festivals a year

A pub called the Falcon, taking its emblem from the crest of former local landowners the St John family, has welcomed travellers at this busy crossroads on the old Guildford coach road since at least 1801. Both passing

Falcon

trade and the local population increased massively with the opening of Clapham Junction station just a few doors downhill, and in 1898 the current large and imposing edifice, originally incorporating a hotel, replaced an older building. Much of the original interior survives, including some of the carved wood and engraved glass screens and the vast curved bar counter, the longest continuous bar in England, which sweeps from a big front area to a sumptuous rear with a huge fireplace and a beautiful arched alcove. The art nouveau tinged skylights are a more recent addition.

The architectural heritage is matched by great beer. Thanks to the support of a keen manager this is one of the leading real ale pubs in Mitchells & Butlers' improving Nicholson's chain. Up to 18 cask choices are normally available which can expand to 40 or more during the quarterly beer festivals, and in 2010 it won Best London Cask Beer Pub in the awards run by trade magazine the *Morning Advertiser*. Regulars are Harveys Sussex Best Bitter and Fuller's London Pride but the rest might come from independents and micros further afield such as Acorn, Lancaster, Thornbridge, Williams Brothers, Wolf or York: check the Nicholson's seasonal beer list leaflet for likely appearances. To assist the undecided the pub operates a 'sip before you sup' policy. Bottled choices such as Meantime Chocolate and Sierra Nevada Pale also pop up. Food is the regular Nicholson's pub grub, including breakfasts, lunches, sandwiches, sharing plates and hearty mains, with sausages heavily featured.

Pub trivia: Don't miss the stained and painted glass, especially the falcon by the entrance lobby and several panels at the back that depict various past incarnations of the pub, including one with funeral carriages that commemorates a former landlord by the name of Mr Death.

≫ ⊖ Clapham Junction ⛖ Local routes Battersea, Balham, Tooting

INK ROOMS

Bar, specialist
14 Lavender Hill, SW11 5RW
📞 (020) 7228 5300, ⊕ www.inkrooms.co.uk,
fbk, tw Ink_Rooms_UK
✪ 5-midnight Mon-Thu; 4-2am Fri; 2-2am Sat; 2-midnight Sun. *Children welcome daytime*
Cask beers ✔ 1 (Nethergate), **Other beers** 8 keg, 70+ bottles, **Also** Small batch spirits, cocktails
🍕 Pizzas ordered in from local suppliers,
🍺 Beer garden
Thu & Sun live music, Fri & Sat DJs, occasional film screenings, quizzes, barbecues

Ink Rooms

This shopfront site on an interesting stretch of Lavender Hill near the Queenstown Road junction deserves at least a footnote in the history of beer in London: in 2001 it became the site of Microbar, arguably the first international craft beer bar in the capital that decidedly wasn't a pub. Restyled in 2009 under new management and a new name as a retro American dive bar, it retains a much shortened but still comprehensive beer list, helpfully divided into user friendly categories like 'refreshing', 'hoppy' and 'session' and actively promoted to a largely youngish (20s-40s) crowd by enthusiastic if occasionally slightly misinformed staff. Classic tattoo art is the decorative theme alongside cars and rock'n'roll, though the working Seeburg jukebox is sadly not plumbed into the sound system. A single handpump usually dispenses Truman's Runner, while the keg taps include novelties like draught Australian Little Creatures. The extensive bottled selection is comprehensive and well chosen – several classic Germans (Augustiner, Gaffel, Jever), Trappists including Orval and Rochefort, Duchesse de Bourgogne and a significant number of bottle conditioned British ales from Burton Bridge, Kelham Island, RCH and St Austell. American brews are unsurprisingly well represented with Anchor, Brooklyn, Dogfish Head, Goose Island and Odell, and the range is due to increase, even stretching to the new breed of taboo-challenging canned craft beers. There's a range of events including bands and DJs playing compatible retro and Americana, and dog friendliness is attested by the hosting of dog fashion shows. Food is ordered in from a couple of decent independent pizzerias nearby.

Insider tip! Stairs to what appears to be the basement lead not only to a more loungey additional space but also, thanks to the hillside geography, to a sizeable and pleasant beer garden, used for barbecues in season.

Clapham Junction Clapham Common, Clapham Junction Cedars Road (numerous from Clapham Junction), Wandsworth Road (137, 345 Clapham Common) LCN+5, local routes Clapham Common, Balham, Tooting

LIGHTHOUSE

Gastropub
414 Battersea Park Road, SW11 4LR
(020) 7223 7721
www.thelighthousebattersea.com
12-11 daily. *Children very welcome*
Cask beers 3 (Sambrook's, occasional guests), **Other beers** 6 keg, 10+ bottles, **Also** Wines
Gastro menu, Beer garden,
Board games, occasional tasting nights

Under the same management as the Roundhouse (below), this place is similarly bright, civilised and welcoming, offering similar beer and food choices without quite the same characterful space. Overspill from its sister's Spanish poster collection brightens the walls, alongside maps and modern art, while the jumble of seating includes some odd padded stools. Sambrook's beers dominate the three pumps, and there are some unusual imported choices including Bavarian Rothaus lager on keg and in bottle, and rare Belgian Viven Ale. Meals might include potted rabbit, coley in beer batter or chestnut pie. The piano is put to good use on occasional live music nights.

Lighthouse

Clapham Junction Battersea Park School (44, 344 Battersea Park, 344 Clapham Junction) Local routes Battersea Park, Clapham Junction Battersea Park paths, Thames Path

MANOR ARMS

Traditional pub
128 Clapham Manor Street, SW4 6ED
(020) 7622 2894
12-midnight daily
Cask beers 5 (unusual guests), **Other beers** 1 keg, 1-2 bottles
Wednesday pizzas, Sunday lunch, otherwise only during special events, Beer garden
Beer festivals several times a year, Wed quiz, big screen sport, pub games

Just off Clapham High Street and a short walk from the Bread & Roses (above), this small, square, one-bar pub has been refurbished in contemporary style – red walls hung with arty pictures, brown bar stools, a cosy sofa-based alcove – but retains the atmosphere of a vivacious community local. Sport, especially rugby, is a major theme and a weekly quiz is supplemented by other events: some raucous carol singing when I visited. Landlord James takes advantage of Enterprise's direct delivery and guest beer arrangements to fuel five handpumps with changing ales: Downton, Loddon, Purbeck and Westerham are favoured, and real cider appears occasionally. The choice widens to over 20 cask ales during the intermittent beer festivals.

Clapham High Street Clapham Common Link to LCN+ Lambeth, Clapham, CS7, LCN+ 5

Nightingale

NIGHTINGALE ☆ 25

Traditional pub
97 Nightingale Lane, SW12 8NX
📞 (020) 8673 1637, ✉ nightingale@youngs.co.uk, ⊕ www.youngs.co.uk, **tw** nightingalepub
🕐 11-midnight Mon-Sat; 12-midnight Sun.
Children until 9pm
Cask beers ✅ 5 (Wells & Young's, Sambrook's), **Other beers** 8 bottles (Wells & Young's, Erdinger), **Also** Wines
🍴 Pub grub, 🪑 Beer garden, ♿
Annual charity walk, darts and other pub games

It's a relatively long stroll past the grand houses of Nightingale Lane but this delightful Young's pub is well worth it – not for nothing did it win trade magazine the *Publican*'s Community Pub of the Year Award in 2009.

It's a single space around a peninsula bar with a lino-floored public bar complete with dartboard at the front, leading to a cosy, carpeted room with an unusual central open fire and one wall covered in awards – including one for Green Pub in recognition of its dedication to recycling and energy conservation. An enclosed conservatory with a fascinating display case leads out to a heated, sheltered terrace at the back. Top quality cask beer consists of the standard Wells & Young's range of Bitter, Special, Bombardier and a seasonal, with Sambrook's Wandle "because it's local". You can sample all of them on a tasting tray, and managers Lee and Keris also aim to stock a comprehensive range of the brewery's packaged beers including bottle conditioned London Ale and London Gold.

Food is home cooked pub grub – sausages, pies and the like. Headlining the community activities is annual fundraising event the Nightingale Walk, now in its 32nd year with almost £500,000 so far raised for a range of mainly small charities. There's a regular newsletter, free WiFi and the pub participates in the Use Your Local scheme, accepting package deliveries on behalf of its neighbours. A gem.

Insider tip! The pub's own beer, called, naturally enough, Nighting Ale, should be available by the time you read this. It's being brewed by Marston's as the prize for winning yet another competition, this time as Britain's Proudest Pub.

🚉 Wandsworth Common ⊖ Balham, Clapham South 🚌 Rusham Road (G1 Clapham South, Balham) 🚲 Local routes Battersea, Tooting 🚶 Clapham Common paths

PROJECT ORANGE
Bar
43 St Johns Hill, SW11 1TT
☎ (020) 7585 1549, ⊕ www.sixxxrecords.com
✪ 5-11 Mon-Wed & Sun; 5-midnight Thu;
5-1am Fri & Sat
Cask beers None, **Other beers** 3 keg, 45 bottles
Monthly live bands, private parties downstairs

When the owners of Project Orange took over
this former Mexican restaurant just along from
Clapham Junction station in 2001, they aimed
to create the sort of place they themselves
would like to drink in, and high on the list of
essentials were good music and good beer.

The result is a long way from a typical
British beer pub – there's no cask, though
there are numerous top quality bottled
options, many bottle conditioned, and a
better class of keg. The range has been
expanded by current manager Liv-Ingrid, who
champions it to customers: BrewDog,
Meantime and Sambrook's are complemented by Flying Dog and Sierra Nevada from
the USA, Australian heritage brewery Coopers
and more.

There's no obvious explanation for the
Space Hopper orange theme of the exterior;
indoors there's graffiti and comic art,
camouflage netting on the ceiling, and a
grungy space downstairs with sofas and table
football. Associated indie label Sixxx Records
promotes the live gigs and the recorded
music runs to retro. As I left, AC/DC were
performing mutely on the video projector
while the sound system struck up, rather
appropriately, with Squeeze's 'Up the Junction'.

≈ ⊖ Clapham Junction ⊶ Local routes
Battersea – Balham and Tooting

ROUNDHOUSE
Gastropub
2 Wandsworth Common Northside, SW18 2SS
☎ (020) 7326 8580
⊕ www.theroundhousewandsworth.com
✪ 4-11 Mon-Thu; 4-midnight Fri; 12-midnight
Sat; 12-11 Sun. *Children very welcome*
Cask beers ✔ 3 (Sambrook's, occasional
guests), **Other beers** 3 keg, 13 bottles, **Also**
1 real cider, wines
🍽 Gastro menu, ☀ Outdoor terrace (though
overlooking main road)
Mon quiz

Roundhouse

This pleasant corner gastropub, with its
curved frontage and distinctive porthole
windows looking across the South Circular to
Wandsworth Common, takes both food and
beer seriously. The food is, in the words of
landlord Alex, "not rocket science" but fresh
and tasty, with a short menu featuring salads,
fish, some unusual meats and good veggie
options. On handpump are Sambrook's
Wandle and Junction plus a guest, also usually
from not too far away – a Hogs Back seasonal
on my visit. This is supplemented by a good
selection of well-chosen bottles from the likes
of Brooklyn, Chimay, Coopers, Little Creatures,
Sierra Nevada and Viru from Estonia, and keg
taps dispensing Czech, Belgian and German
products. A more pubby section leads to a
raised restaurant area but food is identical
throughout, and the pub makes a point of
being family and dog friendly. See also sister
pub the Lighthouse (above).

Pub trivia: Above the mix of reclaimed furniture
hangs a fascinating poster collection, with an
emphasis on enjoyably garish Spanish movie
posters.

≈ ⊖ Clapham Junction ⊶ Local routes
Battersea, Earlsfield, Balham ⤢ Link via
Wandsworth Common to Capital Ring

BRIXTON & STOCKWELL

Brixton is arguably the place where London's cosmopolitan culture sings the loudest and proudest. Like most other suburbs it was remade by the railways and like many inner city areas it slumped into poverty in the 20th century as the middle classes moved on to leafier climes. In 1948, the MV Empire Windrush docked at Tilbury with 492 hopeful immigrants from Jamaica, the first of many Caribbean immigrants to the UK. The new arrivals were temporarily housed in a bomb shelter at Clapham South, and many of them ended up in the decrepit but cheap local housing.

The story since hasn't always been a happy one – the new communities faced racism and the area has twice erupted into major riots. It's long been more than just a major centre of Britain's Afro-Caribbean culture, with an eclectic mix that encompasses a significant lesbian and gay community and notable numbers of artists, revolutionaries and alternative lifestylers. Its street markets are world famous, and include Electric Avenue, the first electrically lit street in the UK. The Ritzy arthouse cinema looks out on a much improved Windrush Square, commemorating those unwitting postwar pioneers that helped change the face of London forever.

Neighbouring Stockwell, to the north, is another wayside village that's been through a similar life cycle, but boasts more obviously gentrified parts, and a very decent specialist pub.

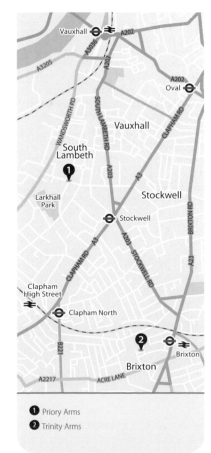

PRIORY ARMS

Contemporary pub
83 Lansdowne Way, SW8 2PB
☎ (020) 7622 1884
⊕ www.theprioryarms.co.uk
☼ 12-11 daily. *Children welcome daytime*
Cask beers ✅ 5 (Hogs Back, Hop Back, Sharp's, 2 unusual guests), **Other beers** 1 Belgian keg, 15 bottles, **Also** Wines
🍴 Tapas and appertizers, enhanced pub grub,
🌳 Front terrace
Thu poker league, Sun quiz, board games, functions

This modest gem of a local free house, just down the road from Stockwell's impressive and architecturally important 1950s bus garage, is a longstanding fine beer haven with a subtle and tasteful continental feel. Big windows shed plenty of light onto a single relatively small space with a separate raised area equipped with leather sofas; the upstairs function room, well used by local groups including Lambeth Cyclists, is also open as overspill at busy times. Food changes daily – a typical menu might include beef stew,

❶ Priory Arms
❷ Trinity Arms

Priory Arms

smoked fishcakes or vegetable terrine. Hop Back Summer Lightning is always among the beer choices, with changing brands from Hogs Back and Sharp's, and two guests that might come from Cottage, Downton or Sambrook's. Two changing Belgian guest kegs – Brugse Zot and Steenbrugge Blond when I called – are supplemented by a shortish bottled list that includes all three Chimays, Anchor Steam, Boon Duivelsbier and lager and wheat beer from Germany's Rothaus. A recent change of management has happily not been reflected in a change of policy.

≋ Wandsworth Road ⊖ Stockwell ⬤⤢ LCN+3 and local link ✸ Brixton Heritage Trails

TRINITY ARMS
Traditional pub
45 Trinity Gardens, SW9 8DR
☎ (020) 7274 4544
⊕ www.trinityarms.co.uk, **fbk**
⊙ 12-11 (midnight Fri & Sat). *Children welcome*
Cask beers ✔ 4 (Wells & Young's), Other beers
4-5 bottles (Wells & Young's)
⏏ Good value pub grub, ⊞ Front terrace, beer garden
Thu quiz, occasional live music, big screen sport, monthly drawing competition, pub games

On a pretty 1850s square hidden between Acre Lane and Brixton Road, this lovely old corner Young's pub is probably the best bet

for good beer in Brixton and a regular *Good Beer Guide* listing. Its pleasant half panelled spaces, hung with yellowed wallpaper, cluster round an island bar where a pub cat takes its ease. Bitter, Special and London Gold are regularly served, with a changing Young's seasonal – an immaculate Winter Warmer when I called – and a few bottles including Special London Ale. Food is simple home-cooked stuff – jackets, fish and chips, macaroni cheese – and the papers rolled into glasses on the tables are entry forms for the drawing competition, the winners of which are exhibited for all to admire.

Insider tip! Investigate the 'secret garden', labelled with a quote from the decidedly unbrixtonian Bruce Springsteen.

≋ ⊖ Brixton ⬤⤢ LCN+6A, link to LCN25 ✸ Brixton Heritage Trails

Trinity Arms

KINGSTON

Kingston, at the confluence of the Thames and the Hogsmill stream and for centuries the first crossing point of the former upstream of London Bridge, was once quite literally 'King's Town', In Saxon times it was a Royal residence where several kings of Wessex were crowned. Enclosed in railings outside the Guildhall is the Coronation Stone on which monarchs are reputed to have sat.

The Thames is starting to take on its classic *Wind in the Willows* appearance and with the Royal Parks of Richmond to the north and Bushy across the bridge to the West the area is well served for green space: you can also walk south along the Hogsmill, on a path that eventually reaches the North Downs. A more contemporary feature is David Mach's memorable sculpture *Out of Order* made of several red phone boxes collapsing against each other, which might cause confusion if you stumble upon it having overindulged at one of the venues listed below.

BOATERS INN

Contemporary pub
Lower Ham Road, KT2 5AU
☎ (020) 8541 4672, ⊕ www.boaterskingston.com, **tw** TheBoatersInn
✪ 11-11 Mon-Sat; 12-11 Sun. *Children welcome*
Cask beers ✔ 5 (Twickenham, unusual guests), **Other beers** 2 keg, 6 bottles, **Also** Wines
🍴 Enhanced pub grub, 🌳 Large riverside terrace, ♿
Mon quiz, Tue wine promotion, Sun live jazz, live rock some other weekend nights, art exhibitions, occasional outdoor events

Wander downstream along the Thames Path from Kingston Bridge or get a bus along Richmond Road, then walk down Woodside Road and keep ahead along the footpath to reach this idyllically-sited, bustling contemporary pub, right on the riverside surrounded by the grass and trees of Canbury Gardens. Customers arriving by boat can take advantage of the pub's own moorings (ring to check availability in advance). In this location some businesses might be tempted to laziness but the Boaters, part of the go-ahead Capital group, works hard to add value, with a busy events programme, sought after food – an inventive British and international menu – and an impressive beer range headlining the drinks offer. The cask ales constantly change

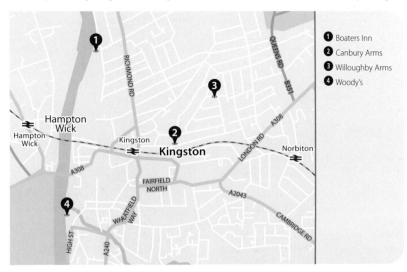

1 Boaters Inn
2 Canbury Arms
3 Willoughby Arms
4 Woody's

but often include local and LocAle micros like Ascot, Hogs Back and the harder to find Pilgrim. A few well known imports like Duvel and Erdinger add some interest to the fridges. It's a biggish place, with bare boards, rugs and the odd sofa, newspapers, restrained background music and a faint boating theme – one corner is dedicated to the nearby Twickenham Boat Club. The extensive terrace is the main attraction on fine days and gets predictably packed. Outdoor events include food markets and, as if that wasn't enough, it's also a major venue on London's modern and contemporary jazz circuit with its long established Sunday night sessions.

Insider tip! Unusually for a pub there's a cake stand on the bar well worth checking out – the chef is especially keen on baking and desserts.

⇌ Kingston 🚲 NCN4 ✹ Thames Path and link to London Loop

Boaters Inn

CANBURY ARMS
Gastropub
49 Canbury Park Road, KT2 6LQ
📞 (020) 8255 9129, ⊕ www.thecanburyarms.com, **fbk**, **tw** thecanburyarms
☼ 9-11 Mon-Sat; 10-11 Sun. *Children very welcome*
Cask beers ✅ 5 (unusual/local guests), **Also** Wines
🍽 Breakfasts, gastro menu, 🌳 Patio, ♿
Community events and coffee mornings, occasional quizzes, wine tastings

Another successful regeneration of a formerly decaying community pub, the Canbury has gone the gastro route. It describes itself as 'food led' but welcomes drinkers too, and makes an effort with its beer. Staff pride themselves on their cellarmanship and their

small but notable range of cask ales from brewers like Harveys, Hogs Back, Otter, Ringwood and Twickenham. The pub interior is now a light, clean space with a modern and very woody look, a roaring fire in winter and a cheerful heated awning to the side, with quirky touches like a large poster of Morecambe and Wise in their prime. Food at slightly higher than average prices runs from breakfasts, brunches and pies to full dinners featuring whitebait, game and pearl barley. The place is embedded in the community and supports numerous local organisations; it runs a loyalty scheme and makes a point of welcoming women. It's particularly popular with local mums for coffee mornings and lunches, and so child-friendly it should win a Child-Friendly Pub of the Year award. In fact it did, in 2010.

⇌ Kingston 🚲 NCN4 ✹ London Loop, Thames Down Link, Thames Path

WILLOUGHBY ARMS
Traditional pub
47 Willoughby Road, KT2 6LN
📞 (020) 8546 4236
⊕ www.thewilloughbyarms.com
☼ 10.30am-midnight Mon-Sat; 12-midnight Sun. *Well-behaved children welcome*
Cask beers ✅ 5 (Fuller's, Surrey Hills, Twickenham, 2 local guests)
🍽 Pizzas, 🌳 Rear patio, ♿
Seasonal beer festivals, monthly acoustic open mike, Mon quiz, functions, darts, pool, table football, big screen sports

This big and rather clunky-looking 1892 street corner pub is deep in the residential streets between Kingston and Norbury. It was in apparently terminal decline in 1997 when Rick and Lysa Robinson turned it round not by going gastro but by restoring its heart as a proper traditional community local. Cask ale is an essential part of the formula – Rick has links to the Society for the Preservation of Beers from the Wood, an organisation that predates CAMRA, and the Kingston branch meets here monthly. Guest beers are from small and often local brewers and three annual beer festivals widen the choice still further. Sport also stars – the bigger sports bar has pool, table football, darts and two big screen TVs – but can be avoided in the slightly smaller and very welcoming space on the other side of

Canbury Arms

the island bar. The wood-panelled rooms are adorned with an eccentric mixture of stuffed animal heads, beer bottles and movie and sport memorabilia. Background music is quiet and there's free WiFi. Welcoming and full of character, it's well worth seeking out.

Insider tip! Make sure you enjoy the free film and sport exhibition on the walls, with a still from *Escape to Victory* marking the transition between the two themes.

≈ Kingston 🚌 Shortlands Road (K5 Kingston)
🚲 NCN4 ✸ Link to Thames Path, London Loop

WOODY'S
Bar
5 Rams Passage, KT1 1HH
📞 (020) 8541 4984
🌐 www.woodyspubco.com, **fbk**
🕐 12-11 Mon-Thu; 12-midnight Fri;
10-midnight Sat; 10-10.30 Sun. *Children welcome*
Cask beers ✔ 2 (Twickenham, Greene King),
Other beers 2-3 keg, 2-3 bottles, **Also** Wines
🍴 Diner style menu, weekend brunch, home made cakes, 🍹 Riverside patio, ♿
Thu quiz, occasional parties

The redevelopment of Kingston's waterfront has provided much enhanced riverside access but has been colonised mainly by middle market chain bars and eateries. Just down from the All Bar One and the Carluccio's, however, is this neat little independent designer bar, which emerged in 2008. It's relaxed and welcoming with an odd collection of furniture harbouring eccentricities such as a glass tabletop resting on two carved stone horse heads, and candy-striped picnic tables outside. It's not the kind of place you might predict would stock real ale, so it's delightful to spot two handpumps dispensing a rotating Twickenham beer and a house beer from Greene King, with its own unique designer label. Keg Freedom Organic Lager and a couple of good bottled options are also on offer. On the menu are sandwiches, salads, wraps, nibbles, sharing platters, simple hot dishes and tempting home made cakes. Books about design and classic albums mix rather incongruously with copies of regional CAMRA magazine *London Drinker* on aforesaid equestrian tabletop.

≈ Kingston 🚲 NCN4 ✸ London Loop,

RICHMOND

One of London's smarter suburbs, Richmond was a link in the chain of Royal Thameside palaces, so named by Henry VII after his ancestral home of Richmond in Yorkshire. Little of the palace survives but much of its adjoining hunting park, Richmond Park, is now London's biggest public park, almost three times the size of New York City's Central Park. It's a magnificent green space combining formal gardens and woodlands with open vistas roamed by deer, an astonishing sight so close to central London. The town itself has a handsome Georgian feel, with a fine open green from which cobbled lanes run down to the picturesque riverfront with its boating activity. A short, pleasant stroll downriver along the Thames Path (or a bus or train ride) brings you to one of London's most popular and celebrated attractions, the Royal Botanic Gardens at Kew, first developed in the 17th century and now a World Heritage Site. Our listings include a pub with one of the finest urban views in Britain. The RealAle.com beer shop is also easily reached from Richmond but is on the other side of the river and therefore listed under West London – see p233.

❶ Brouge
❷ Roebuck
❸ White Cross

BROUGE
Restaurant, bar
5 Hill Street, TW9 1SX
📞 (020) 8332 0055, 🌐 www.brouge.co.uk
🕐 12-11 Mon-Thu; 12-11.30 Fri & Sat; 12-9.30 Sun. *Children welcome*
Cask beers None, **Other beers** 10 keg, 60 bottles, **Also** Wines
🍽 Belgian/international menu
Occasional tutored tastings

This offshoot of Brouge in Twickenham (p230), opened in 2008, has the advantage of a town centre site but although friendly and welcoming lacks the expansive pubby feel of its parent. A pleasant space at the front is set aside just for drinkers though the principal focus is on dining. Food and beer menus are identical to the parent branch's except that cask ale is not available, though there are plenty of bottle-conditioned options on the impressive list. Its location in a vaulted cellar with an attractive skylight, accessed by steps from the street, adds to the continental experience.

🚃 ⊖ Richmond 🚲 Links to NCN4, Richmond Park routes ⚡ Capital Ring, Thames Path

ROEBUCK
Traditional pub
130 Richmond Hill, TW10 6RN
📞 (020) 8948 2329

Roebuck

🕐 12-11 Mon-Thu; 12-midnight Fri;
11-midnight Sat; 12-10.30 Sun. *Children until
early evening*
Cask beers ✔ 4 (Fuller's, 3 unusual/local guests),
Also Wines
🍴 Pub grub, 🪧 Standing room on street only, ♿
Functions

Richmond Hill is a sustained but gentle climb
from the town centre that rewards you with
breathtaking views west across Petersham
Meadows and the Thames valley to Surrey
and Berkshire, with parks, heaths and Windsor
Castle in the distance. Perched right on its
brow is this historic pub and former hotel, in
the 19th century a well-known destination for
day trippers on pleasure boats from central
London. These days it's one of the Punch pubs
recently rebranded Taylor Walker, a name
borrowed from an old London brewery
bought and closed by Ind Coope in 1960.
Thankfully licensee Paul Weymouth is able to
order a wide range of beer through the SIBA
Direct Delivery Scheme and has used this to
build the pub's real ale reputation over his 12
years in office, rotating guests from breweries
like Ascot, Bath and Downton. Given the pub's
heritage the interior feels a little ersatz, not
helped by the pre-printed pub grub menus,
but there are some cosy spaces, the beer is
fine and the view is as good as it was when
Wordsworth and Turner admired it. Richmond
Park is just around the corner, offering some
of the best walks in the capital.

Visitor's note: The pub participates in Richmond
council's community toilet schemes, public-
spiritedly opening its loos to all.

🚃 🚇 Richmond 🚌 American University (371
Richmond, Kingston), Nightingale Lane (65
Richmond, Kingston) 🚲 Links to NCN4,
Richmond Park routes 🚶 Capital Ring, Thames
Path, Richmond Park walks

WHITE CROSS
Contemporary pub
Water Lane, TW9 1TH
📞 (020) 8940 6844, ✉ whitecross@youngs.
co.uk, 🌐 www.youngs.co.uk
🕐 9.30am-11pm Mon-Sat; 9.30am-10.30pm
Sun. *Children welcome*
Cask beers ✔ 5 (Wells & Young's, occasional
guest), **Also** Wines
🍴 Breakfast, brunch, enhanced pub grub,
🪧 Large terrace overlooking river
Functions

This historic, spacious and sturdy-looking
Young's pub is perfectly located on Richmond
riverside not far from the town's lovely green,
with crowds flocking to its outdoor terrace on
fine days. Inside it's had one of those modern,
pastel-shaded makeovers with a series of
distinct but unpartitioned spaces clustered
round an island bar, plus an upstairs room.
Food is posh pub grub with an emphasis on
natural and free range ingredients, offered
alongside consistently well-kept cask ale from
the owning brewery – Young's Bitter, London
Gold and Special, Wells Bombardier, seasonals
and occasional guests from other brewers.

🚃 🚇 Richmond 🚲 Links to NCN4, Richmond
Park routes 🚶 Capital Ring, Thames Path

White Cross

WANDSWORTH

Wandsworth, at the confluence of the Thames and the Wandle, is mentioned in the Domesday book. Beer lovers are likely to know it best as the home of Young's Ram brewery, a real ale stalwart with a history dating back to at least 1533. Sadly the brewery closed in 2007 when Young's merged with Charles Wells in Bedford though some brewing continues on the site (see under Wells & Young's p316 and Ram p277) and Young's pubs still dominate the local drinking scene. Wandsworth today has some handsome corners such as historic Old York Road leading up to Wandsworth Town station, but is rather disfigured by the tangled one way system.

ARMOURY
Contemporary pub
14 Armoury Way, SW18 1EZ
☎ (020) 8870 6771, ⊕ www.thearmourypub.co.uk, **tw** thearmourysw18
🕐 12-11 (10.30 Sun). *Children until 9pm*
Cask beers ✔ 3 (1 Young's, 1 Sambrook's, often local guest), **Other beers** 3-4 bottles (Wells & Young's)
🍴 Pub grub and specials, 🌳 Small beer garden, ♿
Wed quiz, occasional live music

This pub provides a welcome refuge on one arm of the traffic system at the back of the old brewery site. Refurbished in 2010 by youthful new licensees Rebecca Davidson and Nicholas Flook, this is a small but airy single-bar pub decorated with contemporary art and featuring a real fire. Food comprises pies, wraps, sandwiches and interesting good value daily specials. Growing the cask ale trade is a central part of the business plan. Although a Young's house it's also a regular stockist of Sambrook's – the beer range will usually include either Bitter and Junction or Wandle and Special – and guests from the likes of Hogs Back, Hook Norton or St Austell.

⇌ Wandsworth Town ⚲ NCN20, link to NCN4
〽 Thames Path, Wandle Trail

GOTHIQUE
Bar, restaurant
Royal Victoria Patriotic Building, John Archer Way, SW18 3SX
☎ (020) 8870 6567, ⊕ www.legothique.co.uk
🕐 12-midnight daily. *Children very welcome*
Cask beers ✔ 3 (Shepherd Neame, guest, usually Sambrook's), **Also** French wines

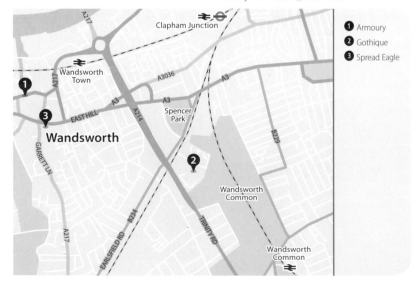

① Armoury
② Gothique
③ Spread Eagle

Gothique

🍽 French bar and restaurant menu, 🪑 Large patio, ♿
2 annual beer festivals, functions, weddings

The Royal Victoria Patriotic Building is a vast Victorian Gothic pile that looms over Wandsworth Common. Its forbidding aspect is matched by some forbidding tales: built as an orphanage, it's allegedly haunted by a the ghost of a girl who died in a fire while locked in solitary confinement, and in World War II the security services used it as an interrogation centre, with Rudolf Hess among its prisoners. Le Gothique has been tucked away in the heart of the complex ever since the mid-1980s, and is also a popular wedding venue. The small bar picks up the architectural theme with a pulpit, Gothic chairs and a huge angel sculpture. Food is French, with full *à la carte* service at the upstairs restaurant and more limited good value options at the bar. The place is also committed to real ale. Three pumps dispense two changing Shepherd Neame beers and a guest which is usually from Sambrook's. The choice expands massively when the marquees go up twice yearly in the adjoining courtyard for a festival offering around 80 beers, in March and around Halloween when the building itself provides a suitably spooky backdrop.

🚆 Wandsworth Town, Clapham Junction 🚌 Windmill Road (77 Clapham Junction, 219 Wandsworth) 🚲 Local routes Battersea, Balham, Tooting 🚶 Capital Ring

SPREAD EAGLE
Traditional pub ☆
71 Wandsworth High Street, SW18 2PT
📞 (020) 8877 9809
✉ spreadeaglewandsworth@youngs.co.uk
🌐 www.youngs.co.uk

🕚 11-11 Mon-Thu; 11-midnight Fri & Sat; 11-11 Sun
Cask beers ✔ 3-4 (Wells & Young's), **Other beers** 5 bottles (Wells & Young's)
🍽 Pub grub and specials, 🪑 Sheltered yard
Wargaming twice a week, monthly 'elderly people's disco', darts, pool, board games

Under the shadow of the towering chimney of Young's former brewery, now sadly derelict and awaiting redevelopment, stands this landmark coaching inn, still offering the opportunity to sample Young's beers in grand surroundings which, in the words of CAMRA's National Inventory of Historic Pub Interiors, give "a very good idea of what a classy pub was meant to look like a hundred years ago". A glass canopy, actually a modern addition, welcomes you into a huge main bar with a sweeping staircase, deep green leather benches, Corinthian pillars and a mammoth original wooden bar back featuring engraved glass and arches with unusual pierced spandrels. To the left is an old public bar with pool table and dartboard, and at the back is the sofa-strewn 'dining room and lounge'. Well kept Bitter, Special and seasonals are on offer as well as bottle conditioned London Ale, while the lunchtime pub grub menu includes snacks, sandwiches, jacket potatoes and home-cooked daily specials. It's looking a little worn round the edges, but still impresses.

Pub trivia: Those customers with an obsessive glint in their eyes may not in fact be beer tickers – gaming fans meet in the upstairs room twice a week to play Warhammer.

🚆 Wandsworth Town 🚲 NCN20, link to NCN4 🚶 Thames Path, Wandle Trail

Spread Eagle

WIMBLEDON

The name Wimbledon is now synonymous with the international tennis tournament held here, but its history as an old rural manor and common long predates Henry VIII whacking a ball with a racquet. The All England Club held its first lawn tennis tournament in 1877 and moved to its present site in the 1920s. The annual Championships in late June and early July is now the most important date in the international professional tennis calendar and the only Grand Slam tournament still played on grass.

Wimbledon isn't all about tennis. There's the New Wimbledon Theatre in its splendid Edwardian building, the Polka children's theatre, the Wimbledon Museum and the large open space of Wimbledon Common. With adjacent Richmond Park the common forms one of the largest areas of public green space in London.

The venues below stretch from the southern edge of the Common to the Victorian suburbs around Collier's Wood and South Wimbledon, reaching almost to Merton Abbey Mills on the river Wandle. From here the Wandle Trail walking and cycling route runs north to Wandsworth and south to Croydon.

BREWERY TAP
Traditional pub
68/69 High Street, SW19 5EE
☎ (020) 8947 9331
⊕ 12-11 Mon-Thu; 12-midnight Fri & Sat; 12-10.30 Sun
Cask beers ✅ 5 (Fuller's, Caledonian, unusual guests), **Other beers** 2-3 bottles
🍴 Home made pub grub
Mon quiz, Tue & Wed big screen football, Thu live jazz

Part sports bar, part real ale free house, this straightforward single-bar high street pub in Wimbledon Village is worth checking out for its interesting range of cask beers chosen by a keen landlord. Fuller's London Pride and Caledonian Deuchars IPA are always on; the rest might originate, among others, from Adnams, Brains, Downton, Everards, Hopback, Slater's or Wandle. Food is good value pub grub all made in house – the bar staff recommend the Loch Fyne fishcakes. It's difficult to escape the big screen sport, mainly football, which takes pride of place midweek, but the small and slightly arty lounge area round the back of the bar provides some respite, and Thursday swaps ball kicking for sax tooting as jazz night comes around.

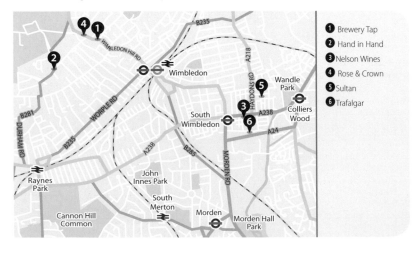

1. Brewery Tap
2. Hand in Hand
3. Nelson Wines
4. Rose & Crown
5. Sultan
6. Trafalgar

Hand in Hand

≠ ⊖ Wimbledon ⌷ Wimbledon ⌷ Wimbledon Village (93, 493 Wimbledon) ⚲ LCN+ Sutton, Wimbledon, Putney Heath

HAND IN HAND
Traditional pub
6 Crooked Billet, SW19 4RQ
☎ (020) 8946 5720
🌐 www.thehandinhandwimbledon.co.uk
⏱ 11-11 Mon-Thu; 11-midnight Fri & Sat; 12-11 Sun. *Children in family room and outdoors*
Cask beers ✓ 9-10 (5-6 Wells & Young's, 2 Sambrook's, unusual/local guests), **Other beers** 2 bottles (Wells & Young's), **Also** Wines
🍴 Enhanced pub grub, 🌳 Front terrace, adjacent common
Mon poker night, Tue 'really very hard' quiz, monthly cellar workshop and tasting, monthly acoustic music night, occasional additional live folk/jazz, 2 beer festivals, occasional morris dancing and mummery

Two picturesquely named Young's pubs stand side by side on their own little triangle of green on the southern edge of Wimbledon Common: the Crooked Billet and the Hand in Hand. The latter, with its rather poignant pub sign, has the edge for the beer lover, and not just for the various beery aphorisms chalked on the walls. Besides a wide range of well kept Wells & Young's regulars and seasonals (Bitter, Special, London Gold, Courage Director's and Bombardier are fixtures), two Sambrook's beers and changing guests are on offer: you might spot the likes of Caledonian, Hook Norton, Sharp's or Twickenham. Monthly cellar workshops and tastings and beer festivals in February and September underline

the commitment to promoting beer appreciation. Given that the autumn fest is timed to coincide with British Food Fortnight, it's unsurprising that the output from 'Caroline's Kitchen' includes hearty pies, salads, sausages and traditional main meals. The building is a delightful, sprawling and very rural low-beamed cottage from 1835 with various cubby holes and spaces, prone to visits from morris men and folk musicians. Three armchairs around an open fire at the front provide a perfect place to ensconce oneself with a pint of Winter Warmer and a good book after a stride across the common on a foggy January afternoon.

Insider tip! In good weather, ask for a plastic glass if you'd rather enjoy your beer on the front green or on the common proper.

≠ ⊖ Wimbledon ⌷ Wimbledon ⌷ West Wimbledon Christ Church (200 Raynes Park, Wimbledon) ⚲ LCN+ Sutton, Wimbledon, Putney Heath ⚶ Wimbledon Common paths linking to Capital Ring

NELSON WINES
Shop
168A Merton High Street, SW19 1AZ
☎ (020) 8542 1558
⏱ 6pm-10.30pm Mon-Fri; 1-4 Sat & Sun
Cask beers None, **Other beers** 500-600 bottles, **Also** Specialist ciders and spirits, wines

Tom McTague is a pioneer among specialist bottled beer sellers in London: he bought out Nelson Wines, then an ordinary street-corner off-license, in 1989 after four years of managing it, and built up the beer range at a time when bottled beer in Britain rarely got more exotic than White Shield. Back then only the Pitfield Beer Shop in Hoxton did anything like it. That shop has now decamped to an Essex farm but Tom keeps going among the rather run down shops that line Merton High Street east of South Wimbledon tube. 500-600 beers are in stock at any one time, mainly from Belgium (Boon, Cantillon, Duvel-Moortgat, Géants, Graal, Silly, Van Honsebrouck, various Trappists), Germany (Andechs, Augustiner, Schlenkerla, Schlösser, Schneider, Weltenburger) and Great Britain (Ascot, Harveys, Hepworth, the delightful Hopshackle, O'Hanlon's, Otley, Sambrook's) dominating. There are some US (Anchor, Brooklyn, Dogfish Head, Odell, Victory) and world beers, including Coopers and some interesting ones from Denmark and Mexico. It's a bit cramped, jumbled and dusty and there's less rare and geek-pleasing stuff than at, say, Kris Wines (p155) or Utobeer (p62), but you're bound to find something of interest and prices are notably keen.

Insider tip! Make sure you have a good look round – beers are crammed in everywhere and you might find a gem where you least expect it.

⊖ South Wimbledon ⅋ NCN20 ♦♦ Wandle Trail

Rose & Crown

ROSE & CROWN
Contemporary pub
55 High Street, SW19 5BA
☎ (020) 8947 4713
⊕ www.roseandcrownwimbledon.co.uk, **fbk**, **tw** Rose_Wimbledon
✪ 11-11 Mon-Sat; 12-10.30 Sun. *Children very welcome*
Cask beers ✔ 5+ (4 Wells & Young's, 1 guest), **Also** Wines
🍴 Enhanced pub grub, 🌳 Sheltered terrace, ♿ *Tue quiz, additional bars and marquees during Wimbledon tournament*

This big old inn at the top end of Wimbledon Village can trace its history back to 1659 and has been a Young's pub since 1832, once counting the poet Algernon Charles Swinburne among its regulars. It's the best placed purveyor of good beer for the All England Club, straight ahead up Marryat

Road, and during Wimbledon fortnight makes the best of it with marquees, big screen coverage and ample supplies of strawberries and Pimms. Readers of this guide will likely prefer the Wells & Young's regulars (Bitter, Special, Bombardier and seasonals) and guests that might come from Hook Norton or Sambrook's. Sausages made with Special are on the menu alongside classic pub grub, sharing platters, salads, pies and desserts at slightly higher than average prices. It's a cheerful, comfortable place done out in dark wood and cream with striking designer lampshades, old photos and a barn-like space heated by a stove at the back. The hotel sign reflects the fact that 13 mid-price bedrooms were added in 2002, highly sought after at tournament time, but the place is still very much a pub.

≋ ⊖ Wimbledon 🚊 Wimbledon 🚌 Wimbledon Village (93, 493 Wimbledon) ⅋ LCN+ Sutton, Wimbledon, Putney Heath

SULTAN
Traditional pub
78 Norman Road, SW19 1BT
☎ (020) 8542 4532, ⊕ www.hopback.co.uk
✪ 12-11 Mon-Thu; 12-midnight Fri & Sat; 12-11 Sun
Cask beers ✔ 4 (3 Hopback, 1 guest, often Downton), **Other beers** 7-8 bottles (Hopback, Downton)
🌳 Beer garden, ♿
Wed beer club (cheap prices on cask ale), occasional barbecues, morris dancing, mummery, annual beer festival, darts, pool

In a residential area between South Wimbledon and Colliers Wood, this pub, named after a racehorse, is the only London house of the Hop Back brewery near Salisbury, one of Britain's most successful new generation micros. It's a showcase for their cask ales – GFB, Entire Stout and the famous Summer Lightning are permanently on draught alongside a guest or seasonal which is often from associated brewery Downton, with polypins, minipins and 4-pint carry out containers available too. Then there's the full range of the brewery's interesting Real Ales in a Bottle, together with some Downton bottles – harder to find and well worth sampling. A wall full of awards demonstrates the success of brewery and pub. The rather plain 1930s red brick exterior looks like it really belongs on a main road but inside is bright and cosy, with two bars, open fires and stripped wood tables. The outdoor patio hosts barbecues in summer and a beer festival in early October, and Morris men and mummers make occasional visits. The saloon bar is named after beer fan Ted Higgins, the original Walter Gabriel in long running radio soap *The Archers*.

Insider tip! Wednesday early evening is Beer Club when all cask ales are sold at a discount.

Colliers Wood, South Wimbledon NCN20 Wandle Trail

TRAFALGAR
Traditional pub
23 High Path, SW19 2JY
(020) 8542 5342, www.thetraf.com
3-11 Mon-Thu; 12-11 Fri-Sun
Cask beers 6 (Ascot, 5 unusual/local guests), **Other beers** 3 keg (Freedom, Riegele), 3-4 bottles (Dark Star, Riegele), **Also** 2 real ciders
Curry on Thu evening or brunch Sat lunchtime, otherwise none, Sheltered standing room
Live music Sat jazz/blues/folk, Sun lunchtime jazz, occasional beer festivals

This small street-corner pub, amid looming tower blocks on a side street off Merton High Street, is a surviving basic old-fashioned neighbourhood local that's neither closed nor gone upmarket. You walk through a front space with a couple of tables and a dartboard and under a ship's wheel suspended from the ceiling into an area with padded benches around a bar decorated with pottery shire horses and a wall mounted TV showing sport. When I visited on a quiet Saturday early evening I got a friendly welcome, but the only woman in the place was behind the bar. Yet it's a multiple winner of the local CAMRA Pub of the Year award for its excellent range of unusual cask ales, always including a dark choice. The house ale, brewed for the pub by Ascot, is the full-bodied darkish bitter Merton Abbey Market Ale, which marks the fact that

Jazz night at the Trafalgar

the Abbey Mills are only a short stroll away. The others are drawn from well reputed micros across the UK – Cottage, Dark Star, Isle of Purbeck, Otley, Palmers, Purple Moose, Tintagel, White Horse and Whitstable might put in an appearance. Two decent imported German lagers include one from rarely seen Riegele, who also provide a bottled Weissbier alongside Dark Star Imperial Stout. Amazingly they manage to squeeze in live bands at least twice a week and there are occasional beer festivals.

Insider tip! Naturally enough, the pub's big day every year is Trafalgar Day on 21 October where they throw a party including a popular quiz.

⊖ South Wimbledon ᛒ NCN20 ✦ Wandle Trail

OTHER LOCATIONS

CARSHALTON

HOPE
Traditional pub
48 West Street, SM5 2PR
☎ (020) 8240 1255
⊕ www.hopecarshalton.co.uk
✪ 12-11 Mon-Sat; 12-10.30 Sun. *Children until 9pm at back of pub*
Cask beers ✔ 5 (King, Dark Star, unusual/local guests), **Other beers** 1 keg, 10 bottles, **Also** 2 real ciders/perries,
⊞ Pub grub and snacks, ⊞ Large beer garden
Occasional live music, pagan festivals, bar billiards, crib, dominoes

When, in 2010, the regulars at this small pub near Carshalton station heard that landlords Punch were intent on selling it off as a restaurant, they literally didn't give up Hope. A group of them including Susanna, the licensee, formed a community company and negotiated a 20-year lease as a free house. The pub was already big on microbrewed real ale and that policy has since expanded, with the two regulars, King Horsham Best and Dark Star Hophead, supplemented by a rotating selection from across the country and usually including a mild and a strong ale. Beers from Bowman, Kelham Island, Leatherbritches, Northumberland, Thornbridge, Titanic and many others have been spotted here. At the

time I called a new and interesting bottled range had recently appeared, including Belgian Géants and Ellezelloise and Farmers Ales from Essex, and they were looking forward to the installation of a new tap for guest specialist keg beers. Lunchtime food is uncomplicated but hearty. The pub itself is a very friendly traditional rustic local with a single L-shaped bar complete with piano around which regulars occasionally burst into song, and well worth the trip to the suburbs.

Insider tip! The pub celebrates Pagan festivals, including a popular harvest do.

⇌ Carshalton ᛒ NCN20 (Wandle Trail) ✦ Wandle Trail

NEW MALDEN

WOODIES FREEHOUSE
Traditional pub
The Sportsground, Thetford Road, KT3 5DX
☎ (020) 8949 5824
⊕ www.woodiesfreehouse.co.uk
✪ 11-11 Mon-Sat; 12-10.30 Sun. *Children welcome*
Cask beers ✔ 7 (Adnams, Fuller's, Young's, unusual/local guests), **Also** 1 real cider
⊞ Pub grub, Sun carvery, ⊞ Terrace, beer garden, ♿
Major annual beer festival, quizzes and live music – generally fortnightly

This unique and welcoming venue claims to be New Malden's best kept secret, with tales of

Woodies Freehouse

people who lived nearby for decades never realising it was there. It is certainly tucked away, a good stroll from the nearest bus stop or station, where the massed acres of suburbia meet the ribbon of playing fields and green spaces alongside the Hogsmill stream. Formerly a cricket pavilion, then a members' club, it's been an independently owned pub since 1982. The drinks offer foregrounds a choice of top cask beers: Broadside, ESB, Pride and Young's Bitter are regulars while the other lines rotate from the likes of Ascot, Cottage, Dark Star, Hepworth, Sambrook's, Welton's and more. Beers can be enjoyed on the extensive outdoor terrace in summer or around an open fire in a still slightly clubby indoor environment in winter. At least as remarkable is the decor: ceiling and wall surfaces are totally obscured by a chaos of stuff that's been accumulating for decades. It's mainly paper – flyers, posters, postcards, photos, press cuttings, whole vintage cricket magazines – but also ties, knick-knacks and breweriana, a bit like one of those fire safety challenging brown cafés found in Dutch cities. The place is child and dog friendly and the annual beer festival is a major event, with stalls and children's activities. A true original, it deserves to be a secret no longer.

Insider tip! Booking is obligatory for the Sunday carvery.

≋ Berrylands, Malden Manor 🚃 Wellington Crescent (131 Kingston, New Malden) 🚶 London Loop, Thames Down Link

PUTNEY

BRICKLAYERS ARMS ☆ 25
Traditional pub, specialist
32 Waterman Street, SW15 1DD
📞 (020) 8789 0222
🌐 www.bricklayers-arms.co.uk
🕐 12-11 Mon-Sat; 12-10.30 Sun. *Children until 8pm*
Cask beers ✔ 12 (Dark Star, Rudgate, Sambrook's, 9 unusual guests), **Other beers** 3 keg, **Also** 1-2 real ciders/perries, English wines 🪑 Small beer garden, ♿ No disabled toilet but can assist
Twice yearly beer festivals (Feb & Sep), annual cider festival (Oct), skittles and shove ha'penny

Bricklayers Arms

Pretty Putney's history was shaped by its role as a river crossing point, first by ferry, then in 1729 by a wooden bridge, the second Thames bridge in London after London Bridge. It is also the starting point of the annual Oxford-Cambridge University Boat Race. Set back just a little from the river is this gem of a real ale pub, a hostelry since 1831. Once known for championing Timothy Taylor beers, it's now lost that link but keeps a loyalty to the white rose county with an annual Yorkshire Beer Festival in February, offering over a hundred beers; a second festival is held in September. The rest of the time its long row of handpumps features a welcome regular mild, Rudgate Ruby, with Sambrook's Wandle and a galaxy of guests that favours Acorn, Dark Star, Downton, Scotland's Fyne Ales, Loddon, Tring and several others – the managers listen out for customer demand. Inside it's basic but comfortable, all white-painted wood and bare brick with an elegant bar counter and open wood fire. A pretty garden completes the amenities for this winner of numerous local CAMRA awards. Those of a certain age will twinge nostalgic at the vintage 70s swimming pool rules poster displayed on one wall.

Insider tip! The boat race takes place either on the last Saturday of March or the first Saturday of April – don't expect a quiet drink that day!

≋ Putney ⊖ Putney Bridge 🚲 LCN+4, NCN Fulham, Wimbledon 🚶 Thames Path, Beverley Brook Walk

STREATHAM

EARL FERRERS
Contemporary pub
22 Ellora Road, SW16 6JF
📞 (020) 8835 8333, 🌐 www.earlferrers.co.uk
⚙ 4-11 Mon & Tue; 4-midnight Wed-Fri;
12-midnight Sat; 12-11 Sun. *Children very
welcome until 7pm*
Cask beers ✔ 5 (Sambrook's, unusual/local
guests), **Other beers** 1-2 bottles, **Also** Wines,
cocktails
🍽 Pub grub/gastro menu, 🌇 Front terrace, rear
patio
*Tue stitch & bitch, Wed quiz, Sun live acoustic
music & jazz, DIY DJ nights, film nights, monthly
book club, board games, pool, darts*

Streatham, on the Roman road that now
forms part of the A23 from London to
Brighton, is another London village that's
managed to hang on to a fair part of its
historic common. In the streets on the other
side of the main road from the Common, is
this delightfully relaxed and friendly
community local with just a hint of gastropub,
advertising "booze, food, good times" on a
board outside. It's an Enterprise tenancy but
landlord Duncan is keen to support local and
regional brewers through the SIBA Direct
Delivery Scheme: Wandle and Junction might
be joined by beers from Brodie's, Fuller's, Hop
Back, Meantime, Pilgrim, Redemption or
Westerham. Very good food could include
mushroom, rocket and blue cheese pastry,
beer battered pollock or a pint of prawns. A
busy events programme, community notice
board and visitors' book underline the
commitment to old style customer care.

Antelope

Pub trivia: An attractive deep red pool room to
the side displays the original rather grim pub
sign depicting the fourth Earl Ferrers under the
shadow of the noose – he was the last British
peer to be executed as a common criminal in
1760, for the murder of one of this staff.

🚆 Streatham, Streatham Common 🚲 Link to
LCN+5 🚶 Capital Ring, Streatham Common
footpaths

TOOTING

ANTELOPE
Gastropub
76 Mitcham Road, SW17 9NG
📞 (020) 8672 3888, 🌐 www.theantelopepub.
com, **fbk, tw** theantelopesw17
⚙ 4-midnight Mon-Thu; 12-1am Fri & Sat;
12-10.30 Sun. *Children until early evening*
Cask beers ✔ 7 (Adnams, Sharp's, St Austell,
Sambrook's, guests), **Other beers** 4 keg, 22
bottles, **Also** Wines, speciality whiskies
🍽 Gastro menu, 🌇 Small beer garden, ♿
Monthly comedy, parties and film nights

This big, bright and quirkily decorated high
street pub is a highly successful fusion of a
gastropub and a beer house. Big engraved
arched windows light a large and pastel-
coloured front space, with inviting sofas on one
side underneath a bright green wall displaying
a plate collection. Behind this is an elegant
wood-panelled dining room and a colonial
club-style Games Room, sometimes reserved
for private functions. The cask beers are solid
stuff from generally well known brewers –
several Adnams beers are normally available
besides examples from Purity, Wells & Young's,
Sambrook's, Sharp's and St Austell. The decently
sized bottled list is remarkable for offering four
hard to find choices from London's tiny Kernel
brewery, alongside Trappists from Chimay and
Rochefort and Austrian lager from Stiegl.
Pleasingly there are food matching suggestions
on the beer list – suggested beers on the food
menu too would be better still. The food in
question changes regularly but might feature
mussels, duck and tasty chunky chips. A
welcome addition to London's beer scene.

⊖ Tooting Broadway 🚲 CS7, link to LCN+
Tooting Bec Common 🚶 Link to Capital Ring

WEST LONDON

West London as outlined here includes both the W and SW postcodes outside the central area and north of the Thames (for the SW postcodes south of the river see Southwest London, p191). It also stretches to western and north western outer suburbs like Brentford, Harrow, Twickenham and Uxbridge.

As a general rule, while London's industry and business has moved east, its accumulated wealth has moved west – a precedent perhaps first set when the monarchy established its London power base at Westminster, upwind of the City, in late Saxon times. The preponderance of well-to-do residential districts here, some of them taking advantage of the picturesque setting provided by the narrowing Thames, is partly the reason why the Underground map looks so unbalanced. Indeed the companies that originally built the Underground are directly responsible for some of the sprawl. From the 1900s the Metropolitan Railway began buying land to develop as housing alongside providing the commuter infrastructure, creating 'Metroland', as wryly celebrated by poet John Betjeman, along what are now the Metropolitan Line routes to the northwest. These lines reach towards fine countryside in the Colne Valley and the edge of the chalk Chiltern Hills, much of it now preserved as green belt. But some sections of West London have more calloused hands, particularly along the arms of the Grand Union Canal. And one of the capital's biggest postwar hives of activity is located just within the western boundary, at Heathrow Airport, where decent beer is, as we'll discover, surprisingly plentiful.

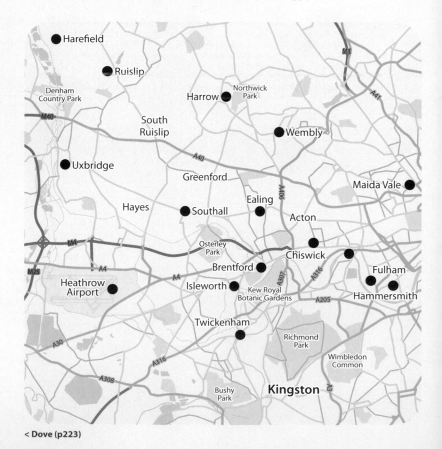

< **Dove (p223)**

CHISWICK

From Tudor times Thameside Chiswick was regarded as a prime site for luxury mansions thanks to its waterway links not only to London but to the palaces upriver at Richmond and Hampton Court. The grandest surviving building is neo-Palladian Chiswick House (1729). Inevitably the place swelled in the railway age and boasted London's first electric trams at the beginning of the 20th century, though subsequent transport developments have seen it severed by the busy A4.

18th century satirical artist William Hogarth lived in Chiswick. One of his most famous works is the diptych that contrasts drunken and degenerate Gin Lane with prosperous Beer Street, an image that's since been appropriated in defence of community pubs. As home to what's now London's only remaining historic craft brewery, the world famous Fuller's (p270), whose Griffin site by the Hogarth Roundabout boasts a 350-year-old brewing legacy, Chiswick is most decidedly on Beer Street.

DUKE OF SUSSEX

Gastropub
75 South Parade, W4 5LF
📞 (020) 8742 8801
🕐 12-11 Mon-Thu; 12-midnight Fri & Sat; 12-10.30 Sun. *Children welcome*
Cask beers ✅ 3 (Fuller's, 2 guests), **Other beers** 8-10 bottles, **Also** Wines
🍴 Gastro-style and authentic tapas, 🌳 Large beer garden, ♿
Sun quiz, Mon bring your own

Overlooking Acton Green Common on the southern edge of late Victorian residential development Bedford Park, the world's first garden suburb, this big mock Tudor corner pub got a gastro makeover in 2007 which still preserves some sense of splendour from its rebuilding in Arts & Crafts style in 1898.

Chiswick Bitter is a regular while cask guests might be from Batemans, Cottage, Hog's Back, Sambrook's, Skinners, St Austell, Triple fff or Wells & Young's, all perfectly maintained by cellarman Ermano. Bottles encompass San Francisco's Anchor Steam Beer alongside Chimay Blanche and Duvel. In good weather you can dine and drink al fresco in a proper garden with flower beds and planters, filling yourself up with an unusual mix of traditional Spanish tapas and British cooking that might even include roast rooks in season.

Pub trivia: The most substantial original feature is the porch onto Beaconsfield Road which still has painted tiles depicting rustic scenes.

🚆 South Acton ⊖ Chiswick Park 🚲 LCN+35 ♦♦ Acton Green footpaths

1 Duke of Sussex   **2** Fox & Hounds / Mawson Arms   **3** Fuller's Brewery Shop

Fox & Hounds / Mawson Arms

FOX & HOUNDS / MAWSON ARMS
Traditional pub
110 Chiswick Lane South, W4 2QA
📞 (020) 8994 2936, ✉ mawsonarms@fullers.co.uk, ⊕ www.fullers.co.uk
⚙ 11-8 Mon-Fri; Closed Sat & Sun. *Children welcome*
Cask beers ✅ 6 (Fuller's), **Other beers** 1 keg, 4 bottles (Fuller's), **Also** Wines
🍴 Pub grub and specials, ⌗ Bench in park opposite
Big screen sport, meeting place for brewery tours

Formerly Alexander Pope's house, now on the corner of Fuller's brewery (p270) and effectively the brewery tap, this pub acquired its two names thanks to an old regulation that stipulated separate licenses for beer and for wines and spirits. It's now a single pleasant space, popular with Fuller's staff and with plentiful historic prints and brewery memorabilia on display. It unsurprisingly offers a good range of Fuller's beers at maximum freshness. Chiswick, Discovery, ESB, Gales' Seafarers and London Pride are always on, while the sixth tap rotates seasonals and specials. There are only a few Fuller's bottles – a more comprehensive range is available to take away from the Brewery Shop (below). Food is pub grub like sandwiches, burgers, steak and ESB pie and veggie pasta. If you're caught out by the unusual hours, a nearby

alternative which also does a good Fuller's range (although it's not actually a Fuller's pub) is the George & Devonshire at 8 Burlington Lane, W4 2QE.

⇌ Chiswick ⊖ Turnham Green, Stamford Brook 🚌 Hogarth Roundabout (190 Richmond, Stamford Brook, Hammersmith) 🚲 LCN+44 and links to NCN4 ⚓ Thames Path

FULLER'S BREWERY SHOP
Shop
Chiswick Lane South, W4 2QB
📞 (020) 8996 2000, ⊕ www.fullers.co.uk
⚙ 10-8 Mon-Fri; 10-6 Sat; Closed Sun
Cask beer None, **Other beers** 20 bottles (mainly Fuller's), minicasks, bulk casks to order, **Also** Wines
Brewery tours

An essential call for Fuller's fans, this is a friendly place in an old building right on the brewery site, and the most reliable source of hard to find specialities. Last time I looked, the Vintage Ale collection covered all but two years back to 1999, and at reasonable prices, though obviously that might vary. It's also an outlet for the Brewer's Reserve and Past Masters series alongside a comprehensive range of the brewery's regular bottled beers. Devotees can equip themselves with glasses, rugby shirts and a host of other promotional items, as well as buy tickets for the brewery tour.

⇌ Chiswick ⊖ Turnham Green, Stamford Brook 🚌 Hogarth Roundabout (190 Richmond, Stamford Brook, Hammersmith) 🚲 LCN+44 and links to NCN4 ⚓ Thames Path

Fuller's Brewery Shop

FULHAM & HAMMERSMITH

Like the Isle of Dogs, Fulham is enclosed by a Thames meander, but couldn't be more of a contrast. It was once the official residence of the Bishop of London, whose former palace grounds are now a park and botanical garden overlooking the long-standing link to Putney on the opposite bank. Just downstream of the Bishop stood Ranelagh Gardens, the 18th century theme park and entertainment venue, which, as a location for amorous assingments and prostitution, had a less pious reputation. At the beginning of the the 20th century Fulham was known as a working class area, and still boasts two major football teams – Fulham and Chelsea – but its proximity to Chelsea proper has seen property prices rocket as the urban dwelling youth of Britain's old money moved west. Numerous celebrities also live locally.

Hammersmith is another former fishing village but its location on the main route west, now the A4, had a huge impact on its subsequent development. In 1961 the highway was hoisted onto Hammersmith Flyover which still dominates the townscape today, skimming through a strip of office blocks occupied by the multinational likes of Coca Cola, Disney, Sony and Universal. Besides a shopping mall it's well endowed with arts and entertainment venues including the Hammersmith Apollo (formerly Hammersmith Odeon), the Lyric Theatre and the Riverside Arts Centre.

DOVE
Traditional pub ★
19 Upper Mall, W6 9TA
☎ (020) 8748 9474, ✉ dove@fullers.co.uk
🌐 www.fullers.co.uk
🕐 11-11 Mon-Sat; 12-10.30 Sun
Cask beers ✔ 4 (Fuller's), **Other beers** 5 bottles (Fuller's), **Also** Wines
🍴 Upmarket pub grub, 🚪 Riverside terrace

A relatively short stroll downriver along the Thames Path from Fuller's brewery and an exemplary stockist of its beers, the Dove is one of London's most favoured pubs in terms of location and historical character. Built in the first half of the 18th century close to Hammersmith's original riverside centre, it fronts onto a cobbled alley and backs straight

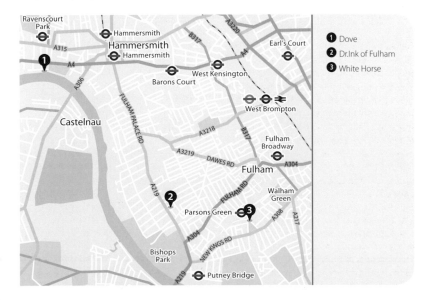

❶ Dove
❷ Dr.Ink of Fulham
❸ White Horse

Dove

onto the Thames. Inside, low-beamed drinking areas with yellowed ceilings cluster round a small bar, while the walls exhibit evidence of connections with Charles II, Nell Gwynne and Scottish poet James Thomson, lyricist of 'Rule, Britannia!'. The woodwork includes what are thought to be some of the oldest purpose built pub fittings still in use, dating back to before 1800. A conservatory leads onto the river terrace where a sheltered spot under a fire escape provides a retreat for amorous couples at quiet times. Pride, ESB, Discovery and a seasonal are the draught choices, with 1845 and Golden Pride among the bottles. Food might include parmesan polenta, steak and ESB pie, London Pride battered fish and chips, roast pumpkin gnocchi and various sharing platters.

Insider tip! Try the door on the right immediately on entering, which leads into what according to *Guinness World Records* is the smallest public bar in Britain, a tiny snug with classic wooden fittings. It's now thought to have been built after 1911 by a licensee who misread a new licensing law requiring some pubs to have at least two rooms.

⊖ Ravenscourt Park NCN4, LCN+35
Thames Path

DR.INK OF FULHAM
Shop
349 Fulham Palace Road, SW6 6TB
(020) 7610 6795, www.drinkoffulham.com,
fbk, **tw** drinkoffulham
Closed Mon; 2-7.30 Tue-Fri; 11.30-8 Sat;
Closed Sun
Cask beer None, **Other beers** 600 bottles,
Also Specialist ciders, fine wines
Curry pastes and spice mixes, vegetarian
farsan snacks, Small front terrace
Occasional tastings

Near-teetotaller Jayesh 'Jack' Patel is one of Britain's more unlikely ambassadors for craft beer, having turned his unassuming Londis corner shop in the Oxfordshire village of Goring-on-Thames into a treasurehouse of beery delights.

Jayesh's cousin Shrila Amin was inspired by the dazzling array of bottles and labels and early in 2010 opened Dr.Ink in a smallish but well-appointed and well-organised shop opposite Bishop's Park, recruiting her cousin as an adviser. The shop's extensive stocks encompass up to 600 beers. As in Goring there's a wide choice of British ales including Burton Bridge, Cropton, Durham, Kelham Island, Marble, O'Hanlon's, RCH, Ridgeway, Saltaire and West Berkshire; Belgians from

Abbaye des Rocs, Caracole, Dolle Brouwers, Dupont, Rochefort, Silly, St Bernardus, St Feuillien, Van Steenberge, Vapeur and lambics from Boon and Oud Beersel; a good few well-chosen Germans and Americans; and even Italian craft beers from the likes of Baladin and Borgo. Prices are very reasonable given the area. Particularly pleasing, though, is the way the place fuses world beer culture seamlessly with the Gujerati background of its owner, with a range of culinary delights – spice mixes and curry pastes during the week, delicious vegetarian savoury farsan finger food at weekends. To top it all, the place is equipped with a limited amount of attractive wooden seating in the front yard where, for an additional £1 per bottle, you're welcome to enjoy a beer on the spot.

Insider tip! Watch out for tastings and meet-the-brewer events.

⊖ Parsons Green, Putney Bridge 🚄 Bishops Park Road (74, 220, 430 Putney Bridge) 🚲 NCN4, LCN+ routes Fulham Broadway, Kensington, Putney 🚶 Thames Path

WHITE HORSE ☆ 25

Traditional pub, specialist
1-3 Parsons Green, SW6 4UL
📞 (020) 7736 2115
🌐 www.whitehorsesw6.com
🕐 9.30am-11.30pm Mon-Wed;
9.30am-midnight Thu-Sat; 9.30am-11.30pm
Sun. *Children welcome*
Cask beers ✅ 8 (Adnams, Harveys, Oakham, 5 unusual guests), **Other beers** 14 keg, 200 bottles (some unique in London), **Also** Bottled ciders and perries, malts, wines
🍽 Gastro menu, 🏡 Small front terrace, ♿
Monthly Beer Academy tastings, four beer festivals annually, other tastings and beer events

This big old former coaching inn overlooking dappled Parsons Green has been a beer-lovers' landmark since the early 1980s when, as a Bass Charrington house, it was renowned for dry hopping its own Draught Bass. On the initiative of cellarman and later manager Mark Dorber it stretched the Bass tie to build one of London's pioneering fine beer ranges, once boasting lists of cellar-aged British and Belgian strong specialities and hosting numerous now-legendary beer and food matching

Dr.Ink of Fulham

White Horse

on offer, presented in 13 categories. They're particularly strong on bottles from Belgium and the USA, with a good few genuine lambics, more unusual Belgian choices such as De Ranke XX Bitter, and beers from Big Sky, Deschutes, Eel River, Green Flash, Lagunitas and Tommyknocker as well as rarer options from more regularly imported Americans like Goose Island. Some of these are at serious prices – a 750ml bottle of the excellent Brooklyn Local 1 will set you back £20. There are some British bottled classics too but the choice (including Coniston, Fuller's, Hop Back, Wells & Young's, White Shield) isn't quite as imaginative, and it's a shame most of the listings under 'British bottle-conditioned beers' are actually filtered and sometimes pasteurised, especially given the attention to detail elsewhere.

Thanks to its prize location in a well-off area the pub is not just a place of pilgrimage for beer devotees – it's known rather unkindly as 'the Sloaney Pony' for its popularity with so-called Sloane Rangers, the younger generation of the British aristocracy.

There is a certain old-style poshness about it: the main drinking area with its leather sofas, ceiling fans and wooden Venetian blinds has a colonial touch. Food is solid modern British with a modest European note, at good value but not bargain prices, and might feature potted pork, stag fillets, pot roast pheasant, lamb shank or wild mushroom pie. Beer matching suggestions have long been included on the menu.

While it's still a good place to listen out for public school accents, the customers are generally a genial mix and the staff remain welcoming, polite and informative even when, as often, they're run off their feet.

dinners. The Bass is long gone, only a handful of aged beers remain and Mark moved on in 2007, but current manager Dan Fox has wisely maintained an impressive focus on beer, including a partnership with the Beer Academy to run regular tasting courses upstairs. Harveys Sussex Best Bitter, Broadside and Oakham JHB are the current regular casks, while guests tend to be quality stuff from respected independents and bigger micros, with a mix of strong and mild, light and dark. They're unafraid to offer stronger stuff from the cask – in season you might catch the wonderful 8.1% Harveys Christmas Ale, for example.

The keg range is bigger still, and stretches beyond now relatively common specialities like Budvar and Blue Moon to US imports from the likes of Great Divide and Left Hand including high gravity specimens.

Bottled beers are still by far the biggest section of the hefty drinks list: around 200 are

Insider tip! I feel most at home in the lovely wood-panelled space to the left of the bar with the beer display cases, but if you're eating, look for the barn-like extension on the right at the back, which can be quiet even when the rest of the pub is heaving. The covered patio at the front accommodates smokers and barbeques in summer.

⊖ Parsons Green ᗛ LCN+ Wimbledon, Kensington, links to NCN4 ✏ Link to Thames Path

HEATHROW AIRPORT

Among the last places you'd expect to find good beer is a major international airport. That's what the managers at JD Wetherspoon thought too when they first went into the airport trade in the 1990s, equipping their outlets with only a token handpump of Boddington's Bitter. Then someone started experimenting with strengthening the cask offer, with surprisingly successful results: real ale is now a core part of the airport trade, and set to grow still further.

It's an iconically British product that's equally valued by overseas visitors, British travellers including expats setting off for another long stint abroad or welcoming themselves back from one, and anyone else that appreciates quality and distinctiveness among the bland globalised chains that dominate the airport retail experience. Interestingly, the strong beers tend to be the preferred options for customers looking forward to dozing on a long flight.

Wetherspoon aren't the only real ale sellers at Heathrow. Geronimo, now part of Young's, offer a slightly less varied but good quality range in their three stylish bars. Some of the other caterers have installed a token pump or two, but aren't covered here. Neither are the Wetherspoon Express bars by the gates, which are currently keg only, although they've been considering ways to incorporate a cask offering at these too.

The bars on 'landside' – before security checks – tend to be quieter, mainly used by greeters, early arrivals and others in the know, including airport and airline staff, who aren't allowed to drink alcohol once 'airside'. And with around 70,000 staff there's a significant market even without all the passengers and visitors.

Tin Goose

London Heathrow Airport (LHR) is the biggest airport in Britain, the busiest international airport in the world and the fourth busiest of all airports, with 66million passengers a year passing through the five terminals. Originally a military airfield during World War I, it was upgraded into London's main airport after a secret wartime decision which, given its proximity to dense residential areas, has caused controversy ever since. A further expansion to a third runway and sixth terminal was cancelled by the current government, though Terminal 2 is being rebuilt and will reopen in 2014 – likely with at least one further outlet selling cask ale.

The **Skylark** at Terminal 1, in the catering area above the checkins, is named after a bird species that's common on nearby Hounslow Health, and is the most Wetherspoon-like in appearance of the company's airport outlets. Greene King Abbot and Fuller's London Pride are regulars, while guest beers tend to be unusual and on the stronger side – they were from Brentwood, Brewster's and Marston's when I called.

On the first floor of Terminal 3, above security and a little tucked away by a Ponti's café, is Geronimo's **Three Bells**. They've worked hard to create a comfortable and loungey environment here with sofas, big armchairs and some tucked away booths. Adnams Bitter, Sharp's Doom Bar and Wells Bombardier are the regulars with an additional guest usually sourced from a better known brewery. A few bottled goodies like Coopers Sparkling Ale and Duvel extend the offer.

The cosiest Wetherspoon, and the one most popular with airport staff which gives it more of a local feel, is the **Windsor Castle** at Terminal 4. Even harder to find than the Three Bells, it's in limbo on a mezzanine between Arrivals and Departures. It has six cask beers – Greene King Abbot, London Pride and one of those Greene King IPA gadgets that offers you the choice of northern or southern heads – plus guests that when I looked came from Acorn, Brains and Hook Norton.

At the posh new Terminal 5, British Airways' home base, is the **Five Tuns**, a smallish Geronimo on the Departures level by check-in area G. Another staff favourite, this boasts the 'last opportunity for a smoke and a pint in quite a while' as the outdoor smoking terrace is right nearby. There's a table service side and a bar side, the latter more loungey with board games. Adnams Bitter, Doom Bar and Bombardier are on offer.

Most departing passengers don't linger landside but head straight for the departure lounge, and beyond the security barriers it's a notably glitzier – and busier – world. Geronimo's airside **Tin Goose** at Terminal 1, in the main departure area near a Boots, is a sizeable corner space with full table service that offers plenty of lounging room, some more private areas and a grand view of the planes. Beside the expected Adnams, Bombardier and Doom Bar is a guest served on gravity and Coopers and Duvel in bottled form.

Wetherspoon's flagship is the airside **Crown Rivers** at Terminal 5, downstairs from security by domestic gate A7. The stylish wood-panelled and mirrored design helps compensate for the fact that a public walkway splits the bar from the bulk of the seating. A house beer, Crown Rivers Ale, is supplied by Loddon brewery, supported by Abbot, IPA, London Pride and two guests, the choice of which is influenced by customer comments but usually includes a dark beer – Titanic Stout when I called. It's a bustling place, the only catering outlet to be allocated more space since Terminal 5 opened.

All these places do food. The Wetherspoon pubs offer a similar menu to high street branches. The Geronimo pubs serve up a version of their high street counterparts' vaguely Gastroish menu, with steaks, pies, ham hock, curries and casseroles. All offer breakfasts and a variety of lighter options. They also

Five Tuns

Skylark

support events like the Wetherspoon and Geronimo beer festivals, although don't expect food promotions from the airport JDWs.

All these pubs have worked hard to find their own solution to the challenge of creating something as ordinary, welcoming and intimate as a pub in the extraordinary and highly stressful environment of a busy airport. None has entirely succeeded, and you probably wouldn't want to make a special trip to any of them, but that's an unfair criticism. More importantly, it's cheering to see good beer being so successfully supported in one of the most unlikely places.

CROWN RIVERS
Terminal 5 Airside, TW6 1EW
☎ (020) 8283 6208
⊕ www.jdwetherspoon.co.uk
✪ Open first flight to last flight. *Children welcome if dining*
✅, ♿

⇌ Heathrow Terminal 5 ⊖ Heathrow Terminal 5

FIVE TUNS
Terminal 5 Landside, TW6 2GA
☎ (020) 8283 5065
⊕ www.geronimo-inns.co.uk/thefivetuns
✪ 6.30am-11pm daily. *Children welcome*
♿

⇌ Heathrow Terminal 5 ⊖ Heathrow Terminal 5

SKYLARK
Terminal 1 Landside, TW6 1PA
☎ (020) 8607 5650
⊕ www.jdwetherspoon.co.uk

✪ 6am-11pm Mon-Sat; 6am-10.30pm Sun. *Children welcome if dining*
Also 1 real cider
✅, ♿

⇌ Heathrow Terminals 1 2 3 ⊖ Heathrow Terminals 1 2 3

THREE BELLS
Terminal 3 Landside, TW6 1AD
☎ (020) 8897 6755
⊕ www.geronimo-inns.co.uk/thethreebells
✪ 6am-10pm daily. *Children welcome*
♿

⇌ Heathrow Terminals 1 2 3 ⊖ Heathrow Terminals 1 2 3

TIN GOOSE
Terminal 1 Airside, TW6 1AP
☎ (020) 8607 5960
⊕ www.geronimo-inns.co.uk/thetingoose
✪ Open first flight to last flight. *Children welcome*
♿

⇌ Heathrow Terminals 1 2 3 ⊖ Heathrow Terminals 1 2 3

WINDSOR CASTLE
Terminal 4 Landside, TW6 3XA
☎ (020) 8759 2906
⊕ www.jdwetherspoon.co.uk
✪ 6am-11pm daily. *Children welcome if dining*
✅, ♿

⇌ Heathrow Terminal 4 ⊖ Heathrow Terminal 4
🚲 Cycle route to Grand Union Canal towpath
🚶 London Loop to ⊖ Hatton Cross

TWICKENHAM & HAMPTON HILL

Twickenham has a long history as a riverside settlement on the Thames' north bank that for centuries was an important ferry crossing point, although it seems that in the mid-18th century the locals were at least as much interested in getting across the water to the Folly, a floating pub "where divers loose and disorderly persons are frequently entertained." The place developed into a sprawling suburban town which is now the headquarters of the London Borough of Richmond, the only borough to straddle both banks of the river. Discerning beer lovers might recognise it as the source of Twickenham Fine Ales (p283) but it's more famous among a world-wide public as the home of English Rugby Union – the RFU is based at the massive Twickenham Stadium, the second biggest stadium in the UK and host of numerous national and international fixtures. When there's a major match on you'll be lucky to find a pub round here that isn't screening it live on a big TV, but at least you'll be able to enjoy a decent pint while you watch. As well as the places below there's a Wetherspoon, the William Webb Ellis, named after the reputed inventor of the game, at 24 London Road, TW1 3RR.

BROUGE

Comtemporary pub, restaurant, specialist
241 Hampton Road, Fulwell, TW2 5NG
☎ (020) 8977 2698, ⊕ www.brouge.co.uk
🕓 12-11 Mon-Thu; 12-11.30 Fri & Sat; 12-11 Sun. *Children welcome*
Cask beers ✅ 2 (1 Sambrook's, 1 often local guest), **Other beers** 10 keg, 60 bottles, **Also** Wines
🍽 Belgian/international menu, 🚪 Front terrace, ♿

Mon quiz, Sun family carvery, beer tastings, occasional live music

If you're looking for a Belgian flavoured beer bistro and are disappointed with Belgo, the answer is to go west – Brouge is more beer savvy, more welcoming and more keenly priced. This original Brouge was fashioned out of a roadside pub close to Fulwell station in 2003 by the owners of beer importer and distributor Pig's Ear, achieving a pleasing

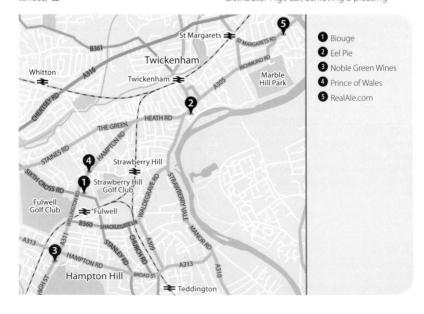

1 Biouge
2 Eel Pie
3 Noble Green Wines
4 Prince of Wales
5 RealAle.com

fusion between a rural Belgian café and a suburban London boozer complete with handpumped cask ale. It's a biggish place with bare floorboards and simple wooden furniture around two sides of the bar, and a more snazzy restaurant at the back, but the same menu is available throughout. It's also very child friendly, particularly at weekends.

The beer choice is impressive, with quite a bit from Van Steenberge who supply the house pils and draught wheat beer Celis White (originally developed in the USA by the man who revived Hoegaarden) alongside bottled Gulden Draak and Leute Bokbier. Other highlights are Boon Oude Geuze, Rochefort trappists and Rodenbach Grand Cru. A welcome addition in 2010 is the world beer list including bottle-conditioned ales from Otley and Sambrook's and American unfiltered delights from Anchor, Brooklyn and Goose Island. There's also a rotating specials list of serious beer geek pleasers from Italy's Borgo (the divine Re Ale was on offer when I visited), Denmark's Mikkeller, De Molen in the Netherlands and Thornbridge in Derbyshire. All this plus two cask ales – Sambrook's Wandle and a rotating guest, sometimes from Twickenham.

Food is a bistro-ey choice of sausages in ale gravy, mussels and chips, ox cheek, rabbit and veggie risotto, and staff can advise on beer and food matching. "Here at Brouge," declares the menu, "we believe that beer deserves its place at the dinner table as well as wine." The Richmond branch (p208) is better located but with much more of a dining emphasis, and doesn't stock cask.

Insider tip! Look out for the various food offers: lunchtime express deals, weekend specials and free food for kids in the early evenings.

⇌ Fulwell 🚆 Sixth Cross Road (numerous Twickenham) 🚲 Link to NCN4 ♦♦ London Loop, link to Thames Path

---

EEL PIE
Traditional pub
9-11 Church Street, TW1 3NJ
📞 (020) 8891 1717
🌐 www.hall-woodhouse.co.uk
🕐 11-11 Mon-Wed; 11-midnight Thu-Sat; 12-10.30 Sun

Noble Green Wines

Cask beers ✅ 4 (Badger), **Other beers** 3 bottles (Badger)
🍴 Pub grub, ⛱ Standing room in alley, 🍖 *Barbecue and 'speed bar' (keg only) during major rugby matches*

Once Twickenham's main thoroughfare, Church Street is now a heritage feature in its own right, lined with specialist shops and lovely old buildings. One of these houses is the Eel Pie pub, named after a privately-owned ait (island) in the Thames nearby which was one of the key sites in the development of British jazz, rhythm & blues and Bohemian culture in the 1950s and 1960s and later home to Who guitarist Pete Townsend's studio.

One of a few London outlets for Dorset's Badger (Hall & Woodhouse) Brewery (p295), the pub is probably the best bet for good beer in Twickenham town centre. The brewery's First Gold, Tanglefoot and K&B Sussex Bitter are regulars while the guest is usually a Badger seasonal. A central bar separates two pleasant spaces with bare floorboards, flagstones and wooden furniture. Predictably decorations have a rugby theme and on match days you can watch the action on the big screen in one half of the bar, followed by a barbecue in the adjacent alleyway. There's no TV in the slightly more luxurious half of the bar but the commentary is relayed all the same.

⇌ Twickenham 🚲 NCN4, NCN+ Twickenham, Hampton Court ♦♦ Thames Path

NOBLE GREEN WINES
Shop
153-155 High Street, Hampton Hill, TW12 1NL
☎ (020) 8979 1113
⊕ www.noblegreenwines.co.uk, **fbk**
⊕ 11-8 Mon-Fri; 10-8 Sat; 11-6 Sun
Cask beers ✔ Up to 6 (Dark Star, Twickenham, unusual/local guests), **Other beers** 250-300 bottles, **Also** Wines, speciality spirits, olive oil
Occasional tastings

This independent off-license in Hampton Hill's village centre, opposite the Playhouse theatre, was opened as its name suggests primarily as a specialist wine merchant but with a small corner of interesting bottled beers. Thanks to customer demand this has expanded to four times its original size, pushing out some of the wine, and is now a major selling point, with window displays and occasional tasting events. The recent addition of cask ales to take away at very keen prices in two pint plastic bottles, minipins, polypins or full size casks has also proved a big success. The bottled range includes several from BrewDog and numerous bottle-conditioned ales with a local-ish slant from the likes of Ascot, Ballards, Dark Star, Hepworth, Hogs Back, and Sambrook's. The Belgians are mainly Trappists and the better-known abbey beers and strong ales with rarer contributions from Ellezelloise, De Graal and Troubadour (Proef), while Germany offers several Bavarians (Andechs, Augustiner, HB,

Kulmbacher) plus quality lager and Kölsch. Staff are helpful and knowledgeable and the shop is spacious and easy to browse. Serious beer hunters will unearth few real rarities here but locals are indeed fortunate to have such a comprehensive range of great beer on their doorstep. It's a shame more wine merchants don't follow this example.

⇌ Fulwell ⊙⊙ Link to NCN4 ⚲ London Loop

PRINCE OF WALES
Contemporary pub
136 Hampton Road, Fulwell, TW2 5QR
☎ (020) 8894 5054
⊕ 4-11 Mon; 12-11 Tue & Wed; 12-midnight Thu-Sat; 12-10.30 Sun. *Children welcome until 9pm*
Cask beers ✔ 8 (Twickenham, Sharp's or St Austell, unusual guests), **Other beers** 1 keg,
Also 20 wines
⑪ Enhanced pub grub, 🎪 Beer garden, 🚻 No disabled toilet but flat access
Tue acoustic night, Thu quiz, Fri steak night, occasional beer festivals

Round the corner from the Twickenham brewery, between Twickenham and Hampton Hill, this medium-sized but quiet and cosy roadside pub was the first to stock its beers, and continues the tradition by featuring at least one or two local brews. Landlord Gavin is a real ale man: Sharp's and St Austell are also regularly favoured while other micros like

Prince of Wales

Salopian and well-loved independents like Adnams come and go. The interior is contemporary with heritage elements such as stained glass and mirrors, and an attractive function room at the back. An extensive menu could include ostrich steak, stuffed aubergine and tapas – the chef grows his own vegetables in the pub garden and makes a point of serving them in season. A roaring fire in winter completes the welcoming picture.

➤ Fulwell, Strawberry Hill ➡ Trafalgar Avenue / Prince of Wales (Twickenham, Fulwell) 🚲 Link to NCN4

REALALE.COM
Shop
371 Richmond Road, TW1 2EF
📞 (020) 8892 3710, ⊕ realale.com, **fbk**, **tw** RealAle_com
✪ 2-8 Mon-Thu; 1-9 Fri; 10-9 Sat; 12-5 Sun
Cask beer None, **Other beers** 80 bottles (mainly UK), gift packs, minicasks, **Also** Specialist cider and perry
Monthly tastings

This 'liquid delicatessen' is the shop window, as its name suggests, for a thriving online shopping business, set up in 2005 with the specific aim of promoting British craft brewed bottle-conditioned ales. Its commitment to this cause was recognised when CAMRA chose it as a partner in developing a beer club scheme for members, while top class imported beers have since been added to the range. The smallish but pleasingly light and well organised shop stocks about 100 beers, about half British bottle-conditioned beers from Ascot, Beowulf, Box Steam, Cheddar, Chiltern, Downton, Otley and Teme Valley among the less commonly found brands. Imported fare runs to Cantillon lambics, Orval and Rochefort Trappists, serious German choices from Andechs and Schneider and American extreme beers from Dogfish Head and Stone. Ever changing gift packs and 'club' boxes remain a feature, and home draught options in minipins and polypins are also available alongside a small range of ciders. Although on the north bank of the Thames and therefore in our West London section, it's only a short stroll from Richmond (p208) across Richmond Bridge.

Insider tip! Keep an eye on Facebook or twitter for regular news of free tastings and competitions.

➤ Richmond, St Margarets ⊖ Richmond ➡ Creswell Road (numerous Richmond) 🚲 NCN4 🚶 Capital Ring, Thames Path

OTHER LOCATIONS

BRENTWOOD

MAGPIE & CROWN
Traditional pub, specialist
128 High Street, Brentford, TW8 8EW
📞 (020) 8560 4570, **fbk**, **tw** MagpieAndCrown
✪ 12-midnight Mon-Wed; 12-1am Thu-Sat; 12-midnight Sun. *Children welcome*
Cask beers ✓ 6 (1 Twickenham, 1 Marble, 4 unusual guests), **Other beers** 5 keg, 20 bottles, **Also** 2 real ciders/perries, malts
🍴 Pub grub daily, 🏡 Small beer garden
Pool table

Brentford, where the road to Bath forded the river Brent just north of its confluence with the Thames, was once a major manufacturing centre, marketplace, transport hub, hotbed of radicalism – the centre of a campaign that elected firebrand politician John Wilkes as MP for Middlesex three times in the 1770s – and poverty hotspot that the local paper once dubbed "the filthiest place in England".

It was also home to several breweries, most of which were taken over and closed by Fuller's in nearby Chiswick by the beginning of the 20th century. The most enduring was the Royal Brewery, run in the mid 19th century by Richard Carrington, an amateur astronomer and an authority on sunspots. This finally closed in 1923 and in the early 1980s the site was redeveloped as the Watermans Arts Centre, today one of the key attractions in what's now an ordinary suburban centre, with pleasant walks along the Thames and the Grand Union Canal.

Housed in an early 20th century mock Tudor building on the high street, the Magpie & Crown has been a real ale stalwart since the 1990s, but recently a rapid turnover in management saw quality slipping. Since autumn 2010 it's been back on track in the

Magpie & Crown

capable hands of new landlady Tam, who has added extra cask pumps and overhauled the longstanding range of imported craft beers. Her convoluted family link to the well-regarded Marble brewery in Manchester explains the regular appearance of their beers in cask and in bottle, alongside local hero Twickenham, the likes of Ossett and Downton and big boned imported classics like St Feuillien Triple and Schneider Aventinus in bottle. The interior is also mock Tudor with bare beams, a horseshoe bar, stained glass and a boat hull hanging from the ceiling.

Insider tip! Use the free WiFi to keep up to date with the pub's regular tweets.

≥ Brentford ☜ Grand Union Canal towpath, CS9 ☞ Grand Union Canal Walk, Thames Path

EALING

QUESTORS (GRAPEVINE BAR)
Bar
12 Mattock Lane, W5 5BQ
☏ (020) 8567 0011
⊕ questors.org.uk/grapevine
✪ 7-11 Mon-Sat; 12-2.30, 7-10.30 Sun. *Children welcome*

Cask beers ✔ 3-4 (1 Fullers, unusual/local guests), **Other beers** 8 bottles (Belgian), **Also** Wines
🚏 Front patio outside theatre, 🚹
Theatre

Too many theatre bars fall back on churning out bland brands to a captive audience. The Grapevine is a shining example of how to do things differently. Since 1959 it's been run by volunteers as a separate undertaking within Ealing's Questors Theatre, a community, fringe and amateur theatre in one of the sprawling mansions overlooking the north side of Walpole Park. Over the years the bar has raised over a million pounds to support the theatre. Two smallish, elegantly decorated and very comfortable muzak-free rooms and a sought-after snug corner also provide wall space for art exhibitions. Fine beer plays a starring role. The guest list mixes local products with more far-flung examples – Inveralmond was on when I called. The concise menu of bottled Belgians includes some excellent rarities like Kapittel and Gouyasse. Customers are unsurprisingly theatrical – I overheard people quoting Shakespeare to each other – and there's still more local thespian connections as the theatre is just round the corner from the legendary Ealing film studios. Strictly speaking it's open only to members and those attending or working at the theatre but you will be welcome with a CAMRA membership card or guide.

Insider tip! It's obviously quieter during performances or when the theatre is 'dark' so check show times beforehand.

≥ Ealing Broadway ↔ Ealing Broadway

HAREFIELD

HAREFIELD
Contemporary pub
41 High Street, Harefield, UB9 6BY
☏ (01895) 820003
✪ 12-11 Mon-Sat; 12-10 Sun. *Children welcome if eating*
Cask beers ✔ 4 (Timothy Taylor, Wells & Young's, guests), **Also** Malts, wines
🍴 Enhanced pub grub, 🚏 Patio, 🚹
Twice monthly quiz, darts, Wed real ale offers, occasional beer festivals

The overgrown village of Harefield, centred on a large village green, sprawls amid the Green Belt of London's northwest corner, not far from the Grand Union Canal and the lakes and wetlands of Colne Valley Park. The village sustains several pubs but the best for beer is this civilised bolthole a little south of the green, declaring its grownup intentions with an 'Over 21s only' sign.

Renamed and refurbished relatively recently in semi-gastro style, it's bright but cosy and informal, with bare floorboards, chunky wooden furniture, newspapers, a second hand book sale and a soundtrack of Amy Winehouse at modest volume. Interesting guest beers come from a range of small brewers mainly from southern England, served with a menu of British classics, veggie options and puddings made from local ingredients. There's a bank holiday beer festival at least once a year.

Insider tip! Catch the weekly Real Ale Wednesday promotions when cask ales are sold at a hefty discount all day.

⇝ Denham ⊖ Northwood 🚌 Merle Avenue (331 Denham, Northwood) 🚲 link to NCN61 🚶 Hillingdon Trail, links to Colne Valley Trail, Grand Union Canal Walk, London Loop

HARROW

CASTLE
Traditional pub ★
30 West Street, Harrow, HA1 3EF
📞 (020) 8422 3155, ✉ castle.harrow@fullers.co.uk, 🌐 castleharrow.co.uk
🕐 12-11 Mon-Thu; 12-midnight Fri & Sat; 12-11 Sun. *Children welcome*
Cask beers ✅ 5 (Fuller's), **Other beers** 8 bottles (Fuller's), **Also** Wines
🍽 Upmarket pub grub, 🌳 Beer garden, ♿
Tue quiz, Fri fish & chip night

Harrow, or more fully Harrow-on-the-Hill, is one of London's ancient villages. Its place on the summit of one of a number of prominent hills in the area was once a site of pagan worship, but is now best known for its famous public school, which counts Winston Churchill among its ex-students. The main school buildings are on the hill, but, unusually, rather than on their own enclosed campus they're mixed in with others, such as this heritage pub tucked down a steeply sloping side street, which still preserves many features installed when it was built in 1901. A mosaic floor in the porch welcomes you to a lovely multi-roomed pub with an island bar and five divided spaces, with plenty of wood

Castle

panelling, old clocks and decorated walls. There's an elegant simplicity to it in contrast to the grander places of the same period listed elsewhere in this guide. Discovery, ESB, HSB and London Pride are fixtures with a changing seasonal, and the excellent range of the brewery's bottles includes rare specials like Vintage Ale and Brewer's Reserve – you might even spot some aged examples. Food might include whitebait, homity pie or beef bourguignon. The station is at the bottom of the hill, so either catch the bus or follow the signed Capital Ring Link footpath to the top.

Pub trivia: Since this is a castle, look for the throne in the garden.

≆ Harrow on the Hill ⊖ Harrow on the Hill ⊟ Harrow School (258, H17 Harrow-on-the-Hill) 🚲 Cycle route to Kenton ⚓ London Loop

ISLEWORTH

RED LION
Traditional pub
92-94 Linkfield Road, Isleworth, TW7 6QJ
☎ (020) 8560 1457, ⊕ www.red-lion.info, **fbk**
✪ 12-midnight daily. *Children welcome*
Cask beers ✪ 9 (unusual guests), **Other beers** 2 keg, 2 bottles, **Also** 5 real ciders/perries
🍴 Pub grub, 🌳 Beer garden, ♿
Mon jazz, Tue ale offers, Wed jam session, Thu quiz, Fri curry night, Sat/Sun live music, regular beer festivals, darts, pool, amateur theatre

A real hidden gem, the welcoming Red Lion has risen to the challenge of its location on an obscure suburban residential street by being both a great community local and a destination pub. One of the main draws is the wide range of well-kept unusual cask ales, which often includes milds and other dark beers. Licensees Paul Andrews and his daughter Luisa take advantage of free house status by constantly rotating beer from the likes of Hampshire, Hop Back, Sharp's, Thornbridge, Whitstable and Wickwar alongside keenly priced session ales from Fuller's and Young's.
    Another draw is the entertainment including jazz, blues and rock gigs and performances from resident amateur theatre company Hiss and Boo. There's a proper

Red Lion

traditional public bar on the right, of the sort that's now all too rare – lino, benches, brown painted wood, an open fire, a dart board, jukebox and pool table round the back. The rest of the pub makes for a loungey contrast with sofas and a fish tank, and there's a pleasant garden too. Food is unpretentious, good value pub grub.

Visitor's note: Don't miss the quiet area at the front left, done out as a 1950s living room with a tiled fireplace, red leather sofa and a TV set on which they might have watched the Coronation.

≆ Isleworth ⚓ Capital Ring, Thames Path

MAIDA VALE

PRINCE ALFRED
Traditional pub, gastropub ★
5A Formosa Street, W9 1EE
☎ (020) 7286 3287
⊕ www.theprincealfred.com
✪ 12-11 daily. *Children until early evening*
Cask beers ✪ 2 (Wells & Young's), **Other beers** 1 keg, 3 bottles
🍴 Gastro menu, ♿
Tue quiz

Not far from picturesque Little Venice on the Grand Union Canal, and within easy walking distance of Paddington (p97), this is one of London's most spectacular heritage pubs. Some customers may think the carved wood and frosted glass partitions that segregate the main drinking area, made barely permeable with perilously low service doors, were installed as a novelty for their benefit, and the pub does well by allowing parties to book the resulting compartments for private use. "We know to stop serving them when they start banging their heads," joked the bar manager. But in fact this was standard pub design practice when the 1865 Italianate end-of-terrace building was refitted in 1898, and it's now the most complete surviving example of its kind in London, with all five compartments around the high peninsula bar still present and correct. One of them even has snob screens, swivelling panels between drinking area and bar, so that the toffs didn't have to look at the bar staff unless absolutely necessary. In contrast is the big modern pavilion-style dining area at the back, decorated with canalside scenes. Food is upmarket – venison steak, duck breast, wild mushroom risotto, with a good value prix fixe menu on offer at less busy times. Beer is well-kept Young's Bitter and another Wells & Young's brand on handpump, supplemented by bottles like London Gold and keg Double Chocolate Stout and Erdinger wheat beer.

➤ Paddington ⊖ Warwick Avenue ⦾ LCN+ Kensal Green, Kilburn, Marylebone, Kensington,

Prince Alfred

Regents Canal towpath ⦿ Jubilee Greenway, Grand Union Canal Walk

RUISLIP

WOODMAN
Traditional pub
Breakspear Road, Ruislip, HA4 7SE
☎ (01895) 635763
⊕ 11–midnight Mon-Thu; 11-1am Fri; 11-midnight Sat; 12-midnight Sun. *Children welcome until 6pm*
Cask beers ✓ 3 (Marston's, Wells & Young's, guest)
🍴 Basic pub grub or Sunday roast, ☷ Patio
Darts and other games, monthly quiz, occasional music nights

The Woodman is a fine and welcoming example of a traditional English country pub on London's urban fringe, with a pretty whitewashed exterior clad in season with dazzling floral displays. It's down a lane which these days is relatively busy with traffic, and right opposite Hillingdon Football Club, with which the landlord has some connection, but the surroundings are some of the greenest in London.

The pub name recalls the fact that this area, like most of England, was once richly wooded; significant stretches of woodland are preserved today in nearby Ruislip Woods National Nature Reserve and Bayhurst Wood Country Park, while the popular woodland lake of Ruislip Lido is just up the lane. The pub preserves its two-bar layout, with a plain, informal public bar and a posher, wood panelled saloon. A former Courage house, it's now owned by Enterprise and stocks the revived Courage Bitter from Wells & Young's, alongside Bass and an ever changing guest tap dispensing beers from Cottage, Exmoor, Otter, Skinners and the like. A perfect stopping point for a countryside walk in London.

Insider tip! Bottled Courage Light Ale is also stocked, so they can mix you a Light and Bitter for an authentic 1960s pub experience.

⊖ Northwood, Ruislip 🚌 Howletts Lane (331 to Northwood or Ruislip) ⦾ Links to David

Woodman

Brough Cycle Trail 🏃 Hillingdon Trail, links to Bayhurst Wood, Ruislip Lido, Ruislip Woods NNR

SOUTHALL

SOUTHALL CONSERVATIVE & UNIONIST CLUB
Social club
Fairlawn, High Street, Southall, UB1 3HB
📞 (020) 8574 0261, **fbk**
🕐 11.30-2.30, 7-11 Mon-Thu; 11.30-3, 6-11 Fri & Sat; 12-3, 7-10.30 Sun
Cask beers ✔ 3 (Rebellion)
🍽 Simple hot lunches, rolls, ☎ Rear patio
Snooker, darts, books and newspapers, internet, upstairs functions

Southall was an important Middlesex market town on a main road before being swallowed by London. Since the 1950s it's become a centre of the capital's Punjabi community, with over half the local population South Asian in origin. It's one of London's best locations for good value Indian food and shopping for specialist ingredients, but has rather less to offer on the beer front. The town's one remaining cask outlet is this small, friendly club in a sprawling Victorian house, Fairlawn, set back from the High Street on a drive between the Old Town Hall and the Habib Bank. Ring the bell for admission – though it's a members' club, card-carrying CAMRA members or those with a CAMRA guide are also welcome, regardless of their politics.

Social clubs like this were once a mainstay of British life but have declined steeply,

especially in southern England – this one keeps going largely by hiring out its function room. The house was the home of a furniture entrepreneur until bought for the club by a consortium of businessmen in 1913. Women weren't allowed as full members until 1968. It's been a cask ale bastion since one of the founders of well regarded Marlow brewery Rebellion happened to wander in 15 years ago, just when the club steward was having trouble with the keg beer supplier. As in many clubs, prices are keen, and the lunchtime rolls on Wednesdays and Saturdays are legendary in their generosity.

Insider tip! The cosiest corner to enjoy a pint is the formerly men only area by the door to the snooker room, under the stern gaze of portraits of Churchill and the Queen.

🚆 Southall ⊖ Ealing Broadway 🚌 Southall Police Station (numerous Ealing Broadway) 🚲 Grand Union Canal Towpath 🏃 Grand Union Canal Walk, Hillingdon Trail

UXBRIDGE

LOAD OF HAY
Traditional pub
33 Villier Street, Uxbridge, UB8 2PU
📞 (01895) 234676
🕐 11-11.45 daily. *Children welcome until 9pm*
Cask beers ✔ 4 (Sharp's, 3 unusual guests), **Other beers** 2-3 bottles, **Also** 4 real ciders/ perries
🍽 Pub grub, ☎ Beer garden, ♿
Sat/Sun live music (rock, blues), Tue quiz, Thu crib, bar billiards, darts

This rather quirky pub on a residential street near the main campus of Brunel University is top beer choice in the suburban town of Uxbridge at one extremity of the Piccadilly Line – though from the tube you still have a good brisk walk or a bus ride to reach it. The unusual building was originally an officer's mess and stables. You enter into a plain, TV-equipped public bar that might look uncomfortably cramped, but past the narrow space alongside the bar is a clubby barn-like room with bare beams, a decorative cartwheel and a cluster of comfy chairs around an open fire. It's a longstanding real ale free house and *Good Beer Guide* entry for its changing guests from the likes of Vale, Cottage, White Horse and Archer's. The pub is popular with students, who get a discount, and the lively menu has a slight student union feel, with plenty of veggie options. But it's also a proper local serving the wider community, with a seniors' discount too. There's live music at weekends, and the carved wood furniture that serves as outdoor seating is truly bizarre.

⊖ Uxbridge ☒ Brunel University (Uxbridge U3); Hillingdon Road The Greenway (Uxbridge, numerous) ಕೆ Link to NCN61; local routes Cowley, Brunel, Hillingdon ✸ Links to Colne Valley Trail, Grand Union Canal Walk, London Loop

WEMBLEY

JJ MOONS
Contemporary pub
397 High Road, Wembley, HA9 6AA
☎ (020) 8903 4923

⊕ www.jdwetherspoon.co.uk
✿ 9am-11pm Mon & Tue; 9am-11.30pm Wed-Sun. *Children until early evening if eating* **Cask beers** ❷ 5-7 (Greene King, Wells & Young's, guests), **Other beers** Usual Wetherspoon keg and bottles, **Also** 1 real cider ⑪ Wetherspoon's menu, ☕ Small patio, ♿ *Wetherspoon beer festivals and promotions*

Wembley achieved world fame in 1924 when it became the site of Wembley Stadium, originally part of the British Empire Exhibition; later came the Empire Pool, now major music venue the Wembley Arena. The stadium became synonymous with English football as the home of the FA Cup Final, and also hosted the Live Aid concert in 1985. The old place with its distinctive art deco twin towers was controversially demolished in 2003; its replacement, on the same site, is Europe's second largest stadium and its 134m-high arch has since become a distinctive contemporary landmark on London's skyline.

If you're in the area the best bet for beer is probably this Wetherspoon outlet, a little way from the stadium complex. It's now something of a veteran, opened in 1991 as one of the chain's then typical conversions from a furniture shop. The beer can include some interesting choices – although there are only five pumps, when busy they put casks on the bar. In deference to the location, the pub screens big local matches in a departure from usual Wetherspoon policy.

⇌ Wembley Central ⊖ Wembley Central ಕೆ Local routes to Wembley Stadium and Wembley Park

JJ Moons

BREWERS & BEERS

THE CRAFT OF BREWING BEER

WHAT IS BEER?

Technically speaking, beer is a fermented alcoholic drink made from cereals. Fermentation is a natural process involving a microorganism called yeast, which grows by feeding on sugars dissolved in water, breaking them down into alcohol and carbon dioxide. The source of the sugars is one factor determining the broad families of alcoholic drinks. Fruit sugars yield wine, cider and perry; while sugars derived from cereal starches yield beer.

That's the technical definition, but beer is also a cultural artefact, the product of a certain western tradition of brewing. Prehistorians point to ancient Sumer, in the 'Fertile Crescent' of the Tigris and Euphrates rivers, part of modern Iraq, where cereal grains were first domesticated about 12,000 years ago. Here, evidence has been found of brewing practices dating back at least 5,000 years. Ancient Egyptians regularly drank a beer-like beverage called *Hqt*, made by fermenting water in which breadcrumbs had been soaked, and flavouring it with dates. By Roman times, brewing had spread across the known world, and the geographical bias familiar today had begun to emerge. Caesar and Tacitus, both wine drinkers, noted beer was a northern European drink.

This association between brewing and northern Europe emerged clearly in the medieval period. The so-called 'beer belt' runs from Ireland to Slovakia, taking in Great Britain south of the Scottish Highlands, southern Scandinavia, the Low Countries, northern France, much of the German-speaking world and the Czech Republic. Here, the moist, temperate climate tends to favour both the cultivation of beer's raw materials and the brewing process itself. In the colder north, various grain spirits became the drink of choice, while the warmer south favoured wine.

Beer brewing never entirely vanished elsewhere. Even today, both north and south of the beer belt you will find intriguing local beverages representing separate lines of the family tree that began in ancient Mesopotamia. Many African countries have 'traditional beers'

made from millet or cassava, while the Baltic region has fermented drinks based on rye and oats, such as *kvass* and *sahti*. But these drinks now occupy a minor niche in the world of brewing, easily eclipsed by the more sophisticated tradition that began to develop in the beer belt in the Middle Ages.

Beer back then was a genuinely everyday drink, and low strength beer was drunk throughout the day, recognised as a safer thirst quencher than water. We now know this is because it was boiled as an integral part of the brewing process, killing off most of the nasty microbes that infested water supplies. Brewing largely took place in a domestic context – in pubs, large houses, monasteries and other institutions – and was generally regarded as women's work. But as medieval gave way to early modern, small-scale 'common brewers' appeared, earning their living from freestanding breweries.

This process accelerated rapidly in the Industrial Revolution, when brewing was transformed from a labour-intensive cottage industry to a capital-intensive factory process, racked up several orders of magnitude in scale and both drove and benefited from successive technological and scientific advances. It's in this period that you can see the recognisable shape of contemporary brewing with its repertoire of beer styles start to emerge.

As described in the introductory section of this book, industrial brewing first flourished in London, with the emergence of the mammoth 18th-century porter breweries like Whitbread and Barclay Perkins. It soon spread elsewhere, and in the 19th century the baton of technological innovation was passed to Germany, Austria, Bohemia and Denmark, while the Dutch and the Irish built their own empires of international brands. Where European beers went, European brewing techniques soon followed, carried by waves of immigration and international investment to every inhabited continent.

Of course the story of brewing since has by no means all been about bigger and more

A perfectly crafted pint of traditional English bitter

high-tech factories making ever more uniform products. In an age of safe water, at least in the developed world, beer has lost much of its functional role, leaving it free to become a means of enjoyment and pleasure. As with other creative industries, beer culture needs artists as well as craftspeople, and spaces where their creativity can flourish. The bloated commercial end of brewing finds it increasingly difficult to nurture such spaces, so they've grown instead in the smaller scale world of independent and 'craft' brewing.

Most people in this sector brew for motives other than profits for shareholders – they will say things like "I wanted to brew something I'd like to drink" or "I brewed it to satisfy my curiosity." Every so often they come up with something that the big brewers pounce on as saleable by the tanker load in a suitably

demotic form. Industrial brewing has helped create the routes to market and provided the technological armoury, but is increasingly looking to the independent sector for inspired innovation.

This book is mainly concerned with beers produced with curiosity, care, inspiration and love, whether they're from conscientious perpetuators of the best of traditional craft brewing, restless innovators on the cutting edge of what it's possible to do with fermented grain sugars, or individuals on the more commercial side of brewing who still take pride in their job despite the accountants setting their agenda – and there are thankfully many still in that last category. In the end, the best answer to the question 'what is beer?' is to get yourself a glass of the stuff these people make, sit back and enjoy it.

BEER INGREDIENTS

GRAINS, MALTS & SUGARS

Cereal grains are the staple ingredient of beer, its principal source of sugars for fermentation. Grains in their raw state don't actually contain much sugar, but they are a good source of starch, another carbohydrate, which can be turned into sugar by the action of chemicals called enzymes. Grains are of course seeds, and left to their own devices they would grow into new plants. As a seed germinates, it releases enzymes which convert its starches into sugars, providing fuel for the growing shoot. The trick is to get the enzymes to do their stuff, and then steal the sugar for your own use.

The most effective way of doing this is by malting. First, the grain is steeped in water to encourage it to germinate and release enzymes. Then just as it is starting to sprout, the process is halted by rapid heating and drying in a kiln. The result is a sweet grain with a taste familiar from every malted breakfast cereal.

Over the millennia, brewers have found one grain, barley, is particularly suited to their purposes. Barley is particularly rich in enzymes. It doesn't lose its husk during threshing so is less likely to turn to porridge and gum up the equipment. It also lends itself well to a range of different malting techniques, helping produce a wide range of flavours.

Malted barley is now ubiquitous in brewing. Even beers that foreground the character of other grains invariably contain barley malt, too. Its use is so widespread that some writers cite it as a defining ingredient of beer, and the term 'malt' on its own usually means malted barley. Beers can and have been made without it, but today they are little more than footnotes: gluten free beers, minor surviving ancient styles or occasional experiments by adventurous brewers.

The bulk of barley used in brewing is kilned to give as light a colour and texture as possible, producing 'pale malt' or even lighter 'pilsner malt'. On their own these will produce golden beers with a clean, sweetish, rounded malt character. But variations of the malting process yield an impressive repertoire of 'speciality malts' in a wide range of colours and flavours.

Increasing kilning temperature and/or time will produce darker and more strongly flavoured malts, though with fewer enzymes. Mild, Vienna, Munich and amber malts are progressively darker and toastier. Brown malt is darker still. Crystal and caramel malts ('caramalts') of various colours, a common ingredient in traditional English ales, are produced using a special technique to bring out caramel and biscuity flavours. Chocolate and black ('patent') malts are highly kilned to give roasted and burnt flavours. Smoked and peated malts, the latter more normally used for whisky, lend distinctive notes to some specialities. Roasted unmalted barley gives a classic bite to Irish stouts.

Although other grains pale into insignificance in terms of volumes, some are important in lending their characteristics to particular speciality styles. Wheat is the next most important brewers' grain, used in both unmalted (Belgium) and malted (Germany and most other places) form. A small amount of wheat is sometimes added to more conventional beers to aid head retention. Rye lends its familiar spicy note to a few beers and oats give an oily, creamy texture to a handful of stouts.

Some grains are used less to add a distinctive character and more as cheap, bland 'bulk'. Certain industrial lagers from the US are notorious for containing high proportions of rice, while AB InBev has been known to boast that the traditional olde worlde ingredients of Stella Artois include the decidedly New World maize (corn). Neither grain requires malting and their use is perhaps more forgivable in places where other grains are hard to grow. Maize in particular can also be deployed more creatively.

Refined sugars can be added directly to beer, a practice sternly proscribed in some worthy brewing traditions – in Bavaria, for example – but almost a defining characteristic of others, such as Trappist brewing. The

Malted barley provides the sugars found in beer. Here it is being ground before use

practice requires discretion to avoid a bland result. Special crystallised sugars like candy and brewing sugar, liquid 'invert sugar', caramel, molasses and honey all find their way into beer. Lactose, extracted from milk, is an unfermentable sugar featured in some sweet stouts, specifically milk stouts.

WATER

Unless you're sampling a dram of Scottish lunacy from a dead stoat (see BrewDog, p288), by far the highest proportion of the liquid in your beer glass will be water, even more of which was used in the brewing process. So it's not surprising that the quality of the water has a significant impact on the quality of the beer.

The local water supply once lent a *goût de terroir* to the local beers. London, sitting on its basin of chalk, has water with a high mineral content including chlorides, which turned out to be perfect for porters and stouts. The local water in Burton upon Trent (and in several other historic brewing centres) is naturally richer in sulphates, better suited to hoppy pale ales. As the latter grew in popularity from the 1840s, the only way the big London brewers could compete was by buying second homes in Burton.

Today, the chemistry of this is better understood, though some brewers still make a virtue of having their own wells and springs. Others simply purify mains water and then tweak its profile artificially to suit the beer being brewed. The practice of adding calcium sulphate – gypsum – to water is still known as 'burtonisation'. Brewers, incidentally, refer to the water used in brewing as 'liquor', while 'water' is something you use for purposes like cooling and cleaning.

HOPS & OTHER FLAVOURINGS

Grains and sugars are rather bland materials and to brew something pleasurable to drink just from these using conventional techniques is quite a challenge. So, they are almost always supplemented with ingredients that are more interestingly flavoured and aromatic.

As with barley malt, one such ingredient is now used so widely that some people include it in the definition of beer, though once again it is perfectly possible, if now very rare, to brew without it. This ingredient is derived from a perennial herbaceous climbing plant, the hop bine. Like its close relative, cannabis, the hop has separate male and female plants, and it's the female that yields the cone-shaped flower clusters rich in bitter resins that have become so essential to the brewer's art.

Hops fulfil three functions: They add bitter, herbal and fruity flavours that balance the blandness of malt; lend an attractive spicy, often slightly piny aroma; and act as a natural preservative.

Since the first records of cultivation in the German Hallertau in the 8th century, many different varieties of hops have been developed. Each has its own characteristics – some are better at bitterness, some at aroma, some at both. Attempts to find an analogue in the beer world for 'varietal' wines have usually focused on hops.

Traditional British brewers favour hops with an earthy, smooth character – the classics are Goldings, developed in East Kent in the late 18th century and popular for its aroma; and Fuggles, a late-19th-century multipurpose hop. In the days before mechanisation, the demand for seasonal labour generated by the Kent hop harvest provided both extra cash and a chance to get out of the city for working class Londoners, including children, as well as reinforcing the cultural links with locally brewed beer.

Challenger, Northdown, Northern Brewer and dwarf hop First Gold are more recent multipurpose hops. Newer notably bitter varieties include Progress and Target. Whitbread Golding Variety (WGV), the last echoes of a once great and now defunct London brewer still sounding in its name, is actually a form of Fuggles. Bramling Cross, a hybrid of Goldings and wild Canadian hops, has a very distinctive blackcurrant flavour.

Mainland European hops tend to be multipurpose, with the grassier, lightly spicy character familiar from classic German and Czech lagers. Five traditional varieties – Hallertauer, Hersbrucker, Spalt and Tettnang from Germany and Žatec (Saaz), originally from Bohemia – are sometimes known as 'noble hops'. Magnum and Perle are more recent German varieties, while Styrian Goldings is a Slovenian-grown substitute for English Goldings, though is actually derived from Fuggles.

North American hops are often more exotic and distinctive, with grapefruit and pine flavours and plentiful bitter acids. The classic example is Cascade, which along with Centennial and Columbus forms the 'Three C's' group of bitter, citric hops. Amarillo, Citra and the piney Chinook are popular for their exotic fruit flavours. More reserved entrants include Crystal and Liberty, which are closer to German hops, and Willamette, a fruitier form of Fuggles. Exotic hops from other places include New Zealand's Nelson Sauvin, its name referencing a resemblance in flavour to Sauvignon Blanc grapes.

The championing of hops by US craft brewers has been one of the most significant developments in brewing over the last couple of decades. "Most working brewers love hops," wrote Michael Jackson in his *Beer Companion* in 1993, "and would use twice as much if the market researchers were not afraid of frightening the customer." Brewers are now getting over that anxiety, as you'll rapidly discover if you taste some of the better US imports or the British beers inspired by them.

Hops are usually used in dried form, though some brewers make a point of commemorating the harvest with fresh hops in annual 'green hop' beers. The finest hop flavour comes from whole cones, but some breweries find hop pellets, which take up less space and have a longer shelf life, easier to deal with. Liquid hop extract is another more convenient but considerably less characterful alternative.

Though hops and beer now seem inseparable, brewing long predates their cultivation and their use developed and

Brewers use multiple varieties of hops, as seen in this brewery's hop store

spread slowly. It didn't reach Britain until the 15th century and was at first staunchly resisted, with hop-free English 'ale' proudly distinguished from continental hopped 'beer'. Other herbs and spices once served the purposes now fulfilled by hops. Herbal mixes for flavouring beer, known as *gruit*, played a significant role in the economy of medieval Europe.

Remnants of these practices persisted into the 20th century, notably in Belgium, where they've been rediscovered by a new generation of brewers and drinkers. Coriander, now probably the commonest brewing herb, is found in numerous Belgian and some British beers. Ginger, chocolate and coffee have found favour with some British brewers. You may also encounter beers containing dried citrus peel, cumin,

mace, pepper, star anise, cloves, sweet gale, chilli, chamomile, nettles, tea, tobacco, juniper, spruce, seaweed, heather and more; but almost always alongside and not instead of hops.

Fruit has added palatability to beer since at least the days of date-infused Egyptian *Hqt*. Steeping with fruit, as still seen in Belgian lambic brewing, was a way of offsetting the sometimes sour results of more primitive brewing processes. Once again craft brewing has extended the traditional repertoire of cherries and raspberries, including native fruits like gooseberries, tayberries and damsons in Britain. Note the results aren't wines, as the fruit sugar isn't essential to fermentation – indeed it's normally added once fermentation has taken place.

YEAST

Yeast spores occur naturally on grape and apple skins, but the raw materials for beer don't come so handily packaged. If you leave a porridge of barley breadcrumbs and warm water out in the air, airborne yeasts might happen along and start fermenting it, and this is likely how brewing was first discovered, but the process is quite haphazard.

It wasn't until the invention of the microscope that we really understood yeast, but long before that, brewers had discovered that if you kept some of the residue of a particularly successful brew and added it to the next, the results became more predictable. Breweries today have their own collections of yeast cultures, sometimes carefully cultivated for generations and essential contributors to the house style. Yeast can survive dormant for many years, and academic and commercial yeast 'libraries' retain thousands of cultures and strains.

Yeast is what distinguishes the two great beer families – ales and lagers. Ales are the older style, fermented with yeasts that work at relatively high temperatures of around 25°C over short periods, forming a foamy crust known as barm that helps protect the beer from infection. Ale yeast cultures are often complex with numerous different strains mixed together, and produce correspondingly complex flavours with fruity notes.

Lagers developed from the practice in Bavaria of storing beer in cold caves – *lagern* means 'to store' in German – where brewers noticed it would ferment over long periods of time at much lower temperatures (5-9°C), with the yeast sinking to the bottom of closed vessels, producing a cleaner tasting and more stable result. Yeast cultures evolved that worked particularly well in these circumstances, and in 1883 brewing scientist Emil Hansen isolated the first single strain lager yeast at the Carlsberg brewery in Copenhagen, ushering in a new era of discipline for the previously unruly microorganism.

Ale yeasts and lager yeasts are sometimes labelled 'top fermenting' and 'bottom fermenting' respectively, for obvious reasons, but yeasts are no longer so neatly classified. Fuller's in Chiswick, like many other British breweries, has replaced its old fashioned open fermenting vessels with closed conical ones, and the house yeast has taken to sinking to the bottom of them, though no one would question that the beers it produces are characteristically ales. A better distinction is between 'warm fermenting' and 'cold fermenting'.

Fuller's use closed conical fermenting vessels in which ale yeast sinks during fermentation

THE BREWING PROCESS

First, the malts and other cereals if used – the 'grist' – are milled to the right consistency. Then they're mixed with hot but not boiling water in a vessel called a mash tun and left to soak while being gently stirred. Mashing releases the enzymes that complete the conversion of starches into sugars.

The sweet liquid, known as 'wort', is run off either directly from the mash tun or via another vessel called a 'lauter tun'. The first runnings have the highest concentration of sugars and will make the strongest beer, but usually further sugars are extracted by 'sparging' – spraying the grains with more hot water. The spent grains may be recycled for animal feed.

The wort is transferred to a 'copper' or 'kettle' (or returned from the lauter tun to a multipurpose mash tun/copper) where it's boiled with hops. These can be added in stages, with those towards the start of the boil contributing more to bitterness, and the 'late hops' near the end towards aroma. Other spices and flavourings, if used, might be added now.

The boiled wort is cooled and put in a fermentation vessel with yeast, known as 'pitching' (see below for Lambic beers). Here the different styles of brewing start to diverge. In traditional ale breweries the fermenters are open to the air (though usually with a loose-fitting lid), but many ale breweries today use closed fermenters with conical lower sections. Lagers are almost always fermented in closed vessels like these, and at lower ambient temperatures. Ales typically ferment for 5-7 days, lagers for up to two weeks.

By the end of this primary fermentation the beer has nearly reached its final alcoholic strength, though may gain a little more through further conditioning. The strength is dependent on the ratio of fermentable sugar in the original wort – the 'original gravity' – and the 'attenuation', the extent to which the yeast has converted this to alcohol. Highly attenuated beers are drier, with nearly all the sugar gone, while lower levels of attenuation leave more residual sugar to give a sweeter flavour. There are various ways of stating

Sweet, liquid wort is boiled in a copper

alcohol content: the most common internationally is the percentage of alcohol by volume (ABV) which is used throughout this book.

After primary fermentation the yeast is separated off and the beer pumped to a separate conditioning tank for a further period of conditioning and maturation to round off the rough edges. For lagers this 'lagering' is a vital part of the process and could take up to three months at cool temperatures, though this is sometimes squeezed to a couple of weeks for the most commercialised brands. One or two weeks of conditioning is adequate for most modern ales. Additional hops can be added directly to the beer during conditioning, known as 'dry hopping'.

Some beer styles rely on very long conditioning, sometimes in wooden vessels that accumulate wild yeasts and other microflora to give a distinctive sour tang, a process vital to 18th-century porter brewing. Wood ageing has been rediscovered by the craft brewing sector, with new twists like using vessels previously holding whisky or port, and the deliberate use of wild yeast strains like *Brettanomyces* to give a funky, farmyard character to beers.

FROM BREWERY TO GLASS

It's possible to serve beer as it comes straight out of the conditioning tank, unfiltered and unpasteurised, so long as travel distances are short and the turnover is quick enough. This is still common practice in some parts of Germany and neighbouring countries. But once out of the tank, beer is vulnerable: prone to going flat, turning stale through oxidation and picking up infections. As brewers looked to distribute their products over wider territories, they had to come up with other ways to ensure it remained drinkable.

The classic solution adopted by British brewers was **cask conditioning**. This depends on a further fermentation in the 'cask', the smaller vessel used for getting the beer to the pub, and ensures it's lively when it reaches the customer. The beer may simply be transferred – 'racked' – into casks direct from the tank, relying on residual sugar and yeast to keep things going. Or it can be filtered, and then dosed with fresh yeast and sugar or unfermented sweet wort. It's often 'fined' with a gelatinous substance like isinglass that sinks to the bottom, carrying stray solids with it. Cask beer is also known as 'real ale' although the term is slightly misleading, as beers other than ales can be cask conditioned.

Cask beer is a live product that needs careful treatment in the pub cellar. After delivery it first has to settle for several days. A porous peg – a shive – is driven through a special bung in the cask so some of the carbon dioxide is released slowly, then replaced by a hard peg. The beer is then either served direct from the cask or drawn through plastic lines from the cellar using a handpump, without the use of additional carbon dioxide. Once the cask is tapped its contents is vulnerable so needs to be sold within a few days.

A similar process, known as **bottle conditioning**, produces 'real ale in a bottle'. The beer might be bottled straight from the tank or additionally dosed with sugars and/or yeast, perhaps after being filtered first. Fermentation then continues in the bottle, though as there's no way of releasing the carbon dioxide until the bottle is opened, the beer is inevitably gassier when served than

cask beer. Some bottle conditioned beers, particularly strong ones, can continue to condition for years, evolving in complexity like fine vintage wines.

At the other extreme, a beer can be filtered, pasteurised, artificially carbonated to replace the sparkle lost during the previous processes, then pumped into a sealed keg to be squirted out using still more carbon dioxide into the customer's glass. This **keg** beer includes all the big name lager brands on sale in UK pubs. Similar treatments can be applied to **bottled** and **canned** beer and indeed many of the beers on sale in British supermarkets, including speciality ales, are filtered and pasteurised even if their draught counterparts are cask beers. The result is a more stable and reliable beer that doesn't need looking after so carefully, but often at the expense of flavour and complexity.

There are several practices that don't fit very easily into any of these categories. For example, beers can be filtered, sometimes very lightly, without being pasteurised. Or they can be made to referment in a keg, making it possible to serve them without additional carbon dioxide pressure. A recently developed system – used by Meantime (p275) and Zerodegrees (p284) – involves conditioning beer with live yeast inside a polythene liner, or 'beer bag' which is then put under external air pressure to serve the beer.

Real ale needs careful treatment in the pub cellar

YES, BUT IS IT CASK?

If I'd been writing this guide twenty years ago, I would undoubtedly be telling you that practically the only beer worth drinking in London was cask ale. These days things aren't quite so straightforward.

Cask conditioning persisted in Britain long after the other brewing nations largely dropped the idea of draught beer that was still fermenting. The big national groups that emerged from the frenzy of post-war consolidation regarded this fact with some irritation. Through the 1960s they attempted to use their marketing might and their control of the majority of British pubs to foist inferior keg ales on the drinking public, rapidly followed by even more egregious faux-Teutonic British-brewed lagers.

Consumer resistance to this led to the formation of the Campaign for Real Ale, CAMRA, in 1971. It was largely thanks to CAMRA that cask beer survived and flourished, and Britain remains the only country where you can find anything like it on such a widespread scale. Indeed, cask ale is currently the only sector of the British beer market that's showing much sign of growth.

Cask ale is Britain's gift to the world of beer, a unique product that, at its best, delivers an incomparable drinking experience. It's no coincidence that the vast majority of outlets in this guide stock cask beer. They can also be relied upon to look after it properly and see

that it's served in top condition – something that sadly can't be said for every cask beer outlet in London. I strongly recommend you take advantage of this and let this guide lead you to as much cask beer as you can responsibly drink.

However not all the beer worth shouting about in London is cask conditioned. Bottle conditioned beers were almost extinct in Britain by 1971, although they persisted in Belgium and among wheat beer brewers in Germany. Interest in fine beer has given the technique a boost and around 1,500 examples are now produced in the UK, with increasing numbers imported from abroad too. Not all brewers have mastered the art of consistent bottle conditioning but the best bottle conditioned beers are world-beating products, particularly those that mature well. CAMRA has long recognised 'Real Ales in a Bottle' (RAIB).

Countries outside Britain that lack a cask tradition are also widely represented in London and it would be wrong to ignore the obvious quality and interest of their products. For example, the unpasteurised lagers of Franconia, made to the strictest quality standards with top quality ingredients and with centuries of craftsmanship behind them, can't be dismissed just because they're not fermenting when we drink them.

A more challenging issue for real ale campaigners is that comparable beers are now appearing closer to home. Listed in this book are two London breweries which, although they produce some cask beer, lavish at least as much tender loving care and top quality ingredients on numerous beers that don't qualify as 'real', including inventive London takes on authentic German styles. These are not big national groups run by accountants, intent on minimising costs and choice and maximising profit, but conscientious independent businesses run by knowledgeable and caring brewers, keen to promote quality and a choice of styles. And they are not alone among British craft brewers. I hope even the most dedicated cask warriors will be able to approach them with an open mind.

TASTING BEERS

Since beer strengths in Britain were slashed during World War I, the British have generally regarded beer as a low strength drink best enjoyed by the pint in hearty quaffs. But, actually, beer is an immensely flavourful drink, offering a far wider range of tasting experiences than wine, despite the respect and intellectual attention paid to the latter. While typical British beer today is indeed low gravity – the so-called 'session strength' of around 3.5%-4.5% ABV – other countries, notably Belgium, regularly produce much stronger beers, and specialist brewers in Britain are also now exploring the higher gravities again. Such beers are not recommended for guzzling by the pint, but for savouring in smaller quantities over a longer period of time. And once you've got the idea, you'll find some of the best of the session beers repay closer attention too.

Here are some basic tips on tasting beer.

1. Get the temperature right. Not all beers benefit from being chilled and no good beer should be served colder than 8°C. Generally the lighter the beer, the cooler the appropriate temperature. Cask ale is normally served cellar cooled at around 12°C, a perfect temperature for traditional English ales. Put beer in the fridge only a hour or so before you drink it, or give it time to warm slightly. Keep it in the door section, which is warmer. Very strong, rich beers can be drunk at room temperature.

2. If tasting several beers, pay attention to the order. You won't be doing a light golden beer justice if you try it immediately after a hefty old ale. The general rule is to taste in order of alcoholic strength but you might need to adjust this if a weaker beer is also darker and more strongly flavoured.

3. Use a good, clean glass. Typical pub glasses are not ideal, especially since in London they're designed to be filled to the brim with no room for a head. Most fancy Belgian glasses are designed for appearance rather

than practicality. Much better is a smaller, stemmed glass with an inward taper to the lip, to help trap the aroma. This type of glass is also easy to warm in the hand if necessary.

4. Pay attention as you open the bottle. Listen for that reassuring release of carbon dioxide. If you don't hear it, the beer may not have conditioned properly, though a handful of beers are intended to be relatively still.

5. Carefully half fill the glass, leaving room for the head and for the aroma to develop. Bottle conditioned beers usually have to be poured in a single motion if you want to leave the yeast deposit in the bottle, so share them with a friend, decant them into a jug first or drink the first glass clear and don't worry about subsequent glasses being cloudy. The yeast won't do you any harm and might even improve the flavour. If the beer is designed to be poured cloudy – a wheat beer for example – swirl the bottle gently before pouring.

6. Admire the beer's colour and head. Swirl it and see what happens to the head – it may leave a 'lace' on the side of the glass.

7. Give at least two good sniffs before you taste: aroma is at least as important as taste. Try swirling before sniffing– some people even put their hand over the glass while swirling to trap the aroma. Successive sniffs can yield different scents. Aromas might be bready, yeasty, malty, hoppy, spicy, grassy, fruity, citric, roasted, liquoricey, sacky, oaky, spirity, minerally, piny, sulphurous, peachy, farmyardy, rubbery and many more.

8. Take a good sip and hold the beer in your mouth. Try slurping some air as you hold the beer on your tongue: this will help release the flavours – but practice over the sink first! Although the tongue can only discriminate a limited range of basic flavours, in combination they give powerful sense impressions. All the tastes mentioned above might come back, and more. Note the balance between the sweet, cereal character of the base malts and the balancing bitter notes provided by hops and, in some dark beers, roasted malts. Fruity flavours might come from hops or yeast. See how the flavour develops over time – hop flavours can take time to emerge.

9. Swallow the beer. You may get 'retronasals' – aromatic substances that find their way back up from your throat to your nose.

10. Don't take another mouthful straight away but pay attention to the aftertaste or finish. This is often when bitterness becomes most intense. Note how long the flavour lingers.

11. Pay attention to the next few sips: you may notice new features on each.

12. Consider how the beer lives up to what it says about itself. What sort of style is it in? Is it a typical example of its style or does it stretch the boundaries? Try to imagine what the brewer intended to achieve from the beer.

13. Take notes. Don't worry about having the right technical vocabulary, just write it down in your own words. You'll start training your palate and be able to review and compare beers more reliably. Read what others have written about the same beer – but don't be too concerned if you seem to disagree!

14. Finally, don't forget to spend at least some time just sitting back and enjoying the beer!

Good beer rewards consideration as well as quaffing. A stemmed, tapered glass is ideal

BEER STYLES

Definitions of beer styles are slippery things, partly because people approach them in different ways. To beer historians they're categories through which we can trace the evolution of brewing. To industry people organising competitions, they're ways of dividing up the field as meaningfully as possible so like can be judged against like. To most brewers and consumers, they're a handy shorthand for talking about intentions and expectations, which is perhaps why this group seems to use them most loosely of all. Just when you think you have a style pinned down, some pesky brewer insists on being creative and pushing the envelope. Some competition organisers deal with this simply by adding new styles – the Brewers Association in the USA now recognises 140!

Bearing all this in mind, the notes below aim to provide some basic navigation through the bewildering variety of beer flavours on offer in London.

Bitter

BITTER

The signature style of British cask beer, and by far the most common, bitter evolved from the hoppy pale ales developed in the late 18th century. It was long regarded as a more middle class drink than proletarian refreshers like porter and mild – a distinction that persisted into the postwar period. Most brewers now make at least two beers classed as bitter, often far more. There's considerable variety – strengths range from 3% to 5.5% or more, though most cluster between 3.7–4.7%, while the colour is classically amber but can run from golden to nut-brown. Some people call the amber and darker ones 'brown bitters' to distinguish them from the increasing number of golden ones, which shade into the 'golden ale' category.

Some brewers previously adhered to a shared system of subdivisions, offering an 'ordinary' bitter at about 3.7%, a 'best' at around 4.5% and perhaps a special at 4.8% or more. Relics of this can still be traced, for example in Fuller's trio of Chiswick, London Pride and ESB (p270). But most modern

micros are nowhere near as structured. There's some grounds for identifying regional variations: Yorkshire bitters are often said to be drier and more 'chalky', although some of the driest old established bitters are brewed in the Southeast, like Harveys (p296).

Classic bitters aim for a rounded flavour with a good balance between fruity, biscuity malt, often with crystal malt in the grist, and a notable hop character achieved with earthy English varieties like Fuggles and Goldings. But the term 'bitter' is relative, and if your tipple of choice is a Californian Quadruple IPA, you won't find most of them very bitter at all.

MILD

Milds are usually assumed to be mild in terms of hop bitterness or strength, but the original distinction was mild in the sense of fresh, as opposed to matured 'stale' beers like porter. Modern milds were developed from the early 19th century by a new generation of London 'ale' brewers like Charrington and Courage, who increasingly challenged the might of the giant porter producers. As a cheaper beer with a more downmarket 'flatcap' image compared to bitter, in upwardly mobile London mild suffered an early fall in popularity, but long retained a hold in the West Midlands and Northern England. Today, it's very much a niche drink, though growing again now everyone's forgotten the class thing, thanks partly to CAMRA-sponsored promotions like Mild Month in May.

Today's milds are typically relatively low in gravity, around 3.5%, restrained in hop character, deep amber to dark brown with a fruity, biscuity and perhaps caramel malt emphasis. Milds from micros seem to be getting increasingly roasty and a bit more hoppy. They don't have to be low strength – a century ago they were much stronger. A number of revivalist versions now reach to 5% and beyond. Light milds, roughly the same colour as bitters but maltier and less hoppy, were once common too. Historic survivors from the Southeast are brewed by McMullen (p301) and Harveys (p296).

Fuller's Discovery – a popular golden ale

GOLDEN ALE

Arguably the first new native style of beer to have emerged in Britain since the 19th century. Driven by the popularity of early examples like Hop Back Summer Lightning (p297), golden ales have become so prevalent that CAMRA's annual Champion Beer of Britain competition has had to create a new category for them, to stop them edging out brown bitters. In fact there have long been light coloured, easy drinking beers in Britain: the old 'Cream of Manchester', Boddington's Bitter, was a notable example.

Golden ales reach out with some success to the mainstream lager drinker though they've also found many fans among existing drinkers of cask ale. They follow the lager model not only in colour, sometimes achieved using pilsner malt, but in their refreshing quality and their often premium strength of 4.5% or more. Some of them are served colder than other casks, though not as chilled as keg lager. They tend to have a clean palate for an ale, and emphasise spicy, floral and fruity hop notes, sometimes from US hops. Their success has encouraged the brewing of paler bitters, blurring the distinction between the styles.

Mild

PALE ALE & INDIA PALE ALE

Pale coloured beers have been around since the invention of coke fuel in the 1640s, which made it easier to control the temperature at which malt was kilned. The best-known pale ales are India Pale Ales (IPAs), the strong, hoppy beers that dominated exports to India in the early 19th century. Their fame ensured similar beers appeared in domestic versions, though their strength and hop character were gradually whittled down. Some long-standing cask beers labelled IPA are still around today, though now indistinguishable from standard bitter. Bottled Worthington White Shield (p319) is one worthy surviving descendant of the golden age of British pale ale.

The past two decades have seen a major revival of interest in the style among craft brewers across the world, and a host of beers with the pale colour, high strengths (perhaps 7% and up) and high hop rates of the original India Pale Ales. In Britain many of these are approximations of the original recipes using traditional hop varieties, while the US versions interpret the style more liberally, making extensive use of American hops, often in massive quantities, to produce intensely bitter and aromatic beers. Standard craft-brewed pale ales in the US tend to be more approachable at about 5–5.5% but still with a characteristic hoppy bite. These beers are now influencing brewers back in the style's birthplace, where several new beers are carving a niche distinct from bitters, with a paler colour, a firm body and a notable but not overwhelming hop character.

PORTER & STOUT

Porter is the first international beer style and the first industrial one, developing in early 18th-century London (see p14). It came in two forms – 'stale' porter matured for months and even years in oak vats, and a fresher 'mild' porter, with the two often mixed at the point of dispense. Porter spread worldwide, proving equally popular in the cold Baltic and the warmer climes of the Caribbean and sub-Saharan Africa. Most famously it spread to Ireland, where the local variant flourished as its parent style declined from the end of the 19th century, struggling to meet the challenge from milds and bitters and further challenged by a restriction on fuel during two world wars – the dark malts required for porter requiring lengthy roasting. The decline was a slow one but, by 1958, porter brewing had ceased completely in Great Britain.

Porter came in a variety of strengths: 'plain' porter was weaker while 'stout' porter was stronger. The stronger version resisted the decline longer and eventually the term 'stout' came to be used in its own right, evolving a range of sub-styles in a variety of different places. The original meaning of 'stout' as 'strong' was eventually forgotten.

In 1978, partly inspired by Michael Jackson's musings on the subject, a few British brewers started to experiment with old recipes, soon joined by colleagues in other countries. Porter has since comprehensively re-established itself as a modern specialist style though almost never matured in oak vats.

Stout and porter are sometimes hard to distinguish from each other but there are a

Worthington White Shield – a classic IPA

Stout

BROWN ALE

Beer historian Martyn Cornell calls brown ale one of the oldest beer styles in Britain, dating from a time when the only malts available produced brown coloured beers. Today, British brown ale is largely a bottled style. Standard traditional brown ales tended to be sweet and low strength, but in the early 20th century a new kind of stronger (4.7%), dry, sappy blended brown ale became popular in the Northeast of England, typified by the famous Newcastle Brown (now brewed in Gateshead). Most examples are pasteurised beers but a few micros produce 'real' beers reminiscent of the style. Belgian brown ales are different again, often soured by long maturation in wooden vessels, like porter once was – the classic example is Rodenbach (p308).

number of distinct sub-styles. Stouts are usually inspired by the Irish variety – black, smooth, coffeeish and dry with the bitterness of roasted barley at around 4.5%. The commercial draught Irish stouts are pasteurised 'nitrokeg' products served with a mix of nitrogen and carbon dioxide to give a soft creamy head, but there are a number of British-brewed 'real' versions. Low alcohol sweet stouts, including milk stouts made with lactose, are an early 20th-century invention that has inspired some craft brewers too.

Imperial stout was a very strong (10%), hoppy variant developed in the late 18th century for export to Russia and the Baltic. Its most famous exponent was Southwark brewer Barclay Perkins, whose successor, Courage, continued to brew it until 1993. Since then, several other specialist brewers worldwide have picked up on the style, and the US brewing community has appropriated the term 'Imperial' for anything strong, hoppy and extreme.

Modern porters tend to be dark brown beers of around 4.5% that share chocolate and coffee flavours with stouts but with more bitterness from hops than from roasted malt. A few stronger 'historical' versions are brewed, often strongly flavoured with a smoky character and perhaps a slightly acidic tang.

Newcastle's famous Brown Ale

OLD ALE

Another style that points back to the days of
porter brewing, old ale implies a beer that has
matured, perhaps picking up winy and acidic
flavours. Today's surviving historic examples
come in a variety of forms and strengths,
including some that contain genuinely
matured beer like Gales Prize Old Ale (Fuller's,
p270) and Strong Suffolk (Greene King, p295),
and some that have some of their character,
like Old Peculier (Theakston, p313). They vary
in colour from amber to dark brown and tend
to be 5.5% or upwards in strength. A few
micros have also experimented with the style.

BARLEY WINE

Used loosely as a general term for any ale,
other than a porter or stout, with a strength
approaching that of wine (7–11%). Strong
beers have a long history in Britain, going
back at least to the 16th century when the
nobility cellared them in their homes. In the
19th century the strongest beers, often
matured in the brewery for a year before
release, were known as 'stock ales'. The term
'barley wine' became familiar in the 1950s

A classic bottled barley wine

through beers like Gold Label Very Strong
Special Beer, which is now only available in
cans. Contemporary British strong ales are
usually sweet with rich fruit and nut flavours.
The best ones, like Fuller's Vintage Ale (p270),
are bottle conditioned so they'll mellow and
gain complexity with age – another
characteristic they share with fine wine.

SCOTTISH ALE

Scotland has its own distinct beer styles.
Traditionally, Scottish ales were slightly darker
and less hoppy than English milds and bitters,
often with a characteristic malty, nutty,
caramel flavour, available in several strengths
denoted by what had once been the standard
price per barrel in the obsolete currency unit
of shillings. The country also brewed India
Pale Ale both for export and in weaker form
for domestic consumption. However, nearly all
the previous upholders of that tradition are
now gone, and though there are many fine
new Scottish microbrewers, if anything they
are even more eclectic than their counterparts
south of the border.

A resuscitated survivor of the IPA days,
Caledonian Deuchars (p290), is often available
in London but is on the tame domestic side
of the style. Several old fashioned malty
Scottish ales are still brewed but sadly rarely
find their way here. One of the most
successful new Scottish brewers, Williams
Brothers (p317), established itself by reviving
some of the country's pre-industrial brewing
practices using ingredients like heather and
spruce. The often remarkable products of
BrewDog (p288) owe more to American
influence and individual eccentricity than to
Scottish brewing heritage. Scotland was also
an early adopter of lager brewing (see below).

WHEAT BEER

Wheat has been used as a brewing grain since
prehistory, giving a characteristic pale yellow
'white' colour and slightly spicy flavour, but
historically its use has often been regulated or
prohibited to protect stocks for baking, and
brewers have found barley more versatile and
easier to work with. Wheat beer was once
common in England, particularly in the

Hoegaarden revived the wheat beer style

Southwest, only finally disappearing in the 1870s. By the 1960s it seemed in terminal decline elsewhere, limited to a few shrinking enclaves in Bavaria, Berlin and Brussels. Then an obsolete style was revived at Hoegaarden (p297) near Brussels and suddenly wheat beer was a young drink again.

Wheat beer is a warm fermented ale style that is most typically served unfiltered, unpasteurised and cloudy with suspended yeast, though some commercialised versions are pasteurised and made artificially cloudy. Belgian white beer (*witbier*, *bière blanche*) on the Hoegaarden model is made with unmalted wheat and spiced, typically with coriander and dried orange peel, giving a smooth milky quality with an orange tang. Bavarian *Weißbier* or *Weizenbier* is made with malted wheat and is unspiced, but has characteristic bubblegum, banana or clove flavours from the yeast. As well as the standard version, there are dark (*Dunkel*) and filtered versions (*Kristall*). Sour, low gravity *Berliner Weisse* is sadly hardly seen in London.

Brewers outside the traditional areas, including British ones, have been inspired by this resurgence to try their hand too, both following traditional styles, as some London

brewers do, or creating their own hybrids – for example St Austell Clouded Yellow (p312) which uses German-style malted wheat, a British ale yeast and added spices. Another Cornish brewer, Sharp's (p310), nods to the ancient wheat beers of the Southwest with Chalky's Bite.

LAMBIC & FRUIT BEER

Brewed in a specific area in and around Brussels now designated by EU law, lambic is an astonishing survivor that links us back to the prehistory of brewing. It's the world's only spontaneously fermented beer still produced on a commercial scale. Like Belgian wheat beer it's made from a mix of unmalted wheat and malted barley, but instead of adding yeast, lambic brewers leave the wort open to the air in vented rooms overnight, trusting that the local microclimate will encourage the right kind of yeasts to colonise it. The resulting beer is sour and acidic, though mellows with

Belgian cherry beer

long ageing of at least a year or maybe three or more. It can be sweetened to make *faro*, or young and old lambics are blended and bottle conditioned to produce sparkling *geuze/gueuze*. Famously, it's also made more palatable by steeping with fruit – traditionally sour cherries for *kriek* or raspberries for *framboise/framboos*.

Consumer interest in fruit lambics has prompted a large number of commercialised, often pasteurised and artificially sweetened versions dosed with ever more exotic fruit syrups. The official designation *'oude'* ('old' in Dutch) marks the most traditional, artisanal interpretations, *oude geuze/gueuze* and *oude kriek*. If you've never tried these beers before, put all your preconceptions on hold. Dry sherry and traditional dry cider are more useful references than anything else discussed in this book. But if you acquire the taste you'll be well rewarded.

Interest in these beers has inspired non-lambic brewers to experiment with fruit – Meantime (p275) makes a raspberry wheat beer while Williams Brothers (p317) uses Scottish fruit in several specialities. There are also a few fruited stouts.

LAGER

To most British drinkers, lager is a particular kind of gold, sparkling beer, invariably pasteurised, with a straightforward, clean, lightly malty, if not bland and boring palate and a bit of grassy hop character. But the term lager designates a whole family of beers brewed using lagering techniques (see p248). Lagers can be gold, black, weak, strong and many other things, including 'real'.

Lager brewing in Britain goes back further than most people think, at least to the 1870s. It gained an early foothold in Scotland: Tennant in Glasgow has been brewing lager since 1885. But lager lagged far behind ale in popularity until the late 1960s when the big brewing groups began to throw their massive marketing weight behind characterless, low gravity keg or canned golden lagers. These were produced domestically from the cheapest possible ingredients but sold at a premium price, sometimes under well-known European names though bearing only a passing resemblance to their namesakes. By 1989, lager sales in Britain overtook those of ale, but at the expense of unfairly besmirching the name of lager in the eyes of discriminating British drinkers.

Most commercial British lagers are very, very approximate interpretations of the pilsner style, but the best examples of this style in Germany and the Czech Republic are another thing entirely, with fine, crisp malt and a notable bite of 'noble' hops. Like most standard beers from this part of the world, they're around 4.8%. *Helles* (which simply means 'light') is a maltier, creamier style with bready notes and less hops. *Kellerbier* ('cellar beer') is an unfiltered, unpasteurised beer, usually a version of a helles. *Märzen* and *Oktoberfest* beers are stronger (5.5%) and slightly darker. Vienna lager is red-amber in colour and notably nutty. *Dunkel* ('dark') is dark brown with lightly roasty and caramel notes. *Schwarzbier* ('black beer') is very dark and quite roasty though rarely bitter like stout. *Bock*, which means 'billy goat', designates a stronger lager, usually a biscuity, malty brown beer at 6.5% or more. German-inspired *bok* has become a seasonal institution in the Netherlands, where versions are also brewed using ale yeasts.

A handful of British brewers now dare to produce craft brewed lager, including three in London. There's no reason why lager can't be cask or bottle conditioned, though a few of the 'real lagers' turn out to be brewed using ale methods with typical lager ingredients.

Pilsner Urquell is an authentic, Czech lager

BREWERIES

A GUIDE TO THE BREWERIES

The listing that follows is intended to help you get more out of exploring London's world of beer by providing background information and notes on selected breweries and their beers. It can't hope to be a comprehensive survey of all the beers you're likely to encounter in the capital, of which there may well be thousands at any one time. Instead, I've picked out the most commonly encountered breweries.

As appropriate for a London guide, all the breweries within Greater London in operation at the time of writing receive extended coverage, and it's particularly pleasing that this list is now more than twice as long as it was just four years ago. As one of the brewers observes below, there's nothing quite like tasting top quality beer close to the place where it was brewed, and I strongly encourage you to take advantage of this by drinking plenty of London beer.

However, drinkers who limited themselves entirely to local beer would be missing one of the greatest and most civilised pleasures of life here. Londoners, like New Yorkers, Parisians, Amsterdammers and many others privileged enough to live in one of the world's great cities, are wont to feel their city

is almost a nation apart. But in reality the city depends for its existence on its connections to the rest of the country and the world. London is the capital of England and the United Kingdom. It may no longer be the capital of an empire on which the sun never sets, but it's still the biggest city in the European Union, and a major world trade and financial centre. It's also one of the most ethnically diverse cities in Europe. People and stuff come to London from all over the country and the known world, as they have done since Roman times.

London's beer scene rightly reflects its diversity and cosmopolitan character, and this book follows suit. Besides breweries from the capital and its immediate hinterland, you'll find representatives below from all over England, from the rest of the British Isles, from mainland Europe, the USA and Australia. This is where Britain, and London in particular, does much better than Europe's other great brewing nations, Belgium and Germany, in showcasing top notch imports beside the domestic product. I recommend you take advantage of this too, and widen your appreciation of the huge variety of styles and flavours offered by brewers across the world.

Casks of Camden Town beer

BEER SELECTION & RATING

Sampling all the beers on offer in London is as impossible a task as cataloguing them, so for those keen to prioritise, I've included a basic rating system. I consider all the beers listed here worthy of your interest. Those particularly worth trying when faced with a choice I've identified with a **single star** (*). A **double star** (**), indicates beers all beer lovers should make a little effort to try at least once. I should stress that, though based on relatively extensive tasting experience and some expertise, these assessments are ultimately personal and subjective ones.

I don't want to give the impression that beers not listed are therefore not worth trying. Some beers have been left out deliberately because I considered others from the same brewery more worthy of consideration in the restricted space available within these pages. But others are absent because they're not readily available in London. Still others aren't here because I haven't tasted them, or didn't

know about them, or because they haven't been invented yet.

For example, there's nothing from Italy – a major omission as the Italian craft brewing scene is currently one of the most exciting in the world. But while some of its products are available from London specialists, supplies can be erratic and no specific brewers and beers have yet established a stable presence. In the meantime, if you see anything from Amarcord, Baladin, Borgo, Ducato or Birrificio Italiano, it's probably worth a go.

This list shouldn't discourage you from taking chances. It's skewed towards regularly produced beers, but brewers are constantly innovating and most produce a stream of specials and seasonals, which may even be more interesting than their standard range. The chances are that you'll find lots of names on pump clips and bottle labels not listed here but don't let that stop you sampling them and making your own discoveries.

BREWERY CATEGORIES

Brewpub. Indicates a brewery on the same premises as a pub or bar, principally to provide beer for sale at that pub or bar.

Microbrewery. I've used this term as a designation of origin and culture rather than size, to indicate an independently owned craft brewery established since the emergence of the modern beer consumer movement in the 1970s. In fact, microbreweries vary hugely in output. And yes, I know it might sound odd to designate Sierra Nevada, with production now approaching 1million hl a year, as a micro-brewery, but I'm not the only one to do so.

Independent. An independently owned brewery – that is, not part of a national or international group – established before the emergence of the modern beer consumer movement. Typically these breweries date back at least to Victorian times, and in Britain

they're invariably vertically integrated, often with extensive estates of pubs. They vary greatly in output: some produce less beer than the bigger 'microbreweries'.

Trappist. A brewery permitted to display the Authentic Trappist Product logo. The beers must be produced within the precincts of a Trappist monastery, under the direction of monks (though secular staff can be involved), and with the proceeds used to fund the monastery and its charitable and religious works. Only seven breweries qualify, one in the Netherlands, the rest in Belgium. The five most often seen in London are listed here. The others are Achel, which is less common, but not unknown; and Westvleteren, which only sells to personal callers.

New national. This is a useful CAMRA-coined term for a small number of national groupings that have emerged through mergers and takeovers over the last decade or so, filling the void left when the previous national groups were carved up by multinationals.

Unlike their predecessors, they retain a strong commitment to cask ale. Although the term originated in the British context, I've extended it to a Belgian brewer that seems to fill a comparable ecological niche.

Subsidiary. A brewery that has its own site and brands, but is owned by a national or multinational group. The owner is named in brackets.

Beer firm. A company that develops and markets its own brands of beer, but doesn't own any kit on which to brew them. Instead beer firms either contract out the brewing or hire brewery facilities as required, making it possible to create and sell new beers without a large capital outlay.

I've borrowed this useful term from CAMRA's sister organisation, PINT in the Netherlands, where such arrangements are more common. Note the multinationals that own most of Britain's historic national beer brands now act mainly as beer firms where cask beer is concerned, contracting out the brewing to others. In these cases I've listed the beer under the brewery where it's actually produced, with a cross reference from the brand name.

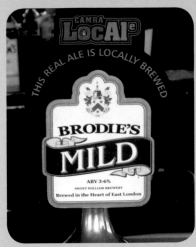

LocAle on sale at the Earl Ferrers (p218)

LocAle is a CAMRA accreditation scheme with the praiseworthy aim of promoting pubs that sell locally brewed cask beer, supporting consumer interest in local products and reducing the environmental impacts of transporting beers long distances. The CAMRA London branches recognise pubs as LocAle ones if they regularly stock at least one beer brewed within a 30 mile (48 km) radius, which effectively includes all breweries within 30 miles of the Greater London boundary. I've aimed to list as many breweries within this wider LocAle zone as I can, but have left out a handful that don't currently sell their beer widely, or at all, within London itself.

LOCATIONS & CONTACT DETAILS

This section isn't intended as a definitive reference work on breweries, so for those outside London you'll find only basic information about location – town; county, province or state; country if not England – plus a web address, indicated by ⊕.

The street address, postcode and phone number, indicated by ☏, is included for all London breweries. Those with relevant entries in the Places to Drink section (for example brewpubs or breweries with a good shop) already have full transport details shown there,

so I've just included a cross reference under Availability here. Otherwise, if the brewery is able to welcome visitors for tours and/or purchases, transport details, in the same format as beer venues, appear at the end of the entry.

Distances from Central London are included as a point of interest. Within Europe, they're distances by road, measured from the traditional central point of Charing Cross. Outside Europe, they're measured 'as the crow flies'. They're only approximate so please don't treat them as a definitive gazetteer.

BEERS & TASTING NOTES

*Forms in which beers are available are indicated
as follows:*

▤ Cask conditioned beer ('real ale')
▲ Bottle conditioned beer ('Real Ale in a Bottle'
or RAIB)
▤ Keg beer – served under gas pressure, may
be filtered and/or pasteurised
◊ Bottled beer – filtered and possibly
carbonated but may be unpasteurised

Sometimes a particular beer may be available
in forms other than the ones shown but I
haven't chosen to comment on these.
Versions of cask beers in particular are
sometimes sold in filtered, carbonated and
often pasteurised bottled form, which may
well have a notably different and usually
inferior character to the cask product.

The percentage shown in brackets after
most beers indicates their alcohol by volume
(ABV). Sometimes different forms of a beer
have different ABVs – usually a stronger
bottled version of a weaker draught beer. So
▤▲ (3.8/4.5%) means that the cask version has
an ABV of 3.8%, the bottle conditioned
version an ABV of 4.5%.

Indications of style and brief tasting notes
are included – again, while based on a certain
amount of expertise and tasting experience,
these are ultimately subjective and personal
and you may well ultimately disagree with
some of them, though hopefully they'll give
you some idea of what to expect.

See the information on the brewing
process, beer tasting and beer styles in the
previous pages for more about some of the
terms used in this section.

AVAILABILITY

These notes give some indication of where to
find the listed beers in London. Named
outlets are only a suggestion and no
guarantee you'll find a particular beer on sale.
Many beers listed are only available as guests
in London and most pubs rotate their guests

rapidly. 'Permanent' beers in non-brewery
pubs can easily be dropped and even
brewery pubs can change ownership. Some
imported bottled beers can be hard to source.

If you're looking for something in particular,
it's always best to ring ahead first.

MORE ABOUT BEERS & BREWERS

Most of the brewery websites shown include
detailed information about that brewery's
beers, including specials and seasonals.

The annual *Good Beer Guide* published by
CAMRA Books includes an extensive and
comprehensive listing of breweries in Britain
and Ireland and their regular cask beers.

Also published by CAMRA is the *Good
Bottled Beer Guide*, a comprehensive source of
information about bottle-conditioned British
beers which also includes selective listings of
imported bottle-conditioned beers.

The excellent and often updated *Good Beer
Guide Belgium*, relatively recent guides to the
US West Coast and the Czech Republic, and a
rather less recent guide to Germany form
CAMRA's foreign Good Beer Guide series.

Comprehensive websites listing brewers
and beers internationally include *ratebeer.com*.
More details about these and other sources of
information are in the More Information
section (p325).

BREW WHARF

Brewpub
Brew Wharf Yard, Stoney Street SE1 9AD
4km/2 miles from Central London
☎ (020) 7378 6601 ⊕ www.brewwharf.com

The name Vinopolis might mean 'city of wine', but this sprawling visitor attraction under the brick arches of an old railway viaduct by Borough Market is notably even-handed in its appreciation of alcoholic drink. The various packages of self-guided tasting tours on offer include gin, whisky, rum, absinthe – and beer.

The source of the suds is one of Vinopolis' four bar-restaurants, Brew Wharf, opened in 2005 by two successful London restaurateurs: Claudio Pulze, who also created the venue's Cantina restaurant, and Trevor Gulliver, of award winning British eatery St John in Clerkenwell, though the latter has since quit the management team. The intention was to

celebrate beer with food, and from the beginning the venue has boasted a five barrel (8.2hl) microbrewery, visible behind glass opposite the kitchen and an equal partner in gastronomic excellence.

In the early days the brewery produced a limited range of traditional British styles, but that all changed in spring 2010 with the arrival of Phil Lowry, manager of online beer shop beermerchants.com and soon to be co-founder of the London Brewers Alliance. He convinced the management that brewing brown bitters was not the best way to grab attention when your neighbours included some of Britain's most exciting beer venues. Phil brought in two fellow beer geeks and former home brewers – Steve Skinner, from Detroit, Michigan, who'd recently done a stint at Gadds' in Ramsgate; and Angelo Scornera, born in Britain but brought up in Houston, Texas.

Since then the brewery has produced a stream of unusual, experimental and strongly flavoured beers, influenced by those the three brewers have discovered on their regular international travels, rarely repeating the same recipe twice. It's also acted as something of a hub for the Alliance, and facilitated numerous collaborations – when I spoke to Steve and Angelo they were busy cooking up something with Stuart Howe of Sharp's. In commercial terms the approach has worked, bringing a raft of new beer aware customers into Brew Wharf and constantly engaging the regulars with something new.

The kit is currently in action about three times a month, according to demand. All the beer is cask conditioned and, apart from occasional festival contributions, is sold only at Brew Wharf, Vinopolis and the Beehive restaurant which is under the same management. Phil and Steve attempted setting up a beer firm called Saints and Sinners with the intention of marketing some of the beers more widely, but Steve has now returned to the US and Phil has found his time taken up elsewhere, so this project has fallen quiet. Meanwhile, Angelo is still in post, continuing to produce diverting and innovative beers which easily hold their own amidst the offerings from the bounteous beer outlets of Borough.

KEY BEERS
These are a few of the more remarkable recent beers. All 🍺.

ABC (3%). Interesting "mid-Atlantic golden ale" rich in grapefruity, coconutty North American hops, but perhaps with not quite the body to support them.
Field of Dreams (4.6%). Developed with Ben Fields of London Amateur Brewers, a grapefruity, refreshing and notably hoppy bitter.
Hopfather * (6.1%). Containing seven American hop varieties, a very fruity and hoppy beer but with good malt to back it up.
How Now Brown Cow * (3.1%). A chocolate milk stout with cocoa nibs, lactose and vanilla beans, with a petrolly note, lots of chocolate and a roasty finish.
Military Intelligence * (6.8%). A so-called Black IPA, malty and dark but generously hopped.

Availability. Usually only at Brew Wharf (p53).

BRODIE'S

Brewpub/Microbrewery
816 High Road E10 6AE
15km/9 miles from Central London
☎ 07976 122853 ⊕ www.brodiesbeers.co.uk

The products of arguably the most fertile imaginations in London brewing fuel a lengthy parade of handpumps on the bar of the sprawling old William IV near Leyton Green. Since brother and sister James and Lizzie Brodie restored brewing to the William in autumn 2008, they've produced over 40 different beers, from traditional British styles and historical recreations to all manner of delightful eccentricities. There's been an East End rye beer made in the presence of a rabbi, a 22% naturally fermented Elizabethan Ale, a strong chilli-infused dark lager named Doppel Dunkel Weizen Heizen, and a Pink Pride beer brewed in solidarity with victims of homophobic violence. The tiny stable block at the back of the pub is the source of a spontaneous and permanently unfinished poem in beer.

James and Lizzie are originally from West London – "I went east to seek my fortune," jokes James. The pair's father Brian Brodie has owned the pub for 13 years, and back in 2000 the family decided a brewery might be a good way of pulling in more custom to this relatively far flung location. In partnership with a third party they set up the Sweet William brewery, fitting out the stables with a new five barrel (8hl) plant designed and installed by Rob Jones of Dark Star (below). But things didn't quite work out and brewing was abandoned in 2005.

The Brodie siblings are longtime homebrewers who had been looking to expand their art, and in 2008 they realised they had an opportunity right under their noses. After a major cleanup and restoration of the derelict plant, the Brodie's brewery sold its first beer in September that year. It has since exceeded all expectations, turning out to be the very attraction it always should have been – they regularly sell 20 9-gallon firkins (1,440 pints or 818l) on a single Sunday and people come from far and wide to sample the brews. The family also owns two central London pubs where real ale sales have doubled since the own brand beers appeared.

KEY BEERS

These are just a few of the brewery's numerous beers. Nearly all are available both ☷ and 🍺.

Amarilla * (4.2%). Named for the local pronunciation of the American hop variety which lends its passion fruit character to this refreshing golden ale.
Citra * (3.1%). Very drinkable pale yellow ale with peppery orange pith flavours well supported by firm malt, along with Amarilla one of the best sellers.
English Best * (3.9%). Traditionally styled fruity-malty brown amber bitter with a spicy hoppy note developing.
IPA (4%). Zesty dry hopped and well balanced golden beer, on the milder side of the IPA style.
Jamaican Stout * (5%). A sappy and very slightly sour near-black beer with a phenolic, thistly note.
Kiwi * (3.8%). Gold and grassy with plenty of New Zealand hops imparting lime and Sauvignon Blanc flavours.
Mild * (3.6%). A chocolatey, notably fruity dark mild with a roasty finish.
Olde Ardour * (5.7%). Winter seasonal, a rich and sappy old ale with a slightly rubbery note.
Red * (4.3%). Well balanced nutty and berry-fruity red ale, offset by a lightly burry hop finish.
Romanov Empress * (12.1%). Chocolate, coffee and grapes fuel this tart, roasty and formidable imperial stout.
Superior London Porter (7.2%). A vivid roast and molasses porter with gravyish malt and a slightly rough finish.

Availability. The Brodie's pubs are the King William IV (p129, with by far the biggest range), the Cross Keys (p75) and the Old Coffee House (p108). The beers are also found at other select outlets especially those keen on local beer.

There are currently around 16 standard beers and many more specials and seasonals, with all the recipes recently redesigned to improve quality. At the weekends, 20 beers are on cask in the pub, with more available bottle conditioned, and the range expands further during festivals. There are beers with American hops, spiced and fruit beers, imperial stouts, and various pleasing nods to the cosmopolitan culture of East London with, for example, real ale versions of Caribbean stouts.

Currently they brew twice a day on four or five days a week, which sometimes means an 18 hour day, but the beer is soon sold. Indeed the brewery is starting to run out of space to mature and condition it all. Despite the volumes James, who devises most of the recipes, still sees brewing as a hobby and works to satisfy his own curiosity as much as anything else. The drinkers of London are the beneficiaries of his restless creativity.

CAMDEN TOWN

Microbrewery
55-58 Wilkin Street Mews NW5 3NN
5km/3 miles from Central London
☎ (020) 7485 1671
⊕ www.camdentownbrewery.com

Spread out in five arches under the London Overground by Kentish Town West station stands a gleaming new computer controlled brewhouse, a tangible and very expensive symbol of faith in the future of craft beer in the capital. And in among the slender stainless steel conical fermenters is a much smaller and more humble vessel clad in old planks, a reminder of how it all started.

This little mash tun was the core of the operation when Australian-born Jasper Cuppaidge honoured his family tradition by installing a small brewery in the cellar of his pub, the Horseshoe. "I did everything in it," recalls Jasper, "and then when all this was put

Camden Town's state-of-the-art brewhouse

in," he says, gesturing to the touch screen monitor from which the whole process can be controlled, "I suddenly realised: I can't brew! It took weeks to learn how to use it. But now we have it, it means we can invest in ingredients and innovation, rather than in extra manpower just to keep the brewing going. It's also extremely efficient, which cuts down the environmental impact."

Jasper's family once owned the McLaughlin brewery in Rockhampton, Queensland. He grew up with brewing and pubs in his blood, and his first brew back at the Horseshoe, a birthday present for his mother, revived both an old family recipe and the brand. The pub is a stylish Hampstead outfit attracting a young and fashionable crowd with a fresh and inventive food menu, some way off the traditional British concept of a real ale boozer. Yet the own-brewed beer proved a hit, holding its own against the British and imported craft beer classics on sale and suggesting there was a growing market for locally brewed quality beer.

Determined to create a freestanding brewery, Jasper found the current site and was originally planning an expansion into one arch. But then he decided to take the plunge with an investment on a much bigger scale which would also give the brewery the ability to guarantee quality and consistency. He'd met Troels Prahl, a renowned yeast expert who runs what's essentially the European branch of US yeast supplier White Labs, at a brewing expo and asked him if he knew of anyone interested in becoming head brewer. Troels volunteered himself, relocating to London, and the pair engaged esteemed Bavarian brewery builders BrauKon to work with them on designing a 20hl brewhouse, finally commissioned in 2010. Since then demand has rocketed: currently they brew about seven times a week, with a staff of six people.

While most British micros concentrate on cask ale, Camden Town does both cask and keg and is now branching into bottling, putting as much quality ingredients and care into all these formats. The kegs are unpasteurised and in the case of the Wheat Beer unfiltered. "Unpasteurised beer in keg still matures and improves, so we now keep batches for several weeks before sending

them out," says Jasper. "There's nothing better than good, well-kept cask beer, and it's lovely when you drink one, but unfortunately that's not as often as it should be. Brewers need to do more to get out to the pubs and ensure better quality. Keg beer is more protected with less risk of bad cellaring and infection. We're now going out to pubs and actually cleaning their lines to ensure the customer gets a good product."

It's always telling to see other people's beers scattered round a brewery and Camden Town has plenty, including Thomas Hardy's Ale vintages going back for years. The beers are there for inspiration. "We drink some of the world's best," says Jasper, "and that's what we aspire to be."

≋ Kentish Town West ⊖ Camden Town 🚴 LCN+6A ✦✦ Links to Jubilee Greenway

KEY BEERS
Some beers also ◊ filtered but unpasteurised.

Bitter * 🍺 (3.7%). The first beer, originally called McLaughlins Horseshoe, a malty brown bitter with sweet fruit and a gritty, spicy finish.
Hells Lager * 🍺 (4.8%). German-style Helles with authentic juicy, honeyed malt character and lightly citric hops.
Pale Ale * 🍺 🍺 (4.5%). The biggest seller, an easygoing US-style pale with sweetish malt and a good pineapple and grapefruit hop character.
Wheat Beer 🍺 (4.5%). Impressively convincing German-style cloudy wheat beer with bubble gum, banana and citrus flavours.
A **porter** and an **Irish red ale** were under development at the time of writing.

Availability. Quality is guaranteed at the brewery's own pub the Horseshoe (p150). The cask beers guest in numerous pubs with a local slant, and the kegs are surprisingly common. Check website for brewery events.

FLORENCE

Brewpub
133 Dulwich Road SE24 0NG
8km/5 miles from Central London
☎ (020) 7326 4987
⊕ www.florenceherne hill.com

The story of brewing at the Florence begins at another pub, the Cock and Hen in Fulham, in 2007. New owners the Capital Pub Company decided that buying a brewery would be a more useful way to spend money on a point of interest than, say, buying a water feature. They recruited Tony Lennon, a recent real ale convert who was London's youngest brewer when he started in the job.

Shortly afterwards Capital took on the sizeable Brockwell Park Tavern in Herne Hill, then an Irish theme bar. The pub underwent a major metamorphosis into the stylish and family friendly Florence, in the process acquiring a second, bigger microbrewery – a 5 barrel (8hl) plant from well-known supplier of brewing kit Dave Porter of PBC. Brewing later ceased at the Cock and Hen, which was sold on to Young's, but continued with great success at the Florence.

Tony moved on late in 2010 and the kit lay silent for a few months, but is now back in action in the expert hands of Peter Haydon, beer writer and long time staff member at Meantime (see below). All the beers are cask conditioned and sold onsite or at one or two other Capital pubs. The plan for the moment is to consolidate the core range.

KEY BEERS
All 🍺

Beaver (4.5%). Slightly cloudy wheat ale with orange-citric notes.
Bonobo (4.5%). Sweetish amber beer with toasty caramel notes.
Weasel (4.5%). Notably hoppy-bitter lively golden ale with cheerful citrus flavours.

Availability. Generally only available at the Florence itself (p185) and occasionally other Capital pubs.

"The brewery is just something really nice to do, as much for fun as for commercial reasons," says Phil Sutton, the Florence manager, who also oversaw the introduction of brewing at the Cock and Hen.

But the Florence beers have proved popular with customers and easily outsell any other cask options, even tempting people who aren't real ale drinkers but are intrigued by the idea of a house-brewed beer. Many of them were concerned about what had happened to the beers during the recent hiatus, but with Peter on board, they can rest easy again.

FULLER'S

Independent
Griffin Brewery, Chiswick Lane South W4 2QB
10km/6 miles from Central London
☎ (020) 8996 2000 ⊕ www.fullers.co.uk

When current brewing director John Keeling first joined Fuller's in 1981, the brewery was a well respected London independent with a modest regional estate, making 70,000 barrels (115,000hl) of beer a year. Today it's the only surviving historic commercial real ale brewery in London, and one of the best known traditional brewers in Britain. Its best bitter, London Pride, is a national brand, its pub estate stretches to Somerset and Birmingham, and its annual output has more than tripled to 220,000 barrels (360,000hl). Beers like ESB have found worldwide fame and helped inspire a new generation of brewers in North America.

Yet at heart Fuller's is still very much a craft brewery, mixing innovation with a dedication to traditional methods. Though the high volume cask brands are its bread and butter, John still finds time to produce the annual Vintage Ale, a world class bottle conditioned barley wine that ages marvellously. Scattered opportunistically in spare corners of the historic Griffin brewery at Chiswick are big wooden former whisky and cognac barrels where the next two editions of the acclaimed Brewer's Reserve beers mature slowly, while the new limited edition Past Masters series is reviving historic recipes with the help of brewing historian Ron Pattinson.

Things could so easily have been different – in the early 1970s the brewery was poised to ditch cask production and convert entirely to keg beers, though the emergence of CAMRA influenced management to drop the plans. Several decades later, in 2005, Fuller's risked raising beer campaigners' hackles by taking over and closing historic Hampshire brewery George Gale. It re-established its heritage credentials by commissioning one last batch of that brewery's classic vintage Prize Old Ale, which has subsequently been blended with Chiswick-brewed beers to keep this historic bottle conditioned brand alive.

Brewing on the site is claimed to date back to a brewhouse in the gardens of Bedford House on Chiswick Mall in the 1650s. Thomas Mawson started the first commercial brewery there in 1701 and a Fuller first became involved in 1829. The founding date of 1845 shown on the brewery logo was when John Bird Fuller got together with Henry Smith and his brother in law John Turner to take over the site. Descendants of the founding partners remain involved, including chairman Michael Turner and sales and personnel director Richard Fuller. Most of the red brick brewery buildings date from the 1870s but parts are older: the wisteria carpeting some of the walls may be the oldest in England, from a Chinese cutting planted in 1816. Perhaps the beer helped it flourish as another cutting

KEY BEERS

Note all 🍺 also available in 🍶, but filtered and pasteurised. There are also seasonals and specials.

1845 ** 🍶 (also occasional 🍺, 6.3%). Old fashioned biscuit malt and orange chestnut-coloured beer with great depth of flavour.
Bengal Lancer * 🍶 (also seasonal 🍺, 5.3%). Subtle 'proper' IPA with firm resins, toast and coconut flavours.
Brewer's Reserve * 🍶 (also occasional 🍺, 7.7%). Blend of 1845, ESB and Golden Pride aged in former spirit casks, each edition different, with a third due by the time you read this. Characteristic orange-tinged Fuller's flavour with a fascinating wood and liqueur edge.
Chiswick Bitter ** 🍺 (3.5%). Much underrated, a beautifully balanced deep golden beer with a sacky malt character and lightly hoppy finish.
Discovery 🍺 (3.9%). Grassy, slightly honeyed golden ale.
ESB (Extra Special Bitter) * 🍺 (5.9%). Classic complex strong bitter with blackcurrant fruit, rich malt, sour orange and peppery hop flavours.
Gales Prize Old Ale ** 🍶 (9%). Intense fruity, vinous and tart deep ruby beer that becomes even more complex with age, released vintage dated.

Gales Seafarers 🍺 (3.6%). Lightly spicy standard bitter with plenty of malt body.
Golden Pride * 🍶 (also occasional 🍺, 8.5%). Intense raspberry fruit, marzipan and orange liqueur flavours are found in this tongue-numbing barley wine.
London Porter * 🍺🍶 (also occasional 🍺, 5.4%). A sharply roasty, quite challenging interpretation with a light yoghurt-like note.
London Pride * 🍺 (4.7%). Lusciously fruity and lightly citric easy drinking best bitter.
Past Masters 🍶. Series of historical recreations from the brewing logs in varying strengths and styles. The first was **XX** * (7.5%), a rich deep amber ale from an 1891 recipe.
Vintage Ale ** 🍶 (8.5%). Based on Golden Pride with a slightly different recipe every year, this limited edition beer always ages magnificently. Bursting with sherbert fruit and hops when young, over the years it acquires porty, cherry, fruit cake and spice flavours of immense complexity.

Availability. The Fox & Hounds / Mawson Arms (p222) is closest to the source, the Mad Bishop & Bear (p98) is more central, but there are lots of other great Fuller's pubs listed here, and London Pride is found in many other pubs. The full selection of bottled beers including aged Vintage Ales is on sale at the Fuller's Brewery Shop (p222) who can also give you details of tours.

from the same batch that went to Kew Gardens later died.

The brewery still makes use of the old practice of 'parti-gyling' – making beers of various strengths from the same basic mash depending on the dilution of the 'runnings' from the mash tun, with some additional variety in the hops added to the copper boil. Four of the brewery's signature beers – Chiswick, London Pride, ESB and Golden Pride – are related in this way.

In a sign of the industry's generosity and the enthusiasm of its workers, Fuller's has slipped easily into the role of elder statesman and mentor of London's developing brewing community. John, a sparkling Mancunian with a wicked taste in music, has been pleased to support the London Brewers Alliance, offering his encyclopaedic knowledge and reliable advice to awestruck young microbrewers. Production manager Derek Prentice has helped two young brewers revive the name of Truman, the brewery where he began his distinguished career (see p281). The current London brewing renaissance would have been so much more difficult without the continued presence of this international treasure, still producing world class beers by the side of the Thames.

HA'PENNY

Microbrewery
8 Aldborough Hall Farm, Aldborough Hatch, Ilford IG2 7TD
24km/15 miles from Central London
☎ (020) 8599 1338
🌐 www.hapenny-brewing.co.uk

In the old stable block of Aldborough Hall Farm, in the green belt surrounds of Thames Chase Community Forest, is London's most rural brewery. It's rather an unexpected location, by a pond complete with ducks and geese and ancient willows, in surroundings patrolled by peacocks. Though within a short walk of two tube stations, until a couple of years back this was a working farm. One of the adjoining houses, Cuckoo Hall, is yet another place that claims to have been a bolthole for peripatetic highwayman Dick Turpin and the brewery building, most recently a pottery, once served as a brewhouse for the nearby Dick Turpin pub

Founders Gavin Happé and Chris Penny were originally drinkers of industrial lager who, bored with lack of flavour, migrated to real ale via Guinness and found themselves wanting to create it too. "We did one brew with a tin of concentrate," recalls Gavin, "and thought this

Fuller's modern bottling line, here producing the bottle-conditioned 1845

isn't how proper beer is brewed, so went straight to full mash." Pleased with the results and determined to set up commercially, they eventually found the stable block and spent three years renovating it, finally installing a 5.5 barrel (9hl) kit that had originally been built as a demonstration model by a company called Malrex in Burton upon Trent.

The first beer flowed in October 2009 and they've been selling seriously since March 2010, with a single brewing day a week, the results of which sell out rapidly. All the production so far is cask and goes out to pubs, not only in East and Central London but also eastwards into Essex and Suffolk, mostly through the SIBA Direct Delivery Scheme. The brewery is proud of its London roots with beers named for local characters and legends.

Look at the founders' last names and you'll soon work out where the Ha'penny name comes from but it has pleasing echoes of a traditional pub game and also – given that the half penny was for many decades the

smallest value coin in circulation in Britain – acknowledges the compactness of the operation. Indeed Gavin and Chris, respectively a barrister and an accountant by profession, haven't yet given up their day jobs, and the fort is held during the week by Gavin's dad Lee. They're determined that should change. "A good day at the office for me usually means somebody gets sent to prison," laments Gavin. "I'd rather earn my living doing something I enjoy and that makes other people happy."

⊖ Barkingside 〃 Thames Chase paths

KERNEL

Microbrewery
98 Druid Street SE1 2HQ
5km/3 miles from Central London
📞 07757 552636
🌐 www.thekernelbrewery.com

The Kernel brewery may only have been founded late in 2009, and its four barrel (6.5hl) plant may be the smallest freestanding brewery in London, but among the beer cognoscenti it's already being talked about in the tones of respect usually reserved for Thornbridge and Dark Star. In 2011 it was listed as one of the top five new breweries in the world by users of the leading international beer rating website, ratebeer.com. Of all the new London breweries, it's the one that most closely pursues the artisanal ideal of a small producer finding self-expression through the creation of individually hand crafted products.

It's a romantic image that sits easily on the shoulders of softly spoken Evin O'Riordan, the creative force who runs the Kernel show. From Waterford in Ireland, Evin studied English Literature as a postgraduate, but ended up working with cheese at Neal's Yard Dairy, a leading distributor and retailer of fine British cheese based in Borough Market. It was on an extended trip to New York City to help set up a Neal's Yard shop that Evin's interest in brewing was engaged.

"With cheese," he says, "we'd know who made it, what day of the week it was made on, what the calves' names were, and we'd care. I realised when we went to the pub after work for a beer, there was almost no thought

KEY BEERS
All 🍺

16 String Jack IPA (3.8%). Actually a fruity bitter with a lightly hoppy and toffeeish finish.
Gogmagog (5.5%). Summer seasonal, an unusual figgy and peachy golden ale with odd spicy notes.
London Stone (4.5%). A traditional English session bitter.
Mrs Lovett's Most Efficacious Stout Porter (5%). A winter seasonal chocolatey and berryish stout with a burnt roast bite, named after Sweeney Todd's pie-making accomplice but thankfully not utilising her favoured ingredients.
Spring Heeled Jack (4%). A winter seasonal plummy porter with caramel, slightly medicinal, fruity and roast notes.

Availability. Look for it in East London pubs. The brewery also stages a beer festival on site in early May.

given to it. And it was only in America that I met people who took beer seriously in the same way I took food seriously." Based in the Borough, he was familiar with venues like the Market Porter and appreciated real ale, but comments, "There's almost a sense there that all the beers are interchangeable, and if there's one you particularly like, you go back to the bar and it's gone, never to be seen again. The Americans shout louder about things that make them passionate, and the really good beers are more vocally appreciated than they are over here."

On his return Evin was determined to start a brewery and began evolving his own beers through home brewing, joining London

Kernel beers are mainly bottled

KEY BEERS

Note recipes may vary. All are 🍶 and very occasionally 🍺.

Export Stout London 1890 ** (7.8%). Based on a Truman recipe, this is a dense and weighty liquorice humbug-tinged mahogany beer with fresh chocolate on a pursing finish.
India Pale Ale ** (6.8%). A version made with four US hop varieties was bursting with passion fruit nectar, with biscuit malt under a resinous peppery finish.
India Pale Ale Black * (6.8%). Actually a deep amber, with rummy malt, Indian spice and a piny, peppery finish.
Pale Ale * (5.5%). An example made with Centennial and Chinook had crisp grainy malt and complex tropical fruit and grapefruit notes.
Porter * (5.6%). Astringent and roasty with malty chocolate and baked vine fruit flavours.

Availability. Kernel bottles are on the list at several discerning pubs and places like the Dean Swift (p54) sometimes have cask too. The brewery is open for direct sales most Saturday mornings from the public entrance at 1 Rope Walk: check website. Mr Lawrence Wine Merchant / Bar (p186) is another good source of bottles.

Amateur Brewers. He then moved into a railway arch in Bermondsey a little east of the market, sharing it with two friends, one a cheesemaker, the other an importer of Italian cheese and charcuterie. The brewery with its three vessels supplied by well known British microbrewery supplier PBC takes up a relatively small space on the south side of the arch. It's currently fired up about twice a week: Evin could brew more but nearly all the beer is bottled by hand, a time consuming process that limits capacity. "Most of the stuff we sell is between here and London Bridge," he says, "so I deliver it by tricycle."

Kernel specialises in two key styles: pale ales and IPAs in the contemporary North American hop accented mode; and British porters and stouts in a much older tradition with its roots firmly in London, although with a well-known historic detour in the direction of Evin's own origins across the Irish sea. These dark delights adapt historic recipes Evin first encountered through amateur historical recreationists the Durden Park Beer Circle. Exact formulations change as the artist constantly renews his palate, with hop varieties and proportions in particular shifting from batch to batch – so far there's no sign of the received brewing wisdom of pursuing stable, distinctive and consistent brands above all. Instead the Kernel label is more like a signature denoting a common personality across diverse individual works, and looks set to become a mark of quality and artistry widely recognised by appreciators of fine beer.

🚆 London Bridge ⊖ Bermondsey **DLR** Tower Gateway 🚲 NCN4 🚶 Thames Path, Jubilee Greenway

MEANTIME

Microbrewery
Blackwall Lane SE10 0AR
13km/8 miles from Central London
☎ (020) 8293 1111
⊕ www.meantimebrewing.com

When Greenwich-born but Heriot-Watt and Weihenstephan-trained brewer Alastair Hook set up on his own in an industrial unit a stone's throw from the Thames Barrier at Charlton in 2000, he chose to follow what for a British microbrewer was then a pretty much unprecedented business plan. Rather than focusing on cask ale, he used his Bavarian experience to brew quality lager in bottles or continental-style bright kegs. He'd spent four summers in the 1980s working in Californian craft breweries and already been involved in creating the Freedom brewery (see p293) among others, so he knew there was a demand that a different approach to craft brewing could satisfy.

Meantime, named for its location not far from the Prime Meridian and its commitment to properly matured beers, originally earned its keep by contract brewing and marketing to restaurants and bars. Production shifted up a gear in 2002 when supermarket giant Sainsbury's commissioned it to produce a range of upmarket European-style beers, and in 2005 it finally launched its own range of bottled beers in impressively varied styles. Some of these proved very forward looking in their use of American hops, while others contributed to the growing revival of traditional styles – two of Meantime's best beers are still its authentic bottle conditioned IPA and London Porter, beautifully presented in champagne style 750ml bottles with wired corks.

Long hampered by a cramped and unattractive site, the brewery underwent an even more ambitious metamorphosis in 2010. First it launched a spectacular new bar-restaurant, the Old Brewery, in the precincts of the Old Royal Naval College, Greenwich, incorporating its own 5hl (3 barrel) automated microbrewery for short run specialities. Then it relocated the main plant to a bigger site on the edge of Greenwich town centre, complete with a new German-

KEY BEERS

Kellerbier and Wheat Beer are sold at the Old Brewery naturally conditioned from polythene-lined tanks under air pressure.

Chocolate * ▲ (6.5%). Well balanced roast, cola and chocolate and a hint of Bailey's.
Helles * ☱ (4.4%). Honeyed pale lager with twists of lime, strawberry and piny hops.
Hospital Porter * ☱ (8%). Brewed at the Old Brewery: fresh beer blended with a stock porter matured in spirited oak – dark, roasty and phenolic.
Kellerbier * ☰ (4.9%). Brewed at the Old Brewery: doughy, lightly grassy and very refreshing pale unfiltered lager. A filtered version is sold as **London Lager**.
India Pale Ale ** ▲ (7.5%). Copper-gold ale with pineapple, grapefruit, peach kernel and a dry finish.
London Pale ☰ ☱ ◊ (4.3%). Actually more US-style with peachy malt and pineapple hops.
London Porter ** ▲ (6.5%). Deep ruby and oozing chocolate mousse, leather and slightly sharp blackcurrant flavours.
London Stout * ▲ (4.5%). Smooth and minerally with a drying coffee finish.
Raspberry * ▲ (5.5%). Refreshing wheat beer with cheerful natural raspberry flavours.
Union * ◊ (4.5%). A rare Vienna-style lager, nutty and toffeeish with burry almond-like hops.
Wheat Beer ▲ ☱ (and ☰, 5%). Sweetish, wheaty and salty with clove and banana flavours.

Availability. The obvious place is the Old Brewery (p180), the only bar to sell Kellerbier and Hospital Porter, but Meantime's first pub the Greenwich Union (p179) is still well worth visiting. The keg beers in particular are becoming increasingly common. Check website or call for details of brewery tours.

Meantime's Old Brewery bar and restaurant

built Rolec 100hl (65 barrel) kit. Currently production stands at around 33,000hl (20,000 barrels) a year but the aim is to grow that to 100,000hl. With Young's now gone, Meantime is easily the second biggest independent brewery in London and one of the most advanced micros in the British Isles.

In 2009, the brewery finally added a cask ale to its repertoire, a version of its London Pale, but Alastair remains unapologetic about an approach that's never endeared him to real ale purists. "I'm a passionate believer in brewery conditioning," he tells me, "because you can't trust the distribution chain. What I learned in Germany was that the most important factor is giving beer enough time to mature, which too few brewers do, including cask brewers – too many of them rush beer out when it's too young. But to spend six or eight weeks lovingly making a beer, so it's properly matured with a nice structure, only to have it ruined by an untrained and uncaring cellarman is just awful. At Meantime we're dedicated to beer brewed with time, care and attention, but we're not preoccupied with the vessel it's dispensed from."

≋ Maze Hill ⨝ NCN1 ⫝ Thames Path, Jubilee Greenway

MONCADA

Microbrewery
5 Grand Union Centre, West Row W10 5AS
5.5km/3.5 miles from Central London
☎ 07775 931321

Former chef Julio Moncada, originally from Argentina, was planning to move into business on his own by opening a specialist delicatessen. But as a keen home brewer, he realised that while a deli requires supplies to be shipped from around the world, all the ingredients for brewing are available close to hand in Britain.

So he's now the proud owner of a six barrel (10hl) brewhouse from PBC, due to start brewing commercially in June 2011 from a site near the Grand Union canal on the northern edge of Kensington, not far from Kensal Green. Julio promises a range of British style ales in both cask and bottle, probably starting with golden and pale ales, still to be named as we went to press.

RAM

Private brewery
Wandsworth High Street SW18 4JT
11km/7 miles from Central London

Unlike the beers of every other brewery listed here, the Ram's products are currently not publically available. But given the extraordinary brewing heritage attached to this site by the mouth of Thames tributary the Wandle, no beer guide to London would be complete without telling its story. And there's a serious chance that in a future edition this entry will no longer be so exceptional.

There's a good case to be made that the Ram site has the longest documented continuous history of brewing in Britain, and certainly in London. Nobody is quite sure when brewing began but an inn with the sign of a ram stood on the site at least as far back as 1533. Inns in those days often had breweries, though the first written records of commercial brewing date from 1581, when the landlord, Humphrey Langridge, not only sold beer to his guests but to other pubs and private houses.

The Young family bought the brewery in 1831, by which time it was a substantial freestanding operation with an estate of 80 pubs. In the 1860s they started to shift the focus from porter towards lighter, more sparkling beers, beginning the evolution of the pale bitter ales for which the Young's name would become famous.

The developing beer consumer movement of the 1970s and 1980s knew Young's as a fortress of brewing tradition and a paragon of real ale virtue. The family retained close control and fiercely defended its independence. Young's always kept the faith with traditional cask ales, retained wooden casks years after most of the industry had converted to aluminium, and still delivered locally using horse-drawn drays. They only finally retired their steam engines in 1976. In an echo of the ancient sign, they kept a ram in the brewery yard as a mascot, and even had the Queen Mother pull their pints.

So it came as a shock to many when, in 2006, chairman John Young admitted he'd let his head rule his heart as he announced Young's was merging with Charles Wells and relocating all production to the latter's big 1970s plant in Bedford. The existing site would be sold for redevelopment. More perceptive observers were less surprised. Young's had been subtly modernising for years, improving its pubs and refreshing its brands, but badly needed to invest in upgrading facilities, an expensive process in its heritage buildings. And the rocketing property values of this up-and-coming inner London town centre were making it increasingly difficult to defend the case for staying.

In a poignant twist, John Young, himself a great-great-grandson of the firm's founder, died aged 85 the very week that Young's brewed its last beer at the Ram. Since then the plan to build a residential and shopping development on the site, centred on two glass towers, has become snarled up in planning and finance issues.

Pay a visit to Wandsworth today (p210) and you can still see how the brewery with its brick chimneys dominated the town centre, not least by the way the Young's brand still plasters practically every pub within walking distance. But the complex at its heart stands gloomily boarded up and apparently lifeless.

Apparently but not entirely. The moment the redevelopment was announced, there was talk of a future new microbrewery on the site. Young's employee John Hatch and some of his colleagues were determined that the lengthy record of continuous brewing should not be broken. As the buildings were stripped, they scraped together a microbrewery from bits and pieces, including tea urns and rubbish bins, and have continued to brew on a very small scale on a regular basis, until such times as commercial brewing can be re-established here. "At which point," says John, "I'll be first in the queue for a job there." It's a touching sign of how much brewers care about their profession, and a fitting example of the indomitable spirit of the ram.

For information on the current Bedford brewed Young's beers, see under Wells & Young's below.

REDEMPTION

Microbrewery
33 West Road N17 0XL
15km/9 miles from Central London
☎ (020) 8885 5227
⊕ www.redemptionbrewing.co.uk

In an industry full of decent people, Andy Moffat stands out as, well, even nicer than usual – dedicated to the work he does, genuinely delighted that it brings pleasure to others, and generous with his time and expertise.

Originally from Glasgow, Andy was a banker who'd lived in London for 18 years, but was keen to start his own business – preferably doing something he felt passionate about and enjoyed. And like an increasing number of young European brewers, he found his inspiration not at home but across the Atlantic, reading *Brewing up a Business*, a how-to book by Sam Calagione, influential US

Sambrook's beers maturing in wooden casks

craft brewer and founder of Delaware's Dogfish Head (below).

Andy was determined to create a genuinely local North London brewery with links to its community, like some of the urban micros he'd encountered in northern England but which, at the time he embarked on the project, seemed curiously absent in London. Following a course at BrewLab in Sunderland he secured his current premises on an industrial estate in Tottenham – and started to hear about all the other new breweries launching in London. "I thought, fine," he says. "Other people think this is a good idea too."

The brewery itself, set up with the aid of consultant Dave Smith, looks more like most people's idea of a micro than, say, the gleaming hi-tech kit at Camden Town (above). It's a 12 barrel (20hl) plant bought second hand from Slater's brewery in Stafford, smallish but not tiny, with a few improvised modifications involving drainpipes and packing tape. But on Dave's advice there are also some features not universal along micros, such as a separate fermentation room where hygiene can be more scrupulously maintained. Definitely artisanal, but serious and businesslike too.

The transatlantic inspiration hasn't left the beers speaking with a particularly American accent, but neither are they cut to the standard British template. Instead Andy has followed his own instincts and tastes in creating beers for contemporary north Londoners. There's an easy drinking pale ale

KEY BEERS

All 🛢 though some bottles are planned.

Fellowship Porter * (5.1%). Late hopped, complex, flowery and herbal, with dry toffee and a long edgy roast finish.
Hopspur * (4.5%). Intriguing blend of British bitter palate with peppery coconut-tinged US hops.
Pale Ale (3.8%). The best seller, a golden ale with a fruity, hoppy aroma, firm oily malt and a citrus peel note in the finish.
Trinity * (3%). Three malts and three hops go into this firm chaffy blond beer with a resinous citrus and rosehip finish.
Urban Dusk * (4.6%). Difficult to classify, a chestnut brown with chocolatey fruit, a slight artichoke note, and a chewy, tangy, bitterish finish.

Availability. Regularly available in discerning pubs particularly in north London, and permanent in places like the Jolly Butchers (p158).

SAMBROOK'S

Microbrewery
1 Yelverton Road SW11 3QG
8km/5 miles from Central London
☎ (020) 7228 0598
🌐 www.sambrooksbrewery.co.uk

When accountant Duncan Sambrook and two university friends combed the beer list at the Great British Beer Festival in 2006, they realised that, aside from Fuller's, not a single London brewery appeared. The obvious way of doing something about it was to start a brewery. As indicated elsewhere, Duncan wasn't the only one moved to such a response but five years on, his is arguably the most successful so far. And there's a certain juicy irony in the fact that, following an unsolicited request, his beers are now available as guests in numerous Young's pubs, as it was that brewery's departure from the capital that tore the biggest hole in the city's brewing fabric.

which is by far the biggest seller, and then there's Urban Dusk, the dark beer which Andy describes as a premium bitter but is not easy to classify, betraying a slight Scottish touch to my taste. Recently some more experimental brews and collaborations with other London brewers have been widening the range. Some bottle conditioned beers are on their way including a Victorian mild brewed jointly with Kernel.

Redemption beers have so far proved as universally affable as their creator. Their distinctive triangular pump clips are now decorating the walls of many of London's traditional real ale pubs, but also look perfectly in place alongside the latest BrewDog weirdness and cutting edge US imports in the new generation of beer bars. Currently production goes up to 80 nine gallon casks a week (5,760 pints, 3,270l) and Andy has taken on a full time brewer, former White Horse cellarman Andy Smith.

"Beer is a British product," said Andy Moffat, "made mainly with local raw materials, much more versatile than wine, but it's been underappreciated. And with people moving away from big brands and towards something more independent, unique and local, not just with drinks but things like music, fashion and food, it's got massive potential. Over the next five to ten years I can see the craft brewing sector doing really well."

🚆 Northumberland Park 🚲 Link to NCN1, LCN+ Wood Green and Lea Valley Path

KEY BEERS
All 🍶 🍺

Wandle * (4.2%). Amber bitter named after the river flowing through nearby Wandsworth and past a certain historic brewery site, with slightly spicy malt, pleasant fruity notes and a gentle hop wash.
Junction * (4.5%). Robust best bitter with a good slightly spicy hop character, named for the brewery's local station, Clapham Junction.
Powerhouse * (4.9%). Named for famous local landmark Battersea Power Station, this very dark ruby porter has slightly liquoricey dark malt and a tasty, chewy finish.
A seasonal **Summer Ale** should be available by the time you read this.

Availability. Widely served in good real ale pubs, including in selected Young's pubs, and in Draft Houses like the nearby Draft House Westbridge (p197). For details of shop and tour times, call or see the website.

Duncan's first attempts foundered on lack of experience. But then came a serendipitous meeting with David Welsh, a veteran brewer and former director of Ringwood (above). Duncan grew up in Salisbury and his formative drinking years had been fuelled by Ringwood beers – when he got over being starstruck he asked David to join him as a partner. Suddenly a new brewery became much more of a practical prospect, and David persuaded him to think much bigger than his original intentions.

The new brewery, in a modern industrial building in Battersea, came onstream in November 2008, the first of the new crop of micros in London. It's a mainly new Canadian-built 20 barrel (33hl) plant, somewhere between the flash of Camden Town and the dressed down practicality of Redemption. Duncan and David have concentrated on using it to brew a limited number of appealing and reliably consistent beers, starting with just two, Wandle and Junction. In winter 2010 they added a seasonal porter which may well become more regular. They're experimenting with maturing in wooden casks and other occasional seasonals may creep in, but they've no intention of overwhelming us with a galaxy of products.

With a staff of eight, they're currently brewing five days a week and a new fermentation tank has upped their output to 140 barrels (40,320 pints, 22,900l) a week. Traditional British malts and hops are used. "The idea was to source all the ingredients as close to the brewery as possible," says Duncan. "We're now getting pretty much all our raw materials from within 100 miles (160km) of the brewery. Most of the hops are from Kent and the malt is Wiltshire-grown from Warminster Maltings." All the beers are also available bottle conditioned, packed at a friendly spirit bottling company. "For brand recognition, it's vital," Duncan affirms.

At the entrance to the brewery is a quirky, pleasant little bar and shop, selling not only Sambrook's bottles but other craft products from local producers. This public face is important, as a local presence and also as the assembly point for brewery tours, already an essential component of the business and booked up weeks in advance. "You can

Sambrook's brew 140 barrels a week

sometimes spot the non-ale drinkers lurking in the background," says Duncan, "and if you can just get them to try, they usually go away saying they're going to try more."

Like most brewers, Duncan is an affable guy, but you can still see the flashes of methodical determination that doubtless pushed him to create the brewery in the first place. Displayed in the bar is a map of London, already relatively densely populated with colour coded pins representing the various Sambrook's accounts. "When I look at that map I just see the gaps," says Duncan, "and I want to fill them." I'm sure he will.

⇌ Clapham Junction 🚲 NCN+ Chelsea, Wandsworth, link to NCN4 ♦♦ Thames Path

STAG

Subsidiary (AB InBev)
Lower Richmond Road SW14 7ET
14km/9 miles from Central London

Although it's not often spoken about for reasons which will become obvious, at the time of writing there is in fact one other historic brewery operating in London besides Fuller's. Commercial brewing at Mortlake, on the south bank of the Thames just upstream of Chiswick Bridge, is first recorded in 1765 when two small breweries under separate ownership stood here, though there are links further back to monastic brewing in the 15th century. By the 1850s the businesses had long since merged, and the much expanded Mortlake brewery was doing very well

TRUMAN'S

Beer firm
Top Floor, 8 Elder Street E1 6BT
📞 (020) 7247 1147 ⊕ www.trumansbeer.co.uk

The first records connecting Joseph Truman with brewing in Brick Lane date from the 1660s, as an employee of another brewer. But by 1697 Truman owned the brewhouse himself, passing it in 1721 to his son Benjamin who began the process of turning it into one of London's biggest and most successful breweries. By the 1830s, now with additional partners as Truman Hanbury & Buxton, it was producing 200,000 barrels (330,000hl) of porter a year and its Black Eagle trademark was known throughout the country. It was also associated with philanthropy, and is mentioned as such by Charles Dickens in David Copperfield: Thomas Buxton was an anti-slavery campaigner and prison reformer who joined the board in 1809.

Like several other London brewers Truman set up a second home in Burton upon Trent when pale ales came into fashion and from the 1870s its brewing in London declined, though the Brick Lane site remained important. The postwar consolidation of the industry sealed its fate – in 1971 it was taken over by the Grand Metropolitan hotel group who used it as leverage to buy out Watney

supplying India Pale Ale to the Army. This financed a major rebuild in 1869 – a date that is still visible on the frontage today.

Then in 1898 the brewery fell to a bigger predator, Watney Combe Reid. That company evolved into Watney Mann, one of the notorious 'Big Six' national brewers of CAMRA's early days (see also Truman's below). Mortlake was the site of Watney's early experiments with keg ale in the 1930s, the first major British brewery to adopt this technique. It later held the dubious distinction of being the principal producer of Watney's Red Barrel, a heavily promoted keg bitter that became a national joke.

Watney was ultimately swallowed by the Grand Metropolitan hotel group, which asset stripped it when it pulled out of brewing in 1989, selling on the Stag among other sites to Scottish Courage (now Heineken). In 1991 the facility was leased to Anheuser-Busch, who converted it into the principal European production plant for Budweiser lager. With the merger of Anheuser-Busch and InBev in 2008, the brewery has been deemed surplus to requirements and is slated to close by the end of 2011, though it's already received one stay of execution thanks to strong sales of its products. Given its current use, lovers of good beer may see the final closure when it comes as putting a once proud brewery out of its protracted misery, and I certainly have no urge to claim the Mortlake version of the industrial rice-based fizz that is 'American' Bud as a London beer. But it is still a notable loss to Britain's brewing heritage, not to mention to the economy of southwest London.

KEY BEERS

Runner * 🍺 4%. So called because it's a 'running beer', the term originally used to distinguish modern-style freshly brewed bitters and milds from long matured 'stale' porters. Deep red-brown, firm and dryish with fruity malts and an edgy twiggy hop note.
A seasonal porter, **Three Threads**, was produced in winter 2010 and a summer ale is planned.

Availability. Seen in a few pubs priding themselves on local beer – try the Carpenters Arms (p102) to enjoy it almost within the shadow of the old brewery chimney.

the following year, creating Watney Mann Truman. Grand Met later lost interest in brewing altogether and finally closed the Black Eagle in 1988 after years of neglect.

And there the story of brewing under the Truman name would have ended, were it not for James Morgan and Michael-George Hemus, university friends who found themselves living in East London and working in and around the old brewery site. Both enthusiasts for fine beer and good pubs, they researched the brewery's history in considerable depth and conceived the idea of reviving the brand. It took almost a year of twice weekly phone calls to various sets of lawyers before the owners, Heineken, took them seriously enough to strike a deal.

One major barrier was a lack of capital for new kit and premises, so after much thought James and Michael-George opted to brew the beer initially outside London, at Nethergate (below). The plan is to build the brand and sales and invest in a brewery later, probably in 2013. "We are very, very keen to bring the beer back to London," says Michael-George. The idea of a microbrewery on the old Brick Lane site is

romantic, but probably not practical, and current options being investigated include the post-2012 Olympic Park.

They've considered recreating old Truman recipes but for their main product have opted to develop a new beer in the spirit of the old. "All the brewing records from 1813 to the 1920s are intact in the archives," explains Michael-John, "but finding more recent records has proved impossible. We think Grand Met actually burned all the paperwork when they pulled out. So we've created a modern beer that at the same time is classically British." Fuller's production manager and former Truman employee Derek Prentice helped them fill in some of the gaps.

Meanwhile the old brewery with its handsome industrial buildings and landmark chimney is dominating Brick Lane once again, but in a rather different way. In the 1990s it was reopened as a centre for arts and creative industries and a shopping and leisure complex, rapidly becoming the centre of gravity of the trendy Hoxton and Shoreditch scene (p100) and providing yet another new face to one of London's most frequently reinvented streets.

Truman's old brewery on Brick Lane

TWICKENHAM

Microbrewery
Ryecroft Works, Edwin Road,
Twickenham TW2 6SP
19km/12 miles from Central London
☎ (020) 8241 1825
⊕ www.twickenham-fine-ales.co.uk

It's easy to miss Twickenham from the list of London breweries and not just because it's in the relatively far reaches of former Middlesex suburbia. Its beers are rarely seen in central London, and although interest is growing slowly, about 80% of production is currently sold within 5 miles (8km) of the brewery, and 95% within 10 miles (16km). And they like it that way. "Customers appreciate a local brewery and beer that hasn't been trucked hundreds of miles," says brewer Tom Madeiros. "And I'm the same – if I'm on a beer tour of Belgium I'd rather go the town where a beer is brewed than drink it in a big city bar that sells 800 beers from all over."

Former IT professional and Twickenham resident Steve Brown used redundancy money to start the brewery in 2004 and intended from the first to give it that local identity, taking particular advantage of the Thameside suburb's association with rugby union, a sport where real ale, and not industrial lager, is the traditional tipple of choice. Tom joined a year later: originally from Cape Cod, Massachusetts, he was a beer-loving electronic engineer until moving into brewing via a BrewLab course. Prior to Twickenham he'd been at Grand Union, a West London micro that enjoyed a brief life in the early 2000s.

Twickenham's forte is traditional cask beer done with flair, an approach that's won them an armful of local CAMRA and SIBA awards and a medal at the Champion Beer of Britain competition. And though the sense of place is indisputable, it doesn't make them parochial. They've been keen supporters of the London Brewers Alliance and have ties further afield too. In 2008 Urbain Coutteau, one of Belgium's innovative Struise Brewers, helped create an oatmeal porter with Tom and Steve, and a version of their best seller Naked Ladies is now being produced by their friends at Alvinne (see p285) in Flanders.

Operations are centred round a 10 barrel (16.5hl) brewing kit bought second hand from the Springhead brewery in Nottinghamshire when the latter was upgrading to a larger plant, and which, despite the lack of a dedicated sales person, is kept going to full capacity supplying their local customers.

Expansion to a 25 barrel (41hl) plant and the provision of off-sales at the brewery is planned and they've also considered small scale bottling but they'll need a bigger site than the old industrial building they currently occupy. In the meantime it's well worth doing what Tom would do, and making that special trip west.

KEY BEERS
All ◉

Grandstand Bitter * (3.8%).
Celebrating Twickenham's internationally known rugby stadium, this is a full flavoured, characterful bronze bitter with tropical fruit notes.
Naked Ladies * (4.4%). A gently perfumed golden beer, rapidly bittering with berryish and herbal hop flavours. The name always catches attention but actually refers to the water nymphs depicted in a famous fountain in the gardens of nearby York House.
Original (4.2%). A notably dark best bitter with a malty body and fruity hops.
Sundancer * (3.7%). Refreshing golden bitter with zesty but rounded grapefruity hops.
Also look out for numerous seasonals and specials.

Availability. Often seen at the better real ale stockists in southwest and west London: the Prince of Wales (p232) is a regular outlet near the brewery. Noble Green Wines (p232) have draught beer to take away. Realale. com (p233) always has a cask beer on tap at the shop. Note there is no sales outlet at the brewery.

ZERODEGREES

Brewpub
29 Montpelier Vale SE3 0TJ
12km/7 miles from Central London
☎ (020) 8852 5619   ⊕ www.zerodegrees.co.uk

Opened in 2001, Zerodegrees is currently London's longest-serving brewpub. It belongs to a small family business that had hitherto run theme restaurants, but one of the directors was intrigued by visits to US brewpubs serving up unusual beers with pizza and mussels, and wanted to experiment with something similar in the UK. So Blackheath gained a stylish new hi-tech bar-restaurant, centred on a semi-automated 15hl (9 barrel) brewhouse built by German company BTB. An American head brewer was recruited, and the four recipes he developed for the regular beers, though modified by successive custodians, have served the place well for a decade.

The brewhouse's current operator is also German-built. Simon Siemsglüss, who started early in 2010, is from Hamburg and got into brewing when living in Canada in 2005, motivated partly by missing the beer of his native land. His last post was in the rather

Zerodegrees' brewer, Simon Siemsglüss

different setting of Shenyang in China, at a brewpub owned by Bavarian giant Paulaner (below). Simon inherited the four regular beers, but the two changing specials are left to his imagination. Perhaps unsurprisingly, so far they've included a Maibock and an Oktoberfestbier, but also rather less traditional styles like a rye ale and a black IPA.

Some real ale purists, noting the non-native styles and the lack of handpumps, might conclude the brewery produces only keg beer, but they would be wrong. All the beers are unpasteurised and unfiltered, naturally lively and dispensed from polythene-lined serving tanks under air pressure without additional gas.

The venture was so successful that the company has become a mini-chain, with branches in Bristol, Cardiff and Reading all following the London model. "The brewery is completely integral to the business," says area manager Wendy Prowse. "Local people absolutely love it. They love the beers and they love the fact that they're actually made in-house."

Zerodegrees may be last on London's alphabetical listing but it's an important and valuable stitch in London's tapestry of beer.

KEY BEERS

All ⬗ (but see explanation above).

Black Lager * (4.8%). A Schwarzbier style with caramel and coffee notes and a smooth finish with sacky hops.
Pale Ale (4.6%). Golden with sweetish nutty malt and a lightly citric and earthy hop bite.
Pilsner (4.8%). Pale gold with cereal notes and a restrained hop character for the style.
Wheat Ale (4.2%). A lightish orange-gold interpretation with banana and citrus notes.
Numerous rotating specials are also brewed.

Availability. At the brewpub – see p168 for details. Occasionally seen elsewhere, for example at Hoopers (p174).

ACHOUFFE
Subsidiary (Duvel-Moortgat)
Achouffe, Luxembourg, Belgium
536km/333 miles from Central London
⊕ www.achouffe.be

Launched in 1982 in the rural Ardennes, the brewery's marketing featuring cheerful gnome-like chouffes helped it become an early Belgian breakthrough in the export market. Bought by Duvel-Moortgat in 2006 but little has yet changed.

La Chouffe (8%) is the soft but zesty flagship blond, sweetish and drinkable with coriander notes. **Houblon Chouffe Dobbelen IPA** * (9%) is a custardy but crisp blond with extra hops for the US market, giving a dry, piney finish. **McChouffe** * (8.5%) is drier, maltier and more complex, with a Scottish influence.

Availability. Belgian and other beer specialists and from bottle shops.

ACORN
Microbrewery
Barnsley, South Yorkshire
285km/177 miles from Central London
⊕ www.acorn-brewery.co.uk

A 2003 offshoot of the now-closed Barnsley Brewery and continuing some of its brands, this is now one of the more respected representatives of the busy South Yorkshire brewing scene.

Barnsley Bitter * (3.8%) is brown with a floral aroma and a dry malty palate, with some cherry notes on the finish. **Gorlovka** * (6%)

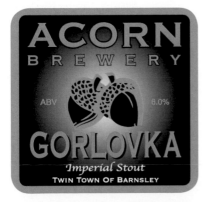

is a leathery scented but light textured Imperial stout with a wallop of hops and roast coffee, named for Barnsley's Ukrainian twin town. **Old Moor** (4.4%) is a charred, creamy porter with raspberry and chocolate notes.

Availability. Pubs with a good changing cask ale list. Try the Dog & Bell (p179).

ADNAMS
Independent
Southwold, Suffolk
183km/114 miles from Central London
⊕ www.adnams.co.uk

In a pretty seaside town, this is one of the most respected of family-owned regional breweries. With brewing on the site since the 14th century, the present company dates from 1857 but now takes a very modern approach to reducing its carbon footprint.

Bitter ** (3.7%) is a beautifully balanced nutty, tart beer with a salty tang. Strong bitter **Broadside** * (4.8%/6.3%) is chewy and nutty with a marmalade note in cask; bottled, it's richer but sadly pasteurised. **East Green** (4.3%) claims to be the UK's first carbon neutral beer: it's blond and sweetish with citric hops. Golden ale **Explorer** * (4.3%) is dry and spicy with grapefruity US hops. Seasonal **Old Ale** * (4.1%) is deep red with a gently liquoricey sweetish palate and a lightly tangy, spicy finish. There are numerous other seasonals and specials; bottled versions are not bottle conditioned.

Availability. The Bridge House (p54) and in many other pubs among both regulars and guest beers.

ALVINNE
Microbrewery
Heule, West Flanders, Belgium
292km/181 miles from Central London
⊕ www.alvinne.be

Established in 2004, this is one of the most experimental and least traditional of small Belgian micros with all sorts of fun small runs and collaborations with other breweries.

Extra Restyled * (7.1%) is the flagship grapefruity, resinous and peppery blond ale with American hops. Also dry but rich, blackcurranty and woody is a big dark ale, **Mano Negra** * ▯ (10%). **Naked Ladies** * ▯ (4.4%) is a yeasty, fruity and herby-hoppy version of the beer of the same name developed at Twickenham brewery (see p283). **Podge** ** ▯ (10.5%), inspired by a British-based beer writer and tour organiser, is a very complex imperial stout with astringently bitter roasty flavours over kiwi fruit and brown sugar. There are also various oak aged versions.

Availability. Specialist pubs and shops; normally stocked at the Rake (p60) and Utobeer (p62) and at CAMRA festivals.

ANCHOR
Independent
San Francisco, California, USA
8,641km/5,369 miles from Central London
🌐 www.anchorbrewing.com

The USA's most important heritage brewery, by 1969 it was barely surviving as the last brewer of 'steam beer' using lager yeast at ale temperatures when businessman and beer lover Fritz Maytag bought and revived it, helping lay the foundations for the American craft brewing revival.

Liberty Ale * ▯ (5.9%) is an amber malty pale with a piney hop note. **Old Foghorn** ** ▯ (8.8%) is a rich, fruity and spirity barley wine. **Porter** ** ▯ (5.6%) has blackcurrant, malted milk and charcoal notes. **Steam** ** ▯ (5%) is a hazy, bready and toffeeish classic with a steely hop finish.

Anchor Liberty Ale

Availability. Steam and Liberty are on the bottled lists of several pubs listed here, though the others are rarer. Try one of the Draft Houses (p55, 196 and 197) or look in shops.

ASCOT
LOCALE
Microbrewery
Camberley, Surrey
54km/34 miles from Central London
🌐 www.ascot-ales.co.uk

This small brewery was taken over and expanded soon after it opened in 2007 and has since been producing some interesting cask and bottle conditioned specialities alongside a solid range of session beers.

Alley Cat ▯ (3.8%) is the dryish citrus-tinged ordinary bitter. **Alligator** * ▯ (4.6%) is a US-hop tinged golden ale. **Anastasia's Exile** ▯ (5%) is a burnt coffee and roast malt stout also available in a bottle conditioned **Imperial** version ▯ (8%) that's rich, plummy and herby but probably needs age for the flavours to settle. Chocolatey, fruity mild **On The Rails** ▯ (3.8%) turns bitterish in the finish. **Posh Pooch** * ▯ (4.2%) is a lightly smoky and chewy best bitter. All also available ▯.

Availability. A regular guest in a number of pubs that support the LocAle scheme, and brews a special beer for the Trafalgar (p215).

BANKS & TAYLOR
Microbrewery
Shefford, Bedfordshire
76km/47 miles from Central London
🌐 www.banksandtaylor.com

One of the first wave of new British microbreweries, founded in 1981, B&T is a reliable source of beers in a wide range of styles.

Black Dragon Mild * ▯ (4.3%) is a fine example of a stronger mild with blackcurrant and liquorice and a smoky, herby note. **Edwin Taylor's Extra Stout** * ▯ (4.5%) is a complex, very malty beer with leathery esters and a refreshingly fruity finish. **Shefford Bitter** ▯ (3.8%) is the pale brown, lightly hoppy and slightly bready session bitter. **SOS** (Shefford Old Strong) ▯ (5%) is a firm, smooth, citric and quite hoppy strong amber ale.

Availability. Often on Wetherspoon guest lists and in several other pubs offering unusual guests. Look for the mild in May.

BASS
See Marston's

BATEMANS
Independent
Wainfleet, Skegness, Lincolnshire
218km/135 miles from Central London
⊕ www.bateman.co.uk

Started in 1874 and almost taken over and closed in the 1980s but saved following a vigorous campaign supported by CAMRA, the brewery is still in the hands of the founding family and lives up to its strapline 'Good honest ales'. Named Regional Brewer of the Year by the *Publican* magazine in 2010.

DM (Dark Mild) * ☰ (3%) is an award winning though slightly dry example of the style, slightly savoury with toffee and vanilla notes. **Salem Porter** * ☰ (4.2%) has rich coffee, chocolate and blackcurrant flavours and a spicy edge. The season bitter **XB** * ☰ (3.7%) is a refined, nutty, russety and also rather bitter mid-amber beer. Deep brown **XXXB** ☰ (5%) is a well-regarded richly fruity and nutty strong bitter. Look out too for some tasty seasonals including lusciously nutty, fruity, date-tinged winter ale **Rosey Nosey** * ☰ (4.9%). There are numerous bottled specialities but none is bottle conditioned.

Availability. A popular brewer on standard guest lists from pubcos, notably Wetherspoon.

BLACK SHEEP
Microbrewery
Masham, North Yorkshire
373km/232 miles from Central London
⊕ www.blacksheep.co.uk

Founded in 1992 by a member of the Theakston family (see Theakston below) to brew good Yorkshire ale in traditional square fermenters.

The **Best Bitter** * ☰ (3.8%) is pale gold and beautifully balanced with notes of peach, blackberry, ginger and honey. Amber **Black Sheep Ale** ☰ (4.4%) is richer and a little astringent, with autumn fruit. **Riggwelter** * ☰ (5.9%) is a tangy darker beer with gum-tingling fruity notes, named after a dialect word for a sheep that can't get up. Bottled versions of the cask beers are regularly seen in supermarkets but are not bottled conditioned.

Availability. Often in pubs that prefer tried and trusted names.

BOON
Part-subsidiary (Palm)
Lembeek, Flemish Brabant, Belgium
371km/231 miles from Central London
⊕ www.boon.be

In the late 1970s Frank Boon became the first person in decades to start a new brewery specialising in spontaneously fermented lambic beers at a time this ancient style seemed in terminal decline. He's since become one of the most successful ambassadors for real lambics, with good distribution through a partnership with Belgian national brewer Palm.

The standard **Kriek Boon** ⬙ (4%) and **Framboise Boon** ⬙ (6%) are sweetened lambics in cherry and raspberry flavours respectively but with natural fruit flavours and genuine sour character. **Oude Geuze** * ⬙ (6.5%) is a proper musty, creamy, lemony, scrumpy-tinged unsweetened gueuze, though milder than some examples. The special reserve **Oude Geuze Mariage Parfait** ** ⬙ (8%) is astonishingly complex, with lemon, clove, kumquat and pear flavours and a long finish. Unsweetened **Oude Kriek** ** ⬙ (6.5%) is deliciously tart with natural cherries and a nutty bite. **Duivels Bier** * ⬙ (8%) is not a lambic but a spicy, winy brown ale with a chocolate orange finish.

Availability. The sweetened fruit lambics are on several bottled beer lists. A fuller range is in shops, specialist and Belgian-themed places, such as the Dove (p126).

BOSTEELS
Independent
Buggenhout, East Flanders, Belgium
360km/224 miles from Central London
⊕ www.bestbelgianspecialbeers.be

Operating from a listed brewhouse in a rural village and still in the hands of the family who founded it in 1791, Bosteels was a successful pils brewer but has made its name internationally with speciality ales.

Deus * ▮ (11.5%) is a cheerful, bready pear-tinged 'champagne beer' at a premium price. **Pauwel Kwak** ◖▤ (8%) is a sweetish amber ale with cherry and cough candy notes, best known for its distinctive stirrup glass. **Tripel Karmaliet** * ▮ (8%), made from four different grains, is a chewy, oily blond beer with spiced orange.

Availability. Several pubs with a specialist Belgian list stock these – try the White Horse (p225).

BRAINS
Independent
Cardiff, Wales
243km/151 miles from Central London
⊕ www.sabrain.co.uk

One of the last remaining historic breweries in Wales, now on a site by Cardiff city centre where Bass once brewed. Also brews the Flowers brands on behalf of AB InBev.

Dark * ▤ (3.5%) is the brewery's malty, sharpish, lightly perfumed mild. **Reverend James** ▤ (4.5%), named after the founder of

Brains Dark

the Buckleys brewery which Brains absorbed, is a cakey, biscuity beer with an orangey finish. **SA** * ▤ (4.2%) is a classic nutty and marmaladey amber bitter, while **SA Gold** ▤ (4.7%) is its apple pie and ice cream-tinged blonde sister. **Flowers IPA** ▤ (3.6%) is a fruity, creamy amber beer with a very light hoppy and cindery finish. Numerous specials and seasonals are also brewed; bottled versions, often spotted in supermarkets, are not bottle conditioned.

Availability. Often on pubco guest ale lists and regularly seen in Wetherspoons.

BRAKSPEAR
See Wychwood

BRENTWOOD
Microbrewery
South Weald, Brentwood, Essex
40km/25 miles from Central London
⊕ www.brentwoodbrewing.co.uk

Not far beyond London's eastern edge, this brewery soon began to win festival awards and expanded rapidly after it was founded in 2006.

Gold ▤ (4.3%) is lightly malty with a citric bite. **Hope and Glory** ▤ (4.5%) is a fruity, caramelly full-bodied best bitter. **Marvellous Maple Mild** * ▤ (3.7%) is a tasty dark brown ale with a hint of maple syrup. **Spooky Moon** ▤ (3.8%) is a fruity golden session bitter with earthy hops. Specially brewed for Wetherspoon is characterful strong bitter **Jolly Decent Wallop** ▤ (5.2%). Most beers are also available ▮.

Availability. Well supported by Wetherspoon, particularly its East London pubs – try the Drum (p129) or the Walnut Tree (p133).

BREW WHARF
See London breweries (p266)

BREWDOG
Microbrewery
Fraserburgh, Aberdeenshire, Scotland
945km/587 miles from Central London
⊕ www.brewdog.com

Founded in 2007 by James Watt and former Thornbridge brewer Martin Dickie, and borrowing the challenging, iconoclastic approach of some Californian breweries, BrewDog has been rattling cages ever since. It's made headlines by achieving soaringly high strengths with the help of freezing techniques – the most outrageous example so far has been the 55% ABV End of History, of which only 12 bottles were made, packaged inside stuffed stoats and squirrels. But don't let all the shenanigans distract you from some decent beer at the more accessible end of the spectrum.

5a.m. Saint * ⊟ ◻ (5%) is a sweetish, chewy amber ale. **77 Lager** ⊟ ⊟ ◻ (4.9%) is a craft-brewed pils with the citric twist of US hops. 'Imperial' **Hardcore IPA** ⊟ ⊟ ◻ (9.2%) is a big hoppy beer which isn't quite as cohesive as the best of its American models. **Paradox** ** ◻ (10%) is a series of imperial stouts aged in various whisky casks, often outstandingly complex beers. **Tokyo** * * ◻ (18.2%) is a rich, viscous, complex oak aged stout with cranberry and jasmine. Golden **Punk IPA** ⊟ ⊟ ◻ (5.6%) is dominated by grapefruity hops. **Trashy Blonde** * ⊟ ⊟ ◻ (4.1%) is the signature copper-gold ale with barley sugar, flowery grapefruit notes and a fruity and peppery finish. Also sought after is the limited edition **Abstrakt** * series ◧, every one different but all generally strong and unusually flavoured.

Availability. Recently opened specialist beer houses are invariably huge fans of BrewDog beers – try the Dean Swift (p54) or Cask (p115). Utobeer (p62) has a range of bottles.

BRODIE'S
See London breweries (p267)

BROOKLYN
Microbrewery
Brooklyn, New York, USA
5,586km/3,471 miles from Central London
⊕ www.brooklynbrewery.com

After over a decade of contract brewing, in 1996 this became the first new brewery in Brooklyn since Prohibition. Globetrotting head brewer Garrett Oliver has helped make it one of the most successful new generation breweries in the US and one of the most highly regarded internationally.

Brooklyn Larger

The rich chocolate, espresso coffee and red fruit flavours of **Black Chocolate Stout** ** ◻ (10.6%) make it a masterpiece. **Brooklyn Lager** ** ⊟ ◻ (5.2%) is a full-flavoured reddish Vienna-style lager recalling pre-Prohibition beers, with hopsack and liquorice notes. **East India Pale Ale** * ◻ (6.8%) has firm but not overwhelming hops with raspberry and meaty notes. **Local 1** * ◧ (9%) is an unusual Belgian-style amber ale with complex herbal and bitter orange flavours.

Availability. The lager is often found in keg in M&B Castle pubs – try the Lyttleton Arms (p142). Bottles are regulars on specialist beer lists including the Ink Rooms (p199).

BUDĚJOVICKÝ (BUDWEISER) BUDVAR
Subsidiary (Czech government)
České Budějovice, Czech Republic
1,369km/851 miles from Central London
⊕ www.budejovickybudvar.cz

Still state owned but under long term threat of privatisation, Budvar is easily the best of the big Czech breweries surviving from before the 1989 'Velvet Revolution'. Its more familiar English name is derived from the German name of its home town, Budweis, but it's been pursued through the international courts for trademark infringement by St Louis megabrewer Anheuser-Busch (now part of AB InBev), and is known as Czechvar in the US and some other territories.

The long-lagered premium golden **Budweiser Budvar** ** ⊟ ◻ (5%, designated *světlý ležák* at home) is crisp but firm, with a good hop character, juicy malt and subtle citric fruit. **Dark** * ⊟ ◻ (4.7%, *tmavý ležák*) is a beautifully drinkable dark lager with mild caramel and chocolate flavours. Some London bars have special taps dispensing a blend of the two called **Half and Half** ⊟ (4.9%) but I'm unconvinced that this is at least equal to the sum of its parts. A hazy, polleny and delicious unpasteurised and unfiltered version of the golden lager, designated **Kroužkovaný ležák** ** ⊟ (5%) is sometimes spotted at beer festivals.

Availability. Budvar is now common in London but the best draught I've tasted is at the Czechoslovak National House (p148). The Half & Half (p177) claims to have originated the blended version.

BUTCOMBE
Microbrewery
Wrington, Somerset
209km/130 miles from Central London
⊕ www.butcombe.com

Caledonian 80/-

One of the UK's oldest established new wave micros, originally set up by an ex-Courage executive in 1978.

The brewery spent its first 18 years perfecting only one beer, **Bitter** ** ⬤ (4%), a superbly balanced flowery, ripely fruity chaffy and resinous example of its style. **Gold** ⬤ (4.7%) is malty and fruity but easy drinking. Bottled versions are filtered.

Availability. A regular at the Doric Arch (p48) and often on the guest list of more discerning pubs.

CALEDONIAN
Subsidary (Heineken)
Edinburgh, Scotland
655km/407 miles from Central London
⊕ www.caledonian-brewery.co.uk

This brewery on the edge of Edinburgh city centre has a fascinating history. Opened in 1869 as Lorimer & Clarke, it spent much of the 20th century in the hands of now closed Sunderland independent Vaux brewing 'Scotch' ales for export to northeast England. Following a management buyout that saved it from closure in 1987 it became one of the most successful craft brewers in Britain. Through a complicated process it's ended up in the hands of multinational Heineken but continues for the moment to produce its established brands by traditional methods.

The brewery's top seller **Deuchars IPA** * ⬤ (3.8%), as drunk by Ian Rankin's Inspector Rebus, is still a fine, delicate, complex and melony-fruity light golden ale when on top form. Less commonly seen in London is **80/-** * ⬤ (4.1%), a fine example of a malty-fruity Scottish amber ale. The bottled versions are filtered.

Availability. Permanently on at the Brewery Tap (p212) and frequently on guest lists elsewhere, including in Wetherspoon pubs.

CAMDEN TOWN
See London breweries (p268)

CANTILLON
Independent
Brussels, Belgium
368km/229 miles from Central London
⊕ www.cantillon.be

The most uncompromising of the authentic lambic brewers and the only one within Brussels itself, also open as a brewery museum.

Gueuze 100% Lambic ** ⬤ (5%) is arguably the benchmark of the style though an acquired taste, bone dry, sour and lemony with a hint of forgiving fruit. **Kriek 100% Lambic** ** ⬤ (5%) is also dry with cherry oil, minerals and lanolin-like flavours. **Rosé de Gambrinus** ** ⬤ (5%), flavoured with raspberries, is a delightfully lively, fruity and slightly petrolly beer. Look out too for excellent grape (**St Lamvinus** *, **Vigneronne** *) and apricot (**Fou'foune** *) flavoured lambics, the **Lou Pepe** ** series of mellower beers, and unusual **Iris** **, made using lambic methods but with 100% barley malt and no wheat – all ⬤.

Availability. At Belgian and other specialists, for example the Euston Tap (p49).

CHIMAY
Trappist
Forges-les-Chimay, Hainaut, Belgium
432km/268 miles from Central London
⊕ www.chimay.be

The longest standing, best known and best-distributed of the current brewing Trappist abbeys, with a working brewhouse since 1862, and the first to commercialise its beers in the postwar period. Recently changes in brewing methods have led to criticism that the beers have lost some of their previous complexity.

Note the beers are know by different names in 330ml and 750ml bottles – two of them are known only by their label colour in 330ml sizes. The names of thr smaller bottles are given first. **Rouge** (Red) / **Première** ⬥ (7%) is a plummy, slightly sweet brown beer. **Triple / Cinq Cents** * ⬥☷ (8%) is an aromatic and liqueurish deep golden ale that works well on draught. Big, cakey and rummy dark brown **Bleue / Grande Réserve** * ⬥ (9%) has raspberry hints and gains complexity as it ages, particularly in big bottles.

Availability. Pubs with a few specialist bottles in the fridge often stock Chimay beers: try the Crown & Greyhound (p172). The Dovetail (p69) has the triple on draught.

COOPERS
Independent
Regency Park, South Australia, Australia
16,260km/10,103 miles from Central London
⬕ www.coopers.com.au

Founded by a Yorkshireman in 1862, this is a remarkable survivor with now-unique brewing techniques that have found a new lease of life on the contemporary scene.

Best Extra Stout ** ⬥ (6.8%) is smooth, fruity and chocolatey, with a dry spicy coffee finish. **Sparkling Ale** ** ⬥ (5.8%) is a cloudy pale beer that's the only remaining example of its style, fresh, fruity and bready with a leafy hop finish.

Availability. Often on speciality bottled lists, for example at the Roundhouse (p202).

COTTAGE
Microbrewery
Lovington, Castle Cary, Somerset
195km/121 miles from Central London
⬕ www.cottagebrewing.co.uk

Started in a garden shed but now one of the most successful southwest England micros, Cottage frequently names its beers using railway themes.

Champflower * ☷ (4.2%) is a mid-brown bitter with a meaty, malty, slightly figgy palate. **Norman's Conquest** ** ☷ (7%) is the brewery's breakthrough beer, a winey dark chestnut old ale rich in dried fruit and chocolate flavours;

the bottled version is now filtered. **Southern** ☷ (3.7%) is the regular bitter, deep golden and nicely hoppy with peach fruit and oily herbs. There are regular specials and seasonals.

Availability. A regular guest brewer for Wetherspoon – try the Crosse Keys (p66).

COURAGE
See Wells & Young's

CROPTON
Microbrewery
Cropton, Pickering, North Yorkshire
405km/252 miles from Central London
⬕ www.croptonbrewery.com

This highly reputed brewery on the edge of the North York Moors began as a brewpub.

Balmy Mild * ☷ (4.4%) is a smoky interpretation with toffee and milky notes. **Monkman's Slaughter** * ☷ (6%) is a big chocolate and caramel strong bitter. Golden bitter **Two Pints** * ☷ (4%) has tart apple and blackberry, good malt and a subtly roasty, mildly bitter finish. Look out too for the seasonal US-inspired beers developed by guest brewer Mike Hall from Michigan. Most of the regular beers are also available ⬥.

Availability. Often on guest lists and the US-style beers may be available in M&B pubs. Try the Princess of Wales (p167).

**Coopers
Sparkling Ale**

CROUCH VALE

Microbrewery
South Woodham Ferrers, Chelmsford, Essex
67km/42 miles from Central London
⬕ www.crouch-vale.co.uk

Founded in 1981 and since developed into one of the biggest craft brewers in its region, Crouch Vale also distributes other brewers' beers.

Rich golden **Amarillo** * ☷ (5%) has apricot and passion fruit hop flavours. **Blackwater** ☷ (3.7%) is a liquoricey, quite austere mild. Award winning, very refreshing and deservedly popular **Brewers Gold** ** ☷ (4%) has flowery, grapey flavours and a lightly resinous finish. **Essex Boys Bitter** * ☷ (3.5%) is a great example of a low gravity ale with smooth malt, tart fruit and sacky hops. The bottled beers are filtered.

Availability. Brewers Gold is widely available, often as a regular, for example at the Pride of Spitalfields (p44). The others appear as guests.

DARK STAR
Microbrewery
Partridge Green, Horsham, West Sussex
74km/46 miles from Central London
🌐 www.darkstarbrewing.co.uk

A brewery with London roots – the original Dark Star beer was developed at the pioneering Pitfield brewery (below), winning Champion Beer of Britain in 1987. In 1994 the name and the beer migrated to 'London-on-Sea', when the Dark Star brewery set up in the cellar of the Evening Star pub in Brighton. Now in a sizeable freestanding plant near Horsham, it's highly respected for its distinctive and flavoursome beers.

American Pale ** 🍺 (4.7%) is an excellent British version of a typical grapefruity, piny but nicely fruity and malty US pale. Made with real coffee beans, **Espresso** * 🍺🍶 (4.2%) has puddingy dark malt and a well-balanced mocha note. An homage to the old King & Barnes Festive, **Festival** * 🍺 (5%) is a classically fruity-malty brown bitter with blackberry and apple pie notes. **Hophead** * 🍺 (3.8%) is a refreshing, gently fruity golden ale with muscat and grapefruit character. **Imperial Stout** * 🍶 (10.5%) has a raisiny, petrolly aroma, winy blackcurrant fruit and a mature Camembert hint in the finish. **Original** * 🍺 (5%) is the current version of the beer that started it all, rich but austere with stoutish roasty malt and dry chocolate. **Partridge** 🍺 (4%) is a more traditional best bitter with gritty but gentle hop notes. There are regular seasonals and monthly specials.

Availability. A regular supplier of house casks to the new breed of London beer bar, for example the Jolly Butchers (p158), and in many other places too.

DOGFISH HEAD
Microbrewery
Milton, Delaware, USA
5,794km/3,600 miles from Central London
🌐 www.dogfish.com

Originally a brewpub founded by legendary US beer guru, brewer and beer writer Sam Calagione, Dogfish Head had to get local licensing laws changed in order to expand. It's since made the best of it by becoming a leading brewer of 'extreme' beers.

60 minute IPA * 🍶 (6%) has 60 hop additions over a 60 minute boil but isn't excessively bitter, with pine and citrus flavours. **90 minute Imperial IPA** ** 🍶 (9%) is inevitably hoppier still but very well balanced with flowery and marmalade tones. **Palo Santo Marron** * 🍶 (12%) is an unusual wood aged beer with rich sherry, tobacco and wood flavours.

Availability. One for the specialists, like Draft House Tower Bridge (p55) or Kris Wines (p155).

DOWNTON
Microbrewery
Downton, Salisbury, Wiltshire
145km/90 miles from Central London
🌐 www.downtonbrewery.com

This small outfit has links to the better known Hop Back brewery (below), also in Downton, but produces distinctive beer in its own right under the Chimera brand.

Dark Delight * 🍺🍶 is chestnut with a moist fruit cake body and a leafy finish. **IPA** * 🍺🍶 (6.8%/7%) turns rapidly hoppy with a peppery, twiggy finish. Golden bitter **Quadhop** * 🍺 (3.9%) is distinctively fruity with an aromatic but not too bitter hoppy note. There's an elderflower-slanted version called **Elderquad** 🍺 (3.9%).

Availability. A regular guest beer supplier to discerning cask pubs: try the Charles Dickens (p111). Bottles can be found at RealAle.com (p233).

Downton IPA

DUVEL-MOORTGAT
New National
Breendonk, Puurs, Antwerp, Belgium
368km/229 miles from Central London
⊕ www.duvel.be

Originally simply Moortgat after the owning family, the brewery has long been synonymous with classic strong golden ale Duvel. In recent years it's expanded by acquiring several other famous specialist brands – Achouffe, Liefmans, De Koninck and a share in Czech brewer Bernard – and has so far proved a trustworthy custodian of their heritage.

Flagship red-labelled golden **Duvel** ** 🍶 (8.5%), named with the local dialect word for 'devil', is complex but perilously drinkable, with lemon sherbert, pear and pistachio; the **Groen** (green) version 🍶🍶 is filtered. The **Maredsous** abbey beers 🍶🍶 are all good examples of their type: grainy **Blond** * (6%), very traditional caramel-coffeeish **Brune** * (8%) and dark golden **Triple** (10%) with banana notes. Premium pils **Vedett** 🍶🍶 (5.2%) is honeyed, resiny and slightly chalky. **Vedett Extra White** * 🍶🍶 (4.7%) is a decent spiced wheat beer with a clean lemon squash note.

Availability. Duvel and one or both of the Vedett beers are stocked by numerous pubs in this guide, but for the full range visit Duvel-Moortgat's own Bar Music Hall (p100).

ERDINGER
Independent
Erding, Bavaria, Germany
1,172km/728 miles from Central London
⊕ www.erdinger.de

Not far from Munich airport, Erdinger is now the biggest specialist wheat beer brewery in the world with an annual output of over 1.45million hl, but is still in independent family hands.

The standard cloudy pale **Weißbier** 🍶🍶 is enjoyable but not especially characterful, with stewed apple and vanilla notes. Dark **Weißbier Dunkel** 🍶🍶 has banana toffee and Dr Pepper

hints. Look out for **Pikantus** * 🍶 (7.3%), a dark Bock with rich tobacco and malt loaf flavours and a nutty, tangy finish.

Availability. The most widely available Bavarian wheat beer in London, though you'll need a specialist bottle shop for the better brands.

FLORENCE
See London breweries (p270)

FLOWERS
See Brains

FLYING DOG
Microbrewery
Frederick, Maryland, USA
5,886km/3,657 miles from Central London
⊕ www.flyingdogales.com

With its distinctive Ralph Steadman-designed labels, this is one of the most successful and widely exported of new US breweries. It started as brewpub in Aspen, Colorado, in 1990 but has since relocated to a large plant in Maryland.

Doggie Style 🍶 (4.7%) is a slightly syrupy pale ale with a smoky note and a dry finish. Imperial porter **Gonzo** * 🍶 (9.5%) shouts with malty and rooty flavours, with a burnt raisin and greasy chocolate finish. **In-Heat Wheat** * 🍶 (4.7%) is big and custardy with citrus and banana notes. 'Belgian IPA' **Raging Bitch** * 🍶 (8.3%) is an interesting spiced orange beer with notes of blue cheese. **Snake Dog** 🍶 (5.8%) is the regular IPA, syrupy with a piney, citric finish.

Availability. Most outlets with an American selection stock this: try Project Orange (p202).

FRANZISKANER
See Spaten-Löwenbräu

FREEDOM
Microbrewery
Abbots Bromley, Rugeley, Staffordshire
226km/140 miles from Central London
⊕ www.freedombeer.com

Another brewery with London roots, Freedom started in Fulham in 1995 as Britain's first new craft brewery specialising in German-style beers made in compliance with the historic Bavarian *Reinheitsgebot* (purity law). One of its co-founders was Alastair Hook, who went on to bigger things with Meantime. At one point it owned two stylish brewpubs in the West End, but London operations ceased in 2005 when it was bought out by Staffordshire-based Brothers Brewery. It's continued to brew quality lagers which are now once more being marketed under the Freedom name.

Organic English Lager 🍺 🍶 (4.8%) is a Helles style, crisply malty with slightly soapy hops. **Pilsner** * 🍺 🍶 (5%) is full flavoured with grassy hops and a sweet cereal base. There's also an **Organic Dark Lager**.

Availability. Discerning pubs like the Bree Louise (p47) have this as an alternative to industrial fizz for lager drinkers. Also at organic pub the Duke of Cambridge (p87).

FRÜH
Independent
Cologne, North Rhine-Westphalia, Germany
587km/365 miles from Central London
🌐 www.frueh.de

Although only dating from 1904, this is one of the best known of the historic brewpubs in Cologne serving regional speciality Kölsch. It now brews at a modern out-of-town site.

Delicate golden **Kölsch** ** 🍺 🍶 (4.8%) has sherbert and bubblegum aromas, a juicy but crisp palate and a lightly nutty finish.

Availability. Although a feature on several more considered specialist beer lists, most likely to be found in German-themed places like Katzenjammers (p58).

FULLER'S
See London breweries (p270)

GOOSE ISLAND
Subsidiary (AB InBev)
Chicago, Illinois, USA
6,377km/3,963 miles from Central London
🌐 www.gooseisland.com

Started in 1988 as a brewpub, Goose Island has developed into one of the US's most respected brewers and branched into barrel aged and Belgian-inspired specialities. In March 2011 it

announced it was financing expansion through a partnership with AB InBev, raising concerns for quality and character in future.

Barack Obama's favourite beer, ultra-pale **312 Urban Wheat** 🍶 (5.1%) is tangy and refreshing with beeswax notes. One of the first successful wood aged beers in the US, **Bourbon County** ** 🍶 (13%) is an immense imperial stout with Belgian chocolate and heady whisky flavours, available in numerous limited edition variants. **Honkers** * 🍶 (5%) is a nutty amber bitter with a syrupy edge and burry hops. **IPA** ** 🍶 (5.9%) is resinously bitter but well balanced with a flowery note. Some beers occasionally 🍺 at specialist outlets.

Availability. Places with a discerning American list, such as the Old Brewery (p180).

GREAT DIVIDE
Microbrewery
Denver, Colorado, USA
7,564km/4,700 miles from Central London
🌐 www.greatdivide.com

Founded by a former homebrewer, whose 'extreme beers' are increasingly widely available in the UK.

Titan IPA * 🍶 (6.8%) has an immense tomato, fruit salad and pepper hop presence. **Hercules Double IPA** * 🍶 (10%) has even more hops but better offset by sweetness and alcohol. **Yeti** ** 🍶 (9.5%) is a big imperial stout with chocolate, raisin and pine flavours, even more complex in its various oak aged versions. Some beers 🍺 in specialist outlets.

Availability. Popular among American specialists – check the White Horse (p225) or the Euston Tap (p49).

GREENE KING
New National
Bury St Edmunds, Suffolk
129km/80 miles from Central London
⊕ www.greeneking.co.uk

Greene King traces its history back to 1799 and was once a real ale icon. It emerged from the takeover wars of the 1990s a claimant to the title of Britain's biggest non-multinational brewery. It's earned the ire of beer campaigners for ruthlessly buying up and closing other independents, swelling its pub estate and cherry picking top brands to recreate, sometimes rather approximately, at its Bury St Edmunds base. Hardys and Hansons, Morland, Ridleys, Ruddles and Tolly Cobbold are all now brewed at Bury, and only its Scottish subsidiary Belhaven has its own production facilities. But the company retains a commitment to cask ale and continues to brew some curious historic specialities.

The once-revered **Abbot Ale** ⬛ (5%) has dried peel and dark cake flavours. **Abbot Reserve** * ⬛ (also occasional ⬛, 6.5%) is a big grainy bitterish beer with sage and stewed fruit notes. At its best **Greene King IPA** ⬛ (3.6%) is a pleasantly fruity and nutty amber session beer but nothing like what contemporary craft beer aficionados expect from the initials IPA. Rarely seen **XX Mild** * ⬛ (3%) has a raisin and plum palate and dark malt dryness. The brewery also makes an old fashioned stock ale, Old 5X, matured in oak casks, which is only released in blended form, most notably in **Strong**

Green King Strong Suffolk

Suffolk ** ⬛ (6%): plummy, vinous and lightly sour with a charred oak and walnut character. **London's Glory**, despite its name, is brewed at Bury for GK's London pubs; all the bottled beers are filtered but unpasteurised.

Availability. The George (p56) carries a range of the brewery's beers, while Abbot and IPA are fixtures in most Wetherspoons. Strong Suffolk is often found on supermarket shelves.

HALL & WOODHOUSE
Independent
Blandford Forum, Dorset
183km/114 miles from Central London
⊕ www.hall-woodhouse.co.uk

Founded in 1777 and once known for very traditional cask ale, the brewery, also known by its Badger trademerk, surprised everyone with a range of unusually flavoured beers for supermarkets in the 1990s, though are all filtered and pasteurised. Some brands are inherited from King & Barnes of Horsham, bought and closed in 2000.

First Gold * ⬛ (4%) is a best bitter with good hop character. **Fursty Ferret** ⬛ ⬛ (4.2%) is a nutty, figgy well balanced summer seasonal. **K&B Sussex Bitter** ⬛ (3.5%) is a lightly hopped, nutty session bitter with slightly astringent rosehip notes. **Tanglefoot** * ⬛ (4.9%) is the sweetish, melon-tinged signature strong bitter. Best of the flavoured range is probably elderflower-infused **Golden Champion** ⬛ (5%).

Availability. Three of the brewery's small estate of London pubs are listed here: the most visually impressive is probably St Stephen's (p117).

HALVE MAAN (BRUGSE ZOT)
Microbrewery
Bruges, West Flanders, Belgium
287km/178 miles from Central London
⊕ www.halvemaan.be

This historic Bruges brewpub was relaunched in 1981, taken over and closed down by a bigger brewery and then revived again by the same family in 2005. It has since recovered the rights to its old Straffe Hendrik brand as its former parent company went bust. In the meantime it's made a great success of its newer Brugse Zot ('Bruges fool') beers.

Brugse Zot Blond * 🍶🍺 (6%) is a cheerful, creamy dry hopped beer with a lemony twist. The dark **Dubbel** 🍶🍺 (7.5%) is sweetish with dried fruit character.

Availability. Several pubs and bars with a strong Belgian list do this – try the Lowlander (p76).

HA'PENNY
See London breweries (p272)

HARVEYS
Independent
Lewes, East Sussex
83km/52 miles from Central London
🌐 www.harveys.org.uk

This classic tower brewery on the banks of the river Ouse houses one of most respected surviving regional family brewers in Britain.

Light amber strong bitter **Armada** 🍺 (4.5%) is malty with gum-tingling citric hops. **Christmas Ale** * 🍶 (also occasional 🍺 **, 8.1%) is deep ruby, lusciously sweet and winey with mint and mincemeat notes. Based on a 19th century recipe developed in London for export to the Russian court, **Imperial Extra Double Stout** ** 🍶 (9%) is heady with cherry, coffee, chocolate, malted milk and slightly sour flavours, a benchmark of its style. Seasonal light mild **Knots of May** * 🍺 (3%) is delightfully nutty and slightly fruity with a lift of hops. **Sussex Best Bitter** ** 🍺 (4%) is a notably dry, bitterish and puckering copper brown beer with soft nut and spiced orange tones. **Sussex Mild** * 🍺 (3%) has a caramel and liquorice palate with a touch of roast and gentle hops. Other 🍶 specialities such as **1859 Porter** * (4.8%), **Tom Paine Ale** * (5.5%) and **Elizabethan Ale** * (8.1%) are worth trying. There are several additional seasonals.

Availability. Harveys pub the Royal Oak (p61) stocks a wide range of the draught and bottled beers, while Sussex Best is a popular guest elsewhere.

HARVIESTOUN
Microbrewery
Alva, Clackmannanshire, Scotland
691km/429 miles from Central London
🌐 www.harviestoun.com

This micro in the historic Scottish brewing county of Clackmannanshire, specialising in innovative blond and dark beers, has been through several changes since it was founded in 1985. In 2005-06 it was a subsidiary of Caledonian (above) but regained independence when the parent fell to the multinationals

Harvieston Old Engine Oil

Bitter & Twisted * 🍺 (4.2%) is nettly dry and grapefruity but softened by a good malt balance. There's liquorice, chocolate and burnt fruit aplenty in dark ale **Old Engine Oil** * 🍶 (also occasional 🍺, 6%), a strong version of which is matured in former Highland Park whisky casks to produce **Ola Dubh** ** 🍶 ('Black oil', 8%), available in various 'expressions' rich in woody, smoky, spirited flavours. **Ptarmigan** 🍺 (4.5%) is a floral, spicy orange golden ale with a bitter bite. Real pils-style lager **Schiehallion** * 🍺🍺 (4.8%) has plenty of elderflower and citric character. There are numerous seasonals; bottled beers are not bottle conditioned.

Availability. The cask beers are regularly featured in Wetherspoon pubs and others that specialise in a good range of guests. For Ola Dubh you'll have to look in specialist bars and shops.

HEPWORTH
Microbrewery
Horsham, West Sussex
58km/36 miles from Central London
🌐 www.hepworthbrewery.co.uk

Set up by former King & Barnes staff when that brewery closed in 2000 (see Hall & Woodhouse above), this highly competent and professional brewery names many of its own beers with railway themes.

Classic Old Ale * 🍺🍶 (4.8%) is a winter treat, very malty and caramelly with liquorice notes and a sticky, roasty finish. **Prospect** 🍺🍶 (4.5%) is a citric organic golden ale. 'First class' bitter **Pullman** * 🍺🍶 (4.2%) is crisp and similarly citric, with a malty base. **Sussex** 🍺 (3.6%) is a traditional, very biscuity bitter. Most cask beers are also available 🍶. There's much contract brewing for other small breweries and beer firms, particularly of 🍶.

Availability. Often on in pubs with a strong local guest policy.

HOEGAARDEN
Subsidiary (AB InBev)
Hoegaarden, Flemish Brabant, Belgium
417km/259 miles from Central London
⊕ www.hoegaarden.com

The distinctive Brabant style of unpasteurised, unfiltered spiced wheat beer returned from the dead in 1966 when Pierre Cells bought this brewery, closed since the 1950s, recreating a local style he recalled from his childhood when he'd helped out part time. The beer became a national success, and the operation was eventually sold to Interbrew, predecessor of AB InBev, who turned it into an international brand, in the process placing the use of wheat and spicing firmly into the repertoire of the emerging craft brewing culture. A huge fuss ensued when in 2006 InBev closed the brewery, moving brewing to French-speaking Belgium. Their U-turn two years later was, according to the brewer, purely in response to production problems at its new home.

Standard **Hoegaarden** * 🍾🍺 (4.8%) inevitably has less character than it did but is still tasty, wheaty and refreshing. Other products are much less seen in Britain but the spicy orange triple-style **Grand Cru** * 🍾 (8.7%) and the dark, fruity **Verboden Vrucht** 🍾 (Forbidden Fruit, 8.5%) are worth exploring.

Availability. Pretty much every pub with specialist kegs serves draught Hoegaarden and it's available in bottle at most supermarkets. Other products are best sourced in specialist shops.

HOGS BACK
Microbrewery
Tongham, Surrey
61km/38 miles from Central London
⊕ www.hogsback.co.uk

A very reliable micro based on an 18th century farm just below an outlying chalk ridge of the North Downs west of Guildford known as the Hog's Back. A longstanding producer of Real Ale in a Bottle as well as cask though some bottled beers are now filtered.

A over T * 🍾 (9%) is a distinctive marmaladey and spicy brown barley wine. Seasonal **Advent Ale** ** 🍾🍺 (4.4%) is dark ruby with red fruit and sappy, rummy notes. **Brewster's Bundle** * 🍺 (7.4%) has sappy fruit and a rich malty finish. **HBB** 🍾 (3.7%) is a lighter bitter with brambly fruit and a hoppy finish. **TEA** * 🍾 🍷 (Traditional English Ale, 4.2%) is a very likeable nutty, mellow amber bitter with a slightly citric note. **Wobble in a Bottle** ** 🍺 (7.5%, also seasonal as Santa's Wobble) is a lovely mid-brown strong ale with banana, toffee and toasted coconut notes and a rounded finish. There are various other seasonal ales.

Availability. TEA is on regularly in numerous pubs like the Priory Arms (p203); other cask beers turn up as guests while a reliable source of the bottles is RealAle.com (p233).

HOOK NORTON
Independent
Hook Norton, Oxfordshire
130km/81 miles from Central London
⊕ www.hook-norton-brewery.co.uk

This surviving Oxfordshire family brewery still uses a steam engine to help make its well regarded traditional beers.

Double Stout * 🍾 🍺 (4.8%) has smooth chocolate and autumn fruit flavours and a roast burry finish. Standard **Hooky Bitter** * 🍾 (3.6%) is straightforwardly fruity and chewy with delicate hops that turn quite peppery. Stronger **Old Hooky** 🍾 (4.6%) is maltier and slightly sticky with a touch of hops. Most bottles are not bottle conditioned.

Availability. Often among the Wetherspoon and Punch Finest Cask guests.

HOP BACK
Microbrewery
Downton, Salisbury, Wiltshire
145km/90 miles from Central London
⊕ www.hopback.co.uk

Hop Back Summer Lightning was the first example of the new style of British golden ale to seize drinkers' imagination on a significant scale. Launched in 1988, it helped turn the

Southampton brewpub where it was developed into a major player among microbreweries. Expansion to a freestanding brewery was inevitable and several other innovative beers followed.

Crop Circle ☕🍺 (4.2%) is slightly floury with lots of citrus and oddly spicy flavours. **Entire Stout** * ☕🍺 (4.5%) is dark with vine fruits and a sticky, quite roasty finish. **GFB** ☕ (3.5%) is a more conventional golden bitter with clean malt and fruity hops. **Summer Lightning** * ☕🍺 (5%) is a refreshing beer with cracker-like malt and gooseberry and tangerine notes. **Taiphoon** 🍺 (4.2%), designed for drinking with Thai food, is wheaty with lemongrass and vanilla notes.

Hop Back Entire Stout

Availability. The full range is on sale at Hop Back's pub the Sultan (p214) and you'll also find the brewery on numerous guest lists, with bottled beers on supermarket shelves.

HUYGHE
Independent
Melle, East Flanders, Belgium
326km/203 miles from Central London
🌐 www.delirium.be

With a history dating back to 1654, this busy Flemish regional brewery is responsible for several cult specialities as well as various rebadgings and contract brewed brands.

Delirium Tremens * 🍺🖥 (9%) with its distinctive pink elephant branding and porcelain effect bottle is a very weighty and sweetish golden ale with quite a hoppy finish. The numerous **Floris** and **Mongozo** sweetened fruit beers are probably best passed over but I confess a weakness for strawberry wheat beer **Früli** 🍺🖥 (4.1%) which is pleasant and refreshing despite its resemblance to strawberry Starburst sweets.

Availability. Relatively common in pubs with an imported beer list as well as Belgian specialists. Note the sign in the Lowlander (p76): "Real men drink Früli"

INNIS & GUNN
Beer firm
Edinburgh, Scotland
655km/407 miles from Central London
🌐 www.innisandgunn.com

The idea for this enterprise came about when Dougal Sharp, then brewer at Caledonian (above), noticed a beer he'd been asked to brew for seasoning barrels destined for whisky production, never intended for consumption, was being enjoyed by distillery staff. Innis & Gunn followed in 2003 as the UK's first commercially marketed beer matured in oak barrels. It's currently contract brewed by Greene King subsidiary Belhaven at Dunbar, East Lothian.

Regular **Innis & Gunn** * 🖥 (sadly not bottle conditioned, 6.6%) is a sweetish mid-brown beer with elusive oaky tones and a complex fruity and slightly smoky finish. Note this is not a whisky beer like those matured in vessels previously used for whisky: new oak barrels are used. There are various special editions at different strengths, though all tend to be sweet.

Availability. Widely on sale in supermarkets – try Waitrose Canary Wharf (p125). Also sometimes on pub speciality beer lists.

ITCHEN VALLEY
Microbrewery
New Alresford, Hampshire
100km/62 miles from Central London
🌐 www.itchenvalley.com

This Hampshire brewery was established in 1997 by two partners who'd just been godfathers at a christening.

Fagins ☕ (4.1%) is a toasty mid-brown bitter with gooseberry and plum fruit. The brewery's first beer, **Godfathers** * ☕ (3.8%), is a pale amber bitter with peach and pear notes and a whiff of rubber. **Hampshire Rose** ☕ (4.2%) is a pungently hoppy and earthy brew with a clean toffee body. **Pure Gold** * ☕ (4.8%) is a golden ale with Czech hops, attractively dry and pineapply. Most beers also 🍺.

Availability. A favourite among pubs with discerning cask guest lists, like the Edgar Wallace (p82).

KELHAM ISLAND
Microbrewery
Sheffield
270km/168 miles from Central London
⊕ www.kelhambrewery.co.uk

One of the stars of a city that's particularly rich in beer culture, the brewery was founded at the Fat Cat pub on Kelham island in 1990 but later expanded to a freestanding site. Things really took off when its flagship brand Pale Rider won Champion Beer of Britain in 2004.

Pale Rider * ⚏ ▲ (5.2%) is a striking golden beer with pineapple and lychee notes, and a definite note of fruity white wine. Other beers are rarely seen in London but catch them if you can.

Availability. Pale Rider is a regular at the Doric Arch (p48) and Kelham Island beers are often on the Mitchells & Butlers Nicholson's guest roster.

KERNEL
See London breweries (p273)

KING
Microbrewery
Horsham, West Sussex
58km/36 miles from Central London
⊕ www.kingbeer.co.uk

Founded in 2001 by Bill King, the last member of the family to run the historic King & Barnes brewery. Now with a head brewer formerly at Harveys (above), the brewery has a reputation for traditional ales.

Based on the old King & Barnes Sussex Bitter is **Horsham Best** * ⚏ (3.8%), rich amber, full bodied and nicely bitter. **Kings Old Ale** * ⚏ (4.5%) is notably smoky and roasty with complex fruit and molasses notes. The equivalent of the old Festival Ale is **Red River** ⚏ (4.8%), with more caramel malt and cherry notes. Most beers also ▲, various seasonals.

Availability. Often stocked by pubs with a local guest ale policy.

KONINGSHOEVEN (LA TRAPPE)
Trappist
Berkel-Enschot, North Brabant, Netherlands
458km/285 miles from Central London
⊕ www.latrappe.nl

The only working Trappist brewery outside Belgium, though operated by an external company, Bavaria. La Trappe beers are brewed under the supervision of the monks and profits go to the abbey for charitable purposes, so they are entitled to carry the Trappist seal.

The following beers are all branded **La Trappe. Blond** * ▲ (6.5%) is a big spicy blond beer with pineapple and banana notes. The caramelly, figgy dark **Dubbel** * ▲ (6.5%) has a bitterish malt finish. The amber-coloured **Tripel** * ▲ (8%) has rich liqueurish apricot tones and a dry finish. Massive deep ruby red **Quadrupel** ** ▲ (10%) is dense with almond, cherry and wood flavours. Wheat beer **Witte Trappist** ▲ (5.5%) is citric, sweetish and slightly medicinal. They also now produce an organic blond and various wood aged beers, as well as various non-Trappist beers, some under contract.

Availability. This is about the best Dutch beer you'll get in Dutch pub De Hems (p106) and is also on other specialist lists.

LEEDS
Microbrewery
Leeds
315km/196 miles from Central London
⊕ www.leedsbrewery.co.uk

Since opening in 2007 this has been Leeds' only independent brewery. Sadly, with the closure of the historic Tetley plant by owners Carlsberg, it's now the city's only brewery.

Best ⚏ (4.3%) is malt-accented and easy going. Award winning strong mild **Midnight Bell** * ⚏ (4.8%) has treacly, spicy vermouth-like notes, caramel and quite a dry finish. **New Moon** * ⚏ (4.3%) is a dark amber winter bitter with creamy toffee and berry fruit. **Pale** ⚏ (3.8%) is a crisp, citric golden bitter.

Availability. Likely to appear on Wetherspoon and Punch Finest Cask lists and among the guests in discriminating real ale pubs.

LEFT HAND
Microbrewery
Longmont, Colorado, USA
7,511km/4,667 miles from Central London
⊕ www.lefthandbrewing.com

Founded by home brewers in 1994 and named after a well known local Native American chief. Known for unusual flavoured beers.

Big marmitey **Imperial Stout** * 🍺 (10.4%) has ripe fruit, roast and olives – the brewery suggests pouring it over vanilla ice cream. **Juju Ginger** 🍺 (4%) has plenty of earthy natural ginger flavour and a mild malty finish. **Milk Stout** * 🍺 (5.2%) has roast coffee and cola flavours with a milk gum note. **Sawtooth** * 🍺 (5.3%) is a malty, gritty and honeyed take on an ESB style. Some beers occasionally appear 🍺.

Availability. On sale at the Ink Rooms (p199), the White Horse (p225) and many other places with a good American list, and in numerous bottle shops.

LITTLE CREATURES
Microbrewery
Fremantle, Western Australia, Australia
14,480km/8,997 miles from Central London
🌐 www.littlecreatures.com.au

Growing out of a harbourside brewpub opened in 2000, this is now one of the most successful of Australian microbreweries. The name refers both to yeast and to the height of the founders.

The brewery makes several beers but the only one regularly exported is the flagship **Pale Ale** * 🍺 (5.2%), fresh with honeysuckle, fruit salad, rosewater and pine notes.

Availability. In places with cool bottled beer lists like the Roundhouse (p202). Also sometimes seen in supermarkets.

LODDON
Microbrewery
Dunsden, Oxfordshire
63km/39 miles from Central London
🌐 www.loddonbrewery.com

Brewing since 2003 in a barn on a rural estate, the brewery has won numerous awards.

Ferryman's Gold 🍺 (4.4%) is a slightly oily and fruity golden ale. **Forbury Lion IPA** * 🍺 (5.5%) is amber and sweetish with floral hop notes. Standard bitter **Hoppit** 🍺 (3.5%) is easy

drinking with light grassy and floral hops. Brewed under contract for a a Kent wholesaler is **Gravesend Shrimpers Bitter** 🍺 (4.1%), a slightly cakey dark amber beer with a pleasantly bitterish finish. Several seasonals and specials are also brewed.

Availability. Makes regular appearances on guest lists. Try the Barnsbury (p145).

MARBLE
Microbrewery
Manchester
324km/201 miles from Central London
🌐 www.marblebeers.co.uk

Opened at the Marble Arch pub just north of Manchester city centre in 2007, Marble has developed into one of Britain's most innovative and interesting small breweries, and recently expanded to a freestanding site.

Chocolate Marble ** 🍺 🍺 (5.5%) is a lusciously intense deep brown beer with toasty malt and a bitterish finish. Very complex and fruity strong stout **Decadence** ** 🍺 (8.7%) has also been released in special fruited versions. **Ginger** 🍺 (4.5%) is blond with distinct but well integrated crystallised ginger notes. Gold-coloured **Manchester Bitter** * 🍺 (4.2%), inspired by the old Boddingtons Bitter in its prime, has weighty creamy malt, tropical fruit and a rooty finish. **Pint** * 🍺 (3.9%) is a very pale beer with plenty of grapefruit hops. **Stouter Stout** * 🍺 (4.7%) is coffeeish with sharp blackcurrant fruit and a wash of hops.

Availability. One of the cask brewers popular with serious specialist pubs like the Southampton Arms (p157) and also seen in the Magpie & Crown (p233).

MARSTON'S
New national
Burton upon Trent, Staffordshire
203km/126 miles from Central London
🌐 www.marstons.co.uk

This historic Burton brewery is the only one still using the traditional Burton Union system where fermenting beer constantly passes through a row of linked casks. In 1999 it was bought up by regional brewer Wolverhampton & Dudley, brewers of Banks's, to create a new national, though the Marston's name was subsequently adopted for the whole group.

Victorian-style IPA **Old Empire** * 🌡 🍺 (5.7%) has apple and custardy malt notes and a bitterish hoppy finish. **Pedigree** * 🍺 (4.5%) is a heritage Burton pale ale with a sweetish nutty palate, well balanced hops and occasionally a note of sulphur on the aroma. Contract brewed for AB InBev is the once legendary **Draught Bass** 🍺 (4.4%), now a thickish, moderately bitter amber ale with brambly fruit. Sadly the bottled versions of the beers are not bottle conditioned.

Availability. Pedigree is much harder to find in London than it once was but is a regular at the Cockpit (p65). Old Empire is often in Wetherspoon pubs while Bass is usually on at the Pineapple.

MAULDONS
Microbrewery
Sudbury, Suffolk
110km/68 miles from Central London
🌐 www.mauldons.co.uk

Bought and closed by Greene King in 1960, the Mauldon brewery was revived just over 20 years later by a new generation of the Mauldon family. It's since been sold on to new owners but still produces quality traditional beer.

Bitter * 🍺 (3.6%) is a thoroughly decent easy drinking bitterish bitter. Dry stout **Black Adder** * 🍺 (5.3%) has dense roasty malt and plum skins. **Micawbers Mild** 🍺 (3.5%) is fruity with a roast and cinder toffee finish.

Availability. Regularly on guest lists – check the Wheatsheaf (p63).

MCMULLEN
Independent
Hertford, Hertfordshire
42km/26 miles from Central London
🌐 www.mcmullens.co.uk

Established in 1827, this family business is now the oldest established brewery in Hertfordshire

AK ** 🍺 (3.7%) is a historic light bitter,

sometimes classified as a light mild, copper with subtle fruit and delicately honeyed finish. **Cask Ale** 🍺 (3.8%) is fruity with mildly citric hops while **Country Bitter** * 🍺 (4.3%) is juicy with tropical fruit notes and a tangy, slightly walnutty finish. Various specials are microbrewed on site under the name of the Whole Hop Brewery.

Availability. Most likely found in McMullen pubs such as the Spice of Life (p109) or the Wonder (p161).

MEANTIME
See London breweries (p275)

MIGHTY OAK

Microbrewery
Maldon, Essex
71km/44 miles from Central London
🌐 www.mightyoakbrewery.co.uk

When the old Ind Coope brewery in Romford closed, brewer John Boyce used his redundancy money to set up his own brewery, which has since become one of the most successful regional micros.

Burntwood Bitter * 🍺 (4%) is an unusual tasty, sweetish and slightly coffee tinged amber beer. **IPA** (3.5%) is golden, easy going and delicately fruity. Popular **Maldon Gold** 🍺 (3.8%) is clean and biscuity with citrus hops. Regular mild **Oscar Wilde** * 🍺 (3.7%), taking its name from rhyming slang, has liquorice and blackcurrant pastille notes and a well balanced slightly roasty finish. **Simply the Best** 🍺 (4.4%) is a caramelly, fruity bitter with malt emphasis. There are changing monthly specials.

Availability. At pubs with a good real ale selection particularly in east and central London. Try the Nags Head (p131). Leyton Orient Supporters Club (p130) are also keen Mighty Oak supporters.

MIKKELLER
Beer firm
Copenhagen, Denmark
1,252km/778 miles from Central London
🌐 www.mikkeller.dk

Former home brewer Mikkel Borg Bjergsø is now the sort of beer producer who sets the world's beer geeks tweeting with his innovative and iconoclastic beers. Based in Denmark but without his own brewery, he describes himself as a "gypsy brewer" working mainly in Belgium and Norway, and collaborating with others including Scotland's BrewDog.

Beer Geek Breakfast * 🍶 (7.5%) is a big stout flavoured with coffee, and rich in red grape, marmitey malt and black pepper notes. Imperial stout **Black** * 🍶 (17.5%, labelled with the Chinese character 黑) is indeed black, and oily, chocolatey and port-like. **Jackie Brown** ** 🍶 (6%) is a figgy, cherryish and notably hoppy dry brown ale. There are many, many others, often in limited editions.

Availability. Look in specialist outlets like Kris Wines (p155), Cask (p115) or the Euston Tap (p49).

MILTON
Microbrewery
Milton, Cambridge, Cambridgeshire
96km/60 miles from Central London
⊕ www.miltonbrewery.co.uk

Opened in 1999, Milton has since built up a large range of beers, many of them with Classically-themed names, although a more recently recruited brewer from the southern hemisphere has added some named from indigenous Australian culture.

Refreshing straw-coloured bitter **Dionysus** * 🍺 (3.6%) has generous fruit and hop flavours. Roasty and sweetish imperial stout **Marcus Aurelius** * 🍺 (7.5%) is an occasional treat. **Minotaur** 🍺 (3.3%) is an inky, lightly roasty and herby dark mild. **Nero** * 🍺 (5%) is a chewy and cherryish dark brown oatmeal stout. **Sparta** 🍺 (4.3%) is a crisp golden bitter with slight roast notes. **Pegasus** 🍺 (4.1%) is a biscuity and fruity amber bitter. There are many others both permanent and seasonal.

Availability. An extensive selection is available at the Pembury Tavern (p127).

MOLEN
Microbrewery
Bodegraven, South Holland, Netherlands
500km/311 miles from Central London
⊕ www.brouwerijdemolen.nl

Working from a disused windmill between Amsterdam and Rotterdam, Menno Olivier has earned an international reputation for fine and unusual beers including historical recreations.

Amarillo ** 🍶 (9.2%) shows off this distinctive fruity hop in an imperial IPA style. **Amerikaans** * 🍶 (4.5%) is a cheerful, citrusy American-style pale. **Bloed Zweet & Tranen** * 🍶 (Blood Sweat & Tears, 8.1%) is a smooth, sweetish beer made with Bamberg smoked malt. **Borefts Stout** * 🍶 (7.7%) is a vivid, well-balanced beer with creamy chocolate and liquorice. **Engels** 🍺 🍶 (4.5%) is a zesty, piney English-style bitter. Made with brown malts, **Hel & Verdoemnis** * 🍶 (Hell & Damnation, 11.2%) is an imperial stout with subtle fruit and malt loaf flavours. **Hemel & Aarde** ** 🍶 (Heaven & Earth, 9.5%) is an astonishing smoky and chocolatey strong stout made with peated malt intended for Bruichladdich whisky. **Rasputin** ** 🍶 (10.7%) is a rich treacly imperial stout with raspberry fruit. **Tsarina Esra** ** 🍶 (11%) is yet another brilliant imperial stout, rich in plums, toffee, tobacco and vanilla. There are many more including wood aged versions, specials and collaboration brews.

Availability. Look in specialist bottle shops and bars: try the Rake (p60) and Utobeer (p62). Menno can normally be found behind the imported beer bar at the Great British Beer Festival with a cask or two of something special.

MILTON BREWERY
NERO
5.0% ABV

MONCADA
See London breweries (p276)

MOORHOUSE'S
Independent
Burnley, Lancashire
352km/219 miles from Central London
⊕ www.moorhouses.co.uk

Originally brewing non-alcoholic malt drinks, Moorhouse's converted to beer in the late 1970s, with remarkable results. Bottled versions are not bottle conditioned.

Well-loved dark mild **Black Cat** * 🍺 (3.4%) is quite stern, roasty and chewy. **Blond Witch** 🍺 (4.5%) is a refreshing, mildly bitter golden ale. Strong amber ale **Pendle Witches Brew** * 🍺 (5.1%) is toffee-apple sweet with a nicely bitter finish.

Availability. On discerning real ale guest lists, for example at the Old Fountain (p95).

NELSON

Microbrewery
Chatham, Kent
52km/32 miles from Central London
🌐 www.nelsonbrewingcompany.co.uk

Based at Chatham's redeveloped Royal Naval Dockyard, this brewery has been through several management changes, and is now dedicated to working with local ingredients including Kent hops.

Friggin in the Riggin 🍺 (4.7%) has sweet malt, a fruity finish and a silly name. **Powder Monkey** 🍺 (4.4%) is a straightforward golden bitter with a lightly hoppy finish. There are numerous specials often with humorous nautical names, and 🍾 versions of some beers.

Availability. On free house guest lists particularly in southeast London – try Rose's (p190). The bottles are often at Mr Lawrence (p186).

NETHERGATE

Microbrewery
Pentlow, Sudbury, Suffolk
117km/73 miles from Central London
🌐 www.nethergate.co.uk

Founded in 1986, Nethergate is one of its region's most successful micros with a well-deserved reputation for quality and consistency. But it's also been unafraid to experiment, helping to reintroduce porter and spiced beers to British brewing. Its beers are often rebadged as house ales and it also

brews for the revived Truman beer firm (above). Under new ownership in 2010 but for the moment continuing business as usual though there's a chance the range may change.

Nethergate Old Growler

Augustinian ** 🍺 🍾 (4.5%) is a complex, seedy and orangey best bitter. **IPA** 🍺 (3.5%) is a light gold, biscuity and lightly honeyed bitter. One of Britain's first revivalist porters, **Old Growler** * 🍺 (5%) is smoothy malty and fruity with burnt biscuit and onion gravy notes. Deep amber **Priory Mild** * 🍺 (3.5%) is a chaffy, drying beer with a nutty finish. Slightly astringent bitter **Three Point Nine** 🍺 (3.9%) has tangy malt and a soft hoppy note. **Umbel Ale** * 🍺 (3.8%) is a toasty, coriander-infused golden ale with a bitter orange finish. **Umbel Magna** ** 🍺 (5%) is an even richer version with coriander. There are numerous specials and seasonals.

Availability. Widely seen as a guest – try for example the Dispensary (p43).

NØGNE-Ø

Microbrewery
Grimstad, Norway
1,616km/1,004 miles from Central London
🌐 www.nogne-o.com

Subtitled 'the uncompromising brewery', the 'Naked Island' was originally set up by homebrewers and has since built a global reputation for unusual beers. Many of the Mikkeller beers (above) are brewed here.

An interpretation of traditional Finnish spruce flavoured beer, **Dugges Sahti** * 🍾 (11%) is pale amber with intriguing spruce, seaweed and medicinal flavours. **Imperial Stout** ** 🍾 (9%) has a dazzling bouquet of roast malt, fruit and hop tones and a smooth, lasting finish. **IPA** * 🍾 (7.5%) has sweet fruity tones and a lasting bitter finish. The **Porter** * 🍾 (7.5%) is intensely coffee flavoured with sweet herbs on an big roasty finish. There are many more regulars, specials and collaborations including the **Dark Horizon** * series of imperial stouts.

Availability. Regularly found at specialist bars and shops like the Rake (p60) and Utobeer (p62).

OAKHAM

Microbrewery
Woodston, Peterborough
134km/83 miles from Central London
⊕ www.oakham-ales.co.uk

This award-winning brewery has expanded several times since it was founded in Rutland in 1993. It's since moved to become the only brewery in the important city of Peterborough, with an additional brewpub in the city centre.

Best selling golden bitter **JHB** * (3.8%) bursts with lychee and kiwi fruit aromas before an elegant bitterish finish. Also aromatic is stronger golden ale **White Dwarf** * (4.3%) with a lager-like body and a firm grapefruit finish. There are numerous specials and seasonals.

Availability. A regular real ale favourite – try the Barnsbury (p145).

O'HANLON'S

Microbrewery
Whimple, Devon
290km/180 miles from Central London
⊕ www.ohanlonsbeer.com

In 1996 John O'Hanlon decided to enhance the attraction of his O'Hanlon's pub in Clerkenwell with own brewed beer, setting up a brewery in Vauxhall. The beer proved so successful he ended up leaving the pub and continuing as a freestanding brewer in the more rural surrounds of south Devon.

The traditional Irish-style **Dry Stout** * (4.2%) is a fine example with burnt cake and sharpish fruit, while the port-spiked version, **Original Port Stout** ** (4.8%) has yet more complexity with wine, geranium and cedar hints. **Firefly** (3.7%) is an orangey-fruity light bitter. Subtly spiced wheat beer **Goldblade** * (4%) has light vanilla and banana notes. **Red Ale** * (4.5%) is a sappy, cherryish, buttery and very distinctive ruby ale. The brewery is no longer making its revived version of legendarily long-lived barley wine **Thomas Hardy's Ale** ** (11.7%) but you may be lucky enough to encounter previous vintage dated editions.

Availability. The former O'Hanlon's pub is now the Old China Hand (p72) and although no longer linked to the brewery regularly stocks its beers. You'll also find them as guests elsewhere, and good specialist shops stock the bottles.

ORVAL

Trappist
Villers-devant-Orval,
Luxembourg, Belgium
584km/363 miles from Central London
⊕ www.orval.be

This handsome red brick abbey in the picturesque Ardennes has been making one of the most unusual Trappist beers since 1931.

Orval ** (6.2%) is a pale amber, figgy, spicy and slightly sour beer with a firm hop bite that becomes notably more complex with age.

Availability. From Belgian specialists and on discerning bottled beer lists elsewhere, for example at the Carpenters Arms (p102).

OTLEY

Microbrewery
Pontypridd, Wales
255km/158 miles from Central London
⊕ www.otleybrewing.co.uk

Founded in 2005 by a small Welsh pub chain, Otley has rapidly made an impression with a series of innovative and strikingly presented beers.

O1 * (4%) is a golden ale with tannic, thistly notes, American hops and autumn fruit. Strong ale **O8** * (8%) is perilously easy drinking with citric hops and an orange liqueur note. **OG** * (5.4%) is a hoppy but smooth strong golden ale. AB InBev-baiting wheat beer **O-Garden** * (4.8%) is complex with orange peel, vanilla, glucose and a firm hop touch.

Availability. Favoured by specialists like Cask (p115) but increasingly on guest lists including in Mitchells & Butlers Castle pubs.

OTTER

Microbrewery
Luppitt, Honiton, Devon
243km/151 miles from Central London
🌐 www.otterbrewery.com

Run to strict environmental standards by a former Whitbread brewer at a farm in the Blackdown hills, and named for the river that runs nearby.

The **Bitter** * 🍺 (3.6%) is a decent amber brew with a good body and bitterish finish. Mid-brown **Head** * 🍺 (5.8%) is rich with complex fruit and cake tones. **Otter Ale** * 🍺 (4.5%) is darkish with berry fruits. Bottled beers are filtered.

Availability. Increasingly familiar on guest ale lists including in Wetherspoon pubs.

PALMERS

Independent
Bridport, Dorset
227km/141 miles from Central London
🌐 www.palmersbrewery.com

In historic buildings with partially thatched roofs and a water wheel, though thoroughly modern inside, this is a treasured survivor with a history dating to 1794.

200 🍺 (5%) is a strong, caramelly and fruity beer developed to celebrate two centuries of brewing. **Best Bitter** 🍺 (also known as IPA, 4.2%) is a smooth, malty brew lighty balanced with hops. **Tally Ho!** * 🍺 (5.5%) is a rich old ale with coffee and wood notes.

Availability. Supplies the house brew at the Claret (p175) and often guests elsewhere.

PAULANER

Subsidiary (Heineken)
Munich, Bavaria, Germany
1,144km/711 miles from Central London
🌐 www.paulaner.de

Founded by monks back in 1631, Paulaner has long been the biggest of Munich's former famous Big Six breweries, now also owning the Thurn & Taxis and Hacker-Pschorr brands. In 2000 it was bought up itself.

Cloudy orange **Hefe-Weißbier** * 🍺 (5.5%) has a tart marmalade finish but isn't as spicy and complex as some of its fellow wheat beers. **Oktoberfestbier** is made to different recipes under the Paulaner and Hacker-Pschorr names: both are straightforward strongish malty lagers. **Original Münchner Hell** 🍺 (4.9%) is a malty golden beer with apricot and light hop notes. **Salvator** ** 🍺 (7.5%) was the world's first double Bock, an oily deep copper with rich marzipan flavours and warming alcohol.

Availability. The Helles and the wheat beer are increasingly seen on keg in places like the Mitchells & Butlers Castle chain. Bottles are regularly found at specialist bottle shops.

PITFIELD

Microbrewery
North Weald, Epping, Essex
45km/28 miles from Central London
🌐 www.pitfieldbeershop.co.uk

First opened in Hoxton in 1981, Pitfield was London's first significant new microbrewery. It was notably fronted by a pioneering specialist beer and homebrew shop that introduced a generation of London drinkers to the riches of Belgian and German craft brewing as well as hard to find British ales. One of the previous partners went on to found Dark Star (above). Pitfield originated the first successful British organic ale in the 1990s and over the past decade the bulk of its production has been organic. It was also an early champion of bottle conditioning and the revival of historic styles. In 2006 high rents forced the brewery out of London and it has now settled on a farm not far away in Essex, where it grows its own organic barley.

Bitter * 🍺 🍾 (3.7%) is a very biscuity amber beer with apple and blackberry fruit. **East Kent Goldings** * 🍺 🍾 (4.2%) is a single varietal deep golden ale with an earthy but rounded hoppy finish. The brewery's first organic beer, **Eco Warrior** 🍺 🍾 (4.5%), is a golden ale with sweetish toffee malt and firm citric hops. **Shoreditch Stout** 🍾 (4%) is chocolatey and slightly spicy with redcurrant notes. The range of **historic beers** 🍾 are all well worth trying:

they include **1850 London Porter** * (5%), **1839 India Pale Ale** * (7%), **1792 Imperial Stout** * (9.3%) and dated **Vintage Stock Ale** ** (10%).

Availability. The Duke of Cambridge (p87) is a regular stockist and Mr Lawrence (p186) regularly has bottles in.

PLZEŇSKÝ PRAZDROJ (PILSNER URQUELL)
Subsidiary (SAB-Miller)
Plzeň, Czech Republic
1,240km/771 miles from Central London
⊕ www.prazdroj.cz

The second part of this famous Bohemian brewery's name in both Czech and German means 'original source', and with some justification. The clear golden hop-accented lager that eventually became the most recognised beer style in the world was first perfected here in 1842. The term 'Pils(e)ner' literally means 'of Plzeň', from the city's German name Pilsen. While the rest of the world did a good job of producing ever more degraded imitations, Pilsner Urquell long remained a beacon of excellence, but has faced accusations of loss of character since current owner SAB-Miller took over and streamlined the brewing process. For all this, it remains a superior example of its style.

Pilsner Urquell

Pilsner Urquell * 🍺 🫗 (4.4%) is golden with vanilla hops over dry, clean and slightly honeyed malt, finishing with a herbal, minerally hop bite. **Gambrinus** is also brewed here but is notably less of a premium product.

Availability. Widely available in pasteurised keg and bottled form in London pubs. Some Czech pubs serve an unpasteurised version known as tankový *('tank beer') and we'd dearly love to hear of any London outlets with similar privileges.*

PORTERHOUSE
Microbrewery
Blanchardstown, Leinster, Ireland
597km/371 miles from Central London
⊕ www.porterhousebrewco.com

Craft brewers in the Irish Republic have struggled to make an impression on a market dominated by industrial stout giant Guinness and its two minor Heineken-owned rivals. Porterhouse is a notable exception: starting in 1989 with a small brewpub in Bray, it expanded to a much bigger place in Dublin's trendy Temple Bar district and now owns other pubs too, enhancing capacity with a freestanding brewery in 2008.

An Brainblásta 🍺 (7%) is an oddly syrupy and perfumed strong ale. **Plain** * 🍺 (4.3%) is a rare example of the near extinct style of 'plain' as opposed to 'stout' porter, with a flavoursome malty palate that finishes pursingly dry but not too roasty. **Red** * 🍺 (4.4%) is a fruity and nutty Irish red ale. **TSB** 🍺 (3.7%) is an easy drinking fruity-malty bitter with an unusual hop note. **Weiss** 🍺 (4.3%) is a wheat beer that's a little heavy on the banana flavour, while **Wrasslers XXXX** * 🍺 (5%) is a classic pungent, meaty and roasty stout.

Availability. A full range is in the London branch of the Porterhouse (p76) and a few beers appear in Draft House pubs.

PURITY
Microbrewery
Great Alne, Warwickshire
193km/120 miles from Central London
⊕ www.puritybrewing.com

Quick to make an impression after opening in 2005, Purity is an environmentally conscientious brewery that also imports from Germany and the Czech Republic.

Mad Goose * 🍺 (4.2%) is warm gold with syrupy malt and a rooty, piney hop bite. Award winning **Pure Gold** * 🍺 (3.8%) is a crisply malty, lightly citric beer with a ginger biscuit note. **Pure Ubu** 🍺 (4.5%) is a malty amber ale with strawberry fruit and nettly hops. Bottled versions aren't bottle conditioned.

Availability. Regularly on sale at the Gunmakers (p70), the Green Man (p79) and many other discerning outlets.

RAM
See London breweries (p277)

REBELLION

Microbrewery
Marlow, Buckinghamshire
53km/33 miles from Central London
⊕ www.rebellionbeer.co.uk

A well-regarded small brewer in a historic brewing town, much expanded since its inception in 1993.

Amber bitter **IPA** * 🍺 (3.7%) is sappy and nutty with complex leafy hops. **Mutiny** * 🍺 (4.5%) is rich and reddish, with rounded hops in a winy finish. **White** * 🍶 (5%) is a spiced wheat beer with caramel, banana and lemon grass notes. There are also numerous seasonals.

Availability. A recurring feature on guest lists, Rebellion is also regular at Southall Conservative & Unionist Club (p238).

RED SQUIRREL
Microbrewery
Hertford, Hertfordshire
42km/26 miles from Central London
⊕ www.redsquirrelbrewery.co.uk

Opened in 2004, this micro has established a good reputation for innovative and tasty beers. It supports the work of the Red Squirrel Survival Trust, helping protect the now rare species, long threatened by North American grey squirrels – but is unafraid to use North American hops in its beers!

Conservation * 🍺🍶 (4.1%) is a notable nutty and gently hoppy bitter. **London Porter** * 🍺 (5%) is very dark ruby with a meaty, marmite palate, ending with sharpish roast and brown sugar. **Redwood American IPA** * 🍺🍶 (5.4%) is a light amber with tasty tangerine and tobacco hops.

Availability. Keep your eye open in places with a good specialist range, like the Old Fountain (p95).

**Red Squirrel
Conservation Bitter**

REDEMPTION
See London breweries (p278)

RINGWOOD
Subsidiary (Marston's)
Ringwood BH24 3AP, Hampshire
156km/97 miles from Central London
⊕ www.ringwoodbrewery.co.uk

This New Forest outfit arguably wasn't the first British micro when it opened in 1978 but it was certainly the one to kickstart the microbrewing movement, and its founder Peter Austin is justly called the 'father of British microbrewing'. It was also one of the biggest micros when it was bought by the Marston's group in 2007. A former director, David Welsh, is now a partner in Sambrook's (above).

Best Bitter * 🍺 (3.8%) is a malty brown bitter with figgy fruit and a clean, twiggy finish. **Fortyniner** 🍺 (4.9%) is a deep gold beer, sweetish with a spicy note. Well known strong bitter **Old Thumper** * 🍺 (5.6%) is a big, nutty, fruity beer with a dry finish, also brewed in the US by Shipyard. **XXXX** * 🍺 (4.7%) is a porter with a slight marmaladey acid tang over caramel and coffee. Bottled beers are filtered.

Availability. Regular at the Jeremy Bentham (p50) and often a guest at Nicholson's pubs.

ROBINSON'S
Independent
Stockport, Manchester
323km/201 miles from Central London
⊕ www.frederic-robinson.co.uk

With a historic brewery dating back to the 1830s, Robinson's is a major regional brewer in northwest England though its cask beers are hardly seen in London.

Old Tom ** 🍶 (and occasional cask, 8.5%) is a rummy, claret-tinged complex strong ale with a dry, tannic finish. Various flavoured versions are not recommended. The dark and light versions of **Hatters** mild are well worth trying if you're lucky enough to spot them down south.

Availability. Old Tom is available in supermarkets and on some more considered pub bottled beer lists.

ROCHEFORT
Trappist
Rochefort, Namur, Belgium
477km/296 miles from Central
London
⊕ www.trappistes-rochefort.com

The smallest, and arguably the
best, of the commercially distributed
Trappist brewers. The beers, all of
which are dark, are identified by their
strengths using an old system of
measurement.

The rare **6** * 🍶 (7.5%) has toffee,
musky yeast, toasted malt and a
herbal, lightly hoppy finish. **8** ** 🍶
(9.2%) has banana and fig tones
and a very long, winey finish. **10** ** 🍶 (11.3%)
is one of the world's best beers, with a
luscious chocolate and raisin palate, and
smoky dark orange and iodine flavours in a
complex finish.

Rochefort 10

*Availability. Belgian specialists and other discerning
stockists should have one or more of these: try Brew
Wharf (p53).*

RODENBACH
Subsidiary (Palm)
Roeselare, East Flanders, Belgium
278km/173 miles from Central London
⊕ www.rodenbach.be

One of the few Belgian breweries, and by far
the biggest and most significant, still ageing
brown ales in wood on a commercial scale,
and then blending them with younger beer
to offset the sourness produced by
microorganisms in the maturation vessels.
The practice ultimately derives from London
porter brewing though it's near-extinct in
Britain, except at Greene King (see above)
and at a handful of experimental micros.
Rodenbach is now owned by Belgian new
national Palm, which has soothed anxieties
by investing in traditional practices.

Rodenbach * 🍶🍺 (5%) is the blended beer,
with a distinct iron filings aroma and a cherry
and orange tinged sweet-sour character.
Grand Cru ** 🍶 is the notably sharper and
woodier unblended aged beer.

*Availability. Should be stocked by any self-
respecting Belgian specialist. The
Dovetail (p69) has the blended beer
on draught.*

ROOSTERS
Microbrewery
Knaresborough, North Yorkshire
338km/210 miles from Central London
⊕ www.roosters.co.uk

This dynamic brewery was one of the first in
Britain to experiment seriously with the
fruity flavours of North American hops.

Yankee * 🍺 (4.3%) is deep gold with
mandarin, lime and honey notes.
YPA * 🍺 (4.3%) is a golden ale vibrant
with pine and grapefruit hops. Also look out for
experimental beers under the **Outlaw** brand.

*Availability. Regular guest at pubs that stock more
unusual casks – try the Horseshoe (p150).*

ROTHAUS
Independent
Grafenhausen, Baden-Württemberg, Germany
937km/582 miles from Central London
⊕ www.rothaus.de

Originating in a Benedictine abbey in 1791
and secularised in the early 19th century, this
historic Black Forest brewery has recently
been much modernised.

Hefeweizen * 🍶🍺 (5.4%) is a wheat beer with a
very spicy and fruity aroma and a creamy body.
Tannenzäpfle 🍶🍺 (5.1%) is a clean, hay-
scented Pils-style lager.

*Availability. Increasingly on speciality lists – try the
Salisbury Hotel (p161).*

RUDGATE
Microbrewery
Tockwith, York, North Yorkshire
333km/207 miles from Central London
⊕ www.rudgatebrewery.co.uk

Founded in 1992, this well regarded micro is
based on a former military airfield where it
shares premises with Marston Moor brewery.

Battleaxe * 🍺 (4.2%) is a stern brown bitter
with autumn fruit and a twiggy, slightly smoky

finish. **Jorvik** ☲ (3.8%) is a very pale blond beer with a biscuity note and a lightly citric finish. **Ruby Mild** * ☲ (4.4%) has light roast chocolate and cereal malt flavours and quite a bracing, chalky finish.

Availability. A regular guest at Mitchells & Butlers Castle and Nicholson's pubs among others.

SAINTS AND SINNERS
See Brew Wharf

SALTAIRE
Microbrewery
Shipley, West Yorkshire
334km/208 miles from Central London
⊕ www.saltairebrewery.co.uk

Impressively sited in a former tram network power station on the edge of the Saltaire World Heritage Site, this innovative craft brewery has won numerous awards since being founded in 2005.

Sammuel Smiths Imperial Stout

Blonde * ☲ (4%) has lots of hops but a slow developing bitterness. **Cascade Pale Ale** * ☲ (4.9%) has a citrus and pine hop character well supported by a sweetish malty palate – it's also available in a blackberry infused version. **Cascadian Black** * ☲ (4.8%) is a so-called 'black IPA', a roasty beer generously hopped with citric notes. **Triple Chocoholic** * ☲ (4.8%) – with chocolate malt, real chocolate and chocolate syrup – has lush chocolate flavours well integrated with charred malt.

Availability. Often on Mitchells & Butlers guest lists, for example at the Southwark Tavern (p62), or at specialist pubs like the Olde Mitre (p83).

SAMBROOK'S
See London breweries (p279)

SAMUEL SMITH
Independent
Tadcaster, North Yorkshire
320km/199 miles from Central London
⊕ www.samuelsmithsbrewery.co.uk

Founded in 1758, the 'Old Brewery' is the oldest brewery in Yorkshire and one of two in Tadcaster founded by bitter rivals from the same family. The 'New Brewery', John Smith, is now Heineken Tadcaster. Rather like its home county, Sam's is traditional, pragmatic and eccentric in equal measure: it retains only one cask beer, sold in its own pubs at a bargain price, but makes an impressive range of bottled specialities originally developed for export. It also keeps a small but significant estate of often landmark London pubs which sell 100% own brand products.

Celebrated Oatmeal Stout * ◊ (5%) is smooth with marzipan and glacé cherry flavours as well as roast. **Imperial Stout** * ◊ (7%) has lots of burnt fruit and coffee notes in a long finish. **Nut Brown Ale** * ◊ (5%) is dry northeast England brown ale with a winy note and a persistent nugget of hops. **Old Brewery Bitter** ☲ (4%) is a distinctive woody, fruity bitter with a stern, seedy and powdery hop note. **Taddy Porter** * ◊ (5%) has cakey fruit and chocolate with a notably dry, roasty bite. If you can find it, oak matured **Yorkshire Stingo** ** ◊ (9%) is a red fruit and spicy toffee monster with oak and pepper notes. The sweet, overcooked fruit beers made at Sam's subsidiary **Melbourn Brothers** are best regarded as a curiosity in my view.

Availability. Two spectacular Central London Sam's pubs are listed here: the Princess Louise (p84) and the Cittie of Yorke (p81). The bottles are regulars in specialist shops.

SCHLENKERLA
Independent
Bamberg, Bavaria, Germany
985km/612 miles from Central London
⊕ www.schlenkerla.de

This classic Franconian brewery developed out of a brewpub founded in 1678, and specialises in beers made from malt smoked over beechwood.

Aecht Schlenkerla Rauchbier Märzen ** 🍺 (5.1%) is a love-it-or-hate-it beer that smells of bacon and sawdust and tastes of smoked cheese softened by caramel and marmalade. **Urbock** * 🍺 (6.5%) has firmer malt, faintly reminiscent of a porter. A wheat version, **Weizen** * 🍺 (5.2%), adds banana, apple and spice to the flavour mix.

Availability. The Märzen in particular is often on specialist beer lists: try Zeitgeist (p113).

SCHNEIDER
Independent
Kelheim, Bavaria, Germany
1,157km/719 miles from Central London
🌐 www.schneider-weisse.de

Arguably the best of the big, old established Bavarian wheat beer breweries, Schneider was licensed in 1850 by the Bavarian royals, who traditionally controlled the monopoly on wheat beer brewing, and is still family owned.

The 'original' standard unfiltered beer is now labelled **Tap 7 Unser Original** ** 🍺📖 (5.4%): it's an amber beer, darker than most in the style, with a beautiful balance of cereal, toffee apple, clove and spicy hop flavours. Aventinus, or **Tap 6 Unser Aventinus** ** 🍺 (8.2%) is a fabulous wheat bock with complex rummy fruit, toffee and pippy hops.

Availability. On draught in quite a few pubs – try the Island Queen (p88) – and in bottle in others with a select list, like the Barnsbury (p145).

SHARP'S
Subsidiary (Molson Coors)
Rock, Cornwall
416km/258 miles from Central London
🌐 www.sharpsbrewery.co.uk

One of Britain's most successful new breweries, expanded from small beginnings in 1994 to selling 60,000 barrels (98,000hl) a year. Besides high volume cask brands, notably Doom Bar, brewer Stuart Howe has also created some impressive bottled specialities. Early in 2011, multinational Molson Coors, which owns the old Bass plant in Birmingham (see Worthington below), bought the

company but has said it intends to keep the brewery in Cornwall with all the existing staff. Bottled versions of the cask beers are not usually bottle conditioned.

Sharp's Chalky's Bite

Unusual spiced wheat beer **Chalky's Bite** * 🍺 (6.8%) is soft and creamy with intriguing herb and orange flavours. **Cornish Coaster** * 🍺 (3.6%) is golden with a sacky, citric palate and a refreshing lagery flowery finish. **Cornish Stout** * 🍺 (4.3%) is a tart, blackcurranty and coffeeish winter seasonal. **Doom Bar** * 🍺 (4%) is the flagship, a likeable amber bitter with a sweetish grapy nutty palate and a slightly chocolatey rounded finish. Burgundy-coloured **Massive Ale** * 🍺 (10%) is heady and herbal with woody and balsamic flavours. **Special** 🍺 (5.2%) is darker and richer with berry fruits and a lightly hoppy finish. **St Enodoc Double** * 🍺 (8%) is brown with fruit, rose and tobacco while **Honey Spice Triple** * 🍺 (9%) is warming with slighty rubbery cinnamon and ginger notes.

Availability. Doom Bar is now ubiquitous in London pubs but for a wider range of casks try somewhere like BFI Southbank (p111). Bottled beers are available from specialist shops and some are served at the Fox & Anchor (p70).

SHEPHERD NEAME
Independent
Faversham, Kent
80km/50 miles from Central London
🌐 www.shepherd-neame.co.uk

A strong claimant for the title of Britain's oldest continuous brewery – the company traces its history to 1698 and there are suggestions of brewing on the site back to the 12th century. Still run with family involvement, it's one of the most important breweries in its region.

1698 * 🍺 (and occasional 🍺, 6.5%) is chestnut coloured with marzipan and fruitcake notes and a sherryish, peppery finish. **Bishop's Finger** * 🍺 (5%) is rich and malty with autumn fruit and orange notes: the name refers to a style of signpost, if you're wondering. **Kent's Best** 🍺 (4.1%) is amber, mellow and marmaladey. **Master Brew** 🍺 (4.1%) is an amber bitter with a lightly hoppy note. **Late Red** * 🍺 (4.5%) is fudgy, sappy and nutty with a blackcurrant note. Flagship brand **Spitfire** * 🍺 (4.7%) is juicy and slightly rummy with a bite of leafy Kentish hops. Organic golden ale **Whitstable Bay** * 🍺 (and seasonal 🍺, 4.5%) has fresh lime and pineapple-tinged flavours. Other seasonal beers are also available; most bottled versions are not bottle conditioned.

Availability. There are several Shep's pubs in London – try the Eleanor Arms (p135) or the Cask & Glass (p116). Bottles are often seen in supermarkets.

SIERRA NEVADA

Microbrewery
Chico, California, USA
8,444km/5,247 miles from Central London
🌐 www.sierranevada.com

This seminal craft brewery was started in 1978 as a spare time project using salvaged plant. It's now one of the biggest and most successful of its kind.

Amber barley wine **Bigfoot** ** 🍺 (9.6%) is a winy and warming beer with bitterish pine, geranium and coconut notes. Hazy golden, piny and spiky but well balanced with fruity malt, **Pale Ale** * 🍺🍺 (5.6%) set the style for much of what was to follow in US craft brewing. **Porter** * 🍺 (5.9%) is sweetish and liquoricey with a notably hoppy and roasty finish. **Torpedo IPA** * 🍺 (7.2%) is notably hoppy, with cutting citrus, warming spice and a bitter chocolate note.

Availability. The pale ale is now everywhere in bottle and/or in keg including in many Mitchells & Butlers pubs. For a wider range you'll need somewhere like the Euston Tap (p49) or bottle shop Dr.Ink (p224).

Sierra Nevada Porter

SKINNER'S

Microbrewery
Truro, Cornwall
440km/273 miles from Central London
🌐 www.skinnersbrewery.com

With its cheerful labelling featuring cartoon characters, this brewery is one of a number in Cornwall to have made a national impression, and is now capable of producing 19,500 barrels (32,000hl) a year.

Amber bitter **Betty Stogs** * 🍺 (4%) has a crisp fruity palate and a lingering lightly bittering marmalade finish. Golden **Cornish Knocker** 🍺 (4.5%) is spicy and bitterish with firm malt and olive notes. **Heligan Honey** * 🍺 (4%) is deep gold with exotic fruit, faint honeyed character and a shortish finish. **Spriggan Ale** 🍺 (3.8%) is golden with a citric malt palate and a cheerfully hoppy finish. Bottled versions are filtered.

Availability. Regularly appearing in cask ale pubs, and occasionally permanent. Try North Nineteen (p163).

SPATEN-LÖWENBRÄU

Subsidiary (AB InBev)
Munich, Bavaria, Germany
1,144km/711 miles from Central London
🌐 www.spatenbraeu.de

In the 1830s two brewer's sons, Bavarian Gabriel Sedlmayr II and his Viennese friend Anton Dreher, toured the breweries of Britain (though apparently not London) equipped with special hollow walking sticks enabling them to take secret samples. Back in Munich they put the results of their James Bond tactics to good use at the Sedlmayr family's Spaten brewery – an ancient foundation with a history starting in 1397, named after the malt shovels regularly in use there. Sedlmayr achieved a consistent technique for creating clean, stable cold-fermented and long-matured 'lager' beer; Dreher is credited with inventing the amber 'red' lager associated with Vienna, a step towards golden 'pilsner' as later perfected in Bohemia (see Plzeňský Prazdroj above). Today Spaten has been coupled with another of Munich's famous former 'Big Six', Löwenbräu, as an InBev subsidiary since 2004. It's long brewed Franziskaner wheat beers, originated by another member of the Sedlmayr family at a site near a Franciscan monastery.

Franziskaner Hefe-Weissbier 🍶🍾 (5%) has the bubblegum and spice notes of the style, with slight chocolate flavours while the **Dunkel** * version 🍶 (5%) has more butter-toffee character. Malty gold **Münchner Hell** * 🍷🍾 (5.2%) is grainy and slightly waxy, with a subtle rooty hop note. Seasonal **Oktoberfestbier** * 🍷 (5.9%) – Spaten's is traditionally the first to be tapped at the famous festival – is mid-golden with generous malt and pear drop flashes. **Pils** * 🍷🍾 (5%) is freshly hoppy over vanilla wafer flavours.

Availability. Franziskaner is increasingly common on draught in pubs with specialist kegs but for a wider range try Zeitgeist (p113) or a good bottle shop.

ST AUSTELL
Independent
St Austell, Cornwall
419km/260 miles from Central London
🌐 www.staustellbrewery.co.uk

Currently one of the most successful of the old regional family breweries, with a very talented head brewer, Roger Ryman.

Brewed using a specially produced single malt, **Admiral's Ale** ** 🍶 (5%) is a lusciously biscuity, nutty and hoppy reddish-brown beer. Spiced with vanilla, cloves and coriander, **Clouded Yellow** * 🍶 (4.8%) is an unusual and very refreshing wheat beer. **HSD** * 🍾 (5%) is a nut-brown slightly winy and marmaladey special bitter. **Proper Job** * 🍶🍾 (4.5/5.5%) is a very flavoursome and tangy golden IPA with fruit salad, strawberry and lime notes. **Smugglers Vintage Ale** * 🍶 (6%) is a spicy, woody dark ale matured in former whisky casks. Best selling premium amber bitter **Tribute** * 🍾 (4.2%) supports leafy and peppery hop character, including a piney note from US hop Willamette, with firm sacky malt.

**St Austell
Admiral's Ale**

Availability. Tribute is very common as a guest, including in Young's pubs. Some of the bottled beers are in supermarkets; for others visit a good bottle shop.

ST PETER'S
Microbrewery
St Peter South Elmham, Bungay, Suffolk

182km/113 miles from Central London
🌐 www.stpetersbrewery.co.uk

Opened in 1996 in the grounds of a 13th century manor house and former Dominican friary, St Peter's has made a great success of a wide range of unusual bottled beers in stylish bottles based on a historic gin bottle design, though none is bottle conditioned.

Best Bitter * 🍾 (3.7%) is brown, nutty and fruity with a bitter finish. Lightly perfumed **Golden Ale** 🍾 (4.7%) is soft and firm with a fruity citric finish. **IPA** * 🍾 (5.5%) is lightly flowery and very grapefruity with a biscuit malt base. Dark brown **Mild** 🍾 (3.7%) has a nutty palate with a slight cheese note and a notably dry finish. **Organic Best** 🍾 (4.1%) is a decent fruity, bitterish brown bitter while **Organic Ale** 🍾 (4.5%) is golden and more citric in character. Ruby **Red Ale** * 🍾 (4.3%) has cough candy and caramel notes with a late hoppy sting. There are numerous spiced and fruit beers of which one of the most regularly available is **Grapefruit** 🍾 (4.7%).

Availability. St Peter's pub the Jerusalem Tavern (p71) stocks a wide range and casks are also occasionally found as guests elsewhere.

STAG
See London breweries (p280)

STIEGL
Independent
Salzburg, Austria
1,291km/802 miles from Central London
🌐 www.stiegl.at

Like many breweries in the German speaking world, Stiegl has a long history, traceable back to a city brewpub opened in 1492. It's now the biggest privately owned brewery in Austria and has recently started successfully exporting to the UK.

Goldbräu 🍷 (4.9%) is a malty and slightly fruity Märzen. **Paracelsus Zwickl** * 🍶🍾 (5%) is a soft, grainy and yeasty unfiltered beer. A very light gold **Pils** 🍾🍷 (4.9%) is clean, crisp and slightly sweetish.

Availability. Relatively widely available in London.

STONE
Microbrewery
Escondido, California, USA
8,782km/5,457 miles from Central London
⊕ www.stonebrew.com

This successful Californian brewery, founded in 1996, has made a virtue of 'extreme' beers explicitly marketed to divide opinions – a tactic since borrowed by some British brewers.

Arrogant Bastard * ▲ (7.2%) has a malty base tinged with vine fruits and a massive hit of citric, vegetal resins. **IPA** * ▲ (6.9%) is full of spiced orange with a slight farmyard note, ending assertively hoppy but controlled. **Pale Ale** * ▲ (5.4%) is an approachable American pale with vanilla and coconut notes and a slightly fudgy palate. **Ruination IPA** * ▲ (7.7%) is very hoppy and resinous with tangerine peel and peppery detergent notes. **Smoked Porter** ** ▲ (5.9%) is firmly smoky and rich in coffee and chocolate flavours. Some beers may also turn up on keg in specialist outlets.

Availability. A favourite of American specialists, often found in the Rake (p60).

SURREY HILLS
LOCAL
Microbrewery
Dorking, Surrey
39km/24 miles from Central London
⊕ www.surreyhills.co.uk

Founded in an old milking parlour in 2005, this brewery has recently relocated to one of southern England's biggest vineyards, the Denbies Wine Estate on the North Downs – a great opportunity to showcase English wine and beer together.

Ranmore Ale ≣ (3.8%) is a golden bitter with a tart apple body and nettly, lychee hop notes. **Shere Drop** ≣ (4.2%) is a more grapefruity deep gold ale. There are also numerous seasonal beers.

Availability. Real ale pubs with a local guest policy, regular at the Willoughby Arms (p206).

THEAKSTON
Independent
Masham, North Yorkshire
370km/230 miles from Central London
⊕ www.theakstons.co.uk

This well loved brewery in a historic brewing town is one of the few to have regained its independence after being swallowed by a national group. It was bought back by the Theakston family from Scottish Courage (now Heineken) in 2003.

Best Bitter * ≣ (3.7%) is substantial with creamy strawberry malt and a classic chalky bitterish finish. The famous dark old ale **Old Peculier** ** ≣ (5.6%) is rich in caramel cake and estery fruit, with a drying roasty finish. Light amber **Traditional Mild** * ≣ (3.5%) is nutty and slightly raspy, with a touch of liquorice toffee. Fruity **XB** ≣ (4.5%) a sweetish, malty special bitter. Bottled beers are not bottle conditioned.

Availability. Mild is a surprising regular at the King William IV (p150) while Old Peculier is reliably found at the Museum Tavern (p51). Other beers pop us as guests elsewhere.

THORNBRIDGE
Microbrewery
Bakewell, Derbyshire
251km/156 miles from Central London
⊕ www.thornbridgebrewery.co.uk

Originally an offshoot of Kelham Island (above) brewing since 2004 at stately home Thornbridge Hall, Thornbridge has quickly developed into one of Britain's best and most interesting breweries. As well as making some world class beer it's also helped seed BrewDog (above). In 2010 it moved to new and bigger premises though brewing continues at a small scale in the Hall. Head brewer Stefano Cossi was deservedly named brewer of the year by British beer writers in 2010.

Bracia ** ▲ (9%) is an unusual sweetish, spicy, peaty and enormously complex dark brew made with Italian chestnut honey and champagne yeast. Stout **Brock** ≣ (4.1%) is coffeeish with vine fruits and rooty hops.

Halcyon * 🍶 (7.7%) is an IPA made with new season green hops, beautifully lettucey, peachy and piny. IPA **Jaipur** ** 🍶🍺 (5.9%) has luscious apricot nectar notes, toasty malt and a controlled peppery finish. Rich gold **Kipling** * 🍺 (5.2%) is fresh, flowery and grapefruity with a citric, rooty finish. **Lord Marples** * 🍺 (4%) is a twist on a classic amber bitter with rich coffeeish malt and fruit. Imperial stout **Saint Petersburg** * 🍶 (7.7%) has cola, blackcurrant and pear drop notes – some of the limited edition **Whisky cask** ** versions are astounding. **Wild Swan** * 🍺 (3.5%) is a delicately pale, flowery and refreshing golden ale with a measured peppery citric bite.

Availability. Now regularly spotted at Wetherspoon and Mitchells & Butlers Nicholson's pubs – try Doggetts Coat & Badge (p111) – with a wider range at specialist outlets like Cask (p115).

Thornbridge Jaipur

Established in 1858, Tim Taylor had long enjoyed the respect of discerning beer drinkers as one of the best of the surviving regional independents when in 2003 a certain musician by the name of Madonna Ciccone told a TV interviewer she enjoyed a pint of Landlord in Soho's Dog & Duck. It has since considerably expanded.

Dark Mild * 🍺 (3.5%) has a long, astringent finish offset by caramel malt, while a rare light mild, **Golden Best** * 🍺 is gently flowery and sweetish. **Landlord** ** 🍺 (4.1%) is indeed a very good beer, a deep golden bitter with fruity malt and a firm, quinine-like bitter orange finish. Dark ruby old ale **Ram Tam** * 🍺 (4.3%) is tannic and chewy with plum and raisin flavours.

Availability. You won't have to look hard to find Landlord but you could follow in Madonna's footsteps and try it at the Dog & Duck (p107). The others are sadly much harder to find in London but try pubs with a good range of cask guests.

THWAITES
Independent
Blackburn, Lancashire
361km/224 miles from Central London
⊕ www.danielthwaites.com

A solid regional family brewery founded in 1807.

Lancaster Bomber 🍺 (4.4%) is a malty and well rounded amber bitter. Dark mild **Nutty Black** * 🍺 (3.3%) is sweetish with cherry and caramel notes and lingering tannic hops. Named after the curmudgeonly Blackburn-born chronicler of the Lake District fells, **Wainwright** 🍺 (4.1%) is a golden ale with a fruity body and citrusy bite. Bottled versions are not bottle conditioned.

Availability. Often in the Punch Finest Cask range – try the Prince Regent (p185).

TIMOTHY TAYLOR
Independent
Keighley, West Yorkshire
344km/214 miles from Central London
⊕ www.timothy-taylor.co.uk

TITANIC
Microbrewery
Stoke-on-Trent, Staffordshire
260km/162 miles from Central London
⊕ www.titanicbrewery.co.uk

Founded in 1985, this successful Potteries brewery derives it names from the fact that Edward Smith, captain of the ill-fated RMS Titanic, was born in Hanley, Stoke-on-Trent.

Golden ale **Iceberg** * 🍺 (4.1%) is complex and fruity with rose scents and a firm hop finish. Tawny **Lifeboat** * 🍺 (4%) is a herbal and nutty dark ale with a bitterish finish. **Mild** * 🍺 (3.5%) is sweetish and fruity with apple and honey notes. **Stout** ** 🍶🍺 (4.5%) has a gravelly coffee aroma and rich coffee, chocolate and roast flavours.

Availability. Often on discriminating guest lists, including Wetherspoon's pubs, or try the Hope (p216).

TRAPPE
See Koningshoeven

TRAQUAIR
Microbrewery
Innerleithen, Scottish Borders, Scotland
606km/377 miles from Central London
⊕ www.traquair.co.uk

Traquair House is the oldest inhabited stately home in Scotland and firmly associated with the Jacobite cause – the main gate has been closed since the 18th century with a pledge that it will only be reopened when a Stuart returns to the throne. In 1965 the laird discovered an old brewery, once a common feature of big houses, in the grounds and decided to revive it, brewing traditional strong Scottish ales. His daughter continues the tradition.

Jacobite Ale * 🍶 (8%) has flavours of liquorice, caramel, coriander and a cough candy note. Classic **Traquair House Ale** ** 🍶 (7.2%) is a dark ruby beer with rummy fruitcake, artichoke and vermouth flavours and a chocolatey note in the finish.

Availability. A feature on some discerning bottled beer lists and a regular at bottle shops.

TRUMAN'S
See London breweries (p281)

TRING
LocAle
Microbrewery
Tring, Hertfordshire
57km/35 miles from Central London
⊕ www.tringbrewery.co.uk

This Chilterns outfit is jointly run by Richard Shardlow, who's also known as a designer and installer of microbreweries for others.

Death or Glory * 🍺 🍶 (7.2%) is a dark amber sweetish, cakey beer with berry fruit notes. Amber bitter **Jack O'Legs** 🍺 (4.2%) is easy going, biscuity and lightly hoppy. **Mansion Mild** * 🍺 (3.7%) has blackcurrant fruit and a malty body reminiscent of a German Dunkel. **Side Pocket for a Toad** * 🍺 (3.6%) is deep gold and refreshingly citrusy, with good biscuit malt in support. There are monthly specials and seasonals; bottled beers are filtered.

Availability. Sometimes on Wetherspoon lists and guesting at other real ale specialists.

TRIPLE FFF
Microbrewery
Four Marks, Alton, Hampshire
87km/54 miles from Central London
⊕ www.triplefff.com

Founded in 1997, this is now one of southern England's highest rated new breweries, expanding several times.

Alton's Pride 🍺 (3.8%) is highly praised as a flavoursome amber bitter, but I find it a little too thin to support its sharply citric hop kick. **Moondance** * 🍺 (4.2%) is deep gold and tasty with a decent citrus bite. Mild **Pressed Rat and Warthog** * 🍺 (3.8%) has a flowery, spicy grape note to its grainy, salty body.

Availability. Often in discerning real ale pubs – try the Castle (p81). The Charles Lamb (p86) stocks Alton's Pride as a regular.

TWICKENHAM
See London breweries (p283)

VALE
Microbrewery
Brill, Buckinghamshire
93km/58 miles from Central London
⊕ www.valebrewery.co.uk

Founded in 1995, this reliable micro expanded in 2007 to a site not far from what was once the furthest extent of the London Underground's Metropolitan Line.

VALE BREWERY CO.
Black Swan
Dark Smooth Rich Mild
ABV 3.9%
Brill Beer
BREWED IN BRILL
BUCKINGHAMSHIRE

Porter **Black Beauty** 🍺 (4.3%) is sweetish with chocolate and a fruity finish. Mild **Black Swan** * 🍺 (3.9%) has blackberry, apple and caramel notes and a very slight smoky hint on the finish. **Edgars Golden Ale** * 🍺 (4.3%) is cheerful and citrusy with complex mineral notes. Cakey, smoky old ale **Grumpling** * 🍺 (4.6%) has a backwash of nutshells and raisin fruit. Golden ale **VPA** 🍺 (4.2%) has pineapply, fruit sherbert flashes. **Wychert** 🍺 (3.9%) is a nutty, apply, lightly tangy amber bitter. Nearly all beers are also available as 🍶.

Availability. Regularly on real ale guest lists including at Wetherspoon pubs.

WELLS & YOUNG'S
New national
Bedford, Bedfordshire
88km/55 miles from Central London
⊕ www.wellsandyoungs.co.uk

A regional brewery founded in 1876, Charles Wells celebrated its centenary by moving to a newly built out-of-town site where it became the biggest family-owned independent in the UK. In 2006 it took advantage of the remaining spare capacity by closing a deal with Young's, keen to realise the capital tied up in their historic but hard to maintain Ram brewery at Wandsworth (see under Ram above). The two companies merged their brewing operations on the Bedford site, moving Young's beers there following a lengthy process of flavour matching that inevitably hasn't convinced some diehard Young's drinkers. In 2008 the group licensed the Courage beers from Heineken and has since partially restored the reputation of a once famous brand. Both partners retain separately branded and managed pub estates, but with some crossover of beers on offer.

The entry level beer of the **Young's** range is **Bitter** * 🍺 (better known, but never labelled, as **Ordinary**, 3.7%), a deep gold refreshing beer with a slightly winy and sour tang. A stronger 🍺 version (4.5%) is crisp with subtle orange fruit and a sulphur whiff. Made with both chocolate bars and chocolate malts, **Double Chocolate Stout** * 🍾 (and occasional 🍺, 5%) has luscious malty chocolate, vanilla and raisin flavours and slightly sharp notes; also available but not as nice on 🍺. **London Gold** 🍺 🍺 (4%/4.8%) has slightly sacky hops over clean lager-like peachy malt. **Special** * 🍺 (4.5%) is pale brown with subtle smooth malt and mulberry-like notes on a raspy bitterish finish. **Special London** * 🍺 (6.4%), originally developed for the Belgian market, has figs, peanuts and almonds and a

tonic water and Granny Smith finish. Dark, complex seasonal **Winter Warmer** ** 🍺 🍾 (5%) has coffee, raisins and treacle-like notes: it's a rare survivor of the old Burton Pale Ale style of the late 19th century.

Of the **Wells** beers, **Banana Bread Beer** * 🍾 (and occasional 🍺, 5.5%) does a good job of balancing banana and cardamom notes, malt and pleasantly citric hops. Amber bitter **Bombardier** 🍺 (4.3%) is notably nutty and biscuity with grape-like fruit and a dry but fudgy finish.

Courage Best * 🍺 (4%) is well-balanced and fruity throughout with a classic biscuity dry finish. **Directors** 🍺 (4.8%) is also fruity but quite light textured with a notable dose of hops.

Availability. You're still never far from a Young's pub in London and several are listed here – we're particularly fond of the Nightingale (p201). There are few Wells pubs and none is included here, but Bombardier turns up regularly in Young's pubs and in others as a guest. Courage beers often appear in former Courage pubs like the Cockpit (p65).

WELTON'S
Microbrewery
Horsham, West Sussex
60km/37 miles from Central London
⊕ www.weltonsbeer.com

Started in 1995 and once sharing premises with Hepworth (above), this interesting micro has now expanded to its own site.

Developed so brewer Ray Welton could have a decent pint as soon as possible after playing rugby, **Pridenjoy** * 🍺 (2.8%) is a great demonstration of how much flavour can be packed into low gravities, with a crisp pineapple palate and a notably bitter finish. Dark brown **Horsham Old** * 🍺 (4.6%) has toffee, chocolate and a drying finish. There are numerous specials and seasonals.

Availability. Another one for discerning real ale stockists who favour local beer. Try Woodies Freehouse (p216) or Rose's (p190).

WESTERHAM
Microbrewery
Crockham Hill, Edenbridge, Kent
43km/27 miles from Central London
🌐 www.westerhambrewery.co.uk

Not far beyond the London boundary on a National Trust property in the North Downs, this quality micro uses yeasts from the long closed Black Eagle brewery in Westerham and also celebrates local links to figures like Winston Churchill, who lived at Chartwell nearby.

Special bitter **1965** * 🍺 🍾 (4.8%) is bitterish, estery and marmaladey with a chewy cereal body. **British Bulldog** * 🍺 🍾 (4.3%) is amber with firm malt, blackcurrant and lychee flavours and a roasty, piney finish. **Finchcocks Original** * 🍺 (3.5%) is a light amber autumnal bitter with complex bacon and olive flavours and a lingering rasp of hops. **Puddledock Porter** * 🍺 (4.5%) is roasty, plummy and a little sternly tannic. Commemorating the anti-slavery campaigner who has local links, **William Wilberforce Freedom Ale** 🍺 🍾 (4.3%) is golden, mellow and a little hoppy, containing Fairtrade ingredients.

Availability. Often on guest lists and a particular favourite at the Dartmouth Arms (p154) and the Eagle (p198).

WESTMALLE
Trappist
Malle, Antwerp, Belgium
403km/250 miles from Central London
🌐 www.trappistwestmalle.be

The second most commercialised Trappist brewery, set amid the woodlands and heaths of the Kempen region, inspired a host of imitators with its influential duo of beers.

Dubbel * 🍾 🍺 (6.5%) is a soft deep burgundy beer with raisin and banana notes and a gently spicy finish. **Tripel** ** 🍾 (9.5%) is golden with meaty and creamy peach notes, complex hops and herbs.

Westmalle Tripel

Availability. Good speciality bottled lists should include this brewery and it's also a mainstay in bottle shops. Try the Greenwich Union (p179).

WHITE HORSE
Microbrewery
Stanford-in-the-Vale, Oxfordshire
127km/79 miles from Central London
🌐 www.breweryoxfordshire.co.uk

Opened in 2004 close to the famous prehistoric white horse figure carved into the chalk of the Berkshire Downs at Uffington.

Black Horse Porter * 🍺 (5%) has blackcurrant, angelica and herb notes, spicy hops and gentle caramel roast. **Oxfordshire Bitter** * 🍺 (3.7%) is a gently hopped, very English bitter. **Wayland Smithy** * 🍺 (4.4%) is a brown bitter with caramel, raspberry and biscuit notes. There are numerous seasonals and specials.

Availability. Regularly seen as a guest in places with a good real ale choice, like the Cleveland Arms (p98).

WHOLE HOP
See McMullen

WILLIAMS BROTHERS
Microbrewery
Kelliebank, Alloa, Clackmannanshire, Scotland
686km/426 miles from Central London
🌐 www.williamsbrosbrew.com

The Forth brewery in Alloa was set up in 1994 as a successor to Maclay, one of the few old established Scottish real ale brewers that had survived into the post-CAMRA era. Elsewhere, Bruce and Scott Williams had been brewing from 1993 to unusual Scottish recipes, beginning with Fraoch Heather Ale. After commissioning beers from Forth, they ended up buying it out in 2004 and relocating all their production there.

Sweetish **Alba** 🍾 (also occasional 🍺, 7.5%) is one of very few beers in the world containing no hops, with Scots pine and spruce twigs doing the job instead. **Fraoch** * 🍺 🍾 (5%) is the Williams' inaugural beer, allegedly based on an old Gaelic recipe for heather ale:

it's mid-gold and sweetish with lavender and sage-toned herbal notes. **Grozet** * 🍾 (also seasonal 🍺, 5%) is a tart, slightly cider-like golden ale laced with gooseberries. **Joker** 🍺 (4.3%) is a peachy, slightly citric golden ale with a rooty hop finish. Porter **Midnight Sun** * 🍺 (5.6%) is tasty but easy drinking with chocolate, coffee and a note of added ginger. **Róisin** * 🍺 (4%) is a refreshing creamy beer flavoured with tayberries. Creamy golden **Seven Giraffes** 🍺 (5.1%) is peachy and fruity. There are also two unusually flavoured dark beers: **Ebulum** 🍾 (6.5%) with elderberries and **Kelpie** 🍾 (4.4%) with seaweed. Bottled beers are not bottle conditioned.

Availability. Often on guest lists including in Mitchells & Butlers Nicholson's pubs, and the bottles are regulars in specialist shops.

WINDSOR & ETON

Microbrewery
Windsor, Berkshire
37km/23 miles from Central London
🌐 www.webrew.co.uk

On St George's Day 2010, brewing returned to Royal Windsor for the first time in 79 years with the launch of this micro. It's the only member of the London Brewers' Alliance that's strictly speaking outside Greater London, though its founders Paddy Johnson and Will Calvert have firm links to London brewing – Paddy served his apprenticeship at the now-closed Courage brewery at Horsleydown in Southwark.

Conqueror * 🍺 (5%) is a 'black IPA' with assertive grapefruit and pine hops over brambly brown malt. **Guardsman** 🍺 (4.2%) is the standard amber bitter with a lightly fruity, nutty palate and some bitterness. Golden ale **Knights of the Garter** 🍺 (3.8%) is lightly hoppy with a toffeeish body.

Availability. A favoured brewery of the Bree Louise (p47) and numerous other places stocking local cask.

Williams Brothers Fraoch

WOLF

Microbrewery
Besthorpe, Attleborough, Norfolk
167km/104 miles from Central London
🌐 www.wolfbrewery.com

One of Norfolk's strong contingent of craft breweries, this was founded on an old cider orchard but has since expanded.

Amber **Best Bitter** * 🍺 (3.9%) is nicely toffeeish with a nettly, lightly hoppy finish. **Golden Jackal** * 🍺 (3.7%) is grapefruity with slightly syrupy malt. Distinctive deep brown **Granny Wouldn't Like It!!!** * 🍺 (4.8%) has mouthfuls of dark marmalade and herbal hops. 'Wild mild' in local dialect, **Woild Moild** * 🍺 (4.8%) has chocolate and blackberry flavours with a dryish spicy finish.

Availability. A likely guest in the better cask ale pubs, regularly favoured at the Dog & Bell (p179).

WOODFORDE'S

Microbrewery
Woodbastwick, Norwich, Norfolk
201km/125 miles from Central London
🌐 www.woodfordes.co.uk

Woodforde's started in Norwich in 1980 but success, acknowledged with multiple awards, saw an expansion to the current rural location.

Persuasive hops lift raisiny, fruity mid-gold **Admiral's Reserve** * 🍺 (5%). Barley wine **Headcracker** 🍺 (7%) is hot, earthy, sherberty and resinous. Subtly complex mid-brown **Nelson's Revenge** * 🍺 (4.5%) is flowery, fruity and chaffy. **Norfolk Nog** 🍺 (4.6%) is dark brown and oily with a roasty, fruity finish. Named after a traditional boat found on the Broads, **Wherry** ** 🍺 (3.8%) is a delightfully delicate golden bitter with blackcurrant, ginger and orange zest notes. All also available 🍾.

Availability. Often among cask ale guests. Wherry is a regular at the Olde Rose & Crown (p132).

WORTHINGTON (WHITE SHIELD)

Subsidary (Molson Coors)
Burton upon Trent, Staffordshire
203km/126 miles from Central London
⊕ www.worthingtonswhiteshield.com

This is one of the remaining relics of the historic Bass brewery, once known the world over for pale ales under the red triangle brand. In one of the final stages of the carve-up of the Big Six national brewers in 2000, Belgian megabrewer Interbrew (now AB InBev) bought both the Bass and Whitbread groups. To regulate competition the government forced it to sell the Bass brewery and some of the brands, though it retains the main Bass brand, commissioning production from Marston's (above). The new owner, US group Coors, now Molson Coors, has turned out to be more supportive of speciality beer than first expected. In 2010 it helped reopen the former Bass Museum as the National Brewery Centre, including a microbrewery on which one of Britain's most admired brewers, Steve Wellington, continues to produce a range of historic specialities.

Red Shield * ▤ (4.2%) is a tasty, easy drinking pale ale with a grapefruity bitter note. **White Shield** ** ▮ (and occasional ▤, 5.6%) is one of the most historic beers in Britain, a direct descendant of 19th century pale ales and one of only two survivors of the five bottle conditioned beers in production when CAMRA was founded. It's a beautifully balanced and complex pale ale with a nutty, fruity body and a firm bite of peppery, almond-tinged hops. There are numerous strong historic recreations too but these generally aren't seen outside the Brewery Centre.

Availability. White Shield isn't on as many pub beer lists as it should be, but is reliably supplied by any decent bottle shop. Look out for Red Shield as a guest beer.

Worthington White Shield

WYCHWOOD / BRAKSPEAR

Subsidiary (Marston's)
Witney, Oxfordshire
114km/71 miles from Central London
⊕ www.wychwood.co.uk
⊕ www.brakspear-beers.co.uk

Revered family brewer Brakspear's abandonment of brewing in 2002 was one of the most striking illustrations in recent years of how even deeply rooted and successful old breweries – Brakspear traced its history to the 17th century – could be tempted to hang up their malt shovels and concentrate on their pubs. Wychwood, founded on the site of an old maltings in 1983, used marketing savvy as well as quality to turn its Hobgoblin into a nationally recognised brand. Enter Refresh UK, a beer firm that commissioned a handful of abandoned Watneys brands from contractors. Refresh bought both the Brakspear brands and the Wychwood brewery, in 2004 installing much of the old Brakspear kit in a separate section of Wychwood's Witney site. The resulting tasty morsel was taken over by Marston's (above) in 2007, though so far both sets of brands continue to be produced in Witney.

Brakspear Bitter * ▤ (3.4%) is a brown bitter with blackcurrant notes and a spicy, lightly astringent finish. Unusual deep amber **Brakspear Triple** * ▮ (7.2%) is notably nutty and toffeeish, with a bitterish finish and a Speyside whisky note. **Hobgoblin** * ▤ (4.5%) is a distinctive marmaladey, lightly bitter dark brown beer with cinder toffee notes. **Oxford Gold** ▤ ▮ (4%/4.6%) has lightly floral and citric hops over a zesty malt body. The brewery also produces the **Duchy Originals** organic beers but none is bottle conditioned.

Availability. The cask beers are regularly seen as guests – try the North Pole (p124) for Hobgoblin or the Jeremy Bentham (p50) for Brakspear.

ZERODEGREES

See London breweries (p284)

APPENDICES

APPENDICES
LONDON BEER FESTIVALS

Beer festivals offer opportunities to try an even wider range of beers than is reguarly available in London's pubs and bars. They fall into two types: events in big venues not normally associated with selling specialist beer; and events in pubs and bars enhancing their regular range.

The biggest organiser of the first kind of event is CAMRA, leading off with the Great British Beer Festival (GBBF), the biggest event of its kind in the world. There are several smaller festivals run by local branches to keep the London drinker happy throughout the year. All are staffed entirely by volunteers, and some are run in partnership with other local organisations. Check the websites for volunteering opportunities.

Beer festivals of this kind usually impose a modest admission charge, with discounts or sometimes free entry at certain times for CAMRA and other European Beer Consumers Union (EBCU) members. Once inside you pay a returnable deposit on a festival glass and buy your drinks with cash, at good value but not heavily discounted prices. Besides cask beer you'll usually find imported and bottle conditioned beers (also available to take away), real cider and perry and food. Draught beers are always available in pints and halves, and sometimes in thirds. Features like bookstalls, games, displays and perhaps entertainment and tutored tastings complete the experience.

The details below are based on recent festivals but these can change from year to year. Check the websites shown for further information, and the listings on the main CAMRA website (⊕ www.camra.org.uk).

Currently the main CAMRA festivals are:

FEBRUARY, 2ND WEEK
Battersea Beer Festival (South West London CAMRA)
Battersea Arts Centre SW11.
180 cask beers, draught and bottled imported beers, ciders and perries.
⊕ www.batterseabeerfestival.org.uk
⇌ ⊖ Clapham Junction

MARCH, 2ND WEEK
London Drinker Beer and Cider Festival (North London CAMRA)
Camden Centre WC1 (though this may change)
100 cask beers including many from London, draught and bottled imported beers, ciders and perries.
⊕ www.camranorthlondon.org.uk/ldbf
⇌ ⊖ Kings Cross St Pancras

MAY, 2ND WEEK
Kingston Beer and Cider Festival (Kingston & Leatherhead CAMRA)
< Bear (p172)

Kingston Working Men's Club KT2
50 cask beers, 12 ciders and perries
⊕ www.camrasurrey.org.uk
⇌ Kingston

MAY, LAST WEEK:
Beckenham Beer Festival (South East London CAMRA)
Beckenham Rugby Club BR3
30+ cask beers, bottled beers, 12 ciders and perries
⊕ www.selcamra.org.uk
⇌ Elmers End

JULY, 1ST WEEK
Ealing Beer Festival (West Middlesex CAMRA)
Walpole Park W5
170+ cask beers, draught and bottled imported beers, ciders and perries.
⊕ www.ealingbeerfestival.org.uk
⊖ Ealing Broadway

Great British Beer Festival, Earls Court

AUGUST, 1ST WEEK
Great British Beer Festival
Earls Court Exhibition Centre SW5 / Olympia
Exhibition Centre W14
Over 700 different beers, ciders and perries: a
huge range of cask, a British bottle
conditioned bar and three imported beer
bars: a mini-festival in their own right under
the name *Bières sans frontières*. Rarities, special
releases, tastings. An essential event on the
international beer connoisseur's calendar.
Earls Court Exhibition Centre is slated for
redevelopment after its stint as an Olympic
venue in 2012 and the future home of the
Great British Beer Festival remains uncertain.

🌐 www.gbbf.camra.org.uk
⊖ Earls Court / Kensington (Olympia)

OCTOBER, 2ND/3RD WEEK
**Croydon and Sutton Real Ale and Cider
Festival**
Wallington Hall SM6
60 cask beers from within a 100-mile (160km)
radius, imported bottled beers, 15 ciders and
perries.
🌐 www.croydoncamra.org.uk
🚆 Wallington

NOVEMBER, LAST WEEK
Heathrow Beer Festival
Concorde Club TW5
35+ seasonal real ales and ciders.
🌐 www.heathrowbeerfestival.co.uk
🚆 Hounslow (then bus) ⊖ Hatton Cross,
Hounslow West (then bus)

DECEMBER, 1ST WEEK
Pigs Ear Beer and Cider Festival (East
London and City CAMRA)
Round Chapel E5
100+ cask beers including several unique
festival brews, draught and bottled imported
beers, British bottle conditioned beers, ciders.
🌐 www.pigsear.org.uk
🚆 Hackney Downs ⊖ Hackney Central

There are numerous beer festivals in pubs –
sometimes quarterly or even more
frequently. These are often referred to in the
pub listings in the Places to Drink section,
but dates are subject to change at very little
notice so I haven't attempted to compile a
definitive list here. Events are often
advertised in the *London Drinker* (More
information, p325)

A pub festival usually involves the pub
offering extra beers, often alongside
entertainment and other activities, but the
choice is likely to be more limited than at a
CAMRA festival. Events themed around a
particular style, region or country are
commonplace. Admission is rarely charged
except possibly for entertainment. A few pub
festivals don't increase the overall numbers of
beers but instead replace regular beers with a
rapidly rotating selection of guests over a
limited period.

The largest scale pub festivals are those
run by Wetherspoon: the **International
Beer Festival** in spring and the **Real Ale
Festival** starting at the end of October.
Over the course of two or three weeks,
Wetherspoon pubs can draw on a wide
range of interesting beers, and some pubs
add temporary stillages or pumps to increase
the variety still further. Top brewers from
overseas are invited to brew cask versions of
their beers at British breweries for the
international event. See 🌐 www.
jdwetherspoon.co.uk for more details.

CAMRA IN LONDON

CAMRA has numerous branches in London running social activities for members as well as campaigning. Activities include pub and brewery visits, talks, tastings, publishing guides and newsletters, running festivals, liaising with breweries, rating beer quality and researching listings for the *Good Beer Guide*. The London branches also jointly publish *London Drinker*, an excellent source of news and information about pubs, beer and beer-related events in the capital (More information, p325).

The branches are run by volunteers and contact details may change so other than websites I haven't attempted to list them here. Information can also be obtained from CAMRA head office, ☎ 01727 867201, ⊕ www.camra.org.uk.

Bexley
⊕ www.camrabexleybranch.org.uk

Croydon and Sutton
⊕ www.croydoncamra.org.uk

East London and City
⊕ www.pigsear.org.uk

Enfield and Barnet
⊕ www.camranorthlondon.org.uk/enfieldandbarnet/

Kingston and Leatherhead
⊕ www.camrasurrey.org.uk/kingston-leatherhead

North London
⊕ www.camranorthlondon.org.uk

Richmond and Hounslow
⊕ www.rhcamra.org.uk

South East London
⊕ www.selcamra.org.uk

South West Essex
⊕ www.essex-camra.org.uk/swessex

South West London
⊕ www.swlcamra.org.uk

West London
⊕ www.westlondon-camra.org.uk

West Middlesex
⊕ www.westmiddx-camra.org.uk

LAGRAD (Lesbian and Gay Real Ale Drinkers)
⊕ www.lagrad.org.uk

London Pubs Group
Promoting pub preservation and good pub design.
⊕ www.londonpubsgroup.org.uk

Regional Director
CAMRA officer with special responsibility for the London branches.
✉ rd.greaterlondon@camra.org.uk

CAMRA's London branches presenting the National Pub of the Year Award to the Harp (p75)

MORE INFORMATION

LONDON

There are numerous histories of London – the ones I've found most useful are:
London: the Biography, Peter Ackroyd, Vintage 1991
London: a History, Francis Sheppard, Oxford University Press 1998

Anyone interested in London history should visit:
Museum of London
150 London Wall EC2Y 5HN
☎ (020) 7001 9844
⊕ www.museumoflondon.org.uk

Good general tourist guidebooks:
London Official Guide, Time Out 2011
Discover London, Tom Masters, Lonely Planet 2011

A fascinating, scurrilous and occasionally unreliable supplement:
Eccentric London, Benedict le Vay, Bradt 2007

London's official tourism services:
Britain and London Visitor Centre
1 Regent Street SW1Y 4XT
☎ 0870 156 6366 ⊕ www.visitlondon.com

An essential source for local events, listings and news:
Time Out, published weekly and sold in newsagents ⊕ www.timeout.com/London

Local and national news, entertainment listings and reviews:
London Evening Standard, daily, free from stations ⊕ www.thisislondon.co.uk

An alternative view from the Blogosphere:
londonist ⊕ www.londonist.com

Essential information on getting around, including journey planner and cycling maps:
Transport for London
☎ 0843 222 1234 ⊕ www.tfl.gov.uk

Walking journey planner:
walkit.com ⊕ walkit.com/london

The best printed street atlases:
A-Z London Street Atlases ⊕ www.a-zmaps.co.uk
You'll need the Greater London atlas, quite a substantial book, to find all the outlying places listed here.

Online mapping:
Streetmap ⊕ www.streetmap.co.uk
Google maps ⊕ maps.google.com

BEER & BREWING
Definitive world surveys and great beer canons:
1001 Beers You Must Try Before You Die, Adrian Tierney-Jones (ed), Quintessence 2010
Beer: Eyewitness Companion, Michael Jackson (ed), Dorling Kindersley 2007
World Guide to Beer, Stephen Beaumont and Tim Webb, Mitchell Beazley 2011

Reliable writings on beer history:
Amber Gold & Black: The History of Britain's Great Beers, Martyn Cornell, History Press 2010
London!, Ronald Pattinson, ⊕ barclayperkins.blogspot.com 2010

Comprehensive sources of information on contemporary breweries and styles:
Good Beer Guide, Roger Protz (ed), CAMRA Books (annual UK beer guide)
Good Beer Guide Belgium, Tim Webb, CAMRA Books 2009
Good Beer Guide Germany, Steve Thomas, CAMRA Books 2006
Good Beer Guide Prague and the Czech Republic, Evan Rail, CAMRA Books 2007
Good Beer Guide West Coast USA, Ben McFarland and Tom Sandham, CAMRA Books 2008
Good Bottled Beer Guide, Jeff Evans, CAMRA Books 2009

A view of cask ale from the industry:
Cask Report 2010-11, Pete Brown, ⊕ www.caskreport.co.uk 2010

The complete guide to tasting beer, written in the USA from an international perspective:
Tasting Beer, Randy Mosher, Storey Publishing 2009

Online information about breweries and beer:
Directory of UK Real Ale Breweries ⊕ www.quaffale.org.uk
BeerMe! (International brewery directory) ⊕ beerme.com
ratebeer (Comprehensive international beer rating site) ⊕ www.ratebeer.com

Regular news of beer and pubs in London:
London Drinker, published bimonthly by CAMRA London branches. Available free in the majority of the places listed in this book.

Great beer blogs by Londoners:
Pete Brown ⊕ petebrown.blogspot.com
Mark Dredge, Pencil and Spoon ⊕ www.pencilandspoon.com
Real Ale Girl ⊕ realalegirl.blogspot.com
...and many more, most of them linked from the pages above

PLACES TO DRINK
The best real ale pubs in London, chosen by CAMRA members, can be found in the London section of:
The Good Beer Guide (annual, see above)
Also available as a mobile app and a POI file
⊕ www.camra.org.uk

Local CAMRA branches produce more comprehensive guides to real ale pubs in their areas, often sold at beer festivals. The following are all available from ⊕ www.camra.org.uk:
Along the Brighton Road: Brixton, Streatham, Mitcham
Clapham Omnibus: Clapham and South Lambeth
A Guide to Real Ale in London WC1 and WC2
Kingston Pub Guide
Real Ale in Hampstead and Highgate
Also check the branch websites listed under CAMRA in London (above) as many have online pub guides.

Sources on pub heritage and history in London:
London Heritage Pubs: An inside story, Geoff Brandwood and Jane Jephcote, CAMRA Books 2008
London Pubs, David Brandon, Amberley 2010
Real Heritage Pubs of London, a listing of CAMRA's National and Regional inventories of historic interiors ⊕ www.heritagepubs.org.uk

Other useful suggestions for interesting London pubs and bars, and alternative takes on some of the pubs listed here:
Around London in 80 Beers, Chris Pollard and Siobhan McGinn, Cogan & Mater 2008
London's Best Bars: 500 Great Places to Drink in the Capital, Time Out (annual)
London's Best Pubs, Peter Haydon, New Holland 2009
London Pub Walks, Bob Steel, CAMRA Books 2009

Cask Marque accredited pubs (p37) including those in London are listed online:
⊕ www.cask-marque.co.uk

Pub reviews by the public can be found at:
Beer in the evening ⊕ www.beerintheevening.com
Fancyapint? ⊕ www.fancyapint.com

UPDATES

If you encounter any closures or significant changes in policy, know about or discover any new or existing venues you believe worthy of inclusion, feel strongly that one of the entries really shouldn't have been included, or have any other comments or feedback, then please email me at des@desdemoor.com or by writng care of CAMRA Books, 230 Hatfield Road, St Albans, Hertfordshire, AL1 4LW.

In the meantime updates to this guide will be published at ⊕ www.desdemoor.co.uk.

ACKNOWLEDGEMENTS

Many, many people participated in various ways in the making of this book, both wittingly and unwittingly.

First and foremost I'd like to thank the owners, managers and staff of all the beer outlets listed in this guide, not only for running great places and making a vital contribution to London's beer culture, but by being so courteous and helpful when I turned up unexpectedly with damn fool questions when they had customers to serve. I'm also extremely appreciative of the owners, managers and staff of all the London breweries, both for making great beer, and for taking time out from doing so to share their stories and views and, in many cases, some of their beers with me.

Numerous volunteers from CAMRA branches also helped out with comments and suggestions for which I am extremely grateful, with a particular nod to Geoff Brandwood for helping me keep in touch through CAMRA's London Liaison Group, Roger Warhurst for his tireless chronicling of London pubs through the Capital Pubcheck in *London Drinker* and a number of tipoffs for this guide, and Christine Cryne for London beer tips. The branches also deserve to be thanked for all the great work they've done over the years in protecting and promoting London's beer culture. Without them I suspect it wouldn't be worth writing a book like this.

Simon Hall, Katie Hunt and Emma Haines, along with designer Ian Midson did a great job of pulling all this together at CAMRA Books. Graham Farr and Barry Brewster of J D Wetherspoon got me airside at Heathrow. Simon Barnett helped me arrange the time I needed for the project and he and other colleagues at the Ramblers uncomplainingly covered for my absence. I'm grateful to them all.

As this is my first book I should thank a few people that weren't directly involved. Tom and Jasper created the Oxford Bottled Beer Database where my beer reviews were first published, Ted Bruning gave me my first paid gig as a beer writer and Sally Toms, Dominic Bates, Adrian Tierney-Jones and Tom Stainer helped me get here too. A whole host of other beer writers provided inspiration, but I'll single out Tim Webb and the late Michael Jackson for special mention. My family clearly played an important role: Phyllis de Moor, Adèle de Moor and Sunil Sohanta de Moor. Thanks to them all.

Last but not least, there's my partner, Ian Harris, who has been unfailingly patient and supportive despite not even liking beer. Ian, I'm writing a book.

PHOTO CREDITS

The publisher would like to thank the pubs, breweries and individuals who have kindly given permission for their photography to be printed in this publication. Specific thanks go to:

Bob Steel: p7, 33, 40 (top), 77 (top), 84, 88 (top), 105, 107, 113, 118, 198, 211, 219, 234, 236, 237

CAMRA archive: p17, 19, 253, 277, 323, 324

Cath Harries: p4-5, 13, 22-3, 37, 39 (top), 40 (bottom), 41, 44, 57, 59, 62, 65, 69, 70, 71, 75, 77 (bottom), 80, 81, 82, 85, 87, 89, 96, 102, 117, 121, 122, 124, 127, 129, 130, 131, 132 (top), 133, 138, 139, 146, 149, 150, 151, 155, 156, 160, 161, 162, 163 (top), 170, 173, 177, 179, 183, 190, 201, 204, 207, 213, 214, 215, 216, 217, 218, 226, 243, 245, 247, 249, 250-1, 261, 282, 284

Des de Moor: p54, 60, 97, 111, 187, 188, 189, 262, 268, 274, 278-9, 280-1

Katie Hunt: p91

Transport for London: p31

visitlondonimages/britainonview: p9, 10-11

www.tiredoflondontiredoflife.com: p76

PLACES TO DRINK BY THEME

ARCHITECTURE

Pub heritage
Argyll Arms (p105)
Blackfriar (p64)
Castle (Holborn) (p81)
Churchill Arms (p94)
Cittie of Yorke (p81)
Dog & Duck (p107)
Falcon (p198)
George (Borough) (p56)
Holly Bush (p149)
Island Queen (p88)
Jolly Butchers (p158)
Museum Tavern (p51)
Palm Tree (p122)
Pineapple (p156)
Prince Alfred (p236)
Princess Louise (p84)
Salisbury Hotel (p161)
Seven Stars (p85)
Southampton Arms (p157)
Spread Eagle (Camden) (p143)
St Stephen's (p117)

Public bars
Anchor & Hope (p137)
Load of Hay (p238)
Palm Tree (p122)
Red Lion (Isleworth) (p236)
Rose's (p190)
Trafalgar (p215)
Willoughby Arms (p206)
Wonder (p161)
Woodman (p237)

Interesting buildings
Barrowboy & Banker (p53)
Betjeman Arms (p45)
Bricklayers Arms (p217)
Coronet (p162)
Crosse Keys (p66)
Dispensary (p43)
Gatehouse (p153)
George (Holborn) (p82)
Gothique (p210)
Jerusalem Tavern (p71)
Katzenjammers (p58)
Knights Templar (p83)
Load of Hay (p238)

Old Brewery (p180)
Old Doctor Butler's Head (p67)
Olde Mitre (Holborn) (p83)
Pilot (p181)
Porterhouse (p76)
Richard I (p182)
Roebuck (p208)
Ship & Shovell (p77)
Spaniards Inn (p151)
Star (p118)
Sun Inn (p194)
Town of Ramsgate (p124)
Wheatsheaf (p63)
Woodies Freehouse (p216)

BEER SPECIALISTS & CHAINS

Adnams
Bridge House (p54)

Belgian
Belgo (see below)
Brouge (Richmond) (p208)
Brouge (Twickenham) (p230)
Dove (Hackney) (p126)
Dovetail (p69)
Lowlander (p76)

Belgo
Bromley (p169)
Centraal (p73)
Clapham (p195)
Kingsway (p74)
Noord (p141)

Brewpubs
Brew Wharf (p53)
Florence (p185)
King William IV (Leyton) (p129)
Old Brewery (p180)
Zerodegrees (p168)

Brodie's
Cross Keys (p75)
King William IV (Leyton) (p129)
Old Coffee House (p108)

Camden Town
Horseshoe (p150)

Cask specialists
Barnsbury (p145)
Birkbeck Tavern (p128)
Boaters Inn (p205)
Brewery Tap (p212)
Bricklayers Arms (p217)
Castle (Holborn) (p81)
Charles Dickens (p111)
Claret (p175)
Cricketers (p176)
Dog & Bell (p179)
Duke of Wellington
(Canonbury) (p145)
Eagle (p198)
Earl Ferrers (p218)
Edgar Wallace (p82)
Grape & Grain (p187)
Harp (p75)
Hope (p216)
Magpie & Crown (p233)
Market Porter (p59)
North Nineteen (p163)
North Star (p132)
Old Fountain (p95)
Olde Mitre (Holborn) (p83)
Olde Rose & Crown (p132)
Pelton Arms (p181)
Pineapple (p156)
Prince of Wales (Highgate)
(p153)
Red Lion (Bromley) (p170)
Red Lion (Isleworth) (p236)
Rose's (p190)
Speaker (p117)
Three Compasses (p163)
Trafalgar (p215)
Wenlock Arms (p96)
Wheatsheaf (p63)
Willoughby Arms (p206)
Woodies Freehouse (p216)

Castle (Mitchells & Butlers)
Commercial (p185)
Crown (Soho) (p106)
Crown & Greyhound (p172)
Crown & Sceptre (p78)
Drayton Arms (p91)
Green Dragon (p177)
Green Man (p79)
Island Queen (p88)

Lyttleton Arms (p142)
Princess of Wales (p167)
Southwark Tavern (p62)
Spaniards Inn (p151)
Sun Inn (p194)

Czech
Bar Prague (p101)
Czechoslovak National House (p148)

Draft House
Northcote (p196)
Tower Bridge (p55)
Westbridge (p197)

Dutch
De Hems (p106)

Duvel-Moortgat
Bar Music Hall (p100)

Fuller's
Anchor & Hope (p137)
Barrowboy & Banker (p53)
Castle (Harrow) (p235)
Churchill Arms (p94)
Doric Arch (p48)
Dove (Hammersmith) (p223)
Fox & Hounds (p222)
Holly Bush (p149)
Mad Bishop & Bear (p98)
Olde Mitre (Holborn) (p83)
Pilot (p181)
Red Lion (Barnes) (p193)
Ship (p109)
Star (p118)

German
Bierschenke (p81)
Katzenjammers (p58)
Zeitgeist (p113)

Greene King
George (Borough) (p56)

Hall & Woodhouse
Eel Pie (p231)
Ship & Shovell (p77)
St Stephen's (p117)

Harveys
Royal Oak (p61)

Hop Back
Sultan (p214)

International
Antelope (p218)
Cask (p115)
Charlotte Despard (p152)
Dean Swift (p54)
Draft House (see above)
Euston Tap (p49)
Half & Half (p177)
Hoopers (p174)
Mason & Taylor (p103)
Priory Arms (p203)
Project Orange (p202)
Questors (p234)
Rake (p60)
White Horse (p225)

McMullen
Spice of Life (p109)
Wonder (p161)

Meantime
Greenwich Union (p179)
Old Brewery (p180)

Milton
Pembury Tavern (p127)

Nicholson's (Mitchells & Butlers)
Argyll Arms (p105)
Bear & Staff (p105)
Blackfriar (p64)
Crown (Soho) (p106)
Crown & Sceptre (p78)
Dog & Duck (p107)
Doggetts Coat & Badge (p111)
Falcon (p198)

Porterhouse
Porterhouse (p76)

Samuel Smith
Cittie of Yorke (p81)
Princess Louise (p84)

Shepherd Neame
Cask & Glass (p116)
Eleanor Arms (p135)
Mabel's (p51)
Old Doctor Butler's Head (p67)

Shops
Bitter End (p170)
Dr.Ink of Fulham (p224)
Fuller's Brewery Shop (p222)
Kris Wines (p155)
Mr Lawrence (p186)
Nelson Wines (p213)
Noble Green Wines (p232)
RealAle.com (p233)
Selfridges Food Hall (p99)
Utobeer (p62)
Waitrose Canary Wharf (p125)

St Peter's
Jerusalem Tavern (p71)

USA
Ink Rooms (p199)
Lexington (p89)

Wetherspoon
Coronet (p162)
Crosse Keys (p66)
Drum (p129)
Gatehouse (p153)
George (Croydon) (p176)
Goldengrove (p136)
Heathrow Airport pubs (p229)
J J Moons (p239)
Knights Templar (p83)
Lord Moon of the Mall (p116)
Metropolitan (p99)
Penderel's Oak (p84)
Pommelers Rest (p60)
Walnut Tree (p133)
Willow Walk (p118)

Young's
Alma (p144)
Buckingham Arms (p114)
Calthorpe Arms (p48)
Duke of Wellington (Notting Hill) (p94)
Founders Arms (p112)

Hand in Hand (p213)
Marquess Tavern (p146)
Nightingale (p201)
Prince Alfred (p236)
Richard I (p182)
Rose & Crown (p214)
Spread Eagle (Camden) (p143)
Spread Eagle (Wandsworth)
(p211)
Trinity Arms (p204)
White Cross (p209)

LANDMARKS NEARBY

Alexandra Palace
John Baird (p164)

Borough Market
Brew Wharf (p53)
Market Porter (p59)
Rake (p60)

Brick Lane
Mason & Taylor (p103)
Pride of Spitalfields (p44)

British Museum
Museum Tavern (p51)

Camden Lock
Black Heart (p142)
Spread Eagle (Camden) (p143)

Canary Wharf
North Pole (p124)

Coliseum
Harp (p75)

Covent Garden
Cross Keys (p75)
Lowlander (p76)
Porterhouse (p76)

Crystal Palace
Grape & Grain (p187)

Dulwich Picture Gallery
Crown & Greyhound (p172)

Earls Court
Courtfield (p91)

Harrow School
Castle (Harrow) (p235)

Hyde Park
Carpenters Arms
(Paddington) (p98)

Koko
Lyttleton Arms (p142)

Leicester Square
Bear & Staff (p105)
Spice of Life (p109)

Leyton Orient Stadium
Leyton Orient Supporters
Club (p130)

London Palladium
Argyll Arms (p105)

London Wetland Centre
Red Lion (Barnes) (p193)

Marble Arch
Carpenters Arms
(Paddington) (p98)

Maritime Greenwich
Old Brewery (p180)
Trafalgar Tavern (p183)

**Museum of Childhood
(V&A)**
Camel (p121)

National Gallery
Harp (p75)
Lord Moon of the Mall (p116)

O$_2$
Pilot (p181)

Olympic Park
Goldengrove (p136)
King Edward VII (p136)

Oxford Street
Selfridges Food Hall (p99)

Palace of Westminster
St Stephen's (p117)

Portobello Market
Duke of Wellington (Notting
Hill) (p94)

Primrose Hill
Landsdowne (p142)

Regent's Park
Spread Eagle (Camden) (p143)

Royal Arsenal
Rose's (p190)

Sadlers Wells
Old China Hand (p72)

St Paul's Cathedral
Cockpit (p65)

Shakespeare's Globe
Founders Arms (p112)

Smithfield Market
Fox & Anchor (p70)

Southbank Centre
BFI Southbank (p111)

Tate Britain
Cask (p115)

Tate Modern
Charles Dickens (p111)
Founders Arms (p112)

Tower Bridge
Bridge House (p54)
Draft House Tower Bridge
(p55)
Pommelers Rest (p60)

Trafalgar Square
Lord Moon of the Mall (p116)

Twickenham Stadium
Eel Pie (p231)

Victoria Park
Eleanor Arms (p135)

Wembley Stadium
J J Moons (p239)

Westminster Abbey
St Stephen's (p117)

Wimbledon (All England Club)
Rose & Crown (p214)

POINTS OF INTEREST

Children very welcome
BFI Southbank (p111)
Barnsbury (p145)
Canbury Arms (p206)
Charles Lamb (p86)
Crown & Greyhound (p172)
Duke of Cambridge (p87)
Earl Ferrers (p218)
Florence (p185)
Gothique (p210)
Green Dragon (p177)
Lighthouse (p200)
Olde Rose & Crown (p132)
Rose & Crown (p214)
Roundhouse (p202)
Thatched House (p138)

Entertainment
Bar Music Hall *Music, DJs* (p100)
BFI Southbank *Film* (p111)
Black Heart *DJs* (p142)
Bloomsbury Bowling Lanes *Bowling, bands, DJs* (p47)
Boaters Inn *Music* (p205)
Duke of Wellington (Canonbury) *Films* (p145)
Horseshoe *Theatre* (p150)
Leyton Orient Supporters Club *Football* (p130)
Lexington *Music* (p89)
Load of Hay *Music* (p238)
North Star *Music* (p132)
Olde Rose & Crown *Theatre, music* (p132)
Pelton Arms *Music* (p181)
Project Orange *Music* (p202)
Questors *Theatre* (p234)
Red Lion (Isleworth) *Music* (p236)
Roxy *Film* (p61)
Southall Conservative & Unionist Club *Social club* (p238)

Spice of Life *Music* (p109)
Wenlock & Essex *DJs* (p89)

Food, serious
Alma (p144)
Antelope (p218)
Bear (p172)
Canbury Arms (p206)
Carpenters Arms (Shoreditch) (p102)
Charles Lamb (p86)
Duke of Cambridge (p87)
Duke of Sussex (p221)
Earl Ferrers (p218)
Fox & Anchor (p70)
Gun (p123)
Junction Tavern (p155)
Landsdowne (p142)
Lighthouse (p200)
Mark's Bark (p107)
Marquess Tavern (p146)
North Nineteen (p163)
Peasant (p72)
Prince Alfred (p236)
Prince Regent (p185)
Roundhouse (p202)
Selfridges Food Hall (p99)
Seven Stars (p85)

Gay pubs
King William IV (Hampstead) (p150)
Queens Head (p92)

Parks and countryside
Belgo Bromley (p169)
Blacksmiths Arms (p188)
Bulls Head (p189)
Cock & Dragon (p160)
Florence (p185)
Grape & Grain (p187)
Hand in Hand (p213)
Harefield (p234)
Kings Head (p137)
Palm Tree (p122)
Prince Regent (p185)
Princess of Wales (p167)
Ramblers Rest (p187)
Roebuck (p208)
Spaniards Inn (p151)
Thatched House (p138)
Woodman (p237)

River and canalside
Anchor & Hope (p137)
BFI Southbank (p111)
Boaters Inn (p205)
Bricklayers Arms (p217)
Doggetts Coat & Badge (p111)
Dove (Hammersmith) (p223)
Founders Arms (p112)
Gun (p123)
Town of Ramsgate (p124)
Trafalgar Tavern (p183)
White Cross (p209)
Woody's (p207)

TRANSPORT TERMINALS

Baker Street
Metropolitan (p99)

Charing Cross
Harp (p75)
Ship & Shovell (p77)

Clapham Junction
Falcon (p198)

Euston
Bree Louise (p47)
Doric Arch (p48)
Euston Tap (p49)

Heathrow Airport (see p229)

Kings Cross/St Pancras Intl
Betjeman Arms (p45)
King Charles I (p50)

Paddington
Mad Bishop & Bear (p98)

Stratford Intl
Goldengrove (p136)
King Edward VII (p136)

Victoria
Willow Walk (p118)

Waterloo
Hole in the Wall (p112)

PLACES TO DRINK INDEX

BOOKS FOR BEER LOVERS

CAMRA Books, the publishing arm of the Campaign for Real Ale, is the leading publisher of books on beer and pubs. Key titles include:

Good Beer Guide 2012
Editor: Roger Protz
The *Good Beer Guide* is the only guide you will ever need to find the right pint, in the right place, every time. It's the original and best-selling guide to around 4,500 pubs throughout the UK. Now in its 39th year, this annual publication is a comprehensive and informative guide to the best real ale pubs in the UK, researched and written exclusively by CAMRA members and fully updated every year.
£15.99 ISBN 978-1-85249-286-1, published September 2011

Good Bottled Beer Guide
Jeff Evans
A pocket-sized guide for discerning drinkers looking to buy bottled real ales and enjoy a fresh glass of their favourite beers at home. The 7th edition of the *Good Bottled Beer Guide* is completely revised, updated and redesigned to showcase the very best bottled British real ales now being produced, and detail where they can be bought. Everything you need to know about bottled beers; tasting notes, ingredients, brewery details, and a glossary to help the reader understand more about them.
£12.99 ISBN 978-1-85249-262-5

London Pub Walks
Bob Steel
A practical, pocket-sized guide enabling you to explore the English capital while never being far away from a decent pint. The book includes 30 walks around more than 180 pubs serving fine real ale, from the heart of the City and bustling West End to majestic riverside routes and the leafy Wimbledon Common. Each pub is selected for its high-quality real ale, its location and its superb architectural heritage. The walks feature more pubs than any other London pub-walk guide.
£8.99 ISBN 978-1-85249-216-8

London Heritage Pubs – An inside story
Geoff Brandwood & Jane Jephcote
The definitive guidebook to London's most unspoilt pubs. Raging from gloriously rich Victorian extravaganzas to unspoilt community street-corner locals, the pubs not only have interiors of genuine heritage value, they also have fascinating stories to tell. *London Heritage pubs – An inside story* is a must for anyone interested in visiting and learning about London's magnificent pubs.
£14.99 ISBN 978-1-85249-247-2

Order these and other CAMRA books online at www.camra.org.uk/books, ask your local bookstore or contact: CAMRA, 230 Hatfield Road, St Albans, AL1 4LW. Telephone 01727 867201

IT TAKES ALL SORTS TO CAMPAIGN FOR REAL ALE

CAMRA, the Campaign for Real Ale, is an independent not-for-profit, volunteer-led consumer group. We promote good-quality real ale and pubs, as well as lobbying government to champion drinkers' rights and protect local pubs as centres of community life.

CAMRA has over 120,000 members from all ages and backgrounds, brought together by a common belief in the issues that CAMRA deals with and their love of good quality British beer. From just £20 a year – that's less than a pint a month – you can join CAMRA and enjoy the following benefits:

A monthly colour newspaper informing you about beer and pub news and detailing events and beer festivals around the country.

Free or reduced entry to over 140 national, regional and local beer festivals.

Money off many of our publications including the *Good Beer Guide* and the *Good Bottled Beer Guide*.

Access to a members-only section of our national website, **www.camra.org.uk**, which gives up-to-the-minute news stories and includes a special offer section with regular features.

The opportunity to campaign to save pubs under threat of closure, for pubs to be open when people want to drink and a reduction in beer duty that will help Britain's brewing industry survive.

Log onto **www.camra.org.uk** for CAMRA membership information.

CAMPAIGN FOR REAL ALE

London Brewers Alliance

The London Brewers Alliance (LBA) was formed in 2010, by a passionate group of brewers, intent on returning London to its rightful place among the world's leading centres for high quality brewing and beer drinking.

Our aim is to unite those who make local beer with those that love it, and represent the vibrant heritage and contemporary scene of beer brewing in the great city of London.

The founding members are:

More information at www.londonbrewers.org
Follow us on twitter @LondonBrewers
www.facebook.com/LondonBrewers